Monuments to Absence

Monuments to Absence

Cherokee Removal and the
Contest over Southern Memory

· ·

ANDREW DENSON

The University of North Carolina Press Chapel Hill

This book was published with the assistance of the Fred W. Morrison Fund of the University of North Carolina Press.

The University of North Carolina Press has been a member of the Green Press Initiative since 2003.

Library of Congress Cataloging-in-Publication Data
Names: Denson, Andrew.
Title: Monuments to absence: Cherokee removal and the contest over southern memory / Andrew Denson.
Description: Chapel Hill: University of North Carolina Press, [2017] | Includes bibliographical references and index.
Identifiers: LCCN 2016021186| ISBN 9781469630823 (cloth: alk. paper) | ISBN 9781469630830 (pbk: alk. paper) | ISBN 9781469630847 (ebook)
Subjects: LCSH: Trail of Tears, 1838–1839—Public opinion. | Cherokee Indians—Relocation—Public opinion. | Collective memory— Southern States.
Classification: LCC E99.C5 D47 2017 | DDC 975.004/97557—dc23
LC record available at https://lccn.loc.gov/2016021186

Cover illustration: Home of Cherokee leader John Ross, with DAR Memorial, Rossville, Georgia, circa 1940. Courtesy Chattanooga Public Library, Paul A. Heiner Collection.

Portions of this book were previously published in a different form. The Introduction and Epilogue include material from "Reframing the Indian Dead: Removal Era Cherokee Graves and the Changing Landscape of Southern Memory," in *Death and the American South*, ed. Craig Thompson Friend and Lorri Glover (New York: Cambridge University Press, 2015), 250–74. Chapters 1 and 2 include material from "Gatlinburg's Cherokee Monument: Public Memory in the Shadow of a National Park," *Appalachian Journal* 37 (Fall–Winter 2009), © *Appalachian Journal* and Appalachian State University. Chapter 4 includes material from "Remembering Removal in Civil Rights–Era Georgia," in *Southern Cultures* 14, no. 4 (Winter 2008). Chapters 4 and 5 include material from "Native Americans in Cold War Public Diplomacy: Indian Politics, American History, and the U.S. Information Agency," *American Indian Culture and Research Journal* 36, no. 2 (2012), © Regents of the University of California. All material used here with permission.

For Kelly Larson

Contents

Illustrations

Acknowledgments

A great many people helped me as I researched and wrote this book. I am very lucky to work at Western Carolina University with fine historians and good people like Gael Graham, Jessie Swigger, Elizabeth McRae, Richard Starnes, Mary Ella Engel, and Jim Lewis, all of whom have helped me in myriad ways. I am also grateful to my colleagues in the Cherokee Studies Program at Western—Tom Belt, Roseanna Belt, Tom Hatley, Brett Riggs, Jane Eastman, Hartwell Francis, and Anne Rogers, all of whom know more about these Cherokee mountains than I suspect I ever will. Thanks also to the university's "scholarly reassignment" program, which allowed me to complete the research.

Tiya Miles, Claudio Saunt, Jace Weaver, Malinda Maynor Lowery, Craig Friend, and Theda Perdue provided sound advice and useful comments at various stages of the project. I am indebted, as well, to my fellow heritage workers in the Trail of Tears Association, who shared their insights on contemporary commemoration of Indian removal: Jack Baker, Jeff Bishop, Shirley Lawrence, Susan Abram, Bobbie Heffington, Michael Abram, Sarah Hill, Alice Murphree, and Patsy Edgar. Mark Simpson-Vos at the University of North Carolina Press supported the project from the start and provided both sound advice and the right mix of patience and prodding. I am grateful to the anonymous reviewers for their rigorous, critical readings of the manuscript. The book is much better for their careful analyses.

Public historians in several places provided invaluable assistance. T. J. Holland with the Eastern Band of Cherokee Indians, David Gomez at the New Echota State Historic Site, Duane King of the Gilcrease Museum, George Frizzell at Western Carolina University, Tom Mooney and Jerry Catcher Thompson at the Cherokee Heritage Center, and the librarians and staff of the local history collections at the Chattanooga Public Library all have my lasting gratitude. I could not have written the final chapter without the work of Daniel Littlefield and the wonderful Sequoyah National Research Center at the University of Arkansas, Little Rock.

Suzette Raney, Ethan Clapsaddle, Jerry Catcher Thompson, and Sharon Sanders helped me find illustrations. I am especially grateful to artist Jeff

Marley, who let me use an image from his excellent "We Are Still Here" project.

I don't know how well John Bodnar remembers me from my graduate school years, but it was during his seminar on public history at Indiana University in the 1990s that I first started thinking about history and memory. That experience has shaped much of my subsequent career.

Finally, my greatest debt is to Kelly Larson, who has lived with this project and my weird obsession with community pageants, roadside markers, and obscure historical monuments for longer than I had a right to ask. I am glad she was there from the start.

Monuments to Absence

Introduction

· ·

This book began with tourism. In the summer of 1994, a friend and I drove from Bloomington, Indiana, where I attended graduate school, to Florida for a short vacation. As we sped along Interstate 75 through northern Georgia, I spotted a brown roadside sign announcing that, at the next exit, we would find New Echota, a state historic site interpreting the history of the Cherokee Nation. For a brief time in the early nineteenth century, New Echota was the Cherokee capital, the seat of the national government created by tribal leaders in the 1820s. The Cherokee National Council met at New Echota in the years prior to removal, and it was the site of the Cherokee Supreme Court. During a time when the United States and the state of Georgia pressured Cherokees to emigrate to the West, the new capital represented the Cherokees' determination to remain in their homeland. It was also the place where, in late 1835, a small group of tribal leaders signed the treaty under which the United States forced the Cherokee Nation to remove. I had recently become interested in the history of Cherokee sovereignty and nationhood, and I concluded that I should probably know about this heritage attraction. We pulled off the highway and followed the signs to the site.

New Echota turned out to be an elaborate reconstruction of the antebellum Cherokee town, spread across a wide meadow near the Coosawatee River. Touring the site, we visited buildings representing the Cherokee Council House and Supreme Court, as well as a model Cherokee farmstead. New Echota included a reconstruction of the office of the Nation's bilingual newspaper, the *Cherokee Phoenix*, complete with a period printing press. It also contained two original structures, a tavern that once belonged to the Cherokee Vann family and the home of Samuel Worcester, a missionary who operated out of New Echota and helped to establish the *Phoenix*. Finally, there was a small museum where exhibits explained the history of the site and recounted the story of Cherokee removal.

Earlier that year, in a seminar on public history, I had first encountered literature on southern memory, academic work that explored the social and political uses of commemoration in the American South. As we toured New Echota I wondered about the context for the creation of the site. Who came up with the idea for a reconstructed Cherokee capital, and when did they begin the project? What did its creators hope to achieve, other than to convince tourists like me to pause awhile in northern Georgia? With the confidence of a novice scholar, I decided that the site must be a recent addition to the commemorative landscape, perhaps from the 1980s. I knew from my reading that recent years had seen an increasing number of public history projects that sought to interpret less celebratory episodes from the American past. Cherokee removal, the infamous "Trail of Tears," seemed to qualify as one of those episodes. I also knew that white heritage workers in the South generally excluded the histories of people of color from public commemoration until after the civil rights movement. Or, to be more precise, I knew that they tended to exclude African American histories. I had not yet seen any literature about the public memory of Native southerners. I was quite surprised, then, when the director of the site told me that, in fact, New Echota opened in the early 1960s. Georgia's state historical commission began work on the reconstruction in the mid-1950s, and the state dedicated the site in 1962. New Echota was not a post–civil rights movement project, but a public commemoration that belonged to the era of massive resistance to desegregation. Why, during the height of resistance to the black freedom struggle, did state authorities in Georgia choose to commemorate the Cherokees, a people their forebears helped to expel from the Southeast? Clearly, New Echota had a story to tell, one that concerned more than Indian affairs in the antebellum era. We left the site and continued on toward the beach and less complicated forms of leisure, but I told myself that one day I would try to find that story. This book evolved from that visit.

The South's Most Famous Indian Story

Cherokee removal is the most famous event from the southern Indian past, an episode that exemplifies a broader history of Native American dispossession and American injustice. In the 1830s, the United States compelled the majority of the Cherokee population to abandon its southeastern homeland and migrate to new territory in the West. In the political maneuvering that led to this action, the United States and the state of Georgia violated American treaties with the Cherokees, forcing the removal policy on an unwilling people. Cherokees offered nonviolent resistance, defending their homeland in federal courts and through the American press. During this period, Cherokees enjoyed a public reputation in the United States as a "civilized tribe," due to the willingness of some to adopt Euro-American economic practices and cultural forms. For sympathetic white Americans, Cherokee civilization proved that Indians and non-Indians could coexist in the East, and removal opponents frequently pointed to the tribe as evidence of the policy's illogic and brutality. In the years prior to removal, meanwhile, Cherokees developed a body of written law and a constitutional government by which they defined themselves as an independent nation. This government provided a strong official voice of opposition as state and federal authorities pressed the tribe to relocate. The United States eventually imposed removal through a fraudulent treaty and military force. This action caused the deaths of several thousand Cherokees due to poor conditions on the journey and during the military's efforts to gather Indians for deportation. Although federal authorities applied the removal policy to a host of Indian nations, the Cherokees became the most significant and well-known test of the campaign. In memory, the Cherokee Trail of Tears came to epitomize the unrelenting effort by the United States to erase Indian nations from the territory east of the Mississippi River.[1]

Modern southerners have sustained the memory of Cherokee removal through frequent commemoration, granting the Trail of Tears a prominent place in the region's public history. Today, at least seven states, from North Carolina to Oklahoma, feature museums and historic sites narrating the removal story. A National Historic Trail, established in 1987, follows the Cherokees' migration routes, and along those routes local communities have erected a host of monuments to removal. Novels and popular histories, pageants and plays, and documentary films have depicted the tribe's removal experience. This is not a recent phenomenon, moreover, but something that took place throughout the last century. I was surprised when I learned that Georgia rebuilt New Echota in the 1950s and early 1960s. When I began looking for other examples, however, I found that southern communities mounted significant efforts to commemorate the Trail of Tears as early as the 1920s. Memorializing Cherokee removal is a southern tradition, not a recent innovation.

In *Monuments to Absence*, I explore the public memory of Cherokee removal as it developed from the early twentieth century through the beginning of the twenty-first. In each chapter I present specific case studies, an approach that allows me to view public commemoration from a variety of different angles. Through these specific examples I document the tourism industry's embrace of Cherokee history in the 1920s and 1930s, the substantial wave of removal commemoration that developed in the decades following World War II, and the national campaign to remember the Trail of

Tears that began at the end of the twentieth century and continues into the present. In addition, I analyze representations of Cherokee history in popular culture, such as the outdoor historical drama *Unto These Hills*, staged each summer in Cherokee, North Carolina, since the early 1950s. I also examine the place of the removal memory in twentieth-century political battles waged by the Eastern Band of Cherokee Indians in North Carolina and the Cherokee Nation in Oklahoma. This book, in short, explores the power and meaning of this most famous southern Indian episode in a variety of modern contexts.

In the past thirty years, students of southern culture have developed a rich and complex literature on public history and historical memory. These scholars suggest that southerners, more than other Americans, have grounded their identities in distinct images of the past, and the literature charts the ways in which southern communities have used, reimagined, and fought over their history.[2] This work overlooks Native American topics almost entirely. Race and the memory of racial injustice form major concerns of this literature, since much of it deals with the Civil War, slavery, and segregation. Yet students of southern memory almost always define race as black and white.[3] In Native American studies, meanwhile, scholars have begun to examine the public memory of the violence of settler colonialism. This literature, however, generally focuses on the American West.[4] In *Monuments to Absence*, I examine public commemoration of Cherokee removal as a means of drawing a Native American subject into a significant area of the literature on southern history and culture. In this way, the book contributes to a growing body of scholarship on the Native South, work that explores Native American history as a central element of the southern experience. Academic writing on southern Indians has expanded greatly in recent decades, but this work has exerted only limited influence on the broader field of southern history. In response, some scholars have looked for Native American topics that allow them to address questions of demonstrated importance to southern historians. The practice of slavery among southern Indians represents one such topic, and recent literature on this subject has gained an audience beyond the ranks of Native American specialists.[5] Public memory bears similar potential, since it, too, forms an established topic for students of southern culture. Examining the commemoration of the Indian removal opens new terrain for Native American scholarship within southern history.

The literature on southern memory suggests that, until very recently, public commemoration excluded the experience of nonwhite communities,

Home of Cherokee leader John Ross, with DAR Memorial, Rossville, Georgia, circa 1940. Courtesy Chattanooga Public Library, Paul A. Heiner Collection.

while shunning topics that might involve the critical depiction of Euro-American elites. Scholars have demonstrated these points quite effectively with regard to African American history. While black communities maintained their own memory rituals, white guardians of tradition worked to exclude these commemorations from public space. During segregation this practice reinforced the power of white elites to dominate the public realm and control black lives and labor.[6] When it came to Indian history, however, white southerners embraced stories of loss and injustice, and they did so in ways that broadcast negative images of their forebears. Some of the same institutions that worked to exclude African Americans from public memory proved willing to recognize and even apologize for the Trail of Tears.

White southerners could offer this acknowledgment because they recounted Cherokee removal as a story of Indian disappearance. The Trail of Tears, after all, led away from the South. In remembering removal, white commemorators placed Native Americans outside of the contemporary region, suggesting that its meaningful Indian history ended in the Age of Jackson. This outlook applied even to the Cherokees of North Carolina, who had not left the region, but whom commemorators defined as an anomaly. African Americans were politically present in the modern South, and their history, if allowed public space, posed a potential challenge to the region's racial order during the era of Jim Crow. Indians, however, belonged elsewhere, in the West or in the past. For white commemorators, Indian history formed a precursor to the development of their own southern communities and, as a result, offered little apparent threat to white authority in the present. The Trail of Tears operated as a "replacement narrative," in the historian Jean O'Brien's evocative phrase. It provided a story of Indian disappearance that established white settlers as the logical possessors of Native American land.[7]

In emphasizing Indian disappearance, removal commemoration functioned as a "racializing practice," an activity that reproduced ideas of racial difference rooted in American settler colonialism.[8] In the United States, white authorities long identified Native Americans as vanishing people. In the antebellum era, the authors of the removal policy insisted that Indians could not long survive in the presence of the white republic, and they promoted forced migration as a supposedly humanitarian alternative to annihilating war or slow decline. Later in the century, participants in the allotment and assimilation campaigns argued that they could only save Indians by destroying Native cultures and dismantling tribal communities. Native Americans might survive as individuals, absorbed into the broader populace, but never as indigenous peoples. In the United States, disappearance defined Indians as a race. They were always going away, always incompatible with modern times. This definition, of course, reflected and supported the project of American expansion and nation building, which demanded the elimination of indigenous peoples as landholders and members of distinct political communities. African Americans formed a permanent presence. The United States required black labor, and the racial definitions imposed upon African Americans expressed that imperative. The role of Indians, however, was to vacate territory, accommodating the creation of new settler communities. During segregation and the era of the civil rights movement, white commemorators excluded African American memory from the public realm. In doing so, they supported the larger project of denying black equality and regulating black labor. When white heritage workers also embraced the story of Cherokee removal, they reminded themselves that most Indians had departed and that their own people had inherited the land. These two practices complemented one another in affirming white authority.

Native Americans, of course, had not disappeared from the South, and the desire of some white communities to commemorate Indian removal represented a potential asset for Cherokee communities. The removal story affirmed Cherokees' original claim to the land, even as it recounted their replacement by white settlers. While the enduring assumption of Indian disappearance helped to sustain white power, it also granted an authority to Indianness and to individuals and communities that could assert a Native identity. In the chapters that follow, I explore white communities' use of the Trail of Tears, while examining how some Cherokees sought to turn the popularity of the removal memory to their own people's benefit.

Tourism, Race, and a Hunger for Memory

The twentieth century witnessed three periods of removal commemoration. In the first, during the 1920s and 1930s, tourism development in southern Appalachia opened new arenas for representations of the Cherokee past. Tourism promoters and regional business leaders sought out cultural attractions to accompany the mountains' celebrated natural environment, and they identified the Cherokee community in western North Carolina as a major tourism asset. This new attention influenced public memory, as tourism promoters recounted episodes from Cherokee history, including the story of removal, in their depictions of the mountains. The Trail of Tears provided a dramatic story to match the stunning landscape, while Cherokee resistance to removal explained why some Indians still lived in the region. During the 1930s, several Appalachian communities, including the Eastern Band of Cherokee Indians, mounted substantial efforts to commemorate removal as part of campaigns to attract visitors. Amplified in this way, Cherokee removal became a more pronounced element of the region's public historical identity.

Appalachian tourism celebrated Cherokees as people of the past. The Eastern Band, boosters promised, had retained its ancient ways and would perform the old culture for visitors. This theme reflected a broader phenomenon in the late nineteenth and early twentieth centuries, whereby Americans looked to Native cultures to provide contact with an authentic premodern existence. It also echoed tourism representations of mountain whites, whom boosters similarly characterized as colorful primitives. In addition, tourism promoters depicted the Eastern Band as an historical aberration, a Native community that persisted in its North Carolina homeland long after most tribes either departed for the West or otherwise faded away.

Removal-era history, as presented within mountain tourism, assured visitors that most Indian people had vanished, while suggesting how a few had managed to remain.

As that last point suggests, the appeal of Cherokee subjects within tourism depended upon a perception of Indian absence from the South. Cherokee people and places attracted tourists because they were unexpected and thus exotic. By the early twentieth century, white southerners came to believe that Native Americans no longer resided in the region to any meaningful extent. Southern writers and artists employed Indian images, but their Indians almost always belonged to the past. The invisibility of contemporary Indian people helped whites to maintain a biracial conception of the region. Native Americans appeared as symbols, old stories, and names on the landscape, but the contemporary South was black and white.[9] Commemoration of the Trail of Tears reflected and reinforced this idea of Indian absence. Removal was a story of Indian people going away. Even when commemoration called attention to the persistence of the Eastern Band, it tended to confirm Indian absence as the southern norm. The Cherokee community in North Carolina presented an attractive anomaly, a small exception that proved the South's racial rule. While tourism magnified the significance of Cherokee history, it sustained this conception of a biracial contemporary South and, with it, the idea of Indian disappearance.

In doing so, it affirmed white supremacy during the era of Jim Crow. As the historian Grace Elizabeth Hale argues, segregation required the continual performance of white superiority. As it emerged in the late nineteenth century, the South's racial caste system rested not only on law and violence, but on a set of cultural forms that enacted racial difference on a day-to-day basis. Public memory formed a significant part of this culture. When whites expressed nostalgia for the antebellum plantation or remembered the Civil War as a heroic "Lost Cause," they reassured themselves of their own superiority and made the region's contemporary racial order seem natural and just. Rooted in this history, segregation became a logical way of organizing a society.[10] Commemorating Indian removal contributed to this practice. Stories of Indian loss and disappearance helped white southerners make indigenous places their own. They confirmed white communities—but never black—as the possessors of Indian land, and they made the Trail of Tears a part of the heritage of those communities, deepening residents' identification with their home places. Removal commemoration, moreover, often involved expressions of regret for Cherokee loss and even apologies for the injustice of the Trail of Tears. This regret demonstrated the moral sensitivity of contemporary white elites, while requiring little from white communities but the apology itself. Remembering removal, then, affirmed white authority. In Hale's terms, it provided an additional stage on which white southerners could perform their racial preeminence.

Cherokees in North Carolina participated in many of the commemorations of the 1920s and 1930s. The growth of Appalachian tourism provided new economic opportunities for citizens of the Eastern Band, while offering Cherokees new ways of asserting their status as an Indian people. That status represented a significant political resource in the segregated South. Under segregation, southern law and culture emphasized the paramount significance of "white" and "colored" as immutable racial designations. This hardening of racial categories encouraged Native communities to emphasize their Indianness and to accept the premise that "Indian" was, itself, a racial category. Public identification as Indian protected these communities from experiencing the degree of control and exploitation suffered by African Americans. It helped them to negotiate a social and political landscape defined by white power over black lives and labor.[11] Cherokee tourism performances in this period affirmed the Cherokees' Indian identity, even if they often involved thoroughly inaccurate depictions of tribal history and culture. A distinct Native people, they announced, persisted in the mountains of the Southeast.

The tourism projects of the early twentieth century set the stage for a second, more substantial period of commemoration in the decades following World War II. In the 1950s and early 1960s, several southern states developed parks and historic sites dedicated to Cherokee removal, while Cherokee communities expanded their own involvement in public memory work. In the book's middle chapters I examine several of these postwar projects in the context of Cold War American culture, the civil rights politics of the South, and midcentury debates over U.S. Indian policy. The Cold War and the struggle over segregation made Cherokee removal a more desirable subject of public memory, as the acknowledgment of Native American dispossession granted some white southerners a politically safe way to consider their region's heritage of racial oppression. In memory, the removal story echoed the modern struggle over black civil rights, but the Cherokee episode lay distant enough from contemporary politics that white communities could memorialize Indian loss without inviting controversy. Indians remained absent from the region and invisible, as far as many whites were concerned. Their history was relevant to contemporary southern politics, but innocuous. Recognizing removal as a crime, moreover, allowed commemorators to express a commitment to American ideals of democracy and equality at a time when civil rights activists condemned the segregated South as profoundly un-American.

If the removal memory served some white southerners' political needs, its popularity also proved to be an asset for Cherokees, who faced their own political struggles in the postwar era. In North Carolina, heritage tourism helped the leaders of the Eastern Band fend off the federal government's termination policy. In Oklahoma, meanwhile, a particular version of the removal story played a significant role in efforts to rebuild a Cherokee national government. There, tribal leaders offered the memory of the reconstruction of the Cherokee Nation *after* the Trail of Tears as a model for political action and as a means of bolstering their own authority. While the broad popularity of Cherokee removal as a subject of public memory reflected non-Indians' needs and political dilemmas, Cherokees proved capable of repossessing this history and applying it to their own purposes.

The book concludes by charting the impressive growth of removal commemoration at the end of the twentieth century and the beginning of the twenty-first. In 1987 Congress designated the Trail of Tears National Historic Trail, adding two Cherokee removal routes to the nation's system of scenic and historic corridors. The national trail became a catalyst for myriad public history projects across the South, as communities along the removal routes sought to participate in this federal project. Cherokee removal became a more prominent feature of the public historical identity of dozens of individual places, some of which figured only briefly in the removal story. As a result of this work, the Cherokee Trail of Tears became one of the most heavily commemorated episodes from American Indian history. This development exemplifies a broader trend in the United States toward the rapid proliferation of memorials and monuments, a phenomenon the scholar Erika Doss calls "memorial mania." In recent decades, Americans have become obsessively concerned with issues of memory and heritage. A growing desire to acknowledge historical trauma and shame has helped to drive this trend. Contemporary Americans display a heightened rights consciousness, and this awareness has made the recognition of past violence and injustice an obligation of American citizenship.[12] The Cherokee Trail of Tears, already a fixture on the southern commemorative landscape, proved a ready vehicle for expressing this intensified concern with shame. It offered a familiar story, but one suitable for containing the new obsessions of memorial mania.

The expansion of heritage work devoted to the Trail of Tears, however, did not always open new understandings of the American past or prompt useful dialogue about the present. Much of the new commemoration, in fact, echoed the monuments and performances of the previous two eras. In many places along the national trail, removal remained a story of Indian disappearance, and non-Indian heritage workers continued to treat the Trail of Tears as their own communities' property. Cherokee removal remained a politically safe subject during this period, even though the development of the national trail took place during the height of the "history wars" of the 1990s. Remembering Cherokee removal helped non-Indians fulfill their obligation to recognize injustice and trauma in the nation's past, but the memory remained politically innocuous. Today, we have more removal commemoration, but our public memories of the Native South are seldom more complicated or more challenging than before.

Contemporary commemoration of the Trail of Tears tends to define Indian removal as a tragic error, an act of injustice that violated American principles of freedom and equality. That premise is certainly reasonable; however, defining removal as a terrible mistake minimizes the significance of Native American dispossession to the history of the United States. Remembering a policy like removal as an aberration suggests that the United States, as we know it, could exist *without* the coercive acquisition of Native American land. It suggests that the roots of American nationhood lie only in a set of liberal political values, rather than in a physical territory constructed from indigenous peoples' homes. Recent literature on settler colonialism offers a different, and more vital, perspective. For scholars in settler colonial studies, the elimination of indigenous peoples as landholders and sovereigns forms the fundamental basis for American nationhood. The foundation of the United States lay in the erasure of Indian peoples and their replacement with settler communities. American principles of liberty and democracy cannot be separated from territorial conquest, insofar as Americans enacted those principles on indigenous land. For American citizens in the nineteenth century, freedom and opportunity depended upon the disappearance of Indian nations.[13] Public commemoration that began with this idea would prove more challenging than the recognition of an old injustice. It might even draw attention to the ways in which colonialism still shapes American life.

Place and Commemoration

In much of the work that follows, I approach commemoration as a form of place making. The public history projects I examine reflect broad political and cultural trends, but they evolved through the work of particular people acting upon discrete locations. When a community erects a monument or establishes a heritage attraction, it selects specific elements of the past and inscribes them on the landscape as the defining characteristics of a particular site. Public history assigns meaning to location, linking stories, events, and values to physical space. In doing so, it creates places.[14] This process is always political, since it involves particular actors or institutions assuming authority to define the historical meaning of a site and can invite counterclaims from others. Place making, moreover, is often an act of possession. When we create a place through public history, we frequently take it as our own, identifying its past as the cultural patrimony of our specific community or population. Any such assertion deflects or subsumes rival claims of ownership. In many of the commemorative projects I discuss in this book, non-Indians embraced the story of Cherokee removal as an element of their own community heritage. They defined certain locations as historically Cherokee, but in doing so took possession of those sites and memories. Acknowledging indigenous histories allowed them to know and hold these places as their homes.

While commemoration creates specific sites, it also connects those locations to larger geographical categories. In the 1920s and 1930s, the tourism industry identified the Smoky Mountains as Cherokee country. In doing so, it tied Cherokee history and the contemporary Cherokee community to the idea of Appalachia as a distinct region. At New Echota, Georgia state officials invoked national patriotic values to define the meaning of the Cherokee capital, while responding to the commemoration in ways that echoed the white South's political crisis during the era of the civil rights movement. The New Echota site proved meaningful within local, state, regional, and national contexts, and each of those contexts shaped the process of its creation. More recently, a variety of local communities across the South have competed for inclusion in the Trail of Tears National Historic Trail. This work has entailed heritage advocates connecting very specific and highly local episodes to regional and national narratives of Indian dispossession. Memorials and exhibits at these sites display conversations between local knowledge and broader conceptions of southern and American history.

Place making is an open-ended endeavor, never fully complete. Memorial sites, once designated as significant, tend to attract multiple narratives over time, as visitors and later generations of heritage workers bring their own perspectives and experiences to bear upon established places. Public history has an accretive aspect, since old monuments and heritage attractions often determine where new rounds of commemoration take place.

When the National Park Service (NPS) developed the Trail of Tears National Historic Trail, for instance, it started by working with existing state and local sites, such as New Echota in Georgia. Old memorials shaped the new commemoration, even as the new commemoration amended the old. In the case of removal monuments, this openness toward revision offers Native Americans opportunities to influence places created by non-Indians, reworking their public meaning. Earlier commemorative acts, however, continue to play a role in defining many of these places, in spite of contemporary efforts at adjustment.

As an example of this general process, consider a site called Moccasin Springs, located in southeast Missouri, on the Mississippi River just north of Cape Girardeau. This area lies hundreds of miles from either the Cherokee tribal lands in North Carolina or the Cherokee Nation in Oklahoma, and it figured only briefly in the history of the Trail of Tears. In the late 1830s, Cherokee detachments passed through the region on their way west. In the mid-twentieth century, however, local white residents chose to highlight this element of the region's past as part of an effort to draw tourists to southeast Missouri. In doing so, they magnified the Cherokee history of this predominantly non-Indian community.

Southeast Missouri witnessed a particularly terrible phase of the Trail of Tears. Removal detachments traveling overland reached the Mississippi in midwinter and had to pause, in some cases for several weeks, as migrants slowly crossed the ice-choked river by ferry. Packed in camps on either bank, Cherokees suffered from exposure and disease, and scores perished as they waited for the journey to resume.[15] Perhaps due to the intensity of Cherokee suffering at this stage, the local non-Indian community retained a memory of removal. In particular, residents recalled one Cherokee death, that of a young woman whose name they remembered as "Otahki." She was the daughter of Jesse Bushyhead, a Cherokee Baptist minister who led one of the removal detachments. According to local tradition, Otahki became ill and died shortly after crossing the Mississippi, and her family buried her on a rise a short distance from the ferry landing. They marked her grave with a wooden cross, and, in the years following removal, local residents chose to care for the gravesite. When a brush fire destroyed the wooden marker, they replaced it with a pile of stones and, later, a cross made of iron. The presence of this marked burial helped to ensure that Cherokee removal remained part of the local community's sense of the past. In the 1940s, Girl Scouts in Cape Girardeau even adopted the name "Otahki" for their troop, and they placed an additional marker at the grave. For more than a century, then, white residents of southeast Missouri maintained this burial site and, with it, a particular memory of the Trail of Tears.[16]

In the 1950s, civic leaders in Cape Girardeau mounted a campaign to establish a state park at Moccasin Springs. This effort had the effect of calling new attention to the removal memory, which, in turn, shaped the character of the place the park preserved. Initially, the campaign had little to do with history or commemoration. The promoters wanted to create a camping and recreation area, making use of a scenic and relatively undeveloped stretch of land along the river to draw visitors to the region. As the park took shape, however, they began to identify cultural as well as natural assets in the landscape, and the memory of Otahki and removal quickly came to the fore. In promoting their plan, they chose to emphasize that Moccasin Springs was not only a beautiful spot but the setting for tragic historical events, personified by the young woman buried by the river. They made the area's fleeting role in the Cherokee removal story one of the justifications for preserving the site, naming the park for the Trail of Tears and proposing the construction of a museum dedicated to Native American history. Thus, a memory of the Cherokee past, fixed on the landscape by Otahki's grave, became a more pronounced element of this non-Indian community's public historical identity. In the context of tourism development, this non-Indian community defined Moccasin Springs as a Cherokee place.[17]

Missouri officially opened its Trail of Tears State Park in the spring of 1962, and one of the highlights of that first season was the dedication of a new monument at the grave. Erected by the Cape Girardeau Rotary Club, it consisted of a bronze tablet set in a stone slab and sheltered within a pagoda-like structure made of iron and concrete. The tablet told of Otahki's death during the Cherokees' "forced exodus" to Indian Territory, identifying her as a "princess" and Jesse Bushyhead as a "chief." At the dedication, a crowd of five hundred listened as Missouri legislator and jurist Rush Limbaugh (grandfather of the radio personality) recounted the Cherokee removal story and described the development of the park. Oklahoma Supreme Court justice N. B. Johnson, representing the Cherokee Nation, offered a formal response, elaborating on the history of the Trail of Tears and thanking Missourians for preserving the memory of this "foul blot" on American history. With this ceremony, local residents and the state government sanctified the site, investing it with moral resonance. More than a recreation area, it became a "shrine," as a local newspaper described it, set apart as a spot suitable for visitors' contemplation of the past.[18]

Dedication of the Otahki Memorial, Trail of Tears State Park, Cape Girardeau County, Missouri, 1962. Courtesy *Southeast Missourian*, Cape Girardeau, Missouri.

This dedication, however, did not fix the meaning of the site permanently. Since 1962, park personnel have applied new narratives to Otahki's grave, prompted first by Cherokee visitors. Descendants of Jesse Bushyhead attended the opening of the park and toured the area in later years, and none could recall a young woman named Otahki. Jesse Bushyhead, they reported, did not lose a daughter on the Trail of Tears. In fact, his wife gave birth to a daughter shortly after crossing the Mississippi, and the family recognized her place of birth by naming her Eliza *Missouri* Bushyhead. Other young women, including a sister of the minister, died during this stage of the journey, but the girl enshrined in local memory never lived. Park personnel responded by recontextualizing the grave. They began to treat the Otahki story as a legend and to suggest to visitors that they view the gravesite memorial as a tribute to all of the Cherokees who died during removal. The park then reworked the monument itself after the NPS included the site on the Trail of Tears National Historic Trail. In 2001 park workers installed new signage at the grave, unveiled during a conference of the Trail of Tears Association, a public advocacy group established to support the national trail. They placed the signs on the approach to the 1962 monument, so that visitors would encounter the new memory just before they met the old. The signs referred to Otahki as a "local legend" and explained that "princess" was merely a title of respect conferred by whites. They suggested, meanwhile, that the person buried in the grave was Jesse Bushyhead's sister. Finally, park officials identified the site as the "Bushyhead Memorial," drawing attention away from the name Otahki, the origins of which were always unclear.[19] Visiting Moccasin Springs today, one encounters competing narratives and evidence of several rounds of place making. The sanctified grave of the "princess" stands in awkward tension with the newer interpretive displays. The "Bushyhead Memorial" revises the older monument, but the romantic story of the dying Indian girl remains a powerful presence. These multiple layers of commemoration confirm the local community's original choice to identify Moccasin Springs as a Cherokee place, but they leave the precise meaning of the site incomplete and open to further revision.

Obligations to the Present

Public commemoration of the Trail of Tears shows few signs of abating. Since the early 1990s, the NPS has designated more than seventy "certified sites" and interpretive centers along the Trail of Tears National Historic Trail, and new requests for certification arrive every year. At each of these sites, local heritage advocates have worked with NPS, tribal authorities, and the Trail of Tears Association to establish interpretive displays, ranging from a few outdoor signs to extensive museum exhibits.[20] The national trail, meanwhile, has grown in recent years. In response to lobbying by heritage groups and tribal representatives, Congress has added hundreds of miles of new routes to those originally designated. These new corridors promise to draw additional communities into the trail project, spurring the creation of new removal places.[21] NPS and its partners, moreover, have worked to expand commemoration of Indian removal to include the histories of multiple tribes, moving beyond the Cherokee experience. One recent project, for instance, interprets sites along removal routes in Arkansas traveled by all five of the large Indian nations of the Southeast.[22] Shaped by the national trail, the public memory of Indian removal continues to grow on the southern landscape.

In the final chapter of the book, I question whether recent commemoration of the Trail of Tears represents a departure from earlier patterns of public memory. Too often, contemporary public history simply confirms the familiar narrative of Indian disappearance, endlessly repeating a story of Native Americans going away. Heritage workers can disrupt that narrative, but only if they find ways to make these places something more than monuments to Indian absence. Removal sites offer opportunities for public dialogue about the persistence and revival of Indian nations in the modern United States and about the contemporary politics of Native American sovereignty. More broadly, they invite discussion of the power of race and colonialism in the present. To embrace those opportunities, visitors and heritage workers alike must approach the Native history of the South as ongoing, rather than as something that ended in the early nineteenth century. They must acknowledge Indian removal not as a tragic mistake in a distant past, but as a foundational moment, an act that helped to create the South as we know it and one that continues to shape privilege and inequality today.

I count myself among those heritage workers who bear this responsibility. In the years since my first visit to New Echota, I have become a participant in the public commemoration of the Native South, as well as a tourist and academic spectator. I belong to the Trail of Tears Association, the nonprofit established in the 1990s to support the development of the national trail. In partnership with the Eastern Band of Cherokee Indians, association members in North Carolina seek to expand and improve public commemoration of removal-era Cherokee history in the western part of the state. Writing this book affected my attitude toward these activities in contradictory ways. The research led me to question my own motivations for participating in removal commemoration, while challenging my belief in the ability of public history to exert a progressive influence on American life. At the same time, it strengthened my conviction that such work is necessary and that academic historians bear an obligation to act as public scholars. I hope that my fellow heritage advocates will find my observations useful as together we look for better ways to put this history to work in the present.

1 Removal and the Cherokee Nation

· ·

The Cherokee homeland lies in the southern Appalachian highlands, with its center in the Great Smoky Mountains. At the time of European contact, Cherokees lived in what is today western North Carolina, the northwestern corner of South Carolina, eastern Tennessee, and a portion of northern Georgia. In the eighteenth century, Cherokees expanded further into Georgia and into northeastern Alabama. They also claimed a much broader expanse of territory in present-day Kentucky and Virginia, where they hunted and gathered wild plants and other resources. With its varied terrain and temperate climate, this country was an immensely rich place, with fertile lands for agriculture and some of the greatest biodiversity in North America.[1] It was a good place for human beings.

Cherokees were farmers, cultivating corn in the valleys made by the rivers and streams that drained the highlands. They lived in permanent settlements, or towns, of several hundred people each. At the center of a Cherokee town stood a polygonal council house, sometimes built upon an earthen mound, which served as both a meeting place and a religious structure. Cherokees viewed some of their settlements as "mother towns," especially significant places that helped to define the surrounding regions. The most important of these was Kituwah (or Kituwha), on the Tuckaseegee River in present-day western North Carolina. Today, Cherokees still identify Kituwah as the *first* Cherokee town, the place where their people learned the proper way of living in this world. At Kituwah, Cherokees entered into the sacred relationship between their people and the land that established this country as their home.[2]

When Europeans began arriving in the Americas, Cherokees first experienced limited encounters with the Spanish before establishing more sustained relations with British colonists operating out of South Carolina and Virginia. In the eighteenth century Cherokees traded deerskins and war captives to the British in return for guns, metal knives and tools, textiles, and other European goods. Cherokees also became British military allies, drawn into the struggles among rival European empires. In the Seven Years' War Cherokees fought on the side of the British until attacks by Anglo-American

Tuckaseegee River valley, looking toward the site of Kituwah. Photo by author.

frontier settlers led some Cherokees to break with the alliance and war upon their former partners. The British responded by invading the Cherokee country, razing more than a dozen towns and burning Cherokee farms and food stores.[3]

When the American Revolution began, Cherokee leaders tried to keep their people neutral. By this time, however, Anglo-American settlers were focusing increasing pressure upon the tribe to cede land. Some Cherokees viewed the Revolution as an opportunity to regain lost territory, aided by the British and their other Native American allies. In the spring of 1776, Cherokee warriors attacked frontier settlements, hoping to drive the intruders from their borders. Colonists responded by invading the Cherokee country, with columns of militia from North Carolina, South Carolina, Virginia, and Georgia all converging upon the Cherokee homeland. The invaders again burned towns and destroyed Cherokee farms, setting much of the population to flight. Cherokees suffered terribly from hunger and disease in the winter that followed. At this point, most Cherokees abandoned the war, but a segment of the tribe fought on, establishing new villages in the vicinity of present-day Chattanooga. Their resistance led colonial militia to mount additional invasions of the Cherokee country, bringing further destruction. Some continued to fight even after the war between the United States and Great Britain ended. The last of the Cherokees made peace with the United States only in 1794, more than a decade after Britain conceded defeat and recognized American independence.[4]

In the Peace of Paris, Great Britain acknowledged U.S. possession of all territory from the Atlantic to the Mississippi, south of Canada and north of Florida. Most of this land, of course, belonged to Indian nations, the Cherokees among them. One of the great questions of early American politics, then, was how the United States could make these expansive claims a reality. Removal was not the first response to this Indian Question, but it became the definitive answer.

Civilizing Indians

Removal was the early nineteenth-century campaign to compel eastern Indian tribes to exchange their lands for territory west of the Mississippi River. After years of piecemeal treaties and land sales, removal advocates sought to open the entire East to non-Indian settlement as rapidly as possible, while eliminating the presence of independent Indian nations within the borders of established states. The idea of Indian removal evolved as an alternative to the approach to Indian affairs first formulated by President George Washington and his secretary of war, Henry Knox, in the early 1790s. Knox and Washington understood that the United States, still recovering from the Revolution, could not fully dominate its Indian neighbors, but they also knew that Americans demanded westward expansion and the opening of new lands. They tried to devise a system that would allow the United States to grow without provoking war along its western borders. The federal government, they decided, would approach Indian tribes as distinct nations, dealing with them through treaties negotiated by the Executive and ratified by the Senate. The United States would purchase lands from Indian people to facilitate westward settlement, rather than expand through war and conquest. At the same time, the United States would encourage Native people to become "civilized," transforming their economies and cultures in emulation of white America. The federal government invited missionary organizations to set up schools and churches in Indian communities, and treaties during this period often included promises by the United States to provide Native Americans with agricultural tools and other materials that would promote economic change. As Indians became civilized, Knox and his supporters believed, they would be willing to sell territory to the United States, since they would no longer need large tracts of hunting land. They also anticipated that frontier trade would leave many Indian communities in debt, forcing them to sell land and alter their economic practices. When fully civilized, Indians would assimilate into American society. Piece by piece, and preferably without conquest, the territory won by the United States in the Revolution would become available to settlers. Historian Robert Berkhofer, with some irony, characterizes this policy as "expansion with honor."[5]

In retrospect, this approach to Indian affairs seems far more benign than forced removal. Certainly, many Cherokees thought it so.[6] It is important to emphasize, however, that "expansion with honor" shared removal's ultimate objective: Indian disappearance and the replacement of indigenous peoples with settler communities. Knox and Washington recognized Indian tribes as distinct nations, but they also anticipated that those nations would soon vanish, their lands absorbed by the United States. Indeed, Indian nations had to vanish for the American republic to prosper and realize its territorial claims. Ideally, Native Americans would disappear through the civilization process, gradually fading into the American populace. If Indians did not assimilate, however, they would likely face destruction. They would find themselves in conflict with their white neighbors, and eventually the more numerous and civilized Americans would overwhelm the tribes. This line of reasoning was more than simply an example of Euro-American ethnocentrism. It represented a core element of American nationhood. The United States required the property of Indian peoples. It could offer its citizens freedom and opportunity only to the extent that it took possession of indigenous territories. This "logic of elimination," to use Patrick Wolfe's phrase, informed all early American Indian policy, Washington's approach no less than Andrew Jackson's.[7]

Cherokee interaction with the United States adhered to Knox's plans. In the late eighteenth and early nineteenth centuries, the Cherokees signed treaties selling large tracts of land to accommodate American expansion. Federal authorities agreed to protect the remaining Cherokee territory from encroachment by American citizens, while Cherokees promised to maintain political relations only with the United States. Under the civilization policy, the federal government provided Cherokees with tools and livestock, and Christian missionaries began to request permission to work in the Cherokee country. While most Cherokees rejected the idea that they had to remake themselves in the image of Euro-Americans, many adopted specific practices of the newcomers. Cherokee men used plows to prepare fields for planting, and Cherokee families raised horses, cattle, and hogs. Cherokee women, who had always made clothing, learned to weave and spin thread. Very few Cherokees converted to Christianity during this period, but many hoped their children might benefit from learning English and other new skills at the mission schools. These changes represented relatively minor adjustments, but they reassured the missionaries and federal agents that the civilization campaign was working as intended. Some Cherokees, meanwhile, embraced a more thorough transformation. Taking white southern planters as their model, they pursued market agriculture on a substantial scale, assembling large tracts of land and acquiring African American slaves. They opened stores and taverns or operated river ferries, taking advantage of increased traffic through the Cherokee territory. By the 1820s, a small but influential economic elite coalesced in the Cherokee country, and many of the Cherokees' leaders during the removal struggle belonged to this class, men such as John Ridge, his father Major Ridge, and John Ross. Elite families often included white men married to Cherokee women. Under the tribe's matrilineal kinship system, the children born to these marriages were Cherokees, but they tended to be conversant in both Euro-American and Cherokee ways. Their bicultural background helped them take advantage of economic opportunities offered by the close proximity of the United States, while making them useful as tribal representatives in Cherokee dealings with the federal government. This elite secured for the Cherokees a public reputation as a "civilized tribe," an image tribal leaders later used to defend their people against removal.[8]

As these economic and social changes took place, Cherokees also altered their political practices. Traditionally, Cherokee political life was a local affair. Cherokee towns were autonomous, with local communities making decisions through consensus. Some political centralization took place during the eighteenth century, as Cherokees conducted trade and diplomacy with Europeans, but power remained widely diffused. In the early nineteenth century, Cherokees departed from this pattern and began building stronger national institutions. They adopted written laws and created a national police, known as Light Horse Guards, to enforce them. They established an executive committee to represent the Cherokee Nation on a day-to-day basis, while organizing a system of districts to select representatives to the Cherokee National Council. Later, in 1827, they drafted a Cherokee Constitution, which established a central government for the tribe modeled on that of the United States, with a chief executive, legislature, and court system. Tribal leaders even designated a national capital, New Echota, as the seat of this new central government. Two motives lay behind this transformation. First, the tribal elite hoped that a national government would help them defend their economic interests. When Cherokees began drafting written laws, many of the early statutes sought to protect individual property and regulate the new economic activities adopted by Cherokee planters. In addition, a strong central government promised to help Cherokees preserve their homeland and contend with American demands for new land cessions. The 1827 Constitution specified that Cherokee land would be held in common and that only the National Council could cede territory. The United States, in other words, could purchase Cherokee lands only with the consent of the Nation as a whole.[9]

One other development from this period is worth mentioning here. In the 1820s, as Cherokee leaders worked to create a national government, a previously obscure man named Sequoyah completed a system for writing the Cherokee language. Sequoyah's syllabary contained eighty-five symbols representing different sounds in spoken Cherokee. By most accounts, native speakers of the Cherokee language could learn the system with relative ease, and its use quickly spread, particularly after it received the endorsement of tribal leaders. In 1828, the Cherokee Nation, aided by missionaries, established a newspaper, the *Cherokee Phoenix*, with material printed in both the syllabary and English. John Ridge's cousin Elias Boudinot became its first editor. During the struggle over removal, Cherokee literacy became a potent symbol of Indian civilization, and the *Phoenix* helped to rally opposition to the policy. Sequoyah, meanwhile, gained considerable fame as a Native American genius, a man who proved the capabilities of Indian people.[10] A century later, Sequoyah and the syllabary would also become common features of the public memory of the Trail of Tears.

From Civilization to Removal

For supporters of the Indian civilization campaign, Cherokees provided ample evidence of the success of Washington's policies. By the early 1820s, however, American political leaders were turning away from "expansion with honor" in favor of the wholesale expulsion of Indian tribes from the East. Several developments explain this change. First, American demand for new territory proved far greater than the eastern tribes' willingness to part with their property. Knox and Washington's approach imagined a gradual, orderly expansion, but the reality was closer to a gold rush. This pressure was particularly intense in the South, where the rise of the cotton kingdom promised wealth and status to any white settler who could secure agricultural land and the slaves to work it. In the midst of an agricultural boom, the continued presence of Indian homelands in the East seemed a criminal denial of opportunity to American citizens. Meanwhile, public faith in Indian civilization faded, as Americans increasingly subscribed to more rigid and hierarchical conceptions of race. In the emerging racial thought of the antebellum era, Indians' cultural difference from Europeans reflected an inherent inferiority, a deficiency no amount of education could ameliorate. If this were the case, Native people could never progress to a level at which they would be ready to enter American society. From this perspective, removal seemed a far more reasonable approach to Indian affairs than continued efforts at civilization. The federal government could simply move Native Americans out of the way of the expanding white republic. Finally, by the early 1820s, the United States possessed greater power to coerce Indian people than during the federal period, making a policy as sweeping as removal more feasible. "Expansion with honor" reflected Knox and Washington's awareness that the large Indian nations of the East still posed a significant military challenge to the United States. After the War of 1812, Native military power was much reduced, and American political leaders could talk of simply imposing their will upon weakened Indian nations. The removal policy, then, emerged from a potent combination of land hunger, white supremacy, and growing imperial power.[11]

The removal campaign received widespread support from white political leaders in the South, but, in the Cherokee case, the government of the state of Georgia forced the issue. In part, this fact simply reflected the size and value of the Cherokee territory claimed by the state, but, in addition, Georgia's leaders believed that the federal government bore a special obligation to eliminate Indian landholding. In 1802 the state entered into a compact with federal negotiators to define its western boundary and settle claims related to the Yazoo land fraud. The state relinquished its western territory (present-day Alabama and Mississippi) in return for 1.25 million dollars and a pledge from the federal government to extinguish Indian land title within Georgia's newly defined borders. Those borders encompassed a portion of the Creek territory, as well as a large section of the Cherokee homeland. As time passed and Creeks and Cherokees refused to cede these lands, Georgia's political leadership felt increasingly aggrieved toward both the Indians and the federal government. Federal authorities seemed to value good relations with Indian tribes more than they did the government's solemn promise to the state.[12]

In the late 1820s, Georgia politicians began pressing the matter. In 1826 and 1827, the state legislature passed resolutions asserting Georgia's sovereignty over all land within its recognized boundaries. This was a warning, of sorts, implying that Georgia would take more direct action to enforce its sovereignty should the Cherokees continue to occupy their land. When no new treaty appeared, the legislature adopted more forceful measures. Beginning in December 1828, it passed a series of laws designed to eliminate Cherokee landownership and political authority within Georgia's borders, while rendering Cherokees incapable of defending themselves against the state's actions. It extended the state's legal jurisdiction over Cherokee territory and declared the Cherokees' own laws nullified. It outlawed the Cherokee national government and began distributing Cherokee lands to Georgia citizens by lottery. Interference with the process of enrolling Indians for removal was made a crime, and the state barred Indians from testifying in Georgia courts against whites. Another law required whites residing in the Cherokee country to swear an oath of allegiance to the state and receive the state's permission to remain, a move aimed at silencing the Cherokees' non-Indian allies. Finally, the state created a militia to enforce the new order, the Georgia Guard. These acts transformed Cherokees into refugees in their own country, stripping them of property rights and legal protection. Georgia erased the Cherokees in law, in preparation for their replacement with settler communities.[13]

In response, Cherokee leaders remonstrated to the federal government, calling upon the United States to protect their people, as guaranteed in the Cherokees' treaties. President Andrew Jackson, however, replied by expressing support for Georgia's sovereignty and urging the Cherokees to negotiate a removal agreement. Federal authorities, he suggested, could not undo Georgia's actions, but they could help the Cherokees escape to the West.[14] In the spring of 1830, as the Cherokee crisis in Georgia deepened, Congress passed the Indian Removal Act, which authorized the president to negotiate the exchange of tribal lands in the East for new territories west of the Mississippi River. The United States would compensate Indians for improvements on ceded land, while defraying the costs of migration. By itself, the act did not force the Cherokees or any other Native people to migrate, but it identified removal as the federal government's primary goal in Indian affairs and established a bureaucratic process for eliminating the Native peoples of the East. To Georgia, it signaled that the state could continue to persecute the Cherokees, while federal authorities stood by, ready to negotiate a removal treaty whenever Cherokee opposition crumbled.[15]

In resisting removal, Cherokees adopted several overlapping strategies. First, they continued to appeal to the federal government for aid, petitioning Congress and the president to uphold U.S. treaty obligations to defend the Cherokees. While Jackson remained intransigent, Cherokee leaders recognized that the president had many enemies. They sought allies in Congress, while hoping to see Jackson replaced by someone more sympathetic to Indian rights in the election of 1832. Cherokees also mounted what we would now call a public relations campaign, cultivating alliances with non-Indian communities in the hope that American public opinion might spur federal authorities to act. The *Cherokee Phoenix*, which circulated widely through exchanges with other newspapers, provided a means of broadcasting the tribal government's opposition to removal. Religious organizations with missionary ties to the tribe also helped to publicize the Cherokee struggle, especially during the early years of the crisis.[16] In their public communications, Cherokee leaders portrayed Georgia's actions as a brutal assault upon a blameless people, one that violated both American law and Christian morality. They reminded non-Indians of the Cherokees' "civilized" achievements—modern agriculture, literacy, education, and constitutional government—and argued that their people proved that Indian communities could exist peacefully within the United States. Removal jeopardized Cherokee progress, they warned, but all could still end well, if the United States would only abide by its promise to protect the Cherokee Nation.[17]

In addition to broadcasting these arguments, Cherokees worked to bring a test of Georgia's laws to the federal courts, hoping to compel federal authorities to intervene on their behalf. This effort provided the context for two Supreme Court cases that helped to establish the foundation of U.S. Indian law. First, in *Cherokee Nation v. Georgia* (1831), the Cherokees' lawyers asked the Supreme Court to grant an injunction halting the enforcement of Georgia's anti-Indian laws on the grounds that they violated international treaties. The Court had the authority to take this action, they argued, under the Constitution's Article III, which allowed the Supreme Court to hear cases between states and foreign nations. The Court's majority, however, refused to consider the request on the grounds that the Cherokees did not, in fact, constitute a foreign country. Chief Justice John Marshall wrote that Indian tribes, instead, were "domestic dependent nations" and declined to address the question of whether Georgia violated the treaties or the Constitution.

In response, the Cherokees and their representatives looked for cases that would fall squarely within the Court's jurisdiction, finding one in the state law that required whites living in the Cherokee country to swear allegiance to Georgia and receive a state permit. Several missionaries defied that law, signing an open letter protesting the state's actions. Arrested by Georgia militia, they were convicted in a state court and sentenced to four years hard labor. Most accepted pardons, but two ministers refused. Samuel Worcester and Elizur Butler chose to appeal their conviction as a test of the anti-Cherokee laws. When the Supreme Court heard the case, *Worcester v. Georgia*, in early 1832, the majority ruled in the missionaries' favor. In his opinion, Marshall still declined to characterize the Cherokees as a foreign nation, but he acknowledged the tribe's right to self-government and recognized that the treaties obliged federal authorities to protect Cherokee land and sovereignty.[18]

For the Cherokees, however, this victory proved empty. Both Andrew Jackson and the state of Georgia refused to act upon the Court's decision, continuing to insist that the Cherokees accept removal.[19] In later public memory, this refusal would help to make Jackson the villain of the Trail of Tears story, although his role in the episode was mostly passive. He simply declined to respond to the Court's decision, leaving Georgia free to continue its harassment. The Cherokees' tactics, meanwhile, would earn them fame and admiration. Their use of the courts and their nonviolent resistance would burnish their reputation as a civilized people. The importance of the court cases to subsequent Indian law, meanwhile, would help to make the Cherokee experience appear more noteworthy than the removal of other Indian peoples. In the 1980s, for instance, the National Park Service cited the Supreme Court cases as evidence that the Cherokee Trail of Tears was significant enough to a broader American history to warrant designation as a National Historic Trail.[20]

As the tribal government searched for ways to push back against Georgia, conditions in the Cherokee country deteriorated. In 1832, Georgia sent surveyors to divide the Cherokee land into individual parcels, which it then distributed by lottery to Georgia citizens. New settlers poured into the Nation that autumn, seizing Cherokee property. State law permitted Cherokees to remain on the lots that held their farms and homes, stipulating that, for the time being, only undeveloped land could be occupied by lottery winners. Many settlers, however, ignored this provision and forced Cherokees from their land, recognizing that state authorities would do little to punish the infraction. According to one newspaper, around two-thirds of the Cherokees in Georgia were homeless by the end of 1835.[21] The discovery of gold in the Cherokee country at the end of 1829 exacerbated these troubles. Several thousand prospectors rushed into what is today northern Georgia, and the promise of mineral wealth made the state's campaign to expel the Cherokees even more urgent.[22] In the twentieth century, popular accounts of the Trail of Tears would often treat the gold strikes as a catalyst for the Trail of Tears, even as its major cause. In memory, the gold rush came to epitomize the greed that drove Cherokees from their homes.

The Cherokee government, meanwhile, also found itself in an increasingly difficult position. Outlawed in Georgia, the national government moved its councils away from New Echota, first to Alabama and then to a place called Red Clay, just over the Georgia line in what is today southeastern Tennessee. Cherokee leaders, meanwhile, had trouble finding the money necessary to maintain their opposition, as Jackson's War Department suspended payment of treaty annuities to the Cherokee government's treasury. The Nation almost immediately ran short of the money necessary to hire lawyers, send delegates to Washington, and otherwise continue its fight against removal.[23] During this time, the Nation also began to lose many of its non-Indian allies, particularly after *Worcester v. Georgia* proved a disappointment. Sympathetic members of Congress advised Cherokee leaders that removal was now inevitable, urging them to negotiate the best possible deal for their land and hope for better fortune in the West. Many of the missionaries came to the same conclusion. Even Samuel Worcester and Elizur Butler capitulated, accepting pardons from Georgia's governor and leaving the state.[24] The great majority of Cherokees still opposed removal, but the Nation seemed powerless to reverse the course of events.

In response to this deepening crisis, some Cherokee leaders began advocating an end to resistance. Led by John Ridge, his father Major Ridge, and his cousin Elias Boudinot, they argued that the Nation must accept removal and negotiate a treaty before conditions grew any worse for the Cherokee population in Georgia. "We found that all our efforts to obtain redress from the General Government, *on the land of our fathers*, had been of no avail," Boudinot later wrote. "Instead of contending uselessly against superior power, the only course left, was, to yield to circumstances over which they had no control."[25] When they presented this position to other Cherokee leaders, however, they faced strong opposition, and the Cherokee government moved to silence them. Ross forced Boudinot to resign as editor of the *Cherokee Phoenix*, and the National Council expelled John and Major Ridge. The council also suspended elections, citing Georgia's ban on the Cherokee government. The Treaty Party, as they came to be known, viewed these actions as an effort by Ross and his allies to prevent political discussion and deny Cherokee people the information necessary to make a decision regarding removal. Ross misled the people, they believed, giving them false hope that removal could still be avoided, even though he surely knew better. Further delay, they argued, could not prevent the loss of the Cherokees' land, but it might lead to the destruction of Cherokee communities at the hands of greedy whites and their unprincipled state governments.[26]

The Treaty Party initially hoped to win Ross over to their position, and they believed that Ross could then persuade the Cherokee people that removal was inevitable. When the chief and his allies remained obdurate, the Ridges and Boudinot began to contemplate making a treaty on their own. In 1835 they met with U.S. Indian commissioner John Schermerhorn to negotiate terms for Cherokee removal. They then presented the terms at a series of public meetings, hoping to persuade Cherokees to back the drafting of a treaty following those guidelines. By this time, Georgia governor Wilson Lumpkin and other state officials spoke openly of expelling the Cherokees by force, and the state legislature passed a law permitting the remaining lottery winners to take possession of Cherokee property, even if Cherokees were still in residence. Ross, meanwhile, submitted increasingly desperate proposals to the United States, hoping to buy time or retain at least a remnant of Cherokee lands in the Southeast, even if it meant Cherokees accepted state citizenship.[27]

Finally, in December 1835, Schermerhorn and the Treaty Party moved to end the stalemate. Meeting at New Echota, the former Cherokee capital, they drafted a treaty based upon their discussions earlier in the year. Under its terms, the Cherokees relinquished all of their land east of the Mississippi and promised to migrate to territory already guaranteed to them under earlier treaties. Removal would take place within two years of the treaty's ratification. The United States would pay the Cherokees five million dollars, along with the costs of removal, and subsidize the Cherokees' subsistence in the West for one year. The federal government also agreed to compensate Cherokees for improvements on lands in the East and to establish funds to support Cherokee schools, relief for destitute orphans, and other projects contributing to the general welfare of the Cherokee people. The United States promised never again to include the Cherokee Nation in an American state or territory without the Cherokees' consent, while pledging to protect Cherokee lands from American intruders and other hostile outsiders. Federal commissioners agreed to add eight hundred thousand acres to the Cherokee Nation's holdings in the West, and the United States would issue a patent in fee simple for the entire Cherokee homeland in Indian Territory.[28] On December 29, the Ridges, Boudinot, and other Treaty Party Cherokees signed this agreement and then organized a delegation to bring the document to Washington. Jackson submitted these terms to the Senate in the spring of 1836. Ross and the Cherokee government protested, insisting that the treaty was a fraud and did not represent the will of the Cherokee people. In May, however, the Senate ratified the treaty by one vote more than the necessary two-thirds majority. The Cherokee Nation now had until May 1838 to depart the Southeast.[29]

The Trail

Some Cherokees left for Indian Territory within a year of the ratification of the Treaty of New Echota. Much of the Treaty Party, for instance, departed in the spring of 1837. They joined Cherokees already living in the West in communities formed by earlier, voluntary migrants. Small numbers of Cherokees had moved west as early as the 1790s, and two significant migrations, totaling about three thousand people, took place following Cherokee land cessions in 1810–1811 and 1817–1819. In addition, some Cherokees moved as the crisis in Georgia intensified, most notably a group of around nine hundred who left in 1834.[30] The majority of Cherokees, however, remained in place. Numbering around fifteen thousand, they refused to comply with the treaty, and many declined even to prepare for the journey. "The Indians are perfectly still," one witness observed, "peacefully working in their fields and gardens, awaiting the arrival of the appointed day, but resolutely refusing to recognize the unjust and unauthorized instrument of New Echota."[31] Ross and other tribal leaders continued to work against removal, petitioning federal authorities to abrogate the treaty. Ross hoped at least to delay their expulsion and renegotiate, securing a better price for the Cherokee homeland. As the May 1838 deadline approached, both the Cherokee government and the great majority of Cherokee people refused to budge. The United States would have to implement removal by force.[32]

Anticipating this resistance, the United States established a network of forts and military camps spread throughout the Cherokee country. It then assembled a force of around seven thousand soldiers under the command of General Winfield Scott. Some of the troops belonged to the U.S. Army, while others were state militia placed temporarily under federal authority. This force began gathering Cherokees for deportation on May 26, 1838, focusing first on Indian communities in Georgia. Small units spread out from each of the forts, seizing Cherokees from their homes in the surrounding area. Typically, the soldiers held Cherokees at the local posts for several days before marching them to larger depots in southeastern Tennessee. In Georgia, this process proved very quick, and within three weeks military commanders reported their work in the state finished. Gathering Cherokees in other states took longer but followed a similar pattern. In North Carolina, for instance, federal troops and the state militia brought captured Cherokees to five small posts spread throughout the mountains and from there to Fort Butler, a somewhat larger installation in the present-day town of Murphy. From Fort Butler, soldiers marched the Cherokees over the Unicoi Turnpike to camps clustered near Fort Cass in present-day Charleston, Tennessee.[33]

From the beginning, captured Cherokees suffered from poor conditions and abuse at the hands of soldiers and white civilians, particularly in Georgia. "Multitudes were not allowed time to take anything with them but the clothes they had on," wrote Evan Jones, a Baptist missionary in the Cherokee Nation. "Well-furnished houses were left a prey to plunderers who, like hungry wolves, follow the progress of the captors and in many cases accompany them. These wretches rifle the houses and strip the helpless, unoffending owners of all they have on earth."[34] Another missionary, Daniel Butrick, described the journey to the camps in Tennessee: "It is evident that from their first arrest they were obliged to live like brute animals," he wrote in his diary, "and, during their travels, were obliged at night to lie down upon the naked ground, in the open air, exposed to wind and rain, and herd together, men women and children, like droves of hogs." Butrick noted numerous Cherokee deaths during this period, and he anticipated more to come. "In this way, many are hastening to a premature grave."[35]

Scott planned to transport Cherokees by water, with groups departing from Ross's Landing, on the Tennessee River in present-day Chattanooga. When the first captives began arriving from Georgia in early June, the army organized them into detachments, loaded them onto boats, and sent them on their way as quickly as possible. Three detachments, numbering around two thousand Cherokees in total, departed in this manner during the summer of 1838. Their route followed the Tennessee River across Alabama and then north through Tennessee and Kentucky to the Ohio River. After a short time traveling west on the Ohio, they took the Mississippi south to the Arkansas River and then moved up the Arkansas toward Indian Territory. Water levels on these rivers varied greatly, and none of the three detachments made the trip entirely by boat. Two groups had to disembark at Decatur, Alabama, and take a train around the Mussel Shoals, a section of the Tennessee River that was frequently impassable. Due to low water levels, one detachment had to walk 250 miles from southeastern Tennessee across much of northern Alabama before boarding boats at the town of Waterloo. Two of the three river detachments also encountered low water levels in Arkansas during the last stage of the journey. Travelers in these groups had to disembark and walk the remaining 150 miles to Indian Territory in stifling midsummer heat.[36]

Back in Tennessee, reports arrived of terrible suffering among the Cherokees traveling by water. Packed together in the boats during warm summer weather, Cherokees fell ill and began to die. The delays caused by low water levels prolonged the journey and added to the travelers' misery. "Driving them under such circumstances, and then forcing them into filthy boats, to overflowing in this hot season . . . is only a most expensive and painful way of putting the poor people to death," Daniel Butrick concluded.[37] The first water detachment, which encountered few problems, made the trip in less than three weeks and reported no deaths. The second took almost eight weeks to complete the same journey, with seventy migrants perishing along the way.[38] When Cherokees in Tennessee learned of poor conditions on the rivers, they asked that removal be postponed until the fall, after the worst of the hot weather passed. Scott agreed, but the delay meant that Cherokees now found themselves confined for several months to the camps in Tennessee, where conditions were just as dire. At one camp in late July, an army doctor speculated that as many as five hundred Cherokees were ill out of a group of around sixteen hundred captives under his supervision. "Their children were sick with [w]hooping cough and dysentery before they left their homes and were traveled here through the heat labouring under those afflictions," he reported. "A considerable number . . . have died since they came here, refusing to take medicine or to have anything done for them."[39]

When tribal leaders requested the delay, they also asked permission to organize the removal of the remaining Cherokees themselves, rather than trust the army any further. The War Department agreed, and John Ross and a committee of tribal leaders assumed control of the migration process. John's brother, Lewis Ross, a successful merchant in southeastern Tennessee, became the main contracting agent, organizing the purchase and distribution of supplies for Cherokee detachments. Ross and the committee abandoned the original water route when a period of drought left portions of the rivers unnavigable. They decided instead that removal would take place over land, starting as soon as the summer heat broke. They organized the remaining Cherokees into thirteen detachments of around one thousand people, each led by a conductor and assistant conductor drawn from the ranks of tribal leaders. The Cherokee minister Jesse Bushyhead, for instance, served as one detachment's conductor, while another group was led by Situwakee, a prominent leader from the Valley River region in North Carolina. The first of these detachments, led by Hair Conrad, set out from the vicinity of present-day Charleston, Tennessee, in late August 1838.[40]

Most of the overland detachments followed a route that led from southeastern Tennessee northwest through Nashville and into Kentucky. Crossing the Ohio River, they moved through the southern tip of Illinois, crossed the Mississippi River, and then traversed southern Missouri, finally turning south to arrive in the new Cherokee territory in present-day eastern Oklahoma. Cherokee leaders selected this corridor, which later came to be known as the "northern route," to make use of existing roads and river crossings and for the presence of towns where Cherokee detachments could secure supplies along the way.[41] Two of the thirteen detachments, however, took alternate paths. A group of 660 Treaty Party Cherokees, led by John Bell, followed a route that ran straight west across Tennessee and Arkansas, passing through Memphis and Little Rock on the way. While more direct, this route required travelers to use lower-quality roads, and it passed through less developed country than did the northern route, making supplies more difficult to secure.[42] A group of around eleven hundred Cherokees, meanwhile, followed a route that ran from northeastern Alabama northwest through Tennessee and the far western corner of Kentucky and then across southeast Missouri and northern Arkansas. This detachment, led by John Benge, consisted of Cherokees whom the army gathered at Fort Payne, Alabama, rather than at the main emigration camps in Tennessee.[43] In total, around thirteen thousand Cherokees migrated by land during the fall and winter of 1838–1839, with eleven thousand taking the northern route. Most detachments required more than four months to complete this journey. Hair Conrad's column left in late August 1838 and disbanded the following January. The final detachment, departing in October 1838, arrived in late March.[44]

While the change to Cherokee leadership probably reassured migrants, it did not, of course, guarantee safe or easy travel. Moving thousands of people nearly one thousand miles on antebellum roads represented a hugely difficult project. Organizers needed to secure vast amounts of food and firewood, while finding sources of clean water and enough forage to sustain the Cherokees' horses and oxen. Under favorable conditions, a Cherokee detachment could cover ten to fifteen miles in a day, but progress was often much slower. When it rained, dirt roads became miry, impeding travel or halting the migrants altogether. Rivers could only be crossed using slow ferries. As the journey wore on, many Cherokees fell ill, weakened by toil and exposure. Measles, dysentery, whooping cough, and other diseases spread through the detachments.

Observers wrote harrowing descriptions of sick, exhausted Cherokees, packed together on the roads or huddled in camp. These accounts established one of the most enduring images of the Trail of Tears—that of a long column of downtrodden, sorrowful people trudging slowly along. "We found the road literally filled with the procession about three miles in length," a correspondent for the *New York Observer* wrote, describing a detachment in Kentucky. "The sick and feeble were carried in wagons . . . a great many ride on horseback and multitudes go on foot. Even aged females, apparently nearly ready to drop into the grave, were traveling with heavy burdens attached to the back, on the sometimes frozen ground, and sometimes muddy streets, with no covering for the feet except what nature had given them." This detachment, he reported, "buried fourteen or fifteen at every stopping place."[45] An even worse stage of the journey lay ahead, on the roads between the Ohio and Mississippi Rivers in southern Illinois. Ice on the rivers prevented the ferries from operating, and Cherokee detachments had to pause, in some cases for several weeks, as they waited for opportunities to cross. Daniel Butrick described the result. "One detachment [has] stopped at the Ohio River, two at the Mississippi, one four miles this side, one 18 miles and one 3 miles behind us. In all these detachments comprising about 8,000 souls, there is now a vast amount of sickness, and many deaths. Six have died within a short time in Major Brown's company and in this detachment of Mr. Taylor's—there are [Cherokees] affected with sickness in almost every tent and yet all are houseless and homeless in a strange land and in a cold region exposed to weather almost unknown in their native country." Later, reflecting on the Cherokee ordeal, Butrick wrote, "O what a sweeping wind has gone over, and carried its thousands into the grave, while thousands of others have been tortured and scarcely survive. . . . For what crime then was this whole Nation doomed to this perpetual death?"[46]

Cherokee losses during removal are difficult to calculate with accuracy. Records related to the detachments organized by John Ross reported around 450 deaths on the journey between Tennessee and Indian Territory. Some detachments did not provide casualty figures, however, and, even if they had, the number would not reflect losses suffered during the military roundup, in the early river detachments, and in the emigration camps in southeastern Tennessee. Most historians report that around four thousand Cherokees died during removal, but this number represents a general estimate at best. It originated with missionary Elizur Butler, who accompanied a Cherokee detachment on the Trail of Tears and served as a physician. Butler provided this number to a Chattanooga newspaper, which the pioneering ethnographer James Mooney then cited in his history of the Cherokees published at the turn of the twentieth century. Subsequent writers treated Mooney's account of removal as authoritative, and, through repetition, four thousand became the established figure. Jerry Clark, a longtime employee of the National Archives, has found sixteen hundred documented fatalities. The demographer Russell Thornton, on the other hand, suggests that, in estimating Cherokee losses, one should include births that removal prevented, as well as deaths directly caused by removal. Using this approach, Thornton places Cherokee losses at around ten thousand for the period between 1835 and 1840. In the absence of clear data, however, Butler's estimate of four thousand seems likely to remain the preferred number.[47]

The Cherokee Nation in the West

For Cherokees, the struggle and hardship of the removal era did not end when the last detachments reached Indian Territory. Cherokees arrived in the West weary and heartsick, facing the daunting task of rebuilding their communities. Securing adequate food proved an immediate challenge. Cherokees had always been productive farmers, but the emigrants needed time to learn how to work the new land. Under the Treaty of New Echota, the United States promised to provide Cherokees subsistence for a year, but the supplies often proved insufficient. Dishonest contractors delivered spoiled grain and meat, or they overstated the amount of food provided. Many Cherokees still lived in tents and other temporary shelters and lacked the means of preserving fresh food. The one commodity in ample supply during this time was whiskey, sold by whites from Arkansas who rushed into Indian Territory to take advantage of the new arrivals. When federal officials proved incapable of halting this trade, Cherokees formed their own police companies to capture whiskey peddlers and destroy their stock.[48]

As they coped with poor living conditions, Cherokees also faced a growing political crisis. The Cherokee majority, still led by John Ross, hoped to reestablish the tribal government in Indian Territory, transplanting it from the southeast to their new home. As one of their final acts before removal, tribal leaders passed a set of resolutions affirming Cherokee sovereignty, condemning the Treaty of New Echota as a fraud, and declaring that the Cherokee constitution and laws would continue to operate in the West, once the Cherokees completed their forced migration.[49] The Nation and its sovereignty, in other words, would be transferred intact from the old homeland to the new. This arrangement worried Cherokees already living in the West. Around three thousand "Old Settlers" resided in Indian Territory, in communities formed by Cherokees who migrated earlier in the nineteenth century. They already possessed a political system, which Ross and his allies now sought to replace, and they worried they would be marginalized in a nation dominated by the recent emigrants, who outnumbered them significantly. Members of the Treaty Party, meanwhile, were even more apprehensive. Numbering around two thousand, they feared reprisals at the hands of Ross's followers and, like the Old Settlers, anticipated that Ross and his allies would dominate any new political arrangement. In councils held during summer of 1839, the emigrants convinced a portion of the Old Settlers to set aside their concerns and endorse an "Act of Union," which declared the Cherokee Nation whole once more. The plan was for the recent emigrants and the Old Settlers to create a new government. In the midst of these meetings, however, all hope of a true reunion departed. On June 22, followers of John Ross carried out coordinated attacks on the leaders of the Treaty Party, killing Elias Boudinot, John Ridge, and Major Ridge. Boudinot's brother, Stand Watie, assembled a group of Treaty Party Cherokees and Old Settlers and vowed to retaliate. Ross's supporters, meanwhile, armed themselves and prepared for a fight. In early September 1839, the emigrants and their Old Settler allies ratified a new Cherokee constitution, which ostensibly signaled the reestablishment of the Nation in the West. In fact, the Cherokees hovered on the edge of civil war, the divisions born of removal having flared into open violence.[50]

For several years, the two factions exchanged raids and killings. Treaty Party vigilantes sought to punish those whom they considered responsible for the deaths of Boudinot and the Ridges, while the Cherokee Nation's police force, the Light Horse Guard, sought to bring the vigilantes to justice. Some of the dissidents, most notoriously a band led by the Treaty Party's James Starr, became little more than outlaws, concerned as much with theft as political violence. Among other consequences, this upheaval encouraged the United States to continue interfering in Cherokee affairs. Sympathizing with the Treaty Party, some federal authorities sought to depose Ross as chief and favored partitioning the Cherokee territory, giving each faction their own land. Others pushed for the allotment of Cherokee land into individual homesteads. At the very least, the violence hindered the Cherokee government's effort to replace the Treaty of New Echota, one of Ross's major goals during this period. Ross still sought to secure better terms for Cherokee lands in the East, hoping the United States would acknowledge the treaty as a fraud. Finally, in 1846, leaders of the Old Settlers and the Treaty Party joined the Cherokee government in negotiating a peace agreement, brokered by the United States. Ross agreed to accept the Treaty of New Echota, and the dissidents received compensation from the federal government for losses suffered since removal. All parties agreed to an amnesty for crimes committed during the troubles. The dissidents accepted the new Cherokee government, and the Cherokee territory remained whole. With this treaty, the removal era seemed finally to come to an end.[51]

In the years that followed, Cherokees rebuilt their economy and created new national institutions. They started a new newspaper, the *Cherokee Advocate*, which, like its predecessor, the *Cherokee Phoenix*, published both Cherokee and English-language material. They established a system of public schools, many of which provided bilingual instruction. That system included two high schools, the Cherokee Male and Female Seminaries. The seminaries became important emblems of Cherokee "civilization," much as the mission schools had in the preremoval era.[52] This period of calm, however, lasted only until the arrival of the American Civil War. The sectional crisis in the United States reignited the Cherokees' old factional divisions. The leaders of the Treaty Party allied with the Confederacy and raised volunteers for the Confederate Army. Ross and his allies tried to keep the Cherokee Nation neutral but eventually negotiated a Confederate treaty when it seemed the United States could no longer protect the Cherokees. Many Ross supporters, however, repudiated that alliance and joined the Union forces, while Ross himself fled the Nation and spent the rest of the war trying to reestablish relations with the federal government. In Indian Territory, Cherokee Confederates fought with Union Cherokee "home guards" for control of the Nation, waging a brutal war that ravaged Indian communities and destroyed much of the Cherokee economy. Cherokee losses during these hostilities were comparable to those of the removal years, and once again Cherokees faced the task of rebuilding the Nation.[53]

The political fissures created by removal only faded after the Civil War, as the Cherokee leaders of the removal era died or retired from public life.

Cherokees rebuilt their communities and institutions after the war, and they developed new political coalitions.[54] By this time, the Nation faced a new threat, the U.S. allotment and assimilation policies. Federal authorities began pressuring the Cherokees and other Indian nations to divide their common lands, dissolve their tribal governments, and accept incorporation into the United States. This campaign sought to eliminate Indian nations as landholders and distinct polities and to assimilate Indian people, once and for all. Cherokees fought allotment with the same spirit and invention they displayed in their resistance to removal. At the end of the nineteenth century, however, federal authorities finally succeeded in forcing the Cherokee Nation to sign an allotment agreement. The United States broke the common lands into individual holdings and dismantled the Cherokee government, and, in 1907, the Cherokee territory became part of the new state of Oklahoma. In a later chapter I discuss the consequences of allotment and the role played by public memory in the Cherokee Nation's twentieth-century revival.[55]

The Eastern Band

Not all Cherokees suffered deportation from the East. In the mid-nineteenth century, as Cherokees in Indian Territory worked to rebuild their communities, those who remained in North Carolina adapted to life in a region transformed by the expulsion of most of its indigenous people. By the end of the century, a distinct Cherokee tribe coalesced in North Carolina, the Eastern Band of Cherokee Indians. These Cherokees managed to build and preserve a tribal land base and gain the recognition of the very federal government that earlier sought to erase Indian people from the Southeast.

The origins of the Eastern Band lie in the early nineteenth century, in the period before removal. In 1817 and 1819, the United States compelled the Cherokee Nation to cede large sections of its territory, including land in present-day western North Carolina that had been the center of the Cherokee country prior to European colonization. This "Middle Town" region held some of the most sacred and significant places in the ancient Cherokee world, most notably Kituwah, the site on the Tuckaseegee River identified as the Cherokee mother town. The treaties included a provision allowing Cherokees who wanted to remain on ceded land to take individual reserves of 640 acres per family. Federal authorities expected individuals who exercised this option to assimilate and become citizens of the states that absorbed the ceded territory. In western North Carolina, around fifty

Cherokees, acting as heads of households, requested these reserves. In selecting their property, they chose some of the best agricultural land along the valleys of the Little Tennessee and Tuckaseegee Rivers, along with the sites of Cherokee settlements and sacred mounds. Kituwah, Cowee, Nikwasi, and other important places, they hoped, could remain in Cherokee possession. In this way, they sought to preserve a Cherokee landscape and, with it, their people's relationship with their homeland. The government of North Carolina, however, had other ideas. The state promised reserved lands to white settlers, and the ceded territory became a target for speculators. Whites squatted on Cherokee reserves and, in some cases, drove Cherokees from their land by force and threat of violence. During this period, some North Carolina Cherokees experienced the kind of abuse suffered by those in Georgia in the years just prior to the Trail of Tears. State courts later upheld the validity of the Cherokee titles to the land, but only after most of the reserves had passed out of Cherokee possession. Eventually, the state paid Cherokees for the land, while securing reimbursement from the federal government.[56]

After the loss of the reserves, some Cherokees moved to territory still within the borders of the Cherokee Nation. Many, however, chose to remain outside of the Nation and form new communities. Quallatown, on the Oconaluftee River, was one such settlement. The Cherokees there lived mainly by subsistence agriculture, adhered to the traditional religion and kinship system, and spoke the Cherokee language almost exclusively. Their principal leader was a man named Yonaguska, or Drowning Bear, who lived in the vicinity of Kituwah before the loss of the reserved lands. The Qualla Cherokees claimed to be North Carolina citizens under the treaties of 1817 and 1819, but they had few dealings with state authorities. They did not maintain a formal relationship with the U.S. government, and neither the Cherokee Nation nor the state appears to have paid them much attention. This small community was the first element of what later became the Eastern Band of Cherokee Indians.[57]

In the 1830s, as Georgia and the United States pressed the Cherokee Nation to accept removal, the Qualla Cherokees asked for an exemption from the policy. They had separated from the Nation, they explained, and now enjoyed North Carolina citizenship. They hoped to receive a share of any funds paid by the United States for Cherokee Nation lands, but they should not be forced to migrate. To argue this position, they employed William Holland Thomas as their legal representative. Thomas was a young merchant and self-taught lawyer who developed close ties to the Quallatown community through his work as a trader. In 1836 he traveled to Washington to represent Quallatown and several other North Carolina Cherokee communities at meetings held to discuss the Treaty of New Echota. The treaty included a provision that allowed Cherokees in Tennessee, Alabama, and North Carolina to stay in the East if they desired to become citizens. Thomas convinced both federal authorities and the leaders of the Treaty Party that the Qualla Cherokees, in fact, were already citizens and should not be subject to removal. He also recruited white community leaders from North Carolina to testify to the Qualla Cherokees' good behavior. In essence, Thomas and the Quallatown Cherokees argued that the United States had already eliminated Indians from this section of North Carolina as landholders and as members of distinct political communities. Those few who remained could be left alone.[58]

Quallatown residents, of course, were not the only Cherokees who hoped to stay in the East. Cherokees still residing in the Nation had two general options when it came to avoiding removal. Under the treaty provision mentioned above, they could declare their willingness to become citizens and request individual exemptions. Federal agents overseeing removal had the authority to issue these permits to Cherokees they deemed worthy, which generally meant those who were more acculturated to the settler society. The commissioners who negotiated the treaty anticipated that few Indians would embrace this opportunity and that fewer still would receive exemptions. In the mountains of North Carolina, however, this loophole inspired one of the more interesting episodes of resistance to removal. In the Valley River region, an emigration agent named Preston Starrett conspired with local Cherokee leaders to issue great numbers of permits, paying little attention to applicants' qualifications for citizenship. The goal seems to have been to preserve a Cherokee community in this section of the mountains, even as the army arrived to seize Cherokees and march them to the camps in Tennessee. One can still find Starrett's permits scattered throughout the removal records. Unfortunately for many of the Cherokees involved, word of this activity reached the military. "Mr. Preston Starret, who signs himself Agent for Emigration, has, as I am informed, granted permissions to some hundreds of Indians to remain in the country," an officer at Fort Butler informed Winfield Scott. "Some time ago I personally cautioned Mr. Starret that he was, in my belief, exceeding the spirit of the letter of his authority, but he did not heed me, and within the last few days he has been more busy than ever, and I am told has given these documents indiscriminately to all Indians who were willing to receive them."[59] Scott responded by ordering his forces to disregard permissions not signed by Scott himself, by the civilian superintendent overseeing removal, or by the general directing the troops in North Carolina.[60] In what must have been a deeply bitter experience, Cherokees who thought themselves secure suffered capture and deportation, their exemptions ignored.

As a last resort, Cherokees could seek refuge in the mountains and attempt to evade the troops sent to take them. While the majority of Cherokees in western North Carolina surrendered when the army arrived in the summer of 1838, several hundred chose to hide. Searching the mountains proved challenging for the soldiers, who knew little of the country and who struggled with the rugged terrain. "After three weeks of the most arduous and fatiguing duty, traveling the country in every direction, searching the mountains on foot in every point where Indians could be heard of we [have] not been able to get sight of a single one," one officer reported. "Their constant vigilance, perfect knowledge of the country, and the rapidity with which that enabled them to communicate intelligence from one camp to another, has rendered all attempts to capture them utterly in vain." The soldiers needed reliable local guides, the officer explained, if they were to have any hope of finding those still in hiding.[61] Some fugitives received aid from Cherokees who had permission to stay in the East and from whites in the region. John Welch, for example, was a prosperous Cherokee farmer in the Valley River area who secured exemptions for himself and his family. His farm, near present-day Andrews, became a center for Cherokee resistance. Welch and his family fed Cherokees hiding in the surrounding mountains, and they kept the fugitives informed of the army's movements. When the soldiers learned of these activities, they arrested Welch and kept him imprisoned at Fort Cass in Tennessee until their campaign in the mountains ended. After removal, Welch purchased land for Cherokees who remained in the area, and this property became the location of a new Indian settlement sometimes known as Welch's Town.[62]

While few people today remember John Welch, another Cherokee who resisted removal gained considerable renown. Tsali, or Charley, was an old man living with his wife and extended family near the Nantahala River. According to his wife, he received permission to stay in North Carolina and become a citizen, but this exemption from removal was ignored or rescinded. When troops arrived to gather Cherokees for the journey west, Tsali and his family sought refuge in the mountains. In late October a small detachment of soldiers found them near the mouth of the Tuckaseegee River. Before they could march the fugitives to the removal camps in Tennessee, however,

Tsali, two of his sons, and a daughter's husband attacked their guards, killing two and wounding a third, and the family escaped. Before this incident, the army was preparing to leave western North Carolina, even though some fugitives remained in hiding. The last of the Cherokee removal detachments were setting out for the West, and there seemed little point in the army continuing operations in the mountains. The killings delayed the army's departure, as American soldiers hunted Tsali and his family, insisting that they be brought to justice. This renewed search placed other fugitives in jeopardy, since the soldiers would most likely deport any other Indians in hiding whom they encountered. Acting on this understanding, Cherokees agreed to aid in the pursuit of Tsali. The searchers included both Quallatown Cherokees, joined by William Holland Thomas, and a group of fugitives, who received a promise of exemption from removal in return for their help. Cherokees finally captured the family in late November, and they executed Tsali and the three others who participated in the assault. In later years, for reasons I explain in greater detail below, Tsali became a symbol of resistance, and his death a case of martyrdom. In memory, he sacrificed his life so that Cherokees could remain in North Carolina. This rather obscure man, then, became one of the state's most famous Cherokee historical figures.[63]

In the wake of removal, around eleven hundred Cherokees remained in the mountains of western North Carolina. Seven hundred lived in the vicinity of Quallatown, a number that included both Yonaguska's original group and others who joined the settlement during the removal era. The remainder lived in smaller communities spread along the rivers to the west and southwest.[64] These settlements did not form a single polity during this period, although kinship, language, and culture provided connections among them. As anthropologist Tyler Howe suggests, Cherokees in North Carolina organized their removal-era communities according to the old model of the Cherokee town, maintaining small autonomous settlements in which residents made decisions through consensus. Qualla itself consisted of several different districts, or townships, with local councils and headmen.[65] William Holland Thomas continued to serve as Quallatown's representative in matters involving government officials and other outsiders. During this time, he also began to help Cherokees purchase land, gradually assembling the large block of land that came to be known as the Qualla Boundary, along with scattered landholdings further west. In later years, local whites would characterize Thomas as the North Carolina Cherokees' "white chief." It would be more accurate, however, to describe him as their legal representative and interlocutor when dealing with non-Indians.[66]

The Cherokees' position in North Carolina remained tenuous during this period, despite their having avoided removal. While they claimed to be citizens, the state did not fully acknowledge that status. During removal, the state merely recognized that some Cherokees would stay in the mountains, without specifying their legal identity. On several occasions after 1839, federal authorities, backed by state officials, encouraged Cherokees to move west to join the Cherokee Nation, suggesting they still expected Indian people to disappear from the mountains.[67] Cherokee status became clearer only after the Civil War. In 1866 the state legislature passed a resolution affirming the Cherokees' right to remain in North Carolina, an act that historians generally interpret as a reward for Cherokees' service in the Confederate Army. Two years later, the federal government recognized the Cherokees in North Carolina as a distinct tribal community, initiating a formal relationship like that maintained with tribes in the West. Cherokee leaders sought this recognition as a way of securing aid for their people in the desperate economic conditions of the postwar South. They also hoped to gain greater access to education for their children. There is a significant irony in the timing of this development. Cherokees in North Carolina received federal recognition as a Native people during precisely the period in which the United States began formulating the allotment and assimilation policies, the great crusade to eliminate Indian peoples as landholders and sovereigns. As federal officials began to press Cherokees in the West to allot their land and accept American citizenship, they acknowledged the presence of a distinct Cherokee people in the East.[68]

During this same period, Cherokees also gained firmer control of their property. When Thomas purchased land on the Cherokees' behalf, he often kept the titles in his own name. This arrangement helped Cherokees protect their property after removal. The Civil War, however, destroyed Thomas's fortune and left him deeply in debt. When Thomas's creditors moved to seize his property, it suddenly appeared that the Cherokees might lose their homes. In this crisis, the Cherokees' new relationship with the federal government proved useful. In 1870 Congress authorized a lawsuit against Thomas to settle the question of Cherokee landownership. Eventually, the matter went to arbitration, which determined that Cherokees still owed Thomas (and, thus, his creditors) several thousand dollars for land purchases made on their behalf. The federal government paid this amount out of funds owed Cherokees since the removal era. Under this arrangement, the Qualla

Boundary became the common property of the tribe, now identified as the Eastern Band of Cherokee Indians. It could not be sold without the tribe's consent and the approval of the federal government. Congress extended similar provisions to other Cherokee lands in North Carolina. This status protected these lands from sale and gave them a standing analogous to that of a reservation.[69]

As Cherokees settled the land question, they created a new tribal government. Federal recognition brought increased relations with the Office of Indian Affairs, later known as the Bureau of Indian Affairs (BIA).[70] This change, in turn, made the development of new political practices expedient. The Cherokees needed a governing structure that federal authorities would recognize as legitimate. In the past, Thomas represented North Carolina Cherokees in their dealings with Washington. After the Civil War, however, he retreated from public life, his fortune gone and his mental health deteriorating. In 1868 a group of Cherokee leaders at Cheoah, a settlement about fifty miles west of the Qualla Boundary, drafted a constitution and formed a council. Two years later, a rival group, led by John Welch's son Lloyd Welch, wrote a new constitution, which had the support of communities on the Qualla Boundary. In the years that followed, federal authorities began treating this second group as the official leadership of the Eastern Band, and the Lloyd Welch Constitution, as it is known today, became the tribe's governing document. Yellow Hill, a section of the Qualla Boundary that today hosts the town of Cherokee, became the seat of the tribal government and the location of the federal agency. By the 1880s, then, the Eastern Band possessed federal recognition, a clearer title to tribal lands, and a new tribal government.[71]

One last political development is worth mentioning in this sketch of the nineteenth-century history of the Eastern Band. In 1889, under the leadership of Chief Nimrod Jarrett Smith, the Cherokees sought a corporate charter from the government of North Carolina, and the common tribal lands became the property of this corporation under state law. Several years later, amendments drew much of the Lloyd Welch Constitution into the terms of the charter, making it the Eastern Band's governing document. The elected tribal government became the directors of this new corporation and tribal citizens its shareholders. This arrangement added an additional layer of legal protection to the Cherokee tribal lands during the era of allotment, when federal authorities sought to dissolve common property and end Indian governments. The charter enabled Cherokees to act as a collective within state law, even if the federal government withdrew its recognition or ignored its responsibility to protect Cherokee land. Tribal leaders could bring suit, for instance, against individuals or companies that illegally expropriated tribal resources, such as timber. The charter promised to insulate the Eastern Band against the worst consequences of the allotment policy. As historian John Finger notes, it meant that Cherokees could continue functioning as a tribe, with or without the help of federal Indian agents.[72] At the end of the nineteenth century, as the Cherokee Nation fought its losing battle against allotment, the Eastern Band managed to solidify its distinct legal status and preserve a body of tribal lands. As I discuss in chapter 2, the presence of this distinct Cherokee tribe became a crucial influence on public memory and heritage tourism in twentieth-century southern Appalachia.

Writing Removal in the Late Nineteenth Century

The Cherokees, of course, were not the only Indian people to experience removal. In the 1830s and 1840s, the United States applied the policy to most of the large Indian nations of the East. The Cherokees, however, provided one of the strongest tests of the removal campaign, and, for the American public, the Cherokee case overshadowed the experience of other tribal communities. The Cherokees' reputation as a "civilized tribe," along with their use of the press and the courts to fight the policy, granted them greater prominence than other Indian nations with similar histories. They became the paramount example of Indian removal, rather than merely one case among many. In the decades following the Trail of Tears, several different genres of American writing perpetuated the memory of removal and the Cherokees' fame. This literature established some of the features of the Trail of Tears story that southern communities would later draw into public commemoration and heritage tourism. I will end this chapter by discussing several key examples of these writings.

In the late nineteenth century, the authors most likely to recite the Cherokee removal story came from the ranks of Indian policy critics and reformers. I am referring here to writers like Helen Hunt Jackson, whose widely read book *A Century of Dishonor* (1881) condemned the violence and chicanery that characterized American Indian relations in the post–Civil War era. These critics often rooted their attacks in historical narratives, and many of them identified the expulsion of the Cherokees from the Southeast as one of the clearest examples of American treachery toward Indian people. In *A Century of Dishonor,* Jackson devoted an entire chapter to the Cherokees, and she described Cherokee removal as the worst of her many examples of American perfidy. There was "no record so black," she wrote. "There will come a time in the remote future when, to the student of American history, it will seem well-nigh incredible."[73] Jackson never fully explained why she considered the Cherokee episode worse than others, but it clearly had something to do with the idea of the "civilized tribe." She speculated that antebellum Cherokees made the quickest progress of any people in history, and this achievement lent particular clarity to Georgia's greed and the federal government's callousness. She listed the familiar markers of Cherokee advancement—productive agriculture, Christian missions, and constitutional government—and she implied that if any Indian people should have been spared the universal experience of abuse and dispossession, then the Cherokee Nation was the one.[74]

Other reformers during this period wrote in very similar terms, lamenting Cherokee removal as one of the darkest chapters of America's long history of cheating Indians. Herbert Welsh, the secretary of the Indian Rights Association, called Cherokee removal "one of the most unjustifiable outrages our history records."[75] William Barrows, another reform writer, remembered the Cherokee controversy as a lost opportunity for the United States. "This was a good time," Barrows wrote, "for our nation to make a move upward to that highest grade of national honor, which develops in a sacred regard for treaty obligations." With the Cherokees, he suggested, the United States might have broken the cycle of treachery, placing Indian affairs on a better foundation. Instead, "the antipathies of race and color and semi-civilization and greed of land" were allowed to rule the day. If the United States could not protect the Cherokees, Barrows asked, how could any tribe "trust in the government, or hope for a permanent home?"[76]

Many of the reformers who lamented the tragedy of removal favored newer policies that most Cherokees themselves opposed. Welsh and Barrows, for instance, supported allotment and the late nineteenth-century assimilation crusade. Their sympathy for the Cherokees did not translate into a willingness to listen to present-day tribal leaders or to support Indian autonomy and self-government. Indeed, part of their criticism of removal was that it prolonged Indian autonomy and delayed assimilation. Henry Dawes, the political leader most associated with the allotment policy, wrote in precisely these terms in the 1890s. He agreed with his fellow reformers that the expulsion of the Cherokees from Georgia was a crime, one of the worst in American history. And for Dawes, one of the reasons it was a crime was that the United States, in prosecuting the removal policy, allowed the Cherokees to go on governing themselves once they arrived in the West. "With a disposition to make atonement for its own outrages upon the Cherokees when they were driven out from Georgia," Dawes recalled, the United States "covenanted with that people that they should be set out in this place and permitted to govern themselves forever." This decision, Dawes argued, delayed Cherokee assimilation, creating conditions that, sixty years later, made allotment necessary. Dawes, then, used the memory of America's violation of Cherokee rights in the 1830s as ammunition for an assault upon the Cherokee Nation at the end of the century.[77]

The leaders of the Cherokee Nation, meanwhile, also invoked the memory of removal during this period, and they used many of the same terms as did the reformers. They recounted the history of Cherokee advancement in the early republic: their embrace of Euro-American education and economic practices and the creation of the Cherokee government. They recalled the hardships of the 1830s, when, as one principal chief of the Nation put it, "a partially civilized but helpless people were dragged by violence from the houses they had built, the orchards they had planted, the farms they had cultivated, and the household goods they had accumulated, and sent as exiles to a new country, of which little was known save the general supposition that it was not worth much."[78] They agreed with the reformers' version of history, with the exception of one crucial point. The reformers almost always depicted Indian affairs as a matter of thinking up policies in the metropolitan East and applying them to Indian communities. Indians were people to be acted upon by good-hearted whites. For Cherokee writers, on the other hand, the lesson of their history was that Indian people had to be allowed to control their own affairs within their own nations. If Euro-Americans truly sympathized with the Cherokees, they would support tribal self-government and help tribal leaders protect their people and lands. This did not require visionary reforms, but rather full respect for treaties and an acknowledgment of Indian nationhood. As Principal Chief Dennis W. Bushyhead wrote in 1881, "if the Indians cannot be permitted to go on working out their own salvation, as they are doing, all laws on the subject will be vain and breaches of faith [and] impotent."[79] As it happened, this was a warning most reformers never heeded.

The reform writers' use of the removal memory featured several themes that would become common elements of twentieth-century commemoration. Like the reformers, commemorators and heritage tourism advocates would frequently depict Cherokee removal as an episode that epitomized the broader American history of Indian mistreatment. The confessional tone adopted by writers like Welsh and Jackson would also become common-place. Books like *A Century of Dishonor* operated like Christian conversion narratives, in which an admission of national sins opened the possibility of change and redemption. Twentieth-century commemoration would fre-quently display a similar dynamic, as commemorators expressed hope that the public recognition of past crimes would help present-day Americans cre-ate a more just and democratic society. Finally, like the tribal leaders who fought allotment, Cherokees in the twentieth century would put the removal memory to their own political uses. In particular, they would invoke the Trail of Tears in debates over tribal autonomy and Indian nationhood.

As reformers debated the future of Indian affairs in the West, other writ-ers ventured into the southern highlands and encountered the Cherokees living in North Carolina. In the late nineteenth and early twentieth centu-ries, southern Appalachia became a popular subject of journalism and travel writing, as authors from outside of the region journeyed through the moun-tains and reported back on the experience to a mainly urban and northern audience. This writing helped to establish many of the enduring images of the southern mountains, contributing to what Allen Batteau calls the "in-vention of Appalachia" as a distinct American region. Authors emphasized the isolation of mountain communities and depicted Appalachian whites as exotic primitives, bound by tradition and cut off from modernity. In many accounts, the southern highlands became a region of the past, a place where people lived in conditions similar to those of the early American frontier. This conception of mountain people as "contemporary ancestors" displayed a deep ambivalence. White highlanders were brave, resourceful, and full of homespun wisdom, but they were also backward, narrow-minded, and prone to violence. Mountaineers needed the help of outsiders to lift them-selves from poverty and ignorance, yet there was something attractive about their simple rural lives, a quality that would likely fade as they embraced progress. These images, of course, closely paralleled those commonly ap-plied to Indians, whom Americans had long depicted as both noble savages and violent primitives. As Anthony Harkins suggests, writings like these es-tablished the mountaineer as a "white other," an exotic figure whose sup-posedly retrograde ways helped urban readers reflect upon their own modernity.[80]

While this literature focused on white communities in Appalachia, some travel writers who passed through North Carolina also described the Cher-okees. In the 1870s, for instance, the author and journalist Rebecca Hard-ing Davis made a point to visit Quallatown, which she described for several popular magazines. For Davis, the North Carolina Cherokees were doubly isolated, a community that seemed remote even to the white residents of this secluded region. While staying in Waynesville, a town some forty miles from Qualla, she heard many different stories and rumors about the Cherokees, but no one seemed ever to visit them. The road to Qualla was poor, and few whites bothered to go there. As a consequence, the Quallatown Indians were a "forgotten tribe." Having managed to avoid removal a generation earlier, Davis observed, they now found themselves thoroughly sequestered from the modern world. "They were, and are, as a rule, unable to speak any tongue but their own; they are barred by the mountains into their wilderness; the surrounding white population is one that scarcely knows that they exist."[81] After Removal, this isolation left them under the control of William Holland Thomas, who handled all of their affairs until his own fortunes collapsed. Thomas may have had good intentions, but, under his "dictatorship," Cherokees remained as isolated and ignorant as the most backward mountain whites. Unlike some of the white highlanders she met, the Cherokees were never vulgar, but they displayed what Davis called "that heavy, hopeless sadness which belongs to races to whom God has given a brain for which the world has as yet found no use."[82] They needed schools, Davis concluded, and should receive the same kind of attention given western Indians by philanthropists and missionaries. "Every religious body in the country has sent teachers to the Western tribes," she wrote, "while this pathetic remnant of Cherokees has all the while been locked up in the hills of one of the oldest States, perishing in our very midst for lack of knowledge."[83] She hoped her writing might encourage the Christian people of the North to take action.

Not all travel writers who visited the Cherokees expressed such a stern outlook, but they generally shared Davis's view of the Eastern Band as a "forgotten tribe" and a "pathetic remnant." Wilbur Zeigler, an Ohio lawyer and author who wrote about western North Carolina in the early 1880s, described the Quallatown Cherokees as a sad reminder of a once-great people. "The ancient nation of the mountains," he wrote, suffered defeat and expulsion in the Jacksonian era, but it left behind "a disevered and withered limb which, like a fossil, merely reminds us of a bygone period of history."[84] In the West, Zeigler noted, Cherokees progressed rapidly after removal, and they now possessed "schools, churches, farms and cattle." The Cherokees in North Carolina, however, advanced very little. According to Zeigler, even their population was declining.[85] A decade later, Henry Melvil Doak reported a more cheerful scene, when he paid a visit to what he termed the "Rip Van Winkle Qualla Reservation." He described the Cherokees as sober and industrious, and he noted that Indian children studied eagerly at the tribe's new Quaker-run boarding school. Still, Doak could not help but add a note of sorrow, remarking that the school offered a "touching spectacle when one reflects upon the sad but inevitable history and lot of this unfortunate race and considers that but a meagre remnant seems now about to redeem the past."[86] For these visitors, the Cherokees were relics, people who should have disappeared from the East long ago but who somehow persisted in this remote corner of the mountains. Like the "frontier" culture of Appalachian whites, the Cherokees provided evidence of the region's isolation and primitive state. Their presence reinforced the travel writers' depiction of Appalachia as a place untouched by modernity. By the start of the twentieth century, this image became a central element of the region's growing tourism economy. As I discuss in chapter 2, tourism boosters marketed Appalachia as a place where visitors would find primeval landscapes and culturally traditional people. They transformed the isolation that writers like Davis lamented into the main source of the mountains' appeal. Experiencing the past became a commodity in Appalachian tourism, and the "remnant" Cherokees emerged as one of the region's biggest attractions.

While journalists helped to define southern Appalachia for the rest of the nation, the traveler most responsible for shaping the public image of the Eastern Band was an anthropologist, James Mooney. In the late 1880s Mooney paid a series of visits to North Carolina on behalf of the Bureau of American Ethnology (BAE). He made contacts among Cherokee cultural authorities, spoke with an aged William Holland Thomas, and began gathering information on Cherokee language, culture, and history. This work resulted in several publications, most notably *Myths of the Cherokee*, which the BAE issued in 1901. This volume, which included a two-hundred-page "sketch" of Cherokee history, proved remarkably influential, not only among anthropologists but with a broader public. In the decades that followed, *Myths of the Cherokee* became a standard source for popular accounts of Cherokee history and culture, including those produced by tourism promoters and groups engaged in historical commemoration. Without intending to do so, Mooney provided a crucial part of the foundation for twentieth-century heritage work involving the Cherokee past.[87]

Mooney shared some of the travel writers' outlook when it came to Appalachia and the North Carolina Cherokees. He described the Eastern Band as a traditional community whose remote location insulated residents from change. The Cherokees in the West, he noted, were "so far advanced along the white man's road as to offer but little inducement for ethnological study," but those in North Carolina were different. "There remained behind . . . in the heart of the Carolina mountains, a considerable body," he noted, "and it is among these, the old conservative Kituwha element, that the ancient things have been preserved." This assessment was almost identical to that of Rebecca Harding Davis, but where Davis saw stagnation, Mooney found cultural persistence (and an opportunity for ethnographers). The Cherokees' isolation safeguarded their culture, Mooney suggested, allowing scholars and other travelers contact with their ancient ways. "Mountaineers guard well the past," Mooney remarked, "and in the secluded forests of Nantahala and Oconaluftee, far away from the main-traveled road of modern progress, the Cherokee priest still treasures the legends and repeats the mystic rituals handed down from his ancestors." In *Myths of the Cherokee*, Mooney sought to record the tribe's ancient knowledge before "modern progress" finally caught up with it.[88]

In explaining why the "old conservative Kituwha element" stayed in North Carolina, Mooney highlighted an episode that later proved ideal for commemoration and tourist consumption. He recounted the story of Tsali, the Cherokee executed for attacking American soldiers during removal, and he made the incident a kind of creation narrative for the Eastern Band by suggesting that Tsali's death explained why Cherokees remained in the Southeast. In Mooney's version, Tsali and his sons only attacked the soldiers after guards abused Tsali's wife, prodding her with their bayonets. The assault was a sudden action by men pushed beyond endurance. Making their "dash to freedom," they joined hundreds of others in the mountains, where they suffered terrible privation. The army mounted a vigorous search for the killers but could not find them until Winfield Scott turned to William Holland Thomas for help. Through Thomas, Scott offered the Cherokees a bargain. If they would give up Tsali and his family, then the army would leave the mountains, ending its search for people still in hiding. Those who remained would be safe from removal. Learning of the proposition, Tsali and his sons surrendered, sacrificing their lives so that some of their people could stay in western North Carolina. "From those fugitives thus permitted to remain," Mooney wrote, "originated the present Eastern Band of Cherokee."[89]

Mooney's main source for this narrative was William Holland Thomas himself, along with Washington, one of Tsali's surviving children (or possibly a grandson). While both men were quite elderly, and Thomas suffered from mental illness, Mooney seems to have considered them reliable informants. They witnessed, after all, many of the events the anthropologist recorded. The documentary record, however, contradicts Mooney's version of the Tsali story in some crucial ways. There is no direct evidence, for example, that soldiers abused Tsali's wife, whose own account of the episode never mentioned such abuse. Moreover, Tsali and his family appear not to have surrendered willingly, but rather suffered capture at the hands of fellow-Cherokees. That conclusion, of course, undermines the most dramatic element of Mooney's narrative, the image of Tsali freely giving his life for his people.[90] The Tsali episode, meanwhile, does not accurately explain the Eastern Band's origins. As I noted earlier, some Cherokees who aided the search for the fugitives were, in fact, allowed to remain. The Quallatown Cherokees, however, received exemption from removal long before the Tsali incident. The Eastern Band evolved both from the "citizen Cherokees" of Qualla and from the people who were supposed to emigrate but managed to stay. In Mooney's account, however, a single act of sacrifice explained the persistence of Cherokees in the Southeast, with Tsali playing the roles of both heroic martyr and founding father.[91]

Mooney never intended to write a definitive tribal history. His goal in *Myths of the Cherokee*, as the title implies, was to transcribe and present the community's oral traditions, and the historical sketch merely offered context for this material. Many subsequent writers, however, accepted Mooney's history as thoroughly reliable. His stature as a pioneering scholar of the Cherokees granted authority to everything he wrote, while the dramatic story of Tsali's resistance and sacrifice appealed to white Americans whose popular culture was already full of noble, dying Indians. Although Mooney could not have anticipated it, his Tsali shaped popular accounts of Cherokee history for decades to come. In the 1920s and 1930s, this romantic story of Eastern Band origins became one of the most common narratives about the Cherokees broadcast within an expanding Appalachian tourism industry. That tourism boom, and the place of Cherokee history within it, form the subject of chapter 2.

2 The Tourists

Basking in Cherokee History in Southern Appalachia

• •

In 1939, *Tennessee Wildlife,* a magazine devoted to outdoor recreation, produced a special issue to mark the completion of the Great Smoky Mountains National Park, located in east Tennessee and western North Carolina. A typical example of park advertising, it offered an extended rhapsody on the beauty of the mountain landscape and the wisdom of the men and women who had worked to preserve this treasure for Americans' enjoyment. The Smokies had the most spectacular scenery in the East, it proclaimed, and a stunning variety of plant and animal life. "Primeval forests and highly varied wildflowers" enchanted visitors, while hundreds of miles of footpaths made the park "a hiker's dream fulfilled." Each season featured its own wonders, from the spring and summer blooms to the rich colors of autumn and winter's "dazzling hoar-frost." All of this natural grandeur, moreover, was located just a moderate drive from most of the nation's urban centers, making the park a convenient destination for millions of vacationers. The Smokies, in short, were "the most interesting and enjoyable mountains in America."[1]

The park's attractions, however, included more than scenery and wildlife, as the region featured a compelling human history to match the landscape. "Romance and legend hang over the Great Smoky Mountains like the haze from which they get their name," the magazine observed, and visitors soon learned that "the story of the Smokies is as beautiful and thrilling as their scenery." As its main example of this exciting past, the magazine told the story of Cherokee removal. It described the gathering of Cherokees by federal troops and their forced migration west, along with the heroic resistance of those Indians who chose to hide in the most remote areas of the Smokies rather than leave their mountain homeland. It recounted the legend of Tsali, the Cherokee said to have sacrificed his life so that a portion of his people might remain in the East. The magazine mentioned several other historical topics, such as the roles played by white mountaineers in the American Revolution, but it devoted the bulk of its history section to the Cherokees. "Tourists bask in history as well as grandeur when they visit the Great Smoky Mountains National Park," it explained, and Cherokee removal provided one of the mountains' most dramatic historical episodes.[2]

This chapter explains how it became possible for travelers to bask in Cherokee history when they visited the southern mountains. In the 1920s and 1930s, Appalachian tourism development, in particular the creation of the Great Smoky Mountains National Park, opened new arenas for the representation of the Cherokee past. As the park took shape, civic and business leaders in the region sought out cultural attractions to accompany the Smokies' celebrated natural environment, and they quickly identified the Cherokee community living just outside the park as a major asset. This new attention influenced public memory, as promoters recounted certain episodes from the Cherokee past, including the story of removal, in their depictions of the mountains. Promotional literature began to highlight the Trail of Tears in sketches of regional history, and journalists often invoked the removal story in their coverage of tourism planning and development. In the 1930s, several Appalachian communities mounted substantial efforts to commemorate removal as part of campaigns to draw more visitors to the mountains. Amplified in this way, Cherokee removal became a more pronounced element of the region's public historical identity.

Tourists leave home in search of unique experience, traveling in order to consume sights and activities outside of their everyday lives. The main product in tourism is the encounter with difference.[3] North Carolina Cherokees could provide such an experience in two related ways. First, as an Indian tribe residing in the Southeast, they represented a supposed anomaly. In the popular imagination, Native Americans left the South long ago, yet here were the Cherokees, still living in the heart of their traditional homeland. Their very presence in the southern highlands offered something different and surprising. In addition, Cherokees proved willing to display elements of a distinctly Indian culture for visitors' consumption. Cherokee handicrafts, traditional dance, and Indian games became important commodities in mountain tourism, promising travelers contact with a unique way of life. Historical thinking informed both of these experiences of Cherokee difference. The idea that the tribal presence in North Carolina was unusual rested upon the assumption that American expansion had erased Indian peoples from the South. The Cherokees' ability to surprise visitors depended on this notion of Indian absence. Tourist consumption of Cherokee culture, meanwhile, also reflected a distinct idea of the past, since promoters almost always marketed cultural attractions as elements of tradition. Cherokee dance and craftwork, they insisted, were ancient Indian ways that persisted into the twentieth century. These practices supposedly offered modern Americans contact with a premodern way of life. Tourism thus encoded Cherokee difference as temporal, as well as cultural, a practice that led promoters to turn to history when advertising Cherokee distinctiveness.[4]

For Cherokees, the expansion of tourism offered new economic opportunities, but it also carried political meaning. Tourism provided a public setting in which Cherokees could demonstrate their community's Indianness. That identity, in turn, helped Cherokees to maintain a political arrangement that protected Cherokee land and secured at least a limited degree of tribal autonomy. As I explained in chapter 1, North Carolina Cherokees managed to confirm ownership of a tribal land base in the decades following the Civil War while also creating a government recognized by both federal and state authorities. American Indian policy, however, still emphasized assimilation and the dismantling of tribal landholdings, and in the early twentieth century, the Eastern Band faced increasing pressure to accept allotment. The politics and culture of segregation made the threat of these policies even more pronounced, since assimilation would mean that Cherokees faced the full force of southern white supremacy. In this context, the Cherokees' ability to broadcast an Indian identity represented a political asset.[5] Tourism performances carried the message that a distinctly Native people remained in western North Carolina, separate from both whites and blacks. Later, in the 1930s, changes in federal policy made this tribal identity even more valuable, as the "Indian New Deal" promised new opportunities to strengthen Cherokee landholding and autonomy. Cherokee images and historical narratives within tourism culture were often quite inaccurate, but they reinforced the idea of Cherokee tribal persistence.[6]

Tourism and the Eastern Band of Cherokee Indians

A tourism industry first developed in southern Appalachia in the antebellum era, when the construction of turnpikes and the removal of most of the Native American population allowed easier travel to the mountain regions of western North Carolina and east Tennessee. Health seekers ventured into the mountains to "take the cure" at mineral springs, and local entrepreneurs developed hotels and spas to serve their needs. Wealthy planters came to the mountains to escape the heat of the lowland summer, and some built seasonal homes. By the start of the Civil War, summer colonies evolved in places like Cashiers, North Carolina, and Asheville, where travelers found both resort hotels and the summer residences of the southern elite. While the destruction of the plantation economy in the Civil War undermined this form of tourism, railroad construction in the postwar era brought new waves of visitors, including middle-class tourists from the urban North. Health-conscious travelers continued to holiday at the various mineral springs, while resorts in Asheville and its surrounding area catered to large numbers of tuberculosis patients, who hoped the region's mild climate and clean air might ease their suffering. Health tourism declined toward the end of the nineteenth century, but mountain communities in North Carolina continued to attract visitors looking for scenic beauty and outdoor recreation. In east Tennessee, meanwhile, substantial resorts appeared in places like Henderson Springs, near Pigeon Forge in Sevier County, and in several spots in neighboring Blount County.[7]

Cherokees living on the Qualla Boundary participated in this burgeoning tourist trade, but only in a limited way. While visitors to the region may have been curious about western North Carolina's Indian community, travel to tribal lands remained inconvenient at the start of the twentieth century. Railroad construction bypassed the Qualla Boundary until 1909, when work began on a spur connecting the village of Cherokee to the Southern Railroad stop at Ela, and the roads to the Boundary were poor. Those travelers who did visit during this period found few amenities once they arrived. Cherokee lacked the hotels and resorts that had become common sights in the region's tourist towns, and, as late as the 1910s, the village supported only a few country stores. In 1914 the tribe began hosting the annual Cherokee Fall Fair, and this event drew crowds of visitors to the Boundary for several days each October. Yet at a time when many nearby communities had become established tourist destinations, the Eastern Band remained on the industry's fringe.[8]

In the 1920s, two developments transformed this situation and set the Eastern Band of Cherokees on a course to become, in the words of one observer, "the most visited American Indian group in the United States."[9] First, the rise of the automobile allowed easier travel to many of the region's more remote communities, including the Qualla Boundary. Cars became much more affordable for middle-class Americans during this period, thanks to assembly-line production and widening consumer credit. In the years between 1915 and 1929, the number of registered automobiles in the United States leapt from around two million to over twenty-three million. Business and civic leaders in the mountain South responded to this development by pushing state governments to improve the region's system of roads.[10] By the middle of the decade, western North Carolina's expanding network of paved all-weather roads reached the Cherokee community. A highway ran from Asheville to Bryson City, a few miles west of the Qualla Boundary, and several dependable routes connected the village of Cherokee to the highway. While many roads on tribal lands remained poor, drivers could now reach the Eastern Band's administrative and economic center with relative ease.[11]

As road building made the Qualla Boundary more accessible, a second development guaranteed that a great many new visitors would soon travel those roads to the Cherokee country. In 1926 Congress approved the creation of the Great Smoky Mountains National Park, which, when complete, would encompass more than a half-million acres of mountain forest on either side of the border between east Tennessee and western North Carolina. This act was the result of an extensive campaign by civic leaders in the region, who had long discussed the idea of establishing such a park in southern Appalachia. In 1899 a group of southeastern politicians, businessmen, and newspaper editors formed the Appalachian National Park Association, the first organized attempt to pursue the idea. While this group met with little success, a more vigorous movement emerged in the early 1920s, led by businessmen in Knoxville and Asheville. In Knoxville, members of the city's automobile club and chamber of commerce formed the Smoky Mountain Conservation Association, while Asheville-based business groups also began to campaign for a park in the Smokies. The advocates' primary goal, from the very start, was to boost tourism, rather than merely preserve the mountain landscape. They hoped that a national park would become a permanent economic engine, an attraction that would guarantee a steady flow of visitors, and their money, into mountain communities. As a song sung by park promoters explained (to the tune of "My Old Kentucky Home"):

The sun shines bright on the Smoky Mountains Park
In summer the tourists are gay
By'n by good roads will bring millions to our Park
And then all will prosper every day.[12]

Fueled by these hopes, park advocates raised millions of dollars to acquire the necessary land while lobbying federal lawmakers and mounting an extensive public relations campaign.[13] The local boosters' outlook meshed well with the goals of the National Park Service (NPS) during this period. Park Service directors insisted that national parks should provide outdoor leisure, as well as preservation. They were "playgrounds" for the American people. This emphasis on recreation made the idea of a park in southern Appalachia particularly attractive. The earliest national parks lay in remote areas of the West, and, for most Americans, they represented expensive and time-consuming journeys. Southern Appalachia, on the other hand, lay only a moderate distance from many of the nation's large population centers, as boosters seldom failed to mention. A park in this region could, in fact, become a playground for a great many Americans. The Smokies' natural beauty might not rival that of Yellowstone, but the average American traveler would find it far easier to consume.[14]

Before the mountain playground could become a reality, however, local organizers had to secure the land. In the 1920s, the federal government did not provide funds for assembling national parks. The 1926 act authorized the park's formation and suggested its boundaries, but state committees in North Carolina and Tennessee had to raise the necessary money and purchase the property. By 1930 the states had secured approximately 150,000 acres, and growing numbers of tourists had begun to visit the future park area. Completing the job, however, absorbed years of work by regional boosters. Powerful timber companies owned much of the land, and gaining this property, in some cases, involved costly condemnation suits and protracted negotiations. After 1933 and the arrival of the New Deal, federal officials became more involved in this effort, and Congress began to appropriate funds to support the completion of the park. Still, the formal dedication did not occur until 1940.[15]

The Eastern Band did not participate in the campaigns that secured federal authorization for the national park. The park's geography, however, ensured that Cherokees would feel the effects of this new attraction. The Qualla Boundary lay just outside the park's proposed southern border, and, shortly after Congress approved the park, work began on a road across the Smokies from Gatlinburg, Tennessee, to the village of Cherokee.[16] While there would be other routes into the park, the construction of this road meant that Cherokee effectively served as North Carolina's gateway to the Smokies, ensuring a large volume of tourist traffic. As the Raleigh *News and Observer* noted in 1930, "this spot [Cherokee] in a year or two will be a focus of interest not only for all North Carolina, but for the great traveling public from all the States of the Atlantic seaboard, North and South. For it is from this focal point that the traveling public will plunge into the great mountain wilderness now known as the Great Smoky National Park."[17] With the creation of the park, the geography of mountain tourism shifted in a way that placed the Cherokee community at its center. No longer on the tourism industry's margins, Cherokees now found themselves living at the very entrance to "one of the great playgrounds of the nation and of the world."[18]

The development of the Cherokee Fall Fair demonstrates the growing significance of tourism on the Qualla Boundary during this period. The fair began as an agricultural exposition. It evolved from a campaign by tribal leaders and the Cherokees' federal agent to encourage the formation of farmers' clubs to improve agriculture on Cherokee land. The earliest fairs included exhibits of "Indian work," artisan objects like baskets and pottery, but they mainly focused on farm produce and livestock. The Cherokee event, in other words, adhered closely to the model of agricultural fairs in surrounding counties.[19] In the 1920s, however, the focus began to shift, as the construction of good roads opened the Boundary to growing numbers of visitors. According to the *Asheville Citizen*, about two thousand people passed through the gates each day of the fair in 1922, and the newspaper estimated that at least half of those attending came from outside of western North Carolina. By 1928, twelve thousand people visited the fair each day, and the next year the *Citizen* recorded a two-day attendance of fifty thousand visitors. People from across the Southeast now attended the event, along with a smattering of tourists from the Northeast and Midwest. Throughout these years, the agricultural exhibits remained important, but, as attendance grew, the fair increasingly featured activities designed to represent distinctly Indian elements of Cherokee life. Exhibits of Cherokee crafts were significant attractions, and games of Cherokee stickball, the tribe's exceptionally rugged version of lacrosse, drew large crowds. Fair organizers added archery and blowgun shooting contests, and, by the mid-1920s, the fair featured exhibitions of traditional Cherokee dance by residents of the Big Cove community. When the dancing proved popular, Birdtown residents joined the performances, and the Big Cove group expanded its repertoire. As the fair's popularity grew, then, the event became as much an overt representation of tribal culture as it was an agricultural show. This change, of course, was not only for the tourists' benefit. Cherokee fairgoers also enjoyed and valued the stickball games, dancing, and archery competitions. As the newspapers indicated, however, these distinctly Indian performances were the features that attracted the crowds of outsiders.[20]

Cherokees organized and directed the fair, as well as participating as performers and exhibitors. Federal agents and the BIA approved of the festival and encouraged its development, but the fair could not take place without substantial contributions and leadership from the Cherokee community.

View of the Cherokee fairground, circa 1930. Courtesy Museum of the Cherokee Indian, Cherokee, North Carolina.

During the early years of the event, the tribe's federal agent served as the president of the fair association. The remaining directors, however, all came from the ranks of Eastern Band community leaders. Non-Indian authorities did not force Cherokees to shift the fair's emphasis toward greater displays of tribal culture. Both Cherokees and federal personnel shaped the event.[21]

A 1929 article in the *Charlotte Observer* offered a particularly vivid picture of the Fall Fair during this period of transition. The author, Henry Owl, was an Eastern Band citizen who grew up on the Qualla Boundary, attended the Indian school at Hampton Institute, and then taught in Cherokee and at Bacone College in Oklahoma. According to historian Theda Perdue, Owl was the first person of color admitted to the University of North Carolina, where he earned a master's degree in history the same year he wrote his essay for the *Observer*. In describing the fair, Owl suggested that it provided an introduction to the Eastern Band. "The visitor," he explained, "will have an opportunity to view the red man both as he has been portrayed in the past by the historian, and in his modern nature." The fair's official purpose, he noted, was "to stimulate a keener interest in farming, in better homes, and in better living among the Cherokees." Most of his essay, however, focused on the traditional dancing, games, and other "Indian features" that had become the fair's main draw for tourists. This year's event, he observed, would include Big Cove residents performing the Green Corn Dance, and he went on to explain that Cherokees had ceremonies for many stages of the agricultural cycle. He described the manufacture and use of blowguns, employed by contestants in some of the marksmanship competitions, and he provided a substantial account of Cherokee stickball, which he named the fair's "most exciting and interesting" event and "the roughest sport in the world." He described the rituals that traditionally accompanied ball games, commenting that, when it came to stickball, "the old practices of the people still exist to a surprising extent." By emphasizing such "old practices," Owl portrayed the Fall Fair as an opportunity for visitors to experience exotic elements of Cherokee culture, persistent traditions from an ancient past. While Cherokees, in many respects, "lived among the mountains as the ordinary mountaineer lives," the fair promised visitors glimpses of a different, older life.[22]

Cherokee cultural performance at the Fall Fair involved more than simply transferring a traditional dance or game to a new setting. Rather, Cherokees adapted these practices to an audience that included large numbers of outsiders. The photographs that accompanied Owl's article gestured toward this process. Alongside pictures of Principal Chief Sampson Owl and the Eastern Band's federal agent, the photos included images of Cherokee performers in "Indian" regalia—Great Plains–style headdresses, blankets, and fringed buckskin. These costumes, of course, bore little resemblance to historic Cherokee clothing styles, but they served to signal the Fall Fair's Indian character to visitors who arrived with little knowledge of Cherokee traditions.[23] During this same period, the practice known as "chiefing" developed on the Qualla Boundary, whereby Cherokee men would dress in Great Plains–style outfits and pose for tourists' photographs in return for tips. While the men who made their living as "chiefs" sometimes experimented with other costumes, they found that only Great Plains regalia guaranteed them customers.[24] At the Fall Fair, Cherokee performers made a similar effort to adapt to audience expectations. In fact, Carl Standingdeer, the Cherokee sometimes credited with having invented the "chiefing" trade, was a frequent performer at the fair. He appeared in one of the photos the

Observer published in 1929, clad in buckskin and identified as the Eastern Band's "champion archer."[25]

In the 1920s, the Cherokees' ability to assert an Indian identity was more than an economic matter. During this period, the United States attempted to implement the allotment policy in western North Carolina, seeking to divide the Cherokees' common tribal lands, sell tribal assets, and dismantle the Eastern Band government. In 1919, after years of pressure, the Tribal Council passed a resolution allowing the United States to make a "final disposition" of Eastern Band affairs, and, in 1924, Congress approved legislation to begin the allotment process. The law placed tribal lands in federal trust, pending their division into individual parcels, and federal agents began drawing up a new Eastern Band roll, which would determine who received a share of tribal property. When enrollment began, however, many more claimants to Eastern Band membership appeared than either tribal leaders or federal officials anticipated. Following a pattern established during the creation of earlier rolls, hundreds of people whom Cherokees did not recognize as members of their community sought enrollment and, with it, a portion of the Cherokees' property. The Eastern Band challenged around twelve hundred names on the roll, arguing that these individuals bore little Cherokee ancestry and few connections to the tribal community. Moreover, tribal leaders quickly realized that if allotment took place, individual members of the Eastern Band would receive very little property. Allotment, it seemed, would impoverish Cherokees, while leaving them exposed to exploitation. The Tribal Council reversed course and asked the BIA to suspend allotment, explaining that Cherokees now strongly opposed the policy. The land should remain in trust as the common property of the Eastern Band. By this time, opinion among legislators and Indian Bureau personnel had begun to turn against the allotment campaign, as a result of a growing awareness of the policy's devastating consequences for Indian communities. Congress agreed to halt Eastern Band allotment, and the North Carolina Cherokees' political status and landholding remained unchanged.[26]

The Eastern Band's growing involvement in tourism took place in the midst of this political crisis. The Fall Fair expanded its overtly Indian features during the years when Cherokees fought over the new roll and turned against allotment. In this context, the performance of Native culture broadcast Cherokees' unwillingness to assimilate. In the Fall Fair, Cherokees issued a clear statement that a distinctly Indian community remained in western North Carolina. This connection between tourism performance and the defense of the Eastern Band's tribal status would persist in the decades to come.

Cherokees and the Promotion of the
Great Smoky Mountains National Park

As visiting the Qualla Boundary grew in popularity, tourism boosters began to pay the Cherokee community greater attention as a feature of the region's economic landscape. One can trace this rising awareness of the tribe by examining the promotional literature for the national park. Early publications generally said very little about the Indian community. They identified the Qualla Boundary as one of the region's points of interest, but it was usually a minor point. In 1928, for instance, Tennessee boosters produced a seventy-page booklet describing the park and advertising the ongoing campaign to raise money for land acquisition. It devoted only one paragraph and a few scattered sentences to the Cherokees, along with a single page of photographs. By way of comparison, the park's wildflowers received three pages of descriptive text and images. "Aside from scraps of pottery and flints," the booklet explained, "the Cherokees have left little to contribute to the history of the Smokies except in the form of myth and legend."[27] A North Carolina publication from around the same time offered a more detailed description, but it was still quite brief, covering only one half-page. It mentioned that the eastern Cherokees were descendants of Indians who "hid out in the wild mountains" to avoid removal, and it told a brief version of the story of Sequoyah's invention of the Cherokee syllabary, stating (erroneously) that Sequoyah completed his great work while living in the Smokies.[28] These early writings seldom did more than note the tribe's existence, offering it as a splash of local color. In the words of the North Carolina booklet, the Cherokees "add the last touch of the picturesque to the park region."[29]

As the development of the park continued, however, the Cherokee presence in the promotional literature expanded, and some writings began to market the Qualla Boundary as an attraction in its own right. In 1933, for example, one of the first NPS-approved guidebooks included a four-page section on the Cherokees, emphasizing the myths and legends the earlier Tennessee pamphlet had dismissed. Drawing on James Mooney's writings, it offered brief versions of Cherokee stories associated with significant places in the Smokies, such as Clingman's Dome, the park's highest peak. It also promoted the Cherokee Fall Fair as a cultural festival and tourist event.[30] A few years later an Appalachian travel magazine produced an issue devoted to the park that included even more Cherokee material. The magazine offered a profile of the Qualla Boundary community, further discussion of the fair, and a description of the Smokies themselves that focused as much on the mountains' historical identity as a Cherokee homeland as it did on the scenery.[31] A Knoxville publisher even produced a short Cherokee-specific guidebook during this period, a twenty-eight-page brochure titled "The Cherokee Indians of the Qualla Reservation." Noting that an increasing number of visitors to the national park were stopping at Cherokee, the guide introduced some of the sights and activities the Boundary offered: unspoiled mountain vistas, the beautiful Occonaluftee River, opportunities to purchase Cherokee baskets and pottery, and, again, the Fall Fair.[32] These writings indicate a growing consciousness of the Cherokee community on the part of tourism promoters. While the mountain forest remained the park's main selling point, the Eastern Band occupied an increasingly significant place in the boosters' conception of the region.

History played a significant role in the promotional literature. As boosters identified mountain communities as potential attractions, they began to include historical narratives in their marketing of the southern highlands. These writings, in other words, were expressions of public memory. In fact, a particular sense of history colored even the literature's discussion of the natural landscape. In making the case that the Smokies merited preservation, promoters often explained that the area contained some of the last "virgin" timberlands in the East. This unspoiled forest made the Smokies a "natural museum," in the words of one guidebook. While urbanization and the industrial economy transformed much of the rest of the nation, here was a place that remained "primeval." This position, of course, ignored the history of industrial logging in the Smokies, but, in doing so, it invested these mountains with a value that went beyond their beauty. The park, by this way of thinking, offered visitors an opportunity to experience a landscape from the past, a remnant of a natural world that modernity had swept from most other areas of the country. A distinct sense of history informed park promoters' arguments for the preservation of the natural landscape.[33]

If the forest represented a remnant of a past world, so too did the Smokies' human communities. As historian C. Brenden Martin observes, tourism promoters depicted southern Appalachia as "a land forgotten by time."[34] Like the late-nineteenth-century travel writers I mentioned in chapter 1, these later writers suggested that the region never progressed beyond a frontier state, and they portrayed the people as relics of an older America. "In this national mountain museum are many quaint people," the *New York Times* stated. "They still guard their heritage and reveal in their present-day customs many characteristics of a hundred years ago."[35] White mountaineers lived in cabins, ate cornpone and crackling bread, and sang centuries-old folk songs. The women still worked with spinning wheels, while the men hunted deer and bears and cooked their own liquor. In addition to being picturesque, promoters suggested, these southern highlanders provided an important link to the national past. Here lived "the American frontiersman," a guidebook explained, "upstanding, clean-cut, independent, resourceful, and brave." Mountain whites were living representatives of the Anglo-Saxon pioneers who conquered the continent and founded the nation. "They belong to that homogeneous racial group that produced such men as Boone, Sevier, Clarke, Robertson, Admiral Farragut, Shelby, Houston, Andrew Jackson, Lincoln, Crockett, and Sergeant York."[36] Living exhibits in the "mountain museum," highlanders offered their tourist countrymen direct contact with a vital element of the national past.

The Indian community also provided a link to older ways. In this case, tourism promoters emphasized that Cherokees were heirs to ancient customs and lore. Some writings recounted Cherokee myths associated with particular places in the Smokies, noting, for instance, that monstrous creatures were said to inhabit the rivers and mountains of the park region. For the Cherokees, one writer explained, "every river bend, striped cliff, deep pool, peak, and trail had its romance. There was a legend for every ridge, cave, waterfall, giant mountain, or impenetrable forest."[37] Including some of these stories in the promotional literature helped boosters portray the Smokies as an ancient place, while adding a sense of "romance" or exoticism to the beauty of the landscape. Other writings focused on the persistence of traditional practices, such as the dancing and stickball Cherokees displayed each year at the Fall Fair. While the federal government maintained schools and promoted "modern methods of living" on the Qualla Boundary, one pamphlet explained, "the ancient ceremonies and sports are still preserved as racial customs."[38] The Cherokees, in other words, offered modern travelers direct contact with a premodern tribal past. Their distinctiveness, and thus their value to the tourism economy, derived from this status as a people out of time.

In addition to broadcasting the general image of the Smokies as a museum, tourism promoters included specific historical narratives in their descriptions of the region, with stories of Cherokee removal figuring prominently. Take, for instance, an essay about the national park written in 1930 by Ben Dixon McNeill, a North Carolina newspaperman and novelist. McNeill began the piece by paying homage to the natural beauty of the Smokies, but he quickly shifted focus to history, depicting the mountains as the setting for the Cherokees' dramatic struggle against removal. He described the early nineteenth-century Cherokees as a peaceful people who were well on their way to becoming civilized, before white pioneers began to covet their land. He placed particular emphasis on the discovery of gold in the Cherokee country, which inflamed the settlers' greed and spurred American demands that Cherokees remove to the West. Andrew Jackson was the villain of the piece. He had once pledged to be a friend to the tribe, Mc-Neill wrote, after Cherokees had helped him defeat the Creeks in 1813 and after one Cherokee, Junaluska, had saved his life at the Battle of Horseshoe Bend. As president, however, he broke his promise, and the United States drove the Cherokees across the Mississippi. Only a small handful of Indians managed to avoid removal by hiding in the wildest and least accessible parts of the Smokies—places now preserved by the park. From this remnant, McNeill explained, came the tribal community tourists would encounter on their visits to the mountains. In creating the park, then, the United States was "preserving a land of tragedy," as well as an area of striking natural beauty.[39]

McNeill's history included a great many errors, but they were errors that served to heighten the importance of the Smokies as the location of historical events. He implied, for example, that the Cherokee Nation in the early nineteenth century consisted mainly of the Smokies and western North Carolina, ignoring Georgia, Alabama, and much of the Cherokee land in Tennessee. While most of the political drama of the removal struggle took place in Georgia, McNeill drew the narrative into the national park area and the vicinity of the modern tribal lands. He cast Junaluska, who lived in western North Carolina, as the principal leader of the Cherokee government in the early nineteenth century, ignoring figures like Major Ridge and John Ross, who lacked Smoky Mountain connections. He even had Junaluska, once removal began, climbing to the top of a mountain in western North Carolina, gazing out over his people's lost homeland, and then dropping dead from grief. According to McNeill, Cherokees buried Junaluska where he fell, and white settlers later named the mountain for the departed chief. There is, in fact, a Junaluska Mountain in North Carolina, but the rest of this story was pure fabrication. It served the apparent purpose of the essay, however, in that it invested the landscape of mountain tourism with romance and historical interest.[40]

Removal stories like McNeill's became a common feature of booster literature during the creation of the national park. Most descriptions of the Smokies included at least a passing reference to the Trail of Tears, and, like McNeill, some writers focused on Cherokee removal as one of the most dramatic chapters of southern Appalachian history. In particular, booster writings began to feature the story of Tsali and his sons, Cherokees who, in October 1838, killed two soldiers while resisting removal and who were later executed for the deed. As chapter 1 described, James Mooney used a version of the Tsali story as an origin narrative for the Eastern Band in his influential *Myths of the Cherokee* (1900). In Mooney's telling, Tsali and his kinsmen surrendered voluntarily and accepted death in return for an American promise that Cherokees still in hiding would be permitted to stay in western North Carolina. That sacrifice, Mooney suggested, explained the continued presence of Cherokees in the Southeast.[41] In the late 1920s and 1930s, tourism boosters embraced the story of Tsali's martyrdom and drew it into the promotional literature for the national park and the broader region. The Cherokee guidebook mentioned above provides an example. After describing the various attractions of the Qualla Boundary, the brochure ended with a historical sketch of the tribe that centered on the Tsali episode. It described American settlers' encroachment on tribal lands and the discovery of gold that, according to this version of events, led the United States to order the removal of the Cherokees to the West. Most Cherokees accepted removal, it explained, once thousands of federal troops arrived to enforce the policy, but "back in the mountains" some Indians continued to resist. "A few of the fighting and determined Cherokee escaped from the pens [the removal forts and deportation camps] and hid out in the mountain fastness." In this version of events, Tsali was not only a member of the "fighting and determined Cherokee," but their leader. This position of authority, rather than the attack on the soldiers, explained why the Americans demanded his capture. After long resistance, the guidebook continued, Tsali finally agreed to surrender, but only if the United States would leave the remaining Cherokees unmolested. In a literary flourish repeated in many promotional writings, the guidebook pictured Tsali's moment of decision. "The old chief gazed silently out over the mountain vastness, visualizing a remnant of his tribe remaining in these glorious hills and then agreed to the supreme sacrifice." American leaders kept their promise and allowed the fugitive Cherokees to stay in the mountains. "This explains the presence today of the small band of 3200 Indians on the 63,000 acre reservation in western North Carolina." When tourists stopped at the Qualla

Boundary on their way to or from the national park, they would encounter the legacy of the Cherokee martyr.[42]

As I noted in chapter 1, this story had serious limitations as an account of Eastern Band origins. It ignored the presence of Cherokees who were legally exempt from removal, not to mention the strong likelihood that Tsali did not surrender willingly. The suggestion that Tsali was a resistance leader or a chief, meanwhile, was simply false. In the 1930s, however, the story suited the needs of tourism promoters quite perfectly. As the Tennessee writer Laura Thornborough stated, visitors to the Smokies often asked why a tribe of Indians still lived in North Carolina rather than in the West. The story of Tsali answered that question in dramatic and highly moving terms, and the tale's action took place in precisely the mountain landscape the boosters worked to advertise. Like McNeill's version of the dying Junaluska, the Tsali episode endowed the Smokies with historical resonance to match the scenery. It offered, in short, a further reason to visit the southern highlands. "The story of Tsali and his sacrifice so that his brothers might live in the land they loved is one of the highlights of this America of ours," one travel writer enthused, "and until the visitor hears the story from the lips of some wrinkled old Cherokee he'll never appreciate the kick there is in it."[43]

While these narratives explained the Cherokee presence in western North Carolina, they were fundamentally stories about Indian disappearance. The Cherokees' appeal within tourist culture derived from their supposedly anomalous position as an Indian tribe that remained in the Southeast. In accounting for their persistence, stories like the Tsali episode reinforced the notion that, as a rule, Native people had vanished. Like the mountain forests, Cherokees represented a remnant, a small relic of a past world. Mountain tourism called attention to the Eastern Band's existence, but only in terms that emphasized the absence of Native people from the rest of the South.

The Spirit of the Great Smokies

In 1935 the directors of the Cherokee Fall Fair decided to add a new feature to that year's festival. Noting that 1935 marked the centennial of the Treaty of New Echota, the agreement that precipitated Cherokee removal, they mounted an elaborate pageant recounting the history of the tribe. Performed on two successive evenings during the fair, "The Spirit of the Great Smokies" depicted the arrival of Europeans, the Trail of Tears, and Cherokee persistence in the decades following removal. Some five hundred citizens of the Eastern Band participated as actors, and members of the North Carolina Symphony Orchestra provided musical accompaniment. The *Asheville Citizen* declared the drama a success, recording an opening night attendance of around three thousand and noting that the amateur cast performed quite well. The Eastern Band's federal agent considered the pageant a big enough hit that he thought it could become a regular attraction. In 1937 he organized a series of performances of "The Spirit of the Great Smokies" during the height of the summer tourist season, and he hoped to do the same in summers to come. The pageant, then, represented a substantial effort to include historical commemoration in the Cherokees' developing tourism economy.[44]

By the 1930s, pageantry formed a well-established genre of public history performance in the United States. The pageant "craze," as historian David Glassberg calls it, developed around the turn of the twentieth century, when communities in the Northeast began to stage increasingly lavish dramas recounting their particular local histories. These pageants typically consisted of a series of episodes representing the chronological development of a given town or city, from the arrival of European settlers up to the modern industrial present. Community members provided the cast, preferably with some citizens playing their own ancestors. These actors generally did not speak. Rather, the pageant directors arranged large assemblies of players in fairly static tableaux, each scene suggesting a particular moment from the town's past. One or more narrators would explain the action as it unfolded, often in rather ornate poetic language. In between episodes, and sometimes within particular scenes, the pageants offered music and dancing. Allegorical dances were particularly popular, with performers representing "Progress" or the essence of a particular locale or simply "The Spirit of Pageantry." By the 1910s, the period of the genre's greatest popularity, these features solidified into a standard model, and a small industry developed to support the mounting of these dramas by providing local communities with costumes, lighting, and sometimes entire productions.[45]

Tourism boosters in southern Appalachia adopted pageantry as an additional way to bring history into their marketing of the mountains. In 1931, for instance, the Rhododendron Pageant, the elaborate finale of Asheville's annual Rhododendron Festival, took as its subject the history of western North Carolina. More than one thousand residents of the state's western counties, including a group of Cherokees from the Qualla Boundary, enacted scenes from the region's past. In one act, a group of Cherokees offered an exhibition of traditional dance, which the local press celebrated as the highlight of the show. The performers included some of the same Qualla Boundary residents who, a few years earlier, introduced Cherokee dance into the Fall Fair. For the Rhododendron Festival, they seem to have simply transplanted a proven Cherokee attraction to the new event, offering the same dances at both the 1931 fair and Asheville's pageant.[46]

Two years later, tourism boosters in Knoxville, on the Tennessee side of the national park, staged a historical drama of their own. Titled "The Spell of the Smokies," the pageant was meant to express, through legend and history, the allure of the southern mountains, with the obvious hope that large numbers of travelers would soon fall under that same "spell." Around half of the scenes involved Cherokee content, with white residents of Knoxville playing the parts of famous Cherokees like John Ross and the eighteenth-century leader Little Carpenter. Early acts dramatized several of the stories collected in James Mooney's *Myths of the Cherokee*, before the pageant shifted to portray warfare between Cherokees and the founders of Tennessee during the Revolutionary Era. The drama also included a substantial Trail of Tears episode. In the removal scenes, John Ross led a long line of weary Cherokees into the West, urged on their way by soldiers on horseback, as the pageant narrator sadly explained how "at last the order came to leave forever the land of his fathers . . . and cross the great Father of Waters to land in the distant and unloved West." The act ended by accounting for the modern-day presence of the Eastern Band in North Carolina. "Not all of the Cherokees crossed the Great Water," the narrator intoned, "for some caught by the Spell of the Smokies, found the delicate chains of their purple-blue mists stronger than the white man's bonds, and breaking away from the march, fled to the deep-hidden coves of the mountains, where the mists and the clouds took them unto themselves, and where they remain today." The scene accompanying this narration included an echo of the story of Tsali's resistance. "There is a sudden tension seen," the stage directions indicated, "and with a great cry the Indians leap upon the nearest soldiers and fell them to the ground. They turn and with women and children following, disappear swiftly into the darkness, going back to the Smokies."[47]

The mounting of these pageants represented a logical extension of the trends I have already discussed in this chapter. As the Qualla Boundary became a more significant part of the tourism landscape, boosters began to include Cherokee culture and history in their promotion of the region. With the pageants, they drew Cherokee history out of the promotional literature and into public tourist events. The Knoxville drama, in particular, suggests that boosters felt that Cherokee stories could invest the southern highlands with a strong attraction. The tribe's oral traditions could fill the landscape with romance, while Cherokee history featured a dramatic struggle to remain in the places promoters now hoped to fill with tourists. For these boosters, the Cherokee community's very existence in the twentieth century advertised the power of the Smokies' "spell."

The Eastern Band's pageant, "The Spirit of the Great Smokies," was equally a product of these regional developments, but it also reflected a political transformation specific to American Indian affairs. The mid-1930s witnessed a significant change in the federal government's relations with Native American peoples, as the Democratic Party's victories in the 1932 elections brought, among other consequences, a new direction in American Indian policy. Franklin Roosevelt's Commissioner of Indian Affairs, John Collier, belonged to a movement of reformers who hoped to modify the assimilation campaigns of the late nineteenth and early twentieth centuries and promote a reinvigorated Indian tribalism. At Collier's urging, Congress passed the 1934 Wheeler-Howard Act, also known as the Indian Reorganization Act (IRA). With this law, the United States repudiated the allotment policy, encouraged Indian groups to draft new tribal constitutions, and offered loans for land purchases and tribal economic development. The BIA, meanwhile, committed itself to supporting certain Native American cultural practices. Collier and his lieutenants insisted that federal agents should no longer interfere with Native American religions, and they directed agents to nurture tribal arts and traditional crafts. While the actual impact of these initiatives on Native American communities varied widely, the "Indian New Deal" marked a profound shift in overall federal policy. After more than a century of working to erode tribal sovereignty and destroy Native American cultures, the government temporarily retreated from complete assimilation as the primary goal of Indian affairs.[48]

The Collier-era policies influenced the Eastern Band in multiple ways. They guaranteed that Cherokees would no longer face the threat of allotment, and they led some tribal leaders to advocate replacing the tribe's North Carolina charter with a new constitution under the IRA.[49] The Indian Bureau's new regard for tribal cultures, meanwhile, complemented the packaging of Cherokee tradition and history as tourist attractions. A planning document drafted by Harold Foght, the Cherokees' federal agent, illustrates this development quite well. Writing in October 1934, Foght outlined a set of initiatives meant to align the Eastern Band with the government's "new program" in Indian affairs. While much of the document dealt with improving Cherokee schools and enlarging the tribal land base, Foght also discussed tourism. He described plans to expand craft instruction at the Cherokee boarding school, and he hoped that Cherokee students could be trained to work as guides to lead visitors through the Boundary and the national park. He also promised changes to the Fall Fair, which had just concluded its 1934 run at the time of his writing. The fair's Cherokee directors would soon dispense with "cheap white shows," he wrote, and make the event "an Indian fair solely." The fair, he hoped, would include only Native American performers and exhibitors, while emphasizing attractions rooted in Cherokee culture, like stickball and traditional dancing. Foght was particularly excited by the prospect of staging a Cherokee historical pageant, already under discussion as an addition to the following year's fair. "Such a pageant," he wrote, "would mean more and attract more tourists than the programs we now offer the public." Applying the Indian New Deal to the Eastern Band, then, involved the further cultivation of Cherokee cultural tourism.[50]

The name of the fair in 1935 suggests an additional influence. While the event was previously known simply as the "Cherokee Fall Fair," in 1935 organizers called it the "Cherokee Fall Fair and Folk Festival." The change offered a further sign that the fair would emphasize cultural performance, while reflecting the emergence of the folk festival as an institution during this period. One of the first modern American folk festivals, in fact, began in Asheville only a few years earlier. In 1928 the city's Rhododendron Festival included a program of Appalachian music and dance organized by Bascom Lamar Lunsford, a lawyer and folklore collector from nearby Madison County, North Carolina. The following year, Lunsford broke away from the Rhododendron Festival and staged the first Mountain Dance and Folk Festival, a yearly event that continues today. Lunsford's example helped to inspire the creation of similar folk celebrations, such as the National Folk Festival, launched by Kentucky native Sarah Gertrude Knott in 1934.[51] By calling the Cherokee fair a "folk festival," organizers indicated that cultural tradition would provide the chief attraction, and they aligned the event with the broader folk revival movement. Lunsford himself may have been responsible for the name change, as he seems to have played a role in the Cherokee fair during this period. In 1936, the *State*, a Raleigh-based magazine involved in tourism promotion, reported that Lunsford helped to stage the music and dance performances at the Indian fair since the beginning of the decade.[52]

To produce the Cherokee historical pageant, Foght called on Margaret Pearson Speelman, a schoolteacher from the West with substantial experience creating Indian-themed dramas. Speelman was a white woman from Kansas, raised in the town of Wakefield and educated at the University of Kansas at Lawrence. She joined the Indian Education Service in 1916, assigned to the Chilocco Indian School in central Oklahoma. There, in addition to teaching, she began to write and produce school plays and pageants, and she continued this work after returning to Kansas and a position at the Haskell Institute, another government-run Indian school.[53] Most of Speelman's pageants dramatized episodes from Native American history, while featuring Indian dances and music, which she learned from her students. "The Pageant of Great Gifts" (1930), for instance, depicted the nineteenth-century "Opening of the West" and featured a series of Pawnee songs, while "Wa-Gthe'ce Shpi-Zho: A Pageant of Indian Education" (1933) attempted to show "the manner of Indian education among the Plains Tribes centuries ago." The latter play included Cheyenne and Dakota songs, along with dances from a variety of Plains tribes. By the early 1930s, Speelman became something like an unofficial drama coach for the Indian boarding school system, well known in the Indian Education Service for her pageant work.[54]

In its basic structure, Speelman's script for "The Spirit of the Great Smokies" adhered to the pageantry genre's conventions. It told a chronological story that began with the appearance of Europeans in the Cherokee country and ended in the present. Narrating such a story from a Cherokee perspective, however, altered the message conveyed by that standard formula. As Glassberg writes, historical pageants generally adopted progress as their central theme. They recounted local histories of steady improvement, from the founding of small settler communities to the development of modern industrial towns.[55] In the Cherokee pageant, however, the settlers were invaders, and many of the historical events Euro-Americans celebrated as mileposts of improvement were disasters for the tribe. "Time after time our war chiefs strive for peace / Time after time we strive to hold our lands," Speelman's narrator explained in an episode on colonial expansion. "But Anglo-folk are greedy for new fields, / And nothing we can do will stem the tide of pioneers / Who force their weary way across our now unhappy Hills."[56] Pioneers, of course, appeared as heroic founders in most community pageants. They were the people who set these tales of progress in motion.

Here they were the villains of the piece, turning the Cherokee hills "un-happy." This same episode ended with the American Revolution, noting the terrible consequences of the Cherokee alliance with the British. "Our towns are burned, our orchards cut, / Our fields lay waste, our cattle killed, / Our warriors slain, our women starved. / So is our nation humbled and brought to sue for peace. / Now a new flag floats above us." Needless to say, the pageant did not depict the founding of the United States as an improvement in Cherokee life.[57]

Rather than progress, the central theme of "The Spirit of the Great Smokies" was persistence. The pageant depicted Cherokee history as a series of terrible challenges posed by outside powers. Cherokees lost each of these battles, but in each they managed to retain their essential tribal identity and a portion of their mountain homeland. The episode on removal, the pageant's centerpiece, provided a case in point. The Cherokees, the narrator explained, recovered from the tragedies of the Revolutionary Era and grew prosperous and civilized, but, as usual, Euro-Americans proved incapable of leaving their Indian neighbors alone. "Greedy whites look on in envy, then in hate," the narrator stated, and soon the United States ordered the tribe's expulsion. Removal visited upon the Cherokees some of the same horrors experienced during the colonial era, yet some Cherokees managed to avoid removal and hold on to a remnant of their mountain domain. Here, like many writers, Speelman employed Tsali ("Charley" in this version) to personify Cherokee resistance, rendering the old man as a kind of guerilla leader. "A few steal out / And make their frightened way back to their loved homeland . . . / They were the folk, the followers of Charley, / Who, when the night was black, called them to steal away." The story of Tsali's surrender and sacrifice explained the survival of Cherokees in the East and provided inspiration for later generations of the tribe. "Well could our young men, the brave hearts of our people, / Learn still greater courage from the story of old Charley, / Who comes, to save his people, down from the mountains, / Giving himself to death, that Cherokee might live."[58] Like the pageant as a whole, the removal episode illustrated the Cherokees' will to remain in the southern highlands.

Only in the very last scene did the pageant embrace the idea of progress, not as a theme of Cherokee history but as a hope for the future. Noting that most of the pageant actors were Cherokee students, the narrator declared, "Before you here now stand the hope of ancient Qualla, / Our young folk, the pride of all our people." The lives of these students, the pageant suggested, could provide a contrast to the grim and violent episodes they had just enacted, provided the young people stayed true to their Cherokee identity. "Teach them, O Spirit, all that it has taken / To keep us truly Cherokee," the narrator concluded. "Restore to us the best that was our fathers', / Help us to use the best our conquerors brought us; / But keep this bit of the Hills forever Indian."[59]

With this emphasis on Cherokee persistence, "The Spirit of the Great Smokies" reflected both the needs of the tourism economy and the policy goals of the Indian New Deal. The pageant reminded spectators that, when they visited the Smokies, they had the rare experience of meeting a distinctly Indian community, and it explained how that community and its culture endured. The pageant was both a tourist attraction in itself and an advertisement for the mountain region. The promise that this corner of the Smokies would remain "forever Indian," meanwhile, echoed the BIA's disavowal of assimilation during the Collier era. Cherokees would not disappear completely into the dominant society, the pageant insisted. They would stay "truly Cherokee" and retain their tribal lands. That future was precisely what Collier and other reformers believed would result from their policies.

The theme of persistence likely also reflected the outlook of the Cherokees who contributed to the pageant's creation. While Speelman based the drama on academic sources (James Mooney, in particular), she also traveled to North Carolina to consult with members of the tribal community. Among these consultants was Will West Long, a widely recognized authority on Cherokee culture who was deeply concerned with the preservation of his people's traditions. Today, Long is best remembered as a contributor to anthropological scholarship. As a teenager in the late 1880s he worked for James Mooney as a translator and guide, and in later years he became a regular collaborator with scholars working on Cherokee topics. As the anthropologist John Witthoft wrote, Long spent most of his adult life engaged in "a systematic study of Cherokee tradition," and he shared some of the resulting knowledge with outsiders in the hope of ensuring its survival. While this scholarship appeared under white academics' names, Long was himself one of the most significant figures in Cherokee studies during the first half of the twentieth century.[60] He was also among the Cherokees who performed for tourists. Long danced with his Big Cove neighbors in the Cherokee Fall Fair, and he led the dancers who performed in the 1931 Rhododendron Pageant. Later, he brought Cherokee dance to even bigger stages, leading performances at the National Folk Festivals in Chattanooga in 1935 and in Dallas the next year.[61] These public exhibitions complemented his work with scholars. In the late 1920s and 1930s, Long and other Big Cove residents demonstrated Cherokee rituals for the anthropologist Frank Speck, work that eventually resulted in Speck and Leonard Broom's important *Cherokee Dance and Drama* (1951). Some of the rituals Speck documented included versions of the same dances Long and other Cherokees performed for tourists.[62] In "The Spirit of the Great Smokies," Long appeared again as a dance leader and as a character called simply "The Chief," and Speelman later remembered him as a particular friend in the Cherokee community. The presence of so significant a cultural revivalist suggests that Cherokee participants, no less than federal agents, shaped the pageant's message of tribal persistence.[63]

Foght's plan to make the pageant a regular feature of Cherokee tourism failed to materialize. In the summer of 1937, the tribe staged a series of six performances, which Foght considered a financial and public relations success, but this season proved to be the pageant's last.[64] According to historian John Finger, "The Spirit of the Great Smokies" fell victim to the Eastern Band's internal political battle over the Indian New Deal. A small but influential group of Eastern Band citizens opposed the Collier-era policies as paternalistic and contrary to American principles of free enterprise. These Cherokees condemned any tourism project organized on a tribal rather than an individual basis, accusing agents like Foght of promoting communism on the Qualla Boundary. These attacks, Finger suggests, made the continued staging of the pageant impossible in the late 1930s.[65] Its disappearance, however, does not lessen the pageant's significance as an example of public memory. Cherokee anticommunists may have disapproved of the drama, but visitors seem to have enjoyed it and considered it a logical addition to Smoky Mountain tourism. With its story of historical persistence, moreover, the pageant reflected the outlook of Cherokees, like Will West Long, who sought to preserve and revitalize their people's distinct cultural practices and identity as a tribal community.

Tennessee's Cherokee Memorial

As Foght labored to make the historical pageant a regular attraction on the Qualla Boundary, a separate effort to commemorate Cherokee removal developed in Knoxville, Tennessee, on the other side of the national park. For several weeks in early 1937, students in the city's elementary and middle schools pooled their money with the aim of erecting a permanent monument to Tsali, the Cherokee martyr. The children formed "penny clubs," one in each public school, with the idea that each student could contribute at least one cent to the effort. Schools competed with one another to gather the most change and to reach full student participation. City newspapers documented the campaign with daily front-page stories, complete with photos of children wearing Thanksgiving-style construction paper headdresses. Adults, meanwhile, responded by creating a Tsali Cherokee Foundation, pledged not only to build the memorial but also to offer aid to Cherokees in North Carolina. While the campaign lasted only a short time, the story of the monument provides a further example of how tourism development could draw elements of Cherokee history into the public memory of Appalachian communities.[66]

As with the Eastern Band's historical pageant, the Tennessee commemoration began with tourism promotion—in this case, a specific item of national park publicity. In February 1937, the *Knoxville News-Sentinel* published a long essay titled "Land of the Cherokee" as the main feature in its Sunday magazine. The author was Herbert Ravenel Sass, a South Carolina–based novelist and travel writer, who originally produced the article for the national weekly *Collier's*.[67] In it, Sass combined a typical booster's portrayal of the national park with a melodramatic rendition of the Tsali story. He described the new park as a paradise hidden in the nation's backyard, containing "the last remnant of primeval Eastern American wilderness." It was "beautiful beyond description," he wrote, "and so rugged and lofty that the advancing tide of civilization fell back daunted before it, flowing around it instead of over it and leaving it all these years unconquered and unspoiled."[68] Eastern Cherokees also represented a remnant for Sass, an echo of an earlier, "unspoiled" time. They had managed to stay in their homeland and avoided the attention of surrounding white communities, much as the area encompassed by the park (in his account) avoided the ravages of industrial civilization. While most Cherokees lived modern lives, Sass continued, "some of them keep in their hearts the red man's ancient lore and maintain the red man's customs."[69] Tsali, meanwhile, linked the people and the place, his legendary sacrifice explaining why this ancient culture still existed in the Smokies. Like most writers, Sass based his version of Tsali on James Mooney's account, describing the impulsive attack on the soldiers, the family's escape, and the fugitives' eventual decision to surrender. The old man and his sons met death with quiet bravery, knowing that they had saved their people and their homeland. "Tsali's eyes, as he faced the rifles, were victorious," Sass wrote. "Perhaps he saw the future—saw the vale of Ocona Luftee once more the home of his people, the smoke rising from hundreds of Indian cabins, the children playing by the river, the small papooses riding on their mothers' backs, as you can see them in Ocona Luftee today."[70]

All of these themes fit well within the conventions of mountain tourism publicity during this period. Toward the end of the article, however, Sass offered a novel flourish by suggesting that a formal monument to Tsali would make a fitting addition to the national park. Visitors to the Smokies should know about Tsali, he reasoned, since the old man's heroism explained why there were still Cherokees in the Southeast. Moreover, "in its valor, its pity, and its triumph," it was "one of the great true stories of America." A memorial would guarantee that a wide audience would learn of Cherokee suffering and persistence. "Perhaps this article will help build it," Sass concluded, "who knows?"[71]

A few days after publishing "Land of the Cherokee," the *News-Sentinel* received a letter from a girl named Jewel Lady, a student at Knoxville's Park Junior High School. She explained that her history class at Park had read Sass's article and that she and her fellow students, moved by the story, wanted to help the effort to erect a Tsali memorial. They had formed a "penny club" to gather contributions. "All of the school children," Lady wrote, "will have a chance to participate and show their admiration for Cherokee Chief Tsali . . . for such heroism knows no race distinction."[72] In fact, there were no plans to build a Tsali memorial, but the editors of the *News-Sentinel* liked the idea and set out to publicize it into reality. A decade earlier, Knoxville children had contributed money to support land purchases for the national park, and the junior high's penny club showed the same spirit. As word spread of the Tsali campaign, other Knoxville schools followed Park's lead, forming fund-raising clubs of their own, and the *News-Sentinel* distributed copies of Sass's article to classrooms across the city. Teachers in many schools used the story as the basis for lessons and class projects, and, according to the newspaper, "so much interest has been created among Knoxville school children that Lawson McGhee Library workers reported their shelves had been 'ransacked' for books about Indian life." Some adults, meanwhile, noted that the memorial campaign might contribute to the region's economic well-being. As Park Junior High's principal observed, "we have everything in the Smokies from the standpoint of scenic splendor and beauty but we need more attractions from the standpoint of human interest and tradition. This unique case of heroism provides that opportunity." A dramatic local history, properly marked and marketed, could provide a further boost to tourism.[73]

For about two weeks, the *News-Sentinel* broadcast the call for children's donations and reported as schools handed their pennies over to the business manager of the Knoxville board of education. By early March, when the campaign ended, the school board reported that it had received more than $150, a sum that, with late submissions, eventually rose to $170. This total may seem small; however, since most individual donations appear to have been literally one penny each, $170 suggests broad participation.[74] At this point, Knoxville's adults took over. City business leaders organized the Tsali Cherokee Foundation, led by Brad A. Lawrence, the head of Knoxville's tourism and publicity bureau, and Clarence Holland, vice president of the chamber of commerce. The foundation promised to build the memorial and staged Cherokee-related events in the city. The Cherokee memorial campaign, which had been inspired by tourism in the first place, thus generated additional efforts to bring Cherokee history and culture into Knoxville's tourism economy.[75]

The foundation began its work by organizing a special "Indian program" in May 1937. Three great-grandchildren of Tsali, Richard, Irma, and Lucille Washington, visited the city's ornate Tennessee Theater, where they recounted the story of their famous ancestor, along with other "legends and stories handed down around Indian campfires for generations." Carl Standingdeer, the Cherokee "chief" and performer, rounded out the program, demonstrating archery and the use of the blowgun "as practiced in the days of Tsali."[76] A month later, the foundation sponsored a much more ambitious event. "Indian Day," a celebration meant to kick off that summer's high tourist season, featured a parade down Gay Street and an afternoon of Cherokee performances at Knoxville's Caswell Park. Before an audience of more than twenty-five hundred spectators, Will West Long led a demonstration of Cherokee song and traditional dance, followed by an archery and blowgun contest organized by Standingdeer. Standingdeer also arranged for Knoxville's first game of Cherokee stickball, which the newspapers of this football-mad college town praised as the world's roughest and fastest sport. Performances like these, of course, were already popular attractions at the Cherokee Fall Fair. Awakened to the tribe's tourism potential, Knoxville simply imported from the Qualla Boundary an established model of Cherokee entertainment.[77]

In sponsoring the Indian Day events, Brad Lawrence and his colleagues merged tourism publicity with a philanthropic outlook. The foundation began to present itself as a group seeking not only to recognize the region's Cherokee history but also "to better the economic condition of the Eastern tribe" in the present. This was perhaps a logical extension of the children's penny campaign, in which the students offered gifts to perpetuate Tsali's memory. In the foundation's case, helping the Cherokees took the form of contributions to the tribe's own efforts at tourism development. Foundation leaders learned of the Eastern Band's plans to stage regular performances of "The Spirit of the Great Smokies" during the summer of 1937, and they offered the tribe six hundred dollars for costumes out of the proceeds from Indian Day. Significantly, the costumes secured by pageant organizers were Great Plains–style outfits from a Wild West show in Oklahoma. The foundation's support, then, led Cherokee performers to continue their adaptation to outsiders' conceptions of "The Indian." Contributing to "The Spirit of the Great Smokies," the Knoxville foundation helped Cherokees present both a distinct tribal history and a universal Indian image.[78]

The Indian Day episode suggests the extent to which tourism and historical memory could shape one another in the shadow of the national park. Tourism development made possible Knoxville's encounter with Cherokee history and the effort to include the Cherokees in the city's public memory. That encounter, in turn, inspired an act of philanthropy that was, itself, an expression of tourism planning. The result was another public representation of Cherokee history and, as suggested by the costumes, the further molding of Cherokee historical images to suit tourist expectations. While Indian Day was a fairly straightforward event, it displayed the kind of complex tangle of economic and commemorative motives present in much historical tourism.

Despite the success of events like Indian Day, several years passed before the foundation could erect the Tsali memorial, and, in the end, it was a very different monument from the one Herbert Ravenel Sass imagined. For one thing, the foundation abandoned its plans to place the monument in the national park. The NPS may have rejected the idea, or perhaps the delays in completing the park encouraged the foundation to look elsewhere. Whatever the reason, Brad Lawrence now hoped that the Tsali memorial could be erected on the Qualla Boundary. He and Clyde Blair, Harold Foght's successor as federal agent, decided that the best site would be on land near the Cherokee boarding school. Placing the monument there would make it a gift from the students of Knoxville to the students of the Eastern Band.

As Lawrence wrote, "it is my feeling that the Cherokee children should obtain whatever inspiration there may be through our perpetuating the memory of this hero of their tribe."[79]

In spring 1939, it appeared that the memorial would soon be completed. The Eastern Band government approved the project, and Blair secured the agreement of BIA commissioner John Collier. Lawrence, for his part, placed an order for a bronze tablet and began planning a dedication ceremony.[80] But then the plan changed one more time, as business leaders back in Knoxville developed second thoughts about the monument's location. Why should a memorial purchased by Tennessee school children, they reasoned, be placed on the North Carolina side of the Smokies, where few, if any, of those children would ever see it? "They raised $170.00," Lawrence explained to commissioner of Indian Affairs John Collier, "which is 17,000 pennies, which represents a sacrifice of the little things that mean so much to the poorer children who had their part in it." Surely, the children deserved a chance to see the product of their campaign. Some in Knoxville added a historical argument. They noted that, back in the 1830s, members of Tennessee's congressional delegation had opposed the removal policy, implying that Tsali's memory, and the memory of Cherokee resistance, belonged as much to Tennessee as to the Cherokees themselves. "I regret," Lawrence wrote to Collier, "that the Indian children at Cherokee will not have such inspiration that would come from the erection of this memorial in a location where they would see it daily." Or see it at all, one could add.[81]

So, in the end, they placed the Tsali memorial in Gatlinburg, their own state's doorway to the national park. The Tennesseans' gift to the Cherokees became a gift to themselves. Their effort to honor the Native American past became an act of possession.[82] The monument stands there today on the main road running from Pigeon Forge to the park entrance, amid the town's famous riot of motels and gift shops. A tablet fixed to a large rock, it features the image of an Indian man in a Great Plains headdress and reads: "To Tsali the Cherokee and his two sons, who gave their lives in 1836, so that their people might remain in the land of the Great Smokies." The date is incorrect (two years early), and the image suggests a performing "chief" rather than a removal-era Cherokee. It is a rather poor memorial, then, to the Trail of Tears. With its own history restored, however, it is a strangely eloquent memorial to the mountain tourism boom of the 1920s and 1930s.

Memorial to Tsali, Gatlinburg, Tennessee. Photo by author.

Cherokees and the Narratives of Mountain Tourism

Storytelling forms an essential activity in tourism development and an important part of the process of making places through commemoration. As the anthropologist Edward Bruner notes, when a community or government designates a particular locale as a travel destination, both planners and tourists themselves devise narratives for the site, stories that explain its attractions and, in doing so, heighten its allure.[83] Those stories, in turn, can reshape the public identity of the place. The master narrative crafted by proponents of the Great Smoky Mountains National Park focused on the protection of a distinct natural environment and its enjoyment by ordinary citizens. Modern civilization destroyed most of the natural wonders of the East long ago, promoters suggested, but this remnant in the Smokies could persist as a "playground" for all Americans. Once they decided that the place was special, tourism planners elaborated on this narrative, identifying human as well as natural assets in the landscape. They attached additional stories to the park area, Cherokee stories among them. Cherokee history gained new meaning to non-Indians like the Knoxville publicity director Brad Lawrence, to the extent that it offered a compelling human experience to match the mountain scenery. As promoters included Cherokee narratives and images in their marketing of the region, the Cherokee past became a central element of Appalachian tourism's commodified sense of place.

The removal episode provided ideal material for this process. The Cherokees' struggle against removal, when translated into tourism literature and performance, became a story about loving the mountains and struggling to remain there. The Tsali legend, in particular, spoke of a powerful bond between this place and its people. Tourism planners, or course, hoped to inspire a similar affection in millions of visitors. The persistence of the Eastern Band, meanwhile, echoed the master narrative promoters devised for the mountains. Like the Smokies environment, Cherokees represented a remnant, an Indian community that had avoided displacement during the era of American expansion. They retained some of their ancient traditions, much as the park preserved a natural abundance long absent from other sections of the East. While this narrative reinforced the assumption that most Indian people had disappeared, it encouraged promoters to raise the public profile of this particular community and its past. In the Cherokees, tourists encountered an unlikely people in an equally surprising landscape, and promoters could only account for the Indian presence by delving into removal-era history.

Cherokees helped to broadcast these tourism narratives by participating in events like Knoxville's Indian Day and performances of "The Spirit of the Great Smokies." The tourism industry provided public settings in which Cherokees demonstrated their community's Indian identity to outsiders. In the 1920s and 1930s, the persistence of that identity represented a political asset, as well as an economic resource. To be clear, Cherokees were seldom the sole authors of tourism performances. Even a production like "The Spirit of the Great Smokies," which involved hundreds of Cherokees, was created by a white educator and expressed the outlook of a particular group of BIA reformers. With their participation, however, Cherokees endorsed the drama's vision of tribal persistence, and, as performers, they influenced how this enduring tribal culture would appear to the visitors attending the play. Cherokees confirmed and elaborated upon tourism narratives when they found such confirmation advantageous, even if they could not rewrite these stories.

3 The Centennial

Chattanooga Marks the One-Hundredth Anniversary
of the Trail of Tears

· ·

In September 1938, Chattanooga, Tennessee, hosted an elaborate commemorative festival called the Chickamauga National Celebration. Ten days long and partly subsidized by the federal government, the event featured daily parades, somber memorial ceremonies, military demonstrations, and a historical pageant that organizers touted as the largest ever produced in the South. As the name implies, the Civil War provided the festival's main focus. September 1938 marked the seventy-fifth anniversary of the Battle of Chickamauga (September 19–20, 1863), in which Confederate forces halted a Union drive into northwestern Georgia, inflicting the federal army's worst defeat in the war's western theater. Two months later, Union forces reversed that loss at Lookout Mountain and Missionary Ridge (November 23 and 25, 1863), victories that opened the way for William Tecumseh Sherman's Atlanta Campaign the following year.[1] In addition to recalling those battles, the 1938 festival also marked the centennial of Chattanooga's founding. In autumn 1838, white settlers chose the name Chattanooga for a small village on the Tennessee River, an event their descendants later identified as the birth of the city. The centennial provided an opportunity for Chattanooga's political and social leaders to celebrate the development of their community from that early settlement into one of the urban and industrial centers of the South. The Chickamauga National Celebration, then, combined two very traditional modes of American public memory, the community anniversary and the memorialization of military sacrifice and valor.[2]

As a final element of the event, organizers included a commemoration of Cherokee removal, noting that 1938 also marked the one-hundredth anniversary of the Trail of Tears. That decision was very much an afterthought, with preparations for the festival well under way before planners thought to incorporate the Cherokee centennial. Once they made the decision, however, they developed an extensive bill of Indian-themed events. Local residents dedicated monuments to Cherokee history at several locations in the

Chattanooga area, and the planners booked Indian performers like Carl Standingdeer to provide entertainment. City newspapers published long essays describing the Trail of Tears, while the removal story occupied a central place in the pageant. More than one hundred Cherokees from North Carolina and Oklahoma attended the festival as either performers or guests, with organizers referring to their visit as a "homecoming," the return of Indian people to this part of the old Cherokee Nation. While the Chickamauga National Celebration began as a Civil War remembrance, it came to include the period's single largest commemoration of Indian removal.

Like the examples discussed in chapter 2, the Chattanooga festival illustrates the emergence of the Cherokee removal story within southern public memory in the interwar period. As the Trail of Tears centennial grew from a minor addendum into an elaborate commemoration, Cherokee history became a more prominent feature of the city's public identity. This process involved not only the recognition of the Cherokee past, but a significant act of possession. The white elites who organized the festival embraced Cherokee history as a part of their own heritage. Removal became a dramatic event that happened in *their* home, with the Cherokee struggle appearing as a stage in the evolution of the white community. Commemorating Cherokee history confirmed white Chattanoogans' control and ownership of this former Indian place and their authority to define the city's past and present. They used that same authority to exclude most aspects of the city's African American history, denying the experience of a community that made up a third of Chattanooga's population. The removal centennial helped white residents know the region as their home, while affirming the place of white elites at the top of the city's social and political hierarchy.

Yet, if the removal centennial left the city's racial power structure unchallenged, it brought a note of doubt into the festival's otherwise celebratory vision of the past. This uncertainty fit a broader cultural pattern in the 1930s. During the Great Depression, American popular culture often expressed a concern for the loss of tradition, a phenomenon that reflected anxiety about the nature of material and technological progress in the modern United States. Depression-era Americans displayed a renewed interest in older ways of life, conducting a wide-ranging search for traditions that could guide or reassure them during unstable times.[3] In most respects, the Chickamauga National Celebration embraced the idea of progress. It identified steady improvement as the essence of American history, and of Chattanooga's history in particular. The inclusion of the Cherokee removal story, however, added a dissonant note to the festival, an edge of uncertainty.

The image of oppressed Cherokees, uprooted and forced from their home-land, troubled the self-congratulatory depiction of Chattanooga's found-ing, complicating the image of the city as a place of progress. Its addition made the festival a more ambivalent commemoration and, in that ambiva-lence, an event better suited to its anxious era.

From Ross's Landing to the Dynamo of Dixie

Chattanooga lies on the Tennessee River near a large gap in the Appalachian Mountains, and this geography made the spot an attractive place to live and a natural corridor for travel and trade long before European settlement. In Cherokee history, the region witnessed particularly significant develop-ments in the late eighteenth and early nineteenth centuries. During the American Revolution, British-allied Cherokees used it as a base from which to war upon American settlements, and the area itself was the site of fight-ing between Cherokees and Revolutionary militia. The Cherokees involved in the war came to be known as "Chickamaugas," after Chickamauga Creek, a tributary to the Tennessee River that later provided the name of the Civil War battle.[4] In the early nineteenth century, the federal government placed its agency to the Cherokees a short distance from the future site of Chattanooga, making this area an important setting for Cherokee political relations with the new United States. The region also became a setting for Euro-American efforts to "civilize" the Cherokees when New England–based clergy founded the Brainerd Mission at a site later encompassed by the city.[5] In the removal era, Cherokees held important political meetings in the area, including their final national councils in the East, and southeastern Tennessee was the site of camps where federal troops gathered and held Cherokees in preparation for their forced migration.[6] This part of Tennessee, then, provided abundant material for anyone wishing to remember the Cherokee past.

Two decades before removal, John Ross and a white business partner established a warehouse and ferry on the Tennessee River, and a small vil-lage known as Ross's Landing developed at the site. As Cherokees departed in the summer and autumn of 1838, new settlers began to crowd into Ross's Landing and the surrounding area. Renamed Chattanooga, the town evolved over the next two decades into a significant transportation hub, first as a river port and later as a railroad center. Its location made the town a natu-ral gateway into Georgia and Alabama, and, by 1860, much of the cargo passing in and out of the Deep South traveled through the growing city.[7] With its economic importance and strategic geography, Chattanooga became a key military target for the Union during the Civil War. In 1863 federal troops led by William Rosecrans occupied the city, forcing a Confederate army under Braxton Bragg to retreat to a more defensible position in northern Georgia. Rosecrans gave pursuit, and, in September 1863, the two armies fought the Battle of Chickamauga a few miles south of the city. In some of the bloodiest fighting of the conflict, Bragg routed the Union force and drove it back into Chattanooga, which he then placed under siege. The Confederates cut off most of the supplies coming into Chattanooga and came close to forcing the Union army to abandon the city. By October, however, substantial reinforcements began to arrive, and federal troops opened a new, reliable supply line. In late November, this augmented Union army, now under the command of Ulysses Grant, dislodged Bragg's troops from key positions on Lookout Mountain and Missionary Ridge, compelling the Confederates to withdraw toward Dalton, Georgia. These victories left the Union in complete control of Tennessee. Chattanooga then became the base from which William Tecumseh Sherman mounted the invasion of Georgia and the Union drive toward Atlanta in the summer of 1864.[8]

After the war, Chattanooga emerged as a significant battleground in the political struggle over Reconstruction and black civil rights. During the military occupation of the city, Union officers took note of Chattanooga's economic possibilities, and, after the war, some elected to settle there permanently. Northern-born entrepreneurs established new factories and commercial enterprises, and by the end of the century Chattanooga became one of the South's most important manufacturing centers.[9] For about twenty years, these northern businessmen controlled city government, making Chattanooga a stronghold of the Republican Party in the South. To maintain their power, they relied upon the support of the city's black population, and, as a consequence, African Americans exercised a significant degree of public influence in Chattanooga in the years immediately following the war. Black residents served as elected aldermen in the city government and enjoyed access to political patronage and municipal jobs. This situation, however, proved unacceptable to the city's white Democrats, who, beginning in the early 1880s, worked steadily to disenfranchise the black population, aided by the passage of state laws designed to eliminate African American voting. By the early twentieth century, Democrats controlled the city government, effectively barring Chattanooga's black community from political decision making.[10]

Chattanooga continued its industrial growth in the early twentieth century, with boosters promoting the city as "The Dynamo of Dixie." In

1899, for instance, a group of local entrepreneurs established the first Coca-Cola bottling plant in Chattanooga, and the company quickly developed into one of the city's most significant employers. The crash of 1929 and the Great Depression curtailed this economic expansion, with the city suffering significant unemployment and the failure of one of its largest banks. With the coming of the New Deal, however, southeastern Tennessee became a major beneficiary of new federal programs, in particular the Tennessee Valley Authority. The influx of federal money into Chattanooga and its surrounding area served to blunt some of the Depression's worst effects.[11] The Chickamauga National Celebration, then, took place in a community that had experienced hard times but had reason to hope for a renewal of its fortunes, and planners intended the festival to express that hope. Though focused on history, it would be a grand promotional event, drawing new visitors to Chattanooga while amplifying the city's "Dynamo of Dixie" image.

Cherokee Monuments in Southeastern Tennessee

By the 1930s, Chattanoogans could boast a significant tradition of public memorialization, with the Civil War battles looming particularly large on the city's commemorative landscape. Even before the war ended, soldiers placed small memorials at various sites, and the city's large military graveyards provided a powerful reminder of the fighting that took place in the region. In the 1880s, Civil War veterans began a campaign to preserve the Chickamauga battlefield, persuading the federal government to transform a substantial portion of the site into the country's first national military park. Veterans groups and heritage organizations erected monuments throughout the new park and within the city, noting the locations of particular actions during the battles and celebrating the contributions of specific units. These activities encouraged further rounds of heritage work. Chattanooga regularly hosted Civil War veterans' reunions, and the dedication of the military park in 1895 inspired a particularly elaborate observance, a three-day commemoration featuring oratory, parades, and ceremony. In mounting the 1938 festival, then, residents continued a well-established practice of celebrating their city's role in the sectional conflict.[12]

Chattanooga and the surrounding area, meanwhile, also featured Cherokee-themed monuments, memorials that wove particular elements of the region's Native American past into the history of the non-Indian community. Local chapters of the Daughters of the American Revolution (DAR) created most of these memorials. In 1923, for instance, DAR members from Chattanooga marked the grave of Nancy Ward, a Cherokee woman remembered as having been a friend of early Tennessee settlers. Daughters from Bradley County erected a monument to "Chief" Jack Walker, a removal-era Cherokee leader, near the site of his home and grave, just outside Cleveland, Tennessee.[13] In Chattanooga, meanwhile, the DAR paid considerable attention to the site of the Brainerd Mission. In 1924, the Daughters placed a monument at the Brainerd cemetery, the only visible remnant of the mission, while convincing Hamilton County to rename the closest street "Brainerd Road." Later, in the early 1930s, the owner of the old mission site deeded the cemetery to the DAR. The Daughters cleaned up the graveyard and protected it with a stone wall, while placing several new bronze tablets that explained the historical significance of the place. By the late 1930s, the Brainerd site became a kind of shrine for Daughters and a significant point of reference for Chattanoogans interested in local history. As one writer noted, the mission "continues to be, in a sense, a part of life to-day, for Brainerd Mission is spoken of almost as though it still existed."[14] While the Civil War dominated commemoration in southeastern Tennessee, the DAR maintained room for certain Cherokee stories, as well.

The DAR's embrace of Cherokee history involved a significant irony. Cherokees, after all, sided with the British in the American Revolution, a fact that would seem to render their history a poor fit for the Daughters' commemorative work. From its formation in 1890, the DAR's central purpose was to foster patriotism through public veneration of the American founders. As lineal descendants of men who fought for American independence, the Daughters believed they bore a special duty to commemorate the Revolution and to use that memory to promote good citizenship and national devotion in the present.[15] Cherokees, however, represented an obstacle to the founding of the United States. Like many eastern Indians, a portion of the Cherokee populace viewed the Revolutionary War as an opportunity to end colonial Americans' encroachment on tribal lands and to push back against Anglo-American expansion. Cherokees allied with the British in the hope of strengthening their own security and independence and, in doing so, became enemies of the Daughters' celebrated ancestors.[16]

Cherokees waged war, in fact, upon the very patriots most venerated by the DAR in eastern Tennessee. There, the Daughters' favorite subjects of commemoration were the "Overmountain Men," Revolutionary militia drawn from the region's earliest white settlements along the Watauga, Nolichucky, and Holston Rivers. The Daughters viewed these settlers as the

founders of Tennessee, and they never tired of honoring the mountain militia's contributions to the Revolutionary War. In 1780 the Overmountain
Men won a decisive victory at the Battle of Kings Mountain in South Carolina, which helped to thwart the British effort to regain control of the southern colonies. In later years, Tennesseans came to view this battle as a major
turning point in the war, a victory that helped to secure American independence. Kings Mountain became Tennessee's contribution to the birth of
the United States, and the DAR turned the memory of the campaign into a
sacred narrative, erecting numerous monuments to "Our Immortals," as one
chapter named the volunteers.[17]

Tennessee's "Immortals," however, spent much of the war fighting
Cherokees. The early Tennessee settlements, established in the late 1760s
and early 1770s, were located in Cherokee territory and violated the British
Proclamation of 1763. Cherokees considered the settlers squatters and
thieves, and their presence became one of the main reasons for Cherokee
involvement in the Revolutionary War. In 1775 Cherokee leaders sold
the territory containing the new settlements as part of a deal known as the
Henderson Purchase. Many Cherokees rejected this agreement and repudiated the leaders who made it, and some began to advocate war to expel the
intruders. A year later, young Cherokee men, led by the warrior Dragging
Canoe, agreed to join a coalition of British Indian allies in assaults on colonial frontier settlements. Among their first targets, they chose the communities of the Overmountain Men, attacking the Watauga settlers in July
1776.[18] As I noted in chapter 1, those attacks inaugurated an immensely de-
structive conflict in the Cherokee country, as several states launched puni-
tive campaigns that resulted in the razing of most of the Cherokee towns
in present-day North Carolina and Tennessee. Following this invasion,
the tribe's established leaders sued for peace and signed new treaties, but
Dragging Canoe and his followers continued to fight. They created new
towns along Chickamauga Creek and, from there, launched fresh assaults
against the Americans. The Tennessee settlements remained Chickamauga
targets, and the mountain militia continued to raid in Cherokee territory.
This Indian war lasted longer than the struggle against Britain, with some
Chickamaugas fighting until 1794. Cherokees, then, were as bitter opponents of Tennessee's founders as were the British themselves.[19]

The DAR refrained from erecting monuments to Dragging Canoe and his
followers. Instead, they memorialized those few Cherokees whom they
could characterize as participants in the sacred narrative of Tennessee's
birth. In Nancy Ward, for instance, they found a Native woman whom they

could place among the founders of their white community. Ward was a Cherokee "Beloved Woman," a title given to individuals who demonstrated particular wisdom and spiritual power. This status granted Ward significant political influence among the Cherokees, whose councils included both women and men.[20] In the Revolutionary Era, Ward advocated peace with Euro-American settlers and, according to tradition, warned the Watauga community of Dragging Canoe's decision to attack frontier whites in the summer of 1776. On several occasions, she prevented her kinsmen from executing white captives, an act that reflected both her desire for peace and her authority as a respected Cherokee woman.[21] Though Ward's goal during this period seems always to have been the preservation of her Cherokee people, her actions allowed later generations of Tennessee whites to remember her as an ally of their own community's founders. "She was a near and sympathetic, though secret, friend of the white settlers," one early state historian explained. "From her they received timely warning by swift messengers of every danger and every bloody design of her savage people."[22] Ward was "the Pocahontas of Tennessee," the DAR memorial at her gravesite declared, and "the constant friend of the American pioneer."[23] The ceremony dedicating the memorial differed little from the exercises Daughters performed when honoring their white heroes. A crowd of local residents gathered at the American-flag-draped monument, sang "My Country 'Tis of Thee," and then listened as a DAR member recounted the story of Ward's heroic service during the Revolution. Two young girls unveiled the marker before the Daughters repaired to the nearby town of Benton for lunch.[24] DAR commemoration emphasized Ward's significance to Tennessee and the United States, while all but erasing her Cherokee identity. It removed her from her own people's history and culture, recasting her as a founding mother of the settler community.

The DAR worked a similar transformation when they commemorated the history of the Brainerd Mission. For the Daughters, Brainerd represented the arrival of Christian civilization on the Tennessee frontier and thus a stage in the evolution of their own Chattanooga. As a newspaper story on one commemoration noted, Brainerd's founding marked "the first time the word of God was taught and a school conducted in the wilderness that later became Hamilton county."[25] The mission's significance came less from its influence on the Cherokees than from this quality of being the first church and school in a place that would later evolve into a modern city. The white missionaries, meanwhile, provided objects of veneration as attractive as the military heroes of the Revolution. In leaving comfortable homes to work on

Gates of the Brainerd Mission Cemetery, with DAR tablets, 1930s.
Courtesy Chattanooga Public Library.

the frontier, Brainerd's "heroic band" of ministers and teachers exhibited the same selfless virtue as had the militia at Kings Mountain. "They were as far from home as the heart of Africa is now," one orator explained at the dedication of a Brainerd monument, and they suffered much hardship. Yet "they were not cast down, nor did they look back." Persevering in their labors, they became worthy of memory. "It is an act of patriotism for the Daughters of the American Revolution to mark this spot," the speaker concluded, "not only as a historic site, but to keep in perpetual remembrance the love, patience, and heroism exhibited here."[26] At Brainerd, the Chattanooga Daughters celebrated white pioneers, rather than the mission's Cherokee hosts or its Cherokee students. They commemorated Brainerd as a step toward the establishment of their own city.

A public argument involving DAR members from Tennessee and Georgia provides a final, particularly vivid example of the Daughters' use of Cherokee history. In the spring of 1935, a few years prior to the Chickamauga National Celebration, the Georgia DAR approved plans to erect a marker indicating the site of Red Clay, where the Cherokee Nation held its final councils prior to removal. Red Clay played a significant role in the Trail of Tears story, as a place where Cherokee leaders debated the removal issue and resisted American demands that they negotiate a removal treaty. As the final seat of the Cherokee Nation government in the East, moreover, it represented a starting point for the Trail of Tears. For anyone interested in Cherokee history, then, Red Clay deserved commemoration. Leola Beeson, the Georgia DAR's state historian, researched the location of the council ground, consulting the writings of James Mooney, as well as various state histories. Based on this work, she selected a spot near Cohutta, Georgia, just south of the Tennessee state line, a few miles from Chattanooga, as the most likely site. The Daughters secured a small plot of land and a large granite boulder, ordered the requisite bronze tablet, and began planning a dedication ceremony.[27]

When residents of southeastern Tennessee learned of the proposed monument, however, they cried foul. The site of the council ground, they insisted, did not lie in Georgia, but in their own state, just to the *north* of the Tennessee line. John Morgan Wooten, a Presbyterian minister and local historian from Cleveland, Tennessee, outlined their position in a letter to the *Dalton Citizen*. Red Clay, he explained, could not possibly be in Georgia, since the Cherokees chose the council site based on its location outside of that state's borders. In the early 1830s, the Georgia legislature passed a law abolishing the Cherokee government as part of its ongoing campaign to force the tribe to accept removal. In response, the Cherokees moved their government meetings away from the capital at New Echota to a site outside of Georgia's jurisdiction. Leaving Georgia, in other words, was the whole point of holding the councils at Red Clay. How, then, could Georgia citizens now claim the council ground as part of their own past?[28] Beeson responded by citing several Georgia state histories, along with Mooney and Charles Royce, who each placed Red Clay in Georgia on maps published by the Bureau of American Ethnology. "Royce and Mooney," she added, "are the very highest authorities." There were "two schools of thought" on the matter, Beeson acknowledged, and she noted that some DAR members favored placing a Red Clay marker directly on the Tennessee-Georgia line as a compromise. In considering this idea, however, "Georgia conceded nothing whatsoever of her own entitlement to the site of the old Cherokee Indian Council Ground."[29]

The "D.A.R. Squabble," as one newspaper called it, continued through the summer and fall of 1935, growing quite heated at times. Zella Armstrong, a Chattanooga journalist and historian, charged the people of Georgia with appropriating Tennessee history in the face of "incontestable proof." Charles Lusk, a Tennessee state judge who grew up in the vicinity of Red Clay, petitioned the DAR's president-general to ask for an investigation into the matter. The national society must intervene, he wrote, "to the end that history not be falsified, and injustices done to the Indians, to Tennessee, and to Georgia itself." Lusk's protest, however, seems not to have had its intended effect. In early November, the Georgians erected the Red Clay monument on their side of the state line. In an article written for the *Chattanooga Times*, Zella Armstrong reported that Lusk and other Tennesseans attended the unveiling. After the ceremony, she noted, they crossed back into their own state and paid a visit to the place they were certain was the *true* site of the council ground.[30]

The Tennesseans, in fact, held the stronger historical claim in this dispute, but that point is less significant than the fierce sense of ownership expressed by advocates on both sides of the argument. As Leola Beeson suggested, the squabble was a question of "entitlement." It was about who could rightly claim this piece of the Cherokee removal story for their own community's history. Moreover, the Georgia monument challenged a particular, cherished element of some Tennesseans' memory of the Trail of the Tears. Georgia, they recalled, had persecuted the Cherokees, driving them from their homes. Tennessee, however, had given them refuge. As Lusk wrote, "neither Tennessee nor any other of our states has much reason to be proud of its record as regards the Red Man; but in this case Tennessee did give the beleaguered and despairing Indians asylum from their oppressors, and did afford them a place for the peaceful and safe holding of their National Councils."[31] In the 1830s, of course, Red Clay was not yet part of Tennessee. It was a section of the Cherokee Nation, the borders of which the United States had guaranteed in its treaties with the tribe. The whole point of the Cherokee struggle against removal was to *prevent* places like Red Clay from being absorbed by Tennessee, Georgia, or any other American state. Tennessee authorities did not grant the Cherokees asylum. They merely proved less active in their pursuit of Indian dispossession than were their neighbors to the south. In memory, however, Tennessee became a protector of "beleaguered and despairing Indians." That identity granted the state a more sympathetic role in the removal saga, while making the Trail of Tears as much an episode of Tennessee history as it was a part of the Cherokee past. Remembering their ancestors as near allies of the tribe, white Tennesseans made the removal story more thoroughly their own.

In scattering Indian monuments through Chattanooga and the surrounding area, the DAR did more than simply document selected elements of Cherokee history. They transformed Cherokee history into Tennessee heritage. Nancy Ward became a founding mother of a state created by some of her people's worst enemies. Brainerd Mission became part of white Chattanooga's early development. And the removal struggle, in which Cherokees fought to preserve an Indian homeland, became a story that belonged to the settler community's past. It is not surprising, then, that the organizers of the Chickamauga National Celebration thought to include Cherokee history in their city's great festival. That history already informed Chattanoogans' own sense of place.

Cherokee History in a Civil War Commemoration

The idea for the Chickamauga National Celebration came from a local organization, the Chattanooga Women's Press Association. In particular, it seems to have originated with the association's president, Zella Armstrong, who a few years earlier participated in the "DAR Squabble" over the location of Red Clay. Armstrong was the editor of the *Lookout*, a weekly society newspaper, and the founder of the "Chattanooga Cotton Ball," the city's main debutante event. She was also a local historian, the author of a respected two-volume history of the city and its surrounding county. In early 1938, she and the press association suggested mounting a festival that would mark both the anniversary of the Civil War battles and the centennial of Chattanooga's founding. Commemoration of local history would celebrate the city's growth and progress over the previous century, while the Civil War remembrances would highlight Chattanooga's role in great national affairs. The city's business and political leaders liked the idea, and by February 1938 a committee formed to plan the event. Richard L. Moore, operator of the Loveman's department store, led the organizers, with Zella Armstrong serving as a vice president.[32]

Moore and his committee worked to make the celebration a national event. They issued official invitations to the governors of twenty-nine states that provided soldiers to the Chattanooga-area battles, and President Franklin Roosevelt promised to attend and deliver a public address. Tennessee's congressmen even managed to secure $35,000 in federal funds to support the festival.[33] With the help of this money, the organizers assembled an extensive program of commemoration. They arranged a solemn memorial service for the Civil War dead at Point Park on Lookout Mountain, along with an elaborate battle reenactment at the Chickamauga National Military Park. They welcomed Confederate and Union veterans to the city, and the United Confederate Veterans held a formal reunion in Chattanooga to coincide with the festival. Heritage groups like the Daughters of the Confederacy and the Daughters of Union Veterans decorated more than 140 monuments scattered throughout the city and within the military park. When heightening political tensions in Europe forced the president to cancel his visit, the organizers replaced his speech with an additional Civil War memorial service, this one held on the Chickamauga battlefield. With the festival placing so much attention on the war, Chattanooga's centennial receded somewhat as a focus of commemoration. The city's founding and development, however, did figure prominently in "The Drums of Dixie," the massive historical pageant staged each night during the celebration.[34]

While history provided the purpose of the event, tourism clearly shaped the planners' work. In addition to commemorative exercises, Moore's committee arranged a host of entertainments that had little or nothing to do with the past but promised to draw visitors to the city. They organized an air show and boat races, band concerts and street dances, and an evening of heavyweight boxing at the city's Memorial Auditorium. They opened the festival with the crowning of a beauty queen, while each night of the celebration ended with an elaborate fireworks display. They advertised widely, going so far as to distribute a short film detailing the event to some 150 movie theaters across the South. They also selected a local teenager, Helen Jones, as the celebration's "theme girl," a kind of mascot and ambassador. Dressed in a drum major's uniform, Jones traveled to communities around the region, promoting the event and inviting all she met to visit Chattanooga in September to enjoy the city's hospitality.[35]

Sometime during the spring of 1938, the organizers added the commemoration of the Cherokee Trail of Tears to this mix of history and tourist spectacle. They arranged for performances by Cherokees like Carl Standingdeer, and they formed a subcommittee to develop this part of the program further.[36] This decision seems to have emerged from discussions of the city centennial. Indian removal, the planners recognized, formed a necessary component of the story of Chattanooga's founding, so, if the city's birth provided a focus of the event, the celebration should include some version of Cherokee history. It was not, of course, a coincidence that 1938 marked the centennial of both the non-Indian community and the Trail of Tears. The creation of Chattanooga and that portion of Tennessee required Cherokee dispossession and the dismantling of the Cherokee Nation in the East. Residents recalled, moreover, that the Trail of Tears began in their section of the state. Cherokees emigrating by river departed from the future site of Chattanooga, and two of the overland routes began nearby. Local histories, like the one written by Zella Armstrong, identified the Chattanooga area as a starting point for the Trail.[37]

In local memory, meanwhile, Chattanooga's history began not simply in Cherokee territory, in a general sense, but at Ross's Landing, a specific Cherokee place with a particular historical identity. As noted earlier, when Chattanooga residents recalled that their city began in 1838, they did not refer to the creation of the first settlement on that spot. Rather, they referred to the selection of the name "Chattanooga," an Anglicized Muskogee word, to replace "Ross's Landing," the English-language name used by the Indian people who were just then being removed. While this focus on the act of naming suggests an erasure of the Cherokee past, Chattanooga residents, in fact, identified Ross's Landing as the city's point of origin. In the early 1930s, for instance, the DAR erected a monument to Ross's Landing, and this marker identified the ferry and trading post as both Chattanooga's birthplace and a point of departure for the Trail of Tears.[38] Local histories, moreover, treated the Ross family, with its mix of European and Cherokee members, as the city's founders, much as the DAR viewed Nancy Ward as a founding mother of Tennessee. Zella Armstrong noted that the first "recorded" marriage in the Chattanooga area was that of John Ross's parents, Scottish trader Daniel Ross and Cherokee Mollie MacDonald, while she dated the history of education in the city to the arrival of a tutor hired by Daniel Ross to instruct young John and his siblings. One of the city's DAR chapters named itself for John Ross, and the chapter history explained that the Daughters chose the name because the "intrepid Cherokee Chieftain . . . founded our city and was her 'first citizen.'" To be sure, these histories employed most of the familiar "savage" images of Native Americans. Indians appeared as primitive precursors to European settlement, obstacles to be overcome by pioneer forebears, and then eventually sad fading remnants of a "once-proud people." Chattanooga histories, however, also accorded certain Cherokees a special role. In local memory, some Indians were founders, as well as mere predecessors.[39]

The prominence of Cherokee stories in local memory meant that, while Trail of Tears commemoration began as an afterthought, Cherokee history quickly became a significant part of the festival. Chattanooga's newspapers, for instance, published substantial stories recounting the region's Indian history in the weeks leading up to the festival and during the event. The *Times* produced a special "Blue and Gray Edition," in which it surveyed the history of the city and southeastern Tennessee. While the Civil War battles dominated copy, the *Times* devoted several long essays to Cherokee subjects. Historian John P. Brown produced a full-page story on the warfare between Chickamauga Cherokees and early settlers during the era of the American Revolution. Brown portrayed the Chickamaugas as cruel warriors but justified in their resistance to Tennessee heroes like John Sevier. He even likened the Chickamaugas to the Confederacy, since they broke with the Cherokees' established leaders over the question of how to respond to frontier settlement. When Dragging Canoe defied the chiefs and called for war, Brown noted, "then and there, he became Tennessee's first secessionist."[40] Local author Robert Sparks Walker, meanwhile, contributed an essay on the Brainerd Mission, based on his 1931 history of the institution, *Torchlights to the Cherokees*. In the *Times*, Walker offered the church and school as evidence that some Euro-Americans wanted to help the Cherokees, rather than defraud and displace them. "This is one of the very few places," he wrote, "that a conscientious white man can stand today with ease and comfort and reflect on our dealings with the Cherokees, for here the Indians received a square deal and justice at the hands of a few people who gave their lives for the welfare of their copper-skinned brothers."[41] In these newspaper supplements, writers like Walker amplified and expanded upon an existing local memory of the Indian past, weaving Cherokee history tightly into the festival's official narrative of the birth and evolution of the city.

The Drums of Dixie

Cherokee history gained even greater attention in the festival's biggest attraction, the lavish historical pageant performed each night during the celebration. "The Drums of Dixie" provided the historical centerpiece of the event, the attraction that brought together the festival's three major subjects—the Civil War, the city of Chattanooga, and the Cherokees. It was created by employees of the John B. Rogers Company, an Ohio-based firm that specialized in helping schools and community groups stage amateur theater. One of the biggest producers of historical pageants in the nation, the Rogers Company developed a system that allowed it to organize these performances rapidly, using large amateur casts. It provided its clients with directors and writers, who would draft a version of the particular community's history in consultation with local authorities. It also furnished costumes and lighting and helped the pageant sponsors assemble casts from the ranks of students and members of civic organizations. The company followed a standard formula for its pageants, inserting local historical episodes into an established national narrative of pioneer struggles, patriotic war, and economic progress. This practice allowed for quick writing and meant that the company could use the same costumes, sets, and props for many different productions. The company also reused certain dance interludes and symbolic tableaux. Most of its pageants, for instance, started with a dance meant to represent the creation of the earth and ended with a routine the company called the "Wheel of Life," in which the pageant's entire cast would form a living wheel rotating around the pageant queen. True to form, "The Drums of Dixie" began with the creation dance and ended with the great wheel, renamed the "Wheel of Progress" in this particular version.[42]

American historical pageantry tended to relegate Indians to marginal roles at the very beginning of community narratives. Tribal peoples represented the dangers and hardship overcome by founding settlers, and their primary purpose was to disappear, making way for the Euro-American progress that formed the pageants' dominant theme.[43] "The Drums of Dixie" certainly showed the Cherokees going away, but it granted the story of their displacement much more space than was typical of this kind of entertainment. The pageant writer, a Rogers Company worker named Mary Cecilia Freeland, based the drama on Zella Armstrong's history of Chattanooga, and, like Armstrong, she made Cherokee history a central concern of her narrative, not simply a prelude to the main action. In fact, around half of the pageant's episodes included Cherokee material, with Freeland emphasizing Indian assimilation, as well as Cherokee displacement. One early scene, for instance, recounted the Nancy Ward story. Freeland showed Ward dispatching her warning to the Watauga settlers and then intervening with her people to save white captives from torture and execution. At the end of the scene, a rescued settler "takes Nancy into her home as the Indians depart." With this last gesture, the episode literally removed the Beloved Woman from the Cherokee people, assimilating her into the ranks of the pioneers in the saga of Tennessee's early development. Following Armstrong's lead, "The Drums of Dixie" also included a scene portraying the wedding of Daniel Ross and Mollie MacDonald, and Freeland wrote an episode about Brainerd Mission that featured the baptism of Catherine Brown, an early Indian convert who became famous for her Christian piety. The Brainerd scene even included a brief appearance by Sequoyah, who represented the mission's work to translate the Bible into the Cherokee syllabary.[44]

Removal provided the subject for the most elaborate Cherokee scenes. In one, U.S. commissioner John Schermerhorn reads the Treaty of New Echota to Treaty Party leaders assembled within Elias Boudinot's home. As Schermerhorn calls their names, Boudinot, Major Ridge, John Ridge, and Andrew Ross step forward to sign the removal agreement. An accompanying "historical note" in Freeland's script described the factional dispute over removal, the illegitimacy of the treaty, and the Cherokee government's effort to prevent its ratification. The next episode shows Winfield Scott directing the gathering of Cherokees in preparation for removal. The scene has armed soldiers retrieving groups of Indians and confining them within an onstage stockade. The soldiers abuse some of their captives, including John Ross and his wife Quatie, as they herd them into the fort. Freeland included a reference to the Tsali story in this scene. At the front of the stage, an old man, his sons, and their families walk toward the fort, when one of the soldiers prods the old man's wife with a bayonet. The man, who of course is Tsali, cries out in Cherokee and kills the soldier. His kinsmen join the attack, and together they make their escape. The removal scene ends with the imprisoned Cherokees emerging from the stockade, "some boistrous [sic] and angry—others in tears," as they begin their long walk into the West and out of Chattanooga history.[45]

The inclusion of these removal scenes added an ambivalent note to the pageant's portrayal of early Chattanooga. In some parts of the drama, Cherokees clearly played the role of obstacles, primitive warriors who must experience defeat before the city's progressive history could begin. In the last removal scene, however, they appeared as innocent victims of Euro-American cruelty. The pageant presented removal as a "journey of misery and sorrow" and implied, with the reference to Tsali, that Cherokee resistance had been warranted. "The Drums of Dixie," then, came close to suggesting that the city's history began not in progress, but in violence and injustice.[46]

This potential for moral ambiguity may explain a chronological anomaly in the pageant script. "The Drums of Dixie" included a short scene portraying the selection of the name "Chattanooga" to replace "Ross's Landing." In this scene, a gathering of white residents discusses various options, before agreeing on the Muskogee name for Lookout Mountain. Together, the crowd chants: "(Softly) 'Chattanooga'—(Questioningly) 'Chattanooga?'—CHATTA NOOGA! HURRAH!"[47] Residents made this decision in the summer of 1838, as the army gathered Cherokees for deportation, and the local post office adopted the new name shortly after the last Cherokee detachment departed. The city's birth, then, coincided with removal quite precisely. In the pageant, however, Freeland interposed a scene depicting "An Early School" between the somber "Trail of Tears" episode and the celebratory "Chattanooga" scene. Featuring several dozen singing children, the scene served to dispel the dismal mood of the removal tableaux ("misery and sorrow") and prepare the audience for the happier material to follow ("CHATTA NOOGA! HURRAH!"). This maneuver, of course, also disentangled the memory of Chattanooga's founding from the memory of Cherokee suffering, obscuring their very direct historical relationship.[48]

Cherokee Homecoming

Other elements of the Chickamauga National Celebration also included Cherokee material and events. Organizers dedicated an entire day of the festival to Cherokee activities, and they invited Cherokee people from both North Carolina and Oklahoma to attend. Carl Standingdeer came with a group of performers from the Qualla Boundary, and Will West Long participated. Principal Chief Jarrett Blythe of the Eastern Band made an appearance, accompanied by members of the tribal council, as did Jesse Bartley Milam, who would later be appointed principal chief of the Cherokee Nation in the West.[49] The city received descendants of John Ross, Sequoyah, and other prominent removal-era Cherokees, as well as non-Indian dignitaries like Clyde Blair, the Eastern Band's federal agent. Organizers styled their Cherokee-themed day as a "homecoming," an occasion for Chattanooga to welcome Cherokees back to this portion of the former Indian nation.[50]

Like much of the festival, the Cherokee events featured a mix of historical commemoration and tourist spectacle. "Cherokee Commemoration Day," September 21, began at the Brainerd Mission Cemetery, where Indian visitors attended the unveiling of two new historical markers by the Daughters of the American Revolution. One identified Cherokee students and supporters of the mission, including Charles Hicks, Catherine Brown, and Elias Boudinot. The other honored Stephen Foreman, a Cherokee minister who worked with the Brainerd missionaries, traveled the Trail of Tears, and served in the Cherokee government in the West. Descendants of Foreman, led by his only surviving child, Arminta Foreman, sponsored this monument and participated in the unveiling.[51] Commemoration then yielded to performance in the afternoon, as Carl Standingdeer led a group of North Carolina Cherokees in a demonstration of dance, archery, blowgun shooting, and stickball for crowds gathered at the city's baseball stadium. Will West Long and the Big Cove dancers may have joined in this performance. While the journalists covering the show did not identify the dancers by name, a photo in the *Times* captured Long dressed in the Plains-style regalia he wore for tourist events. His participation would certainly have been in keeping with his other tourism work during this period. Long's presence notwithstanding, the entertainment failed to impress Chief Jarrett Blythe. He remarked to a reporter that the performers' costumes did not accurately represent traditional Cherokee dress and that the stickball that afternoon was subpar. "It would have been fine," he noted, "if they had played like they do at home."[52]

Later, some of the visiting Cherokees joined in that evening's historical drama. They offered a short pageant called the "Trail of Tears" as an opening act before the regular performance of "The Drums of Dixie." In other words, the audience that night witnessed two versions of Indian removal— one acted by whites playing Cherokees, the other by Cherokees playing their own exiled relations.[53] Unfortunately, newspapers failed to describe the Cherokees' version in any detail, so it is impossible to compare their performance with the Trail of Tears scenes in "The Drums of Dixie." Yet even if the two depictions of removal were identical, the Cherokee presence that night surely added a new dimension to the drama. Anthropologist Laura Peers argues that the inclusion of indigenous people in historic reconstructions creates opportunities to disrupt the frontier myths that have traditionally shaped Euro-American conceptions of Indian history, in particular the idea that Indian disappearance was inevitable. When Indians "play Indian," she suggests, their presence can remind tourists that Europeans settled the continent through violent force, rather than through the working out of some preordained process. At the same time, she notes, Indian inclusion often grants authority to historical representations that otherwise adhere quite closely to those same tenacious myths. The presence of "real Indians" lends an appearance of greater authenticity to narratives that absolve settler societies of responsibility for Indian marginalization.[54] In the Chattanooga drama, either result (or both) seems possible. Cherokee participation, and the addition of another Trail of Tears scene, called greater attention to the injustice of removal, undermining the pageant's focus on progress. Yet it also reinforced the authority of the pageant's overall conception of the past, which in most respects still followed the old frontier models. Despite its potential for moral ambiguity, "The Drums of Dixie" remained a story of Indian disappearance, and Cherokee participation suggested an Indian endorsement of that narrative.

The Cherokee portion of the festival concluded the next day, when organizers led their Indian guests on a "pilgrimage" to significant Cherokee sites in the Chattanooga region. They began by traveling to the council ground at Red Clay (the Tennesseans' Red Clay, not the Georgia site). Gathered at the natural blue spring on the site, they listened as historian John P. Brown

Visitors from the Cherokee Nation to the Chickamauga National Celebration, 1938. Arminta Foreman is third from the right. Courtesy Chattanooga Public Library.

once again told the story of the Trail of Tears, emphasizing the wrongs done to the visitors' forebears. Arminta Foreman responded, thanking the Tennesseans on behalf of her people and remarking that "we believe they are sincere" in their expressions of regret and their desire to honor the Cherokees.[55] From Red Clay, the party drove a short distance to Flint Springs, where they helped to unveil a marker at the site of John Ross's last home in the East. The new memorial noted that Flint Springs was near the spot where Georgia militia had arrested Ross in 1835, along with his guest, John Howard Payne, the scholar and writer of the song "Home, Sweet Home." As part of the dedication ceremony, some of the Indian pilgrims sang "Home, Sweet Home" in the Cherokee language.[56] The group ate lunch in nearby Cleveland and joined in a parade through the town's business district before heading to Charleston, a few miles to the north. There, they attended the unveiling of another marker, this one indicating the sites of the early nineteenth-century Indian agency and Fort Cass, which served as Winfield Scott's headquarters during the gathering of Cherokees in the summer and fall of 1838. The pilgrimage ended at Benton, where the party visited Nancy Ward's grave and a settlement-era fort on the grounds of the local school.[57]

The Cherokee pilgrimage provides an example of the accretive nature of public memory, the extent to which the placement of particular stories on a given landscape tends to draw further memorial activity. When the festival organizers decided to include acknowledgment of removal in the Chickamauga National Celebration, they looked to local memory to guide their choice of particular commemorative subjects, much in the way that Cecilia Freeland used Zella Armstrong's writings as material for the pageant. Assembling an itinerary for their Cherokee guests, organizers chose spots that already featured prominently in their community's understanding of the past. Tennesseans knew something of the history of Red Clay, for example, thanks to the "DAR Squabble" a few years earlier. Area residents had memorialized Nancy Ward and the Ross family in recent years. As the pilgrims traveled to these sites, they conducted new ceremonies and unveiled new memorials, reinforcing the importance of these places and the individuals associated with them. In this way, memories of the Cherokee Nation accumulated on the landscape, following a pattern established in the years before the festival.

Visiting Cherokees, however, exercised little authority over that pattern. While commemoration affirmed the region's Cherokee identity, white residents' sense of the past determined the expression of that identity. Tennesseans honored Indian people who, like Nancy Ward, could be defined as helpers of white pioneers or, in the case of the Cherokees at Brainerd, partners in an acculturative enterprise. They defined Cherokee sites in relation to national historical figures like Winfield Scott or Euro-American friends of the tribe like John Howard Payne. The Cherokee Foreman family did manage to influence commemoration by having Stephen Foreman included among those memorialized at Brainerd, but Foreman, as an Indian minister, readily fit the established local memory of the mission. White commemorators remained the primary authors of Cherokee history, a power that reflected and confirmed their ownership of these Indian lands, while the Cherokee pilgrims acted mainly as spectators, witnesses to the honor paid their ancestors. Cherokee removal, in this scenario, became a set of dramatic events that occurred in the history of a non-Indian community. The Cherokee homecoming took place at someone else's home.

Ambivalent Commemoration

Despite the dominance of this non-Indian sensibility, the inclusion of the removal commemorations did alter the festival by adding a dissonant element to its overall portrayal of the past. Both the Civil War ceremonies and the observance of Chattanooga's founding emphasized unity and worked to erase memories of conflict and injustice. The city centennial celebrated progress, showing the world "the panorama of Chattanooga's vital history, from obscure beginning as a river landing to its metropolitan present."[58] The history supplements published by local newspapers, for instance, offered glowing accounts of the development of the city's educational institutions, hospitals, and industries, and they praised the wise leadership of Chattanooga's political and economic elites. The general image was one of steady improvement by a cohesive community, a story that erased any hint of conflict among Chattanooga residents. Like other industrial cities, Chattanooga experienced labor disputes and strikes in the late nineteenth and early twentieth centuries, but this history was nowhere to be found in the 1938 celebration. Likewise, the recent history of African American disenfranchisement disappeared from public memory, as did black efforts to resist the imposition of state segregation laws on their city.[59] In the festival's vision of the past, all Chattanoogans worked together to better their community, a memory that served to legitimate the city's existing economic and social structure.

The Civil War commemorations, meanwhile, emphasized the patriotism of both Union and Confederate soldiers, while celebrating the ending of sectional differences in the decades since the war. At the memorial service held at Point Park, the national commanders of the United Confederate Veterans and the Grand Army of the Republic shook hands and "agreed smilingly that they were happy to meet as fellow-citizens of the greatest nation on earth."[60] Union and Confederate veterans praised one another's valor and declared that the true lesson of Civil War remembrance should be national unity. That message, they suggested, had become especially important in 1938, when the world seemed poised on the brink of another terrible conflict.[61] This theme of national reunion dominated Civil War public memory in the United States in the early twentieth century. Commemorations emphasized that both Union and Confederate soldiers fought heroically on behalf of thoroughly noble principles and that, after the war, the antagonists quickly reconciled. As historian David Blight states, "everyone was right, no one was wrong, and something so transforming as the Civil War had been rendered a mutual victory" through reunion.[62] This memory worked to minimize slavery as the cause of the conflict, while disavowing any connection between the war and the persistence of racial violence and inequality in a segregated society. These tributes to unity, then, provided part of the ideological foundation for Jim Crow.[63] The Chattanooga commemorations in 1938 fit this pattern quite closely, with some speakers pointing to the city itself as a model of sectional reconciliation. As noted earlier, Union veterans helped to direct Chattanooga's postwar industrial expansion and dominated its politics for a time, and some speakers pointed to that phenomenon as evidence that the city had led the way toward national reunion. The power of these northern-born Republicans, in fact, had proven a significant source of conflict, particularly since it depended upon the political participation of Chattanooga's African Americans. Democrats regained full control of the city only when they managed to deny black citizens a role in public life. In the commemorations, however, the postwar era became a seamless narrative of reunion and economic development.[64]

Within this celebration of harmony, the Cherokee removal centennial struck a different note. Commemoration of the Trail of Tears acknowledged a history of violence and injustice. Indeed, that acknowledgment appears to have been the commemoration's primary message. Journalists and speakers at the ceremonies emphasized the cruelty of removal and expressed regret for their forebears' part in the Cherokees' expulsion. Some speakers suggested that Tennesseans bore a responsibility to remember removal, an obligation to bear witness to this historical wrong. Judge Charles Lusk, for instance, argued at one ceremony that Cherokee history should be taught in all Tennessee schools. Lusk, who had participated in the debate over the location of Red Clay, "spoke feelingly of the atrocious manner in which the United States Government had treated the Cherokee Indians" and noted that "information on the subject among young people of today was sadly deficient in comparison with its importance."[65] So while the city centennial and the Civil War events worked to deny conflict and difference, the removal commemorations highlighted precisely those themes. With the inclusion of the removal centennial, Chattanooga named itself a site of injustice, as well as a place of progress.

It is tempting, then, to interpret the removal commemoration as a sign that this southern community had begun to confront the legacies and burdens of white supremacy. Such a conclusion, however, seems implausible when one compares the acknowledgment of Cherokee removal with the festival's near-erasure of the city's black community. African Americans constituted around 30 percent of Chattanooga's residents, but they were all but absent from the Chickamauga National Celebration. Take, for example, the *Chattanooga Times*' "Blue and Gray" edition, the history supplement published to accompany the festival. It contained a single article describing black Chattanooga. That essay emphasized the material and educational improvements experienced by African Americans under segregation, and it credited this progress to the city's "fine racial relationships" and to the fact that black residents had "let their buckets down where they were."[66] This last remark, of course, referred to Booker T. Washington's 1895 "Atlanta compromise" address, which advised African Americans to seek economic improvement within a segregated South rather than pursue political power and equality. In Chattanooga, African Americans had, in fact, sought and exercised political power, and they had resisted segregation. Black residents formed an important voting bloc following the Civil War, and black politicians had served in the city government. Ordinary African Americans had challenged the state's segregation laws. The 1938 festival, however, ignored these elements of Chattanooga's history. Mary Cecelia Freeland's script for "The Drums of Dixie" never mentioned African Americans, and the most detailed press description of the pageant noted their presence in only one scene. In the tableaux depicting Chattanooga in 1861, the *Times* observed, a black choir sang spirituals, while, on a raised stage to one side, several African American men played dice. This scene ended with a messenger arriving to announce the coming of the Civil War, and, after this point, African Americans seem not to have played a noticeable role in the drama. Not surprisingly, the festival also ignored the substantial history of black slavery in the Cherokee Nation. It confirmed Cherokees like John Ross as founders, but did not acknowledge the contributions of enslaved workers to the development of the Cherokee Nation and its "civilized" institutions.[67]

This exclusion of black history represented the norm in southern commemoration during this period. As W. Fitzhugh Brundage writes, historical memory represents a struggle over public space, a contest that reproduces the social and political fissures of a given time and locale. During the era of Jim Crow, white heritage groups worked to marginalize African Americans in their representations of southern history, an activity that reflected a broader effort to preserve and strengthen white supremacy. Black southerners maintained their own memory rituals but found themselves excluded from the public realm.[68] In creating the Chickamauga National Celebration, organizers adhered to this pattern quite thoroughly. The Civil War rituals focused on white heroism. The Chattanooga centennial celebrated the supposed unity of a segregated city. African Americans, meanwhile, disappeared.

Yet if black history was off-limits, why did these same commemorators embrace the story of Cherokee removal? I have already suggested a partial answer to the question in this chapter. The white elites who shaped the city's public memory treated Cherokee history as an element of their own past. By the late 1930s, they had substantial experience memorializing Cherokees, and the central dynamic of this memory work was to transform indigenous history into Tennessee heritage. The removal centennial continued that process. It reinforced white Chattanoogans' sense of the past, rather than challenging it. In the process, it strengthened their authority over this part of the old Cherokee Nation, a power denied Chattanooga's African Americans. Like the Civil War battles, Cherokee removal was a dramatic story that took place in and around the commemorators' own city. Acknowledging this Indian past deepened their appreciation for the place where they resided, even if it also required them to express regret for their forebears' role in removal. Expressing regret, in fact, appears to have made the experience more satisfying, since apologizing allowed them to feel that they had somehow atoned for old crimes. Remembering Cherokee history, then, strengthened white residents' ties to a land their people conquered. It helped them to possess this place as a home.

Commemorators could use the removal story in this way, because it demanded very little from them beyond expressions of regret. White commemorators barred black memory from the public realm because its inclusion promised to challenge white supremacy in the present. Cherokee history, on the other hand, was politically safe. White Tennesseans like Charles Lusk felt obliged to remember removal, but apparently memory was enough. The Cherokees who participated in the Indian "homecoming" would return to their real homes once the festival ended. Their visit might call attention to injustice in the past, but they would not demand social or political change in present-day Chattanooga. Contemporary Indian politics happened elsewhere. While acknowledging the evils of black slavery or segregation could point toward the remaking of southern society, acknowledging removal required only monuments.

This political neutrality, however, rendered the Trail of Tears a more likely vehicle for expressing other anxieties during this period. As the historian Lawrence Levine observed, the Great Depression traumatized Americans, not only because it caused them physical deprivation, but because it upset some of their most cherished beliefs about the nature and direction of their history. Americans expected progress, and, by the early twentieth century, they generally defined progress in material terms. Each generation would be wealthier than the last, and, despite occasional economic downturns, the United States would always provide talented and disciplined individuals with opportunities for advancement. These ideas formed a secular faith and a crucial element of American national identity. The Depression delivered a terrible shock to those who carried such expectations, a psychological blow that, in Levine's terms, left them bewildered and profoundly anxious. "Americans had been living in what they had assured themselves was a supremely rational and progressive society," Levine wrote. "Suddenly they found themselves inhabiting a land whose cruel incongruities and ironies could no longer be ignored."[69]

Americans responded to the shock of the Depression in a variety of ways. The literature scholar Morris Dickstein identifies a sustained questioning of the "American Dream" in the culture of the 1930s, a profound uneasiness with the traditional belief in social mobility and material improvement. He suggests that, while relatively few Americans embraced radical politics during the Depression, a great many came to doubt the old ideologies.[70] Other scholars, like Levine, document a powerful strain of traditionalism in Depression-era America, an assertion of old values in the face of upheaval.[71] For my purposes, the important point is simply that American progress was open for debate. The Depression made the idea of progress something that required attention. It was a concern, a point of anxiety, regardless of whether one sustained the notion or rejected it. Chattanooga's commemorative festival embodied that concern. The organizers created an event that explicitly affirmed the old faith in inevitable improvement. They promised that, despite recent troubles, their city would once again become the "Dynamo of Dixie," since progress was the essence of their history. By including the removal centennial, however, they also allowed the commemoration to suggest that their progressive community began in an act of unnecessary violence against a blameless people. The festival, then, was a celebration of progress that expressed doubt in its own central premise. With the introduction of this doubt, the commemoration cohered with one of the more prominent cultural patterns of the era.

For some observers, meanwhile, the story of Cherokee removal may have invited comparison with their own communities' struggles in the 1930s. Some of this period's most successful popular culture texts dealt with historical crises offering parallels to the Depression. One of the clearest examples of this phenomenon was *Gone with the Wind*, Margaret Mitchell's best-selling novel, and its film adaptation. *Gone with the Wind* depicted a happy and prosperous plantation South and a vibrant, if often frivolous, planter culture. War plunged that society into chaos, much as the crash shattered the hopeful America of the 1920s, and Mitchell showed her central characters struggling to survive and then create new lives. The Civil War romance, then, offered a metaphor for the Depression, articulating the pain and anxiety of those living through the modern crisis.[72] The Trail of Tears served a similar function at events like the Chickamauga National Celebration. Here was the story of a community threatened by forces beyond its control, a people uprooted and dispossessed. The removal scenes in "The Drums of Dixie," for instance, emphasized the disruption of family life and the misery of those who lost their homes, familiar experiences for many during the Depression. The Trail of Tears, moreover, was a story of the sorrows of migration, recounted only a few years after the crash had forced thousands of Americans to take to the roads. While Chattanooga's removal centennial belonged to a long American tradition of depicting Indian disappearance, this particular disappearance narrative may have resonated with the emotional experience of the 1930s.

At Chattanooga, then, the Trail of Tears was a safe topic for memorialization, but still a relevant one, and that dynamic helps to explain the remarkable popularity of removal as a subject of public memory among whites in the twentieth-century South. Removal was distant, but familiar—politically unthreatening, but still emotionally powerful. This phenomenon would become even more apparent in the decades after World War II, when, in the midst of the Cold War and the civil rights movement, southern communities mounted an even greater round of Cherokee commemorations.

4 The Capital

Remembering Cherokee Removal in Civil Rights–Era Georgia

. . . .

In the spring of 1962, legislators in Georgia voted unanimously to repeal a set of anti-Indian laws passed in the late 1820s and early 1830s. These were the statutes that precipitated the Cherokees' final removal crisis. Beginning in 1828, the state unilaterally extended its jurisdiction over Cherokee territory, nullified tribal laws, and outlawed the Cherokee government, among other actions. The purpose of this legal assault was to make life in Georgia so terrible for Cherokees that tribal leaders would have no choice but to negotiate a treaty with the United States to sell their land in the East and migrate to Indian Territory. These laws provided the focus for the Cherokee removal debate in the early 1830s. They formed the basis, for instance, of the Supreme Court's groundbreaking "Cherokee Cases": *Cherokee Nation v. Georgia* (1831) and *Worcester v. Georgia* (1832). By repealing the laws, the state's political leaders acknowledged Georgia's central role in destroying the old Cherokee Nation and facilitating the removal policy.[1]

The legislature took this step as part of a historical commemoration. That same spring, Georgia opened a state historic site at New Echota, the former Cherokee Nation capital near present-day Calhoun, in Gordon County. A decade earlier, local business leaders had launched an effort to rebuild the town, identifying a section of farmland once occupied by New Echota, raising money to purchase it, and then petitioning the state government to turn it into a historic site and recreation area. The Georgia Historical Commission (GHC), a newly formed state agency, ended up managing the project, and, as work proceeded, New Echota became one of the GHC's most important and highly publicized ventures. By the early 1960s, it reconstructed a portion of the town, and planning began for a museum dedicated to Cherokee history and the removal story. The General Assembly timed the repeal of the old anti-Indian laws to coincide with the state's formal dedication of that site.[2]

In striking the laws, Georgia politicians emphasized the injustice of their forebears' actions, offering the repeal as an apology for the Trail of Tears. The anti-Indian statutes had been "harshly restrictive of the inalienable

rights of the Cherokees," the legislators declared. If enforced in the present, they would "cause such gross injustice as to shock the consciences of
all who believe in equality under the law."[3] Representative Charles Pannell,
who introduced the repeal bill, called the acts "asinine laws passed to protect people doing a great wrong," and he likened Georgia's assault upon the
Cherokee Nation to Communist China's treatment of Tibet.[4] By condemning removal and commemorating Cherokee history, Georgia's modern leaders demonstrated that they regretted their ancestors' treatment of the
Indian population. "In doing this," the legislature declared, "Georgia atones
for the wrong done to these worthy people."[5]

This apology, and the commemoration that prompted it, came at a
time when other "harshly restrictive" laws—those maintaining racial
segregation—had become the most significant public issue in the South. By
early 1962, the same Georgia politicians who sought atonement for the
state's part in Indian removal waged an increasingly bitter struggle to maintain Jim Crow. Georgia dedicated New Echota while elsewhere in the state
civil rights activists fought the Albany campaign, maintained a bus boycott
in Macon, and labored for the desegregation of public facilities in Atlanta.
A short time before the dedication, state and local officials debated the question of whether to close public schools and the University of Georgia rather
than accept the enrollment of black pupils in white institutions.[6] In fact, during the very session in which the state legislature repealed the nineteenth-
century anti-Indian laws, students from Atlanta's black universities
demonstrated outside of the statehouse. Several days before, police had
ejected students from the capitol for attempting to desegregate the General
Assembly galleries, and students responded by picketing the building.
Charles Pannell decried the unjust laws of the past in a Jim Crow capitol,
while black activists marched just outside the door, demanding an end to
legal segregation in the present.[7]

Georgia's apology, and the heritage work that inspired it, offer insight
into the culture of the white South during a crucial period of struggle and
transformation. The New Echota project belonged to a significant wave of
removal commemoration in the 1950s and 1960s. During these decades,
communities in several southern states mounted ambitious projects devoted
to remembering Cherokee history. This work, of course, took place in the
midst of the black civil rights movement, and the timing represents something more than an interesting coincidence. Civil rights politics made
Cherokee removal a more desirable subject of public memory, as the acknowledgment of Native American dispossession granted some white

southerners a politically safe way to consider their region's heritage of racial oppression. In memory, the removal story echoed the modern struggle over black civil rights, but the Cherokee episode lay distant enough from contemporary politics that white communities could memorialize Indian loss without inviting controversy. Apologizing for removal, moreover, allowed commemorators to express a commitment to an American ideal of equality at a time when civil rights activists condemned the segregated South as profoundly un-American. Projects like the New Echota restoration, then, reflected the central political conflict of the era and the white South's deepening dilemma. While commemoration did little to alter political opinion in the region, it allowed white southerners to experience the conflict anew.

New Echota was one of the most extensive commemorations of Cherokee history attempted during the postwar period, and the capital today remains one of the more impressive Native American historic sites in the Southeast. The fact that Georgia sponsored the restoration, moreover, meant that the state government that had labored most vigorously to achieve Cherokee removal was now, a century later, working to acknowledge that episode. At New Echota, commemorators had little choice but to confront the political morality of the removal story, since their own forebears had done so much to push the Cherokees out of the Southeast. As a consequence, the project elicited particularly vivid apologies and expressions of regret.

Tourists on the Trail

By the end of the 1930s, as chapters 2 and 3 described, the Trail of Tears became an established, if still minor, feature of southern public memory. Communities in southern Appalachia had commemorated removal as part of their promotion of mountain tourism, and several substantial events, most notably the Chickamauga National Celebration, had included the recognition of Cherokee history. This work set the stage for more extensive commemoration in the post–World War II decades. In the 1950s and 1960s, communities in northern Georgia not only initiated the New Echota project, but also restored the antebellum mansion built by Joseph Vann, a prominent Cherokee planter, as well as a house once owned by Principal Chief John Ross.[8] During this same time, in western North Carolina, white civic leaders, along with Cherokees from the Eastern Band, founded the Cherokee Historical Association (CHA), most famous for producing the long-running outdoor drama *Unto These Hills*. In chapter 5, I discuss the CHA and the drama in detail.[9] Tennesseans, meanwhile, set up numerous markers to

Cherokee history, continuing a practice that evolved before the war. They also began to explore the idea of a historic site at Red Clay, the place where Cherokees held their council meetings just prior to removal and the subject of the "DAR Squabble" I discussed in chapter 3. The state did not complete the Red Clay project until the 1970s, but local civic leaders pursued the idea beginning in the 1950s.[10] White residents of Cape Girardeau, Missouri, developed the Trail of Tears State Park, which I described in the introduction, while other communities in the state built monuments at points along the Cherokee migration route. In eastern Oklahoma, Cherokee Nation leaders partnered with non-Indian interests in developing events like the Cherokee National Holiday, which marked the rebuilding of the nation after removal.[11] Throughout this period, the Civil War remained the dominant subject of southern public memory, but Cherokee history received significant attention.

Almost all of these projects began as efforts to promote tourism. They belonged to a broader trend in the South, in which civic leaders and business interests sought to capitalize on America's midcentury boom in automobile travel. Auto ownership in the United States increased rapidly in the postwar decades and, with it, domestic travel for recreation. Growing affluence and the shrinking of the average American workweek meant that some form of tourism lay within reach of a large and steadily increasing number of Americans. In 1963 the Census Bureau estimated that 43 percent of all American families took long-distance vacations each year, with the average journey covering six hundred miles. The great majority of these trips were made by car. State and federal governments facilitated auto travel by improving roads and building new freeway systems, and by the early 1960s drivers could cross around one-third of the continent using four-lane highways.[12] The South participated in this expansion, and, in some states, the tourism industry grew to rival agriculture in size and economic significance. By the late 1950s, tourism revenues in the South totaled an estimated $2 billion per year. State authorities cultivated the trade by forming publicity bureaus and tourism associations and by actively encouraging the development of new parks and attractions. As the Kentucky historian Thomas Clark observed in 1961, a friendly attitude toward tourism was one of the few positions a public figure could take in the postwar South and expect near-universal support.[13]

Memorials and historic sites formed an important component of this tourism boom. As the historian Michael Kammen notes, the postwar years witnessed rising public interest in history and tradition in the United States.

Popular histories of the founding of the nation and the Civil War gained a wide audience, and the success of *American Heritage* magazine testified to public fascination with the national past. The preservation movement experienced a revival during this period, helped by the founding of the National Trust for Historic Preservation in 1949, and state and federal governments sponsored a variety of historically themed celebrations, from the two-hundredth anniversary of John Marshall's birth (1955) to the centennial of the Civil War (1961–1965). The historian Michael Kammen interprets this phenomenon as a response to widespread anxieties over social and political stability in the postwar era. He suggests that the Cold War, in particular, encouraged Americans to seek purpose and a secure national identity in the past.[14] Whatever its origins, the trend certainly helped to spur the rapid growth of heritage tourism. In Virginia, Colonial Williamsburg's annual attendance expanded from 94,000 in 1945 to more than 340,000 in 1956, and the figure then doubled over the next decade to well over 700,000. Partly owing to Williamsburg's success, this period saw the steady propagation of living history museums in the United States. Preserved homes like Monticello and Mount Vernon likewise reported significantly increased visitation, and this popularity encouraged new preservation efforts involving historic houses, both in the South and in other parts of the country. During the 1950s and 1960s, Americans marked a number of significant national anniversaries, and these commemorative festivals also contributed to the growth of southern heritage tourism. In 1957, for instance, the celebration marking the 350th anniversary of Jamestown's founding drew large numbers of visitors to the Chesapeake, while the centennial of the Civil War a few years later inspired Americans to visit a host of southern battlefields. The past was a growth industry in the postwar decades, a fact that encouraged communities to search their histories for distinctive features and marketable narratives.[15]

Restoring the "Cherokee Williamsburg"

At New Echota, local tourism boosters partnered with the state of Georgia to rebuild a portion of the removal-era Cherokee capital. In the early 1950s, business leaders in Calhoun organized a new Chamber of Commerce, and this group immediately identified the construction of a park and historic site at New Echota as one of its primary goals. While few visible signs of the Cherokee town remained, members of the chamber believed that this element of the local past offered an opportunity to develop a major attraction in close proximity to their community. New Echota was a unique place, the seat of a Native American government. It also occupied a favorable location, close to Calhoun's downtown and only a short distance from Highway 41, an important autoroute connecting the cities of Atlanta and Chattanooga. At a time when automobile travel and heritage tourism were growing in popularity, a historic site must have seemed like a guaranteed boon for the local economy.[16]

New Echota served as the capital of the Cherokee Nation for only a short time, and, in appearance at least, it was never a particularly grand place. The Cherokee Nation constructed several small public buildings there, the most famous being the office of the *Cherokee Phoenix*, the bilingual national newspaper. A handful of homes and businesses surrounded the village center, and, at a slight remove, Samuel Worcester kept a house and missionary station. During sessions of the national council, a great many Cherokees stayed temporarily at New Echota, but only a handful lived there year-round. Despite its small size, the town had great significance as a symbol during the period before removal. It exemplified the Cherokees' effort to forge an Indian republic; it was a new capital for a nation reborn. Moreover, it broadcast the message that the Cherokees were a "civilized tribe," an Indian people who embraced a Euro-American concept of progress. New Echota, of course, also represented a key location in the struggle over removal, being both the capital during key stages of resistance and the place that gave its name to the 1835 removal treaty.[17] After the Trail of Tears, the town all but disappeared. The land's new owners dismantled the buildings for their materials and established new farms on the site of the Cherokee capital. By the 1950s, local residents possessed only a general idea of New Echota's location. A small cemetery remained, containing the graves of the prominent leader Pathkiller and Harriet Boudinot, wife of *Cherokee Phoenix* editor Elias Boudinot, among others. Of the original buildings, only a section of the Worcester house survived into the twentieth century, and fire and additional construction altered even that remnant quite significantly.[18]

Gordon County residents began discussing the idea of a New Echota historic site some time prior to the 1950s. In 1915 the Calhoun Women's Club purchased and preserved the New Echota cemetery, and this act encouraged further commemoration of the area's Indian history. In 1930, Calhoun residents, working through their congressman, secured federal funding for a memorial to New Echota, erecting a granite obelisk at the approximate location of the Cherokee capital. Like the Chattanooga residents described in chapter 3, the people of Calhoun had an established tradition of commemorating the Cherokee capital, and they appear to have begun discussing a more elaborate historic site during the Great Depression. The war interrupted these plans, but, in the economic boom of the postwar years, the Chamber of Commerce revived the idea in an effort to expand Gordon County's tourism industry.[19]

The chamber began by sponsoring research to identify the capital's exact site. Henry Malone, an Atlanta-based historian, conducted this work. He gathered maps and other records that indicated the location of the town and found descriptions of the public buildings. The chamber, meanwhile, began to raise money for land purchases and obtained options to buy some of the property thought to include the town site. Malone and Robert D. Self, president of the Chamber of Commerce, presented the project to the Georgia Historical Commission, while J. Roy McGinty, a sometime politician and editor of the *Calhoun Times,* promoted it locally.[20] Convinced of the site's potential, the GHC allocated funds for an archeological survey, while supporting additional research by Malone and ethnohistorian Clemens de Baillou. By early 1954, the Chamber of Commerce assembled 145 acres of farmland for the historic site, and the archeological work began. For the first phase of the project, the local promoters planned to reconstruct the Cherokee council house, the Supreme Court building, and the print shop that produced the *Cherokee Phoenix.* Ideas for later additions included a museum, the restoration of the Worcester house, and the reconstruction of Elias Boudinot's home. They also considered planting historical gardens to demonstrate Cherokee agricultural practices of the early nineteenth century.[21]

Initially, the local leaders hoped to manage the site's development themselves, with the state historical commission merely providing research assistance and technical support. Shortly after the Chamber of Commerce purchased the land, Calhoun residents formed a nonprofit foundation for this purpose, led by the president of one of county's largest banks. Work on the project, however, quickly outstripped the foundation's ability to raise funds, while the complexity of the restoration led the GHC to become far more deeply involved than its officers originally intended. After several years, the Chamber of Commerce deeded the land to the historical commission, and the state agency assumed formal direction of the site. Local business and civic leaders continued to participate, but, from this point forward, New Echota became a state project.[22]

Management by the commission, however, did not ensure a smooth operation. The state government funded the GHC irregularly, with appropriations varying widely from year to year. At times, the commission managed to continue its work only by receiving last-minute infusions of cash from the governor's office. This erratic budgeting led to delays and complaints that the commission neglected its obligations to communities like Calhoun.[23] Equally serious, New Echota became the subject of a bitter argument among GHC personnel only a short time after the agency took possession of the site. In 1957 the commission hired Atlanta-based architect Thomas Little to direct the reconstruction of Cherokee public buildings and the restoration of the Worcester house. Little decided that the goal of the project should be to represent the Cherokee capital during its brief high point in the late 1820s, before Georgia and the United States moved to dismantle the Cherokee Nation. The site, in other words, would feature buildings that were historically appropriate but that appeared newly constructed, since the capital was, in fact, a new town in the 1820s. Little hoped that the site might eventually become a fully-fledged living history museum. Before moving to Atlanta, he worked at Colonial Williamsburg, and this experience clearly shaped his conception of New Echota, which he envisioned as a model historical village filled with costumed Indian interpreters. In promoting the project, he sometimes compared the Cherokee town to the popular Virginia site, suggesting that New Echota might become a "little Williamsburg." A visitor to the site, he wrote, should be "carried back to the very hour of the town and to feel that he is living in an active part of history." Creating this effect would require not only reconstructed buildings, but "authentic living craft displays," preferably conducted by "Indians of Cherokee descent, in appropriate dress of the period."[24]

While Little's overall goals did not meet with opposition, some GHC workers objected to his manner of pursuing them. In particular, Clemens de Baillou, who conducted initial research on the site, criticized Little's reconstructed buildings as historically inaccurate. He made them too pretty, de Baillou complained, with far too much ornamentation. By modern standards, de Baillou noted, New Echota was a frontier village. The buildings would have appeared quite plain, even crude, to the eyes of a twentieth-century American. Little, however, seemed intent on having New Echota match a modern tourist's idea of a picturesque old town, with neat avenues and quaintly decorated structures. For his first building, the *Cherokee Phoenix* print shop, Little planned to include a porch with decorated benches, wrought-iron ornamentation, and even a picket fence. Such "flamboyant" detail "is perhaps permissible in Williamsburg," de Baillou wrote, but the historical record could not support this approach at New Echota.[25] Georgia-

Reconstructed print shop of the *Cherokee Phoenix* newspaper, New Echota State Historic Site. Photo by author.

based archeologist Arthur Kelly described the issue in more strident terms, calling the print shop "an obscene gesture" and "a bastard conception of no apparent 'period' or structural integrity."[26] Little responded to this criticism by arguing that his designs reflected the Cherokees' effort to represent themselves as a civilized people. He cited the Vann family's plantation house and John Ross's home as evidence that the Cherokees could employ refined building practices and suggested that constructing crude buildings would make the Cherokees appear primitive. "The Cherokee Indian had by this date," he wrote, "completely copied the way of the 'white man,'" and travelers' accounts demonstrated that Euro-American visitors were quite impressed with the town. "Why should we attempt to reconstruct it in any other feeling?"[27]

De Baillou and Kelly were correct to question Little's version of the newspaper building, which did take considerable liberties with the available documentary descriptions of the shop.[28] This dispute, however, reveals a deeper clash between varying notions of historical authenticity, and here Little's position deserves consideration. De Baillou and Kelly objected to Little's designs because no hard evidence existed for the kind of ornamentation the architect proposed to include and because the historical context suggested that such detail would be inappropriate. They wanted the buildings to remain plain rather than incorporate features that they could not verify in the historical record. Little, on the other hand, worried more about the "feeling" of the New Echota project. He wanted the site to tell visitors that the Cherokees were a refined people who achieved great things, rather than the primitive savages of popular imagination, and he recognized that a rustic frontier village might fail to communicate that sentiment. Little, in other words, was willing to stretch the limits of historical accuracy in the interest of cultivating what he considered an authentic emotional experience of Cherokee history. His preferred message, in fact, echoed the one removal-era Cherokee leaders themselves hoped to send when they created their new capital. They wanted New Echota to display their "civilized" status and their determination to remain in their homeland. A more polished design, Little believed, would express those aspirations to the traveling public. A few years later, another GHC worker stated the matter in this way: "I feel that the actual dream of [the Cherokees], their eloquence, their fine Constitution and Laws, plus known skills of the period, give us the right and actual obligation to make the place [New Echota] as nice as we can within the limits of our actual knowledge."[29] Authentically representing the Cherokee "dream," it seems, could require a less authentic physical restoration.

By early 1962, GHC directors felt that enough work had been completed at New Echota to justify the site's formal opening. In addition to recreating the *Cherokee Phoenix* print shop, the agency had restored the Worcester house to an approximation of its original appearance, and it reconstructed the building that housed the Cherokee Supreme Court. Workers relocated an authentic Cherokee structure to the site, a tavern once operated by the Vann family. The commission acquired this building in the mid-1950s, moving it to New Echota when the creation of the Lake Lanier reservoir threatened it with inundation.[30] One very significant building was missing, thanks to a further disagreement among the technicians. The GHC postponed the planned reconstruction of the council house, after researchers failed to reach a consensus regarding its dimensions and appearance.[31] Still, the agency and its local partners implemented most of their original proposal, and the GHC concluded that the time had come to dedicate the site and open it to the public.

Civil Rights Politics in Postwar Georgia

The creation of the New Echota historic site coincided with one of the most intense periods of the postwar struggle over black civil rights. Calhoun residents purchased the land for the project the same year the Supreme Court delivered its decision in *Brown v. Board of Education* (1954), and the GHC reconstructed the principal Cherokee buildings as the initial legal challenges to school segregation in Georgia moved through the courts. The completion and opening of the site took place during the first waves of direct action protest by civil rights activists in Atlanta, Savannah, and other Georgia cities.[32] Throughout this period, the state government fought strenuously to preserve Jim Crow. As in other southern states, Georgia officials responded to *Brown* by pledging "massive resistance" to integration. "Come hell or high-water," Governor Marvin Griffin promised, "races will not be mixed in Georgia schools." State officials promised to enforce an existing law denying funds to integrated schools, and in 1955 the legislature strengthened that prohibition by making it a felony for a school official to spend state revenue on integrated institutions. Georgia's justice department, meanwhile, harassed segregation opponents, launching a campaign aimed at driving civil rights activists out of the state or into quiescence. Attorney General Eugene Cook accused the NAACP of subversive activities and argued that any teacher found to be a member of the group should be blacklisted. He led a move to classify barratry (litigation for the purpose of harassment or profit) as a felony and threatened to use this rule against those who filed lawsuits in pursuit of school desegregation. At one point, he even suggested that the General Assembly pass a bill making it a capital offense for anyone not employed by the federal government to assist in carrying out the *Brown* decision.[33]

This was the state government that rebuilt New Echota. The GHC began its support for the project during the administration of Herman Talmadge, one of postwar Georgia's most vehemently white supremacist governors. The commission assumed control of New Echota while Marvin Griffin held the governor's office. Griffin, in fact, personally helped to revive the New Echota project at a time when work had flagged due to a lack of funding. In 1958 the governor attended a dinner at the Calhoun Elks Club, where J. Roy McGinty and other New Echota supporters discussed the restoration, expressing their concern that the project had foundered. Griffin responded by releasing $54,000 to the GHC for use in rebuilding the Cherokee capital. These funds allowed the commission to continue work on the Worcester house, begin the reconstruction of the Cherokee Supreme Court, and conduct further research on the council house.[34] This transaction had no explicit bearing on the ongoing battle over black civil rights. Griffin simply intended to show his support for tourism in the northern part of the state. The episode demonstrates, however, that the leaders of Georgia's defense of white supremacy directly facilitated the commemoration of Indian history and the Cherokee Trail of Tears. The New Echota site not only developed during Georgia's resistance to integration; it owed its existence to some of the leaders of that resistance.

By the time the GHC finished the first phase of the Cherokee capital, Georgia's battle over black civil rights had reached an important watershed. In 1959 a U.S. District Court ordered the desegregation of Atlanta's public school system and gave city and state officials one year to develop an integration plan. This decision placed Governor Ernest Vandiver in a serious political dilemma. Elected the year before, he had promised to resist any form of school desegregation, holding the line established by his predecessors Talmadge and Griffin. Under Talmadge-era laws, moreover, the state government could not provide funding to integrated institutions. The court order left Vandiver with the choice of either shutting the public schools or reversing course and working to amend the law to allow integrated education. A special state commission, appointed by Vandiver to examine the matter, recommended that Georgia accept the court's decision while striving to "secure the maximum segregation possible within the law."[35] Before Vandiver and the assembly could act on this advice, however, a second education crisis erupted, this one involving the University of Georgia. In January 1961 a federal judge ordered the university to admit two black students, a decision met with outrage around the state and rioting on the university's Athens campus. Vandiver and his political allies now faced the prospect of closing not only Atlanta's schools but the state's beloved college, and, in the end, the governor chose to back down. Addressing the state legislature, he recommended the repeal of the laws barring state funding for integrated schools and endorsed the special commission's report. By the end of the month the assembly passed legislation embracing those recommendations, and Atlanta's schools officially integrated later that year.[36]

This shift in policy did not amount to a repudiation of Jim Crow. Georgia's government backed away from massive resistance, but it retained its commitment to preserving segregation. The acceptance of court-ordered school integration was, at most, a tactical retreat. It did not end Georgia's struggle over civil rights; it merely forced segregation's defenders to find new methods.[37] To frame the matter in somewhat different terms, the public school debate reflected the state government's predicament in the early 1960s. Vandiver and his allies sought to maintain the South's racial caste system, which white citizens continued to support, while working to avoid confrontations with the federal government. Federal law, however, increasingly favored racial equality, or at least it required the abandonment of avowedly white supremacist state practices. Georgia's leaders, then, faced the challenge of maintaining a segregated reality in the absence of strict segregation laws.

That issue, in turn, reflected a broader ideological dilemma. For much of the nation's history, white supremacy in the United States coexisted quite comfortably with an American national identity that emphasized democracy and human equality. In the postwar era, however, maintaining this contradiction became increasingly difficult. From the founding of the republic, Americans cultivated dual traditions of nationalism. On one hand, they defined the United States according to its founding principles of liberty, equality, and government by consent of the people, an ideology the historian Gary Gerstle labels "civic nationalism." On the other hand, many white citizens conceived of the nation in racial terms, believing that only Europeans (and usually only particular kinds of Europeans) were fit to enjoy full democratic participation. According to this tradition of "racial nationalism," American democracy required the exclusion or subordination of members of the less fit, nonwhite races. Within this outlook, legal segregation in the South was compatible with democracy. It was necessary, in fact, for the republic's continued well-being.[38] In the mid-twentieth century, several developments undermined the racial nationalist tradition. The awareness of Nazi racism during World War II encouraged Americans to question white supremacy at home, while granting new political ammunition to advocates of racial equality. American white supremacy then became a liability in the Cold War, as the United States found itself competing with the Soviet Union to influence emerging nations in Africa and Asia. The leaders of the postwar State Department quickly realized that the continued existence of a racial caste system in the South sullied America's international image. This understanding helped to compel the federal government to take its first tentative actions in support of the civil rights movement. Civil rights activists, meanwhile, employed the language of civic nationalism against Jim Crow, insisting that opposition to segregation represented the

highest form of American patriotism. As Gerstle writes, these developments encouraged Americans to view the founding ideals of freedom and
equality as forming the only legitimate basis for national identity.[39]

Racial nationalism, of course, did not disappear during this period. White
supremacists continued to defend segregation as essential to the proper
functioning of southern society and to condemn black activism and federal
intervention as threats to the rights and liberty of white southerners. Cold
War politics, meanwhile, informed both sides of the struggle over black civil
rights, with supporters of Jim Crow charging civil rights activists with sub-
version.[40] For my purposes, however, the significant point is simply that
these midcentury developments made southern white supremacy an increasingly visible problem in American public life. The contradiction between racial and civic nationalism grew more apparent in the postwar
political environment, and it became less sustainable. Critics and activists
condemned segregation as un-American and the white South as an obstacle to the nation's progress.[41] By the early 1960s, politicians like Georgia's
Ernest Vandiver faced not only the practical challenge of finding new methods of keeping the South segregated, but also the ideological problem of
defining the still-segregated region within a nation ostensibly committed
to racial equality. As the remainder of this chapter documents, this dilemma
left its imprint on public memory.

Sanctifying New Echota

On May 12, 1962, Georgia dedicated the New Echota site in an elaborate ceremony that drew journalists, Cherokee tribal representatives, and a host of
state politicians to Gordon County. Joseph Cumming, an Augusta lawyer
and chairman of the historical commission, presided, while Governor Vandiver and Secretary of State Ben Fortson delivered the principal speeches
of the day. Earl Boyd Pierce, legal counsel for the Cherokee Nation, attended
on behalf of the governor of Oklahoma, and N. B. Johnson, who also spoke
at the unveiling of the Otahki memorial in Missouri that same month, represented the Cherokee Nation and the Oklahoma Historical Society. Mollie
Blankenship, a North Carolina Cherokee, attended on behalf of Osley Saunooke, the principal chief of the Eastern Band. Charles Pannell, who had
sponsored the bill striking Georgia's anti-Indian laws, read the repeal
resolution to the crowd and presented copies to the Cherokee representatives. N. B. Johnson responded by presenting Joseph Cumming with a cer-
tificate thanking the GHC and declaring Cumming an "Ambassador of the

Dedication of the New Echota State Historic Site, 1962. The ceremony took place at the restored home of missionary Samuel Worcester. Courtesy Georgia State Archives, Vanishing Georgia Collection, gor527.

Cherokee Nation." In honor of the historic site's opening, the state of Oklahoma flew the Georgia flag over its capitol building on the afternoon of the ceremony, and Georgia flags were also raised in the cities of Tulsa, Muskogee, and Tahlequah, the capital of the Cherokee Nation in the West. Not surprisingly, the dedication attracted a great deal of attention from the press, and newspapers across the state covered the event, praising the GHC and celebrating Georgia's newest history attraction.[42]

During construction of the site, public discussion of New Echota had mainly concerned the logistics of the restoration. Calhoun residents and GHC personnel worried about state funding, accurate research, and finding the proper materials for the reconstructed buildings. With the first phase of the project complete, however, conversation turned to the site's meaning. At the dedication, state officials and the GHC sought to explain New Echota, indicating the lessons visitors should learn there. Journalists did the same, offering digests of Cherokee history and anticipating visitors' experiences of the site. In doing so, they "sanctified" the restored capital, to use a term employed by the cultural geographer Kenneth Foote. By "sanctification" Foote means the process whereby a community not only acknowledges a memorial site, but sets it apart on the landscape, placing it outside of normal life and protecting it as a spot suited for contemplation. Sanctification almost always involves an effort to derive some kind of clear moral message from the events that took place there. Preserved battlefields, for example, will usually emphasize the virtue of sacrifice for the nation.[43] At New Echota, that interpretive effort drew upon the civic nationalist tradition and focused on two broad themes: admiration for the Cherokees' achievements in becoming a "civilized tribe" and regret for Georgia's part in removal. "New Echota," the governor explained, "was the scene of an intense drama in which an Indian nation took upon itself all the monumental responsibilities of modern civilization, created for itself a written language, established a national newspaper, evolved a code of written laws and created a supreme court to administer these laws." With the reconstruction of the town, modern visitors could experience "the panorama of Cherokee achievement."[44] Many journalists emphasized the disparity between the picture of Cherokee life provided by the historic site and the Indian images spread by popular culture. As the *Rome News-Tribune* pointed out, a visitor coming to New Echota expecting "an Indian wigwam village with a few painted and synthetic savages lurking about with bows and arrows is in for a big disappointment."[45]

Antebellum whites' assault upon this Indian civilization had been a terrible crime, and the dedication ceremony depicted the New Echota commemoration as a public act of atonement for Georgia's part in the removal episode. "This restoration," Vandiver declared, "is more than the mere reconstruction of an historic area as a tourist attraction." Rather, it "offers honor and dignity to the descendants of those proud people so shamefully banished from our borders 128 years ago." The governor identified "the unbridled avarice of our ancestors" as the cause of Cherokee removal, and he condemned the "harsh, oppressive laws passed by our ancestors to harass the Cherokee people." Admittedly, the historic site was "small compensation for the anguish of the 'trail of tears,'" but perhaps it would help to "heal the wounds of resentment" left by removal and create a new sense of friendship between Cherokees and the people of their former homeland. If nothing else, New Echota would convey an important lesson about the dangers of greed and intolerance. The historic site, Vandiver stated, would serve as a "reminder that greed, avarice and lust for power cannot be allowed to take control of any of our people, or our state and national governments, if all of our people are to progress and prosper."[46] Secretary of State Ben Fortson reinforced this last message and, in doing so, provided the ceremony's clearest example of the rhetoric of civic nationalism. New Echota, he declared, "will make us better Americans, for Americans use their mistakes as stepping stones for something more worthwhile."[47]

The "civilized tribe" image long provided a prominent theme in the public memory of Cherokee removal. As earlier chapters demonstrated, commemoration of Cherokee history during the interwar years almost always presented some version of the familiar story of the progress of the Indian nation. The emphasis on atonement, however, represented something new in this period. Earlier commemorators had sometimes expressed the idea that southern communities bore a public responsibility to acknowledge the injustice of removal, but this idea became a much more prominent theme in the commemorations of the 1950s and 1960s. When Georgia restored the Vann House, for instance, a Cherokee visitor from Oklahoma described the site as "a partial apology for the maltreatment of the Cherokee people perpetrated by a previous generation of Georgia people," while another Cherokee observed that Georgians "seemed to be trying to do everything to make amends."[48] The main organizer of the restoration of John Ross's home near Chattanooga described her work in similar terms. The house should become "a shrine to honor Chief Ross and his people who were so ruthlessly forced to leave this part of the country," she wrote. "Even at this late date we can atone for this cruel treatment of the Cherokee by restoring the home of their old chief."[49] Like New Echota, these projects began as efforts to promote tourism and to highlight distinctive elements of the local history of particular southern communities. When it came time to sanctify the sites, however, participants chose to interpret them as apologies for old crimes. As Vandiver observed of the restored Cherokee capital, these places were more than tourist attractions. They represented efforts by white southerners to bear witness to acts of oppression.

A Good Place to Reflect on Our Ideals

This moral tone may surprise twenty-first-century readers. The literature on southern memory suggests that, until very recently, public commemoration in the South has excluded the experience of nonwhite communities, while shunning topics that might involve criticism of Euro-American elites. Those rules clearly applied to African American history, which continued to receive very little attention from institutions like the GHC.[50] Yet the region's Native American past was a different matter. Some of the same commemorators who kept black history at the margins of public memory embraced the story of Cherokee loss, and the fact that removal was a crime and an injustice appears to have made the episode more, rather than less, attractive. It is difficult to imagine the government of a southern state sponsoring a public commemoration that recognized a history of injustice toward African Americans during this period. Could the governor of Georgia apologize for slavery in 1962? For some white southerners, however, contemplating a historic crime against the Cherokees proved not only permissible, but satisfying.

It is worth noting, meanwhile, that Georgia's removal commemoration did not encounter public opposition. Other GHC projects during this period drew complaints from state residents who felt that the agency portrayed their ancestors in a negative light. Some Georgians, for instance, criticized the commission's Civil War marker program for expressing insufficient veneration of the Confederacy. The GHC, they argued, memorialized too many Union actions and Yankee victories. At one point in the early 1950s, Herman Talmadge halted plans to erect markers tracing the Union army's "march to the sea," judging that episode too shameful to deserve recognition.[51] Indian removal was a very different matter. In the case of New Echota, the project's few critics grumbled that the state had failed to put enough money into the site and that work proceeded too slowly. They did not take issue with the commemoration's focus or moral message.[52]

In chapter 3, while discussing the Chickamauga National Celebration, I observed that Cherokee removal represented a politically safe memory in Depression-era Chattanooga. It formed an established element of the white community's sense of its own past, and its commemoration did not imply a need for significant change in the present. While the greater inclusion of black history in the 1938 festival might have challenged white supremacy in Chattanooga, the public recognition of injustice toward Cherokees offered no such threat. In postwar Georgia, Cherokee history proved an equally safe subject. Cherokee people lived in the state in the 1950s and 1960s, along with individuals who could claim Cherokee ancestry, but no formally recognized tribes resided there. Later in the century, the state government would acknowledge a number of Georgia communities as Indian tribes, but that practice had not yet begun. As a result, Georgia had little involvement in the politics of Indian affairs during this period.[53] The commemoration depicted the state's Cherokee history as having ended in the late 1830s. In Georgia, as in much of the South, removal was a story of Indian absence, another in a long line of disappearance narratives, and an absent people could have little effect on the state's political life. After the dedication, the Cherokee dignitaries who visited for the ceremony would return home, away from Georgia and outside of its public affairs. The state government could commemorate Indian history precisely because it seldom participated in contemporary Indian politics.

This lack of controversy, however, did not mean that the removal story was politically irrelevant in the mid-twentieth century. On the contrary, the Trail of Tears resonated with postwar Americans' heightened awareness of the politics of race relations, and that quality granted new pertinence to this particular version of the disappearing Indian. The memory of Cherokee removal, in other words, was politically innocuous but broadly relevant. It suited, for instance, a Cold War environment that encouraged Americans to consider the history of racial inequality in the United States. As noted earlier, race became an element of the Cold War's propaganda battles, with the Soviet Union and its allies citing racial discrimination as proof of Western hypocrisy and the flawed nature of democracy and capitalism. That argument compelled American politicians and international representatives to acknowledge the presence of racism in the United States, while always insisting that the nation was advancing toward a more open and just society. When applied to the struggle over black civil rights, that position involved a particular kind of historical thinking. American spokesmen could not deny the existence of Jim Crow laws or southern whites' massive resistance to desegregation. They could, however, depict the events of the fifties and sixties as one chapter in a longer American history that tended toward progress. They acknowledged the country's record of racial oppression, discussing slavery and segregation, but they reassured their audiences that life for black Americans had steadily improved in more recent times and would continue to improve, as the American political system responded to the just appeals of black citizens. They suggested, moreover, that only American-style democracy could enable this kind of peaceful change. Racial equality, in other words, could not be achieved through revolution or political radicalism, but only through patient reform. In this way, American representatives worked to transform the nation's troubled history of race from a Cold War liability to an advantage.[54]

Most scholars who examine race in the Cold War focus on African Americans, yet Indian people also figured in this ideological debate.[55] Take, for example, the media productions created by the U.S. Information Agency (USIA). The USIA was America's Cold War public diplomacy service, charged with explaining American politics and life to international audiences. Its broadcasts and publications, circulating around the world, formed one of the American government's principal tools for influencing overseas opinion during the Cold War.[56] When discussing race in the United States, the USIA often included Native American subjects, and its approach to Indian history and federal Indian policy followed the model used in discussing black civil rights. The agency did not deny that Native communities had suffered terrible injustices in the past, but it insisted that Indian life had greatly improved, and continued to improve, in modern times. "Very few Americans would defend the treatment the Indians have received in the past," one radio broadcast began. Early settlers drove them from their land, it explained, and the United States frequently broke treaties. Americans warred upon the tribes for many years, until even the bravest resistance collapsed. The present, however, offered a very different picture. "From the beginning," the program continued, "there had been some Americans who protested the treatment of the Indians. As the years went by more and more Americans began to feel this way—in other words, the American conscience became awakened. As a result, the people of the United States, through their federal government . . . began making amends." Today, it noted, Indian people enjoyed equality before the law, protection in the use of their property, and a host of federal programs to help them become full participants in American life.[57] As another broadcast put it, the United States had a "bad conscience about its Indian people," but the nation was "working very hard to make up for lost time . . . and to offer the Indian of the future some of the opportunities he was denied many years ago."[58] The history of the United States might not be spotless, the USIA suggested, but Americans were people who recognized their errors and corrected them through the operation of their democratic system.[59]

The New Echota commemoration echoed that message and the idea of history that informed it. The restored capital represented Georgia's acknowledgment of an old misdeed and a promise to do better in the future. It expressed regret and indicated the state's "bad conscience" regarding Cherokee removal, while proposing that the memory of the Trail of Tears, if properly maintained, would help Georgians and other Americans create a more just society. A progressive conception of history lay at the heart of the commemoration, as it did the USIA's discussions of race and Indian affairs. By recognizing Cherokee removal as an oppressive act, commemorators demonstrated that modern Americans had improved upon the society and politics of their forebears, and they suggested that the very act of recognition would help to ensure continued progress. As Secretary of State Ben Fortson observed, remembering the Trail of Tears would "make us better Americans." Participants in removal commemorations seldom referred directly to the Cold War, so it is impossible to know whether visitors at New Echota found themselves contemplating U.S. international rivalries. The commemorators' general outlook, however, fit this Cold War cultural pattern. Georgia's apology to the Cherokees, in other words, suited a postwar political culture that promoted the measured acknowledgment of racial conflict and injustice.

The public memory of Cherokee removal bore a similar relationship to the politics of civil rights. The black freedom struggle did not inspire commemorative projects like the New Echota site, but it heightened the removal story's relevance in the postwar South. Press coverage of New Echota suggests that part of what made the Cherokee capital interesting was that observers could readily, if indirectly, connect the Trail of Tears to contemporary civil rights battles. As recounted in Georgia newspapers, the Cherokee story echoed many details of the South's modern crisis. It involved unjust state laws and the rejection of federal court decisions by southern politicians, an experience familiar to the region during the era of "massive resistance." At New Echota, Georgia apologized for defying federal law in the removal era during a period when the state government similarly defied court-ordered desegregation. The removal issue, meanwhile, sparked an argument over states' rights and a moral debate in which northern reformers leveled harsh criticism at southern people and institutions.[60] When describing the New Echota site and its history, journalists frequently made offhand or indirect references to the fight over segregation. One editor, for example, observed that the Cherokee experience showed that Georgia's record of racial tension extended far into the past. Or as the *Rome News-Tribune* put it, "Indians had racial troubles, too." The *Atlanta Constitution* noted the irony of the General Assembly repealing anti-Indian statutes while black students picketed outside of the capitol building. An Associated Press story, which local papers across the state reprinted, described New Echota and the repeal resolution as "a move to put Georgia's racial house in order from early beginnings," while admitting that the action came "a little late."[61] None of these items truly discussed the movement, but they suggest that observers' thoughts could move easily from the memory of removal to contemporary civil rights politics. New Echota did not force visitors to draw comparisons with the black freedom struggle, but it offered a setting that invited them to consider race and justice as general subjects in American history. As the *Atlanta Constitution* noted, the site provided "a good place for us to go and reflect upon our ideals."[62] At a time when the civil rights movement had become the most prominent public issue in the South, surely some travelers joined journalists in considering segregation and black activism while exploring the restored capital.

Civil rights politics, in other words, helped to create the conditions in which the public contemplation of episodes like removal became more satisfying. The American studies scholar Erika Doss notes that shame and apology have become prominent themes of historical commemoration in the twenty-first century, and she asks why Americans today find "sites of shame" so very attractive. She argues that a "heightened attention to moral accountability" in contemporary public culture has inspired a powerful longing to remember historical injustices and express the collective shame inherited from old crimes.[63] Doss, of course, describes memorialization after the rights revolutions of the postwar era, but sites like New Echota suggest that a form of this commemorative desire emerged earlier, as well, in the midst of those revolutions. The civil rights movement, after all, demanded the kind of moral accountability Doss considers significant. It insisted that white southerners confront their communities' history of racial oppression and their failure to live up to American ideals of freedom and equality. In a small safe way, they could meet that demand by remembering Native American loss. They could "put their racial house in order," at least when it came to absent Indians, aligning themselves with the civic nationalist tradition at a time when activists condemned the South as un-American. They could even apologize for one old crime, offering a racial confession impossible and undesirable for most when it came to the current struggle over Jim Crow.

This is not to argue that projects like New Echota encouraged sympathy toward black activism. One logical reading of the commemoration is that it gave whites an opportunity to feel wise and magnanimous with regard to race without forcing them to confront injustice and racial violence in their own time. Or perhaps visitors, if they thought about civil rights at all, concluded that these were simply different cases, that Cherokees and African Americans were different peoples entirely and that whites still enjoyed the right to define the differences. The "civilized tribe" story, so prominent a feature of the memorial, could encourage that conclusion, insofar as it implied that the Cherokees had been unique in their achievements. Apologizing to one group of Native Americans, moreover, reinforced white leaders' moral authority at a time when black activists challenged the legitimacy of southern governments and institutions. Scholars of public memory like to describe how commemoration in the United States has often cleaned up the past, ignoring wrongs in American history. They note that sanitized memories reinforce the authority of governments and social elites. Something similar, however, can be said of the acknowledgment of injustice. Historical confessions empower those who offer them. They imply that the confessor has achieved a level of moral consciousness necessary for better behavior in the future and, therefore, that one can trust them. White elites needed this kind of authority in the 1960s—not when it came to Indian affairs, but in the realm of black civil rights.

When they memorialized Cherokee removal, white southerners acknowledged an American history of racism and, in doing so, endorsed the general principle of racial equality as an American ideal. Their apologies to Native Americans, however, left white supremacy untouched in the mid-century South. This style of commemoration complemented and reinforced white supremacy by reassuring southern elites of their own propriety and sound moral judgment. In Gerstle's terms, the removal memory allowed white southerners to express their allegiance to the ideals of American civic nationalism while maintaining a tradition of racial nationalism. Their apologies for the injustice of removal, then, did not represent a politically meaningful disavowal of racism. Rather, they expressed their predicament, their contradictory position, as Americans devoted to both democracy and white supremacy. White southerners could not resolve that dilemma through public history projects like New Echota. For a moment, however, they could hold the contradiction in balance, sustaining it in a manner that was becoming increasingly difficult in the broader public arena.

The memory of the Trail of Tears could perform this work because white southerners treated removal as the end of the region's Indian history. The absence of Indian people, their invisibility within the contemporary South, made the removal story a safe subject of commemoration and a ready vehicle for expressing the concerns and contradictions of the postwar era. The story proved relevant to a region convulsed by the struggle over Jim Crow, but it was harmless as long as southerners remained unconcerned with contemporary Indian affairs. Cherokee representatives might attend the opening of commemorative sites like New Echota, but they did so as visitors. Removal commemoration did not challenge white southerners' assumption of Indian absence. If anything, it reaffirmed the idea.

Yet Cherokees, of course, had not disappeared, and Native American politics could still matter in some parts of the region. The postwar era was a crucial time of debate and activism among Indian people, no less than among African Americans. The 1950s and 1960s witnessed a significant dispute over federal Indian policy and the beginning of what scholars now recognize as the modern revival of Indian nations. As chapters 5 and 6 suggest, the broad popularity of the removal story became an asset for some Cherokees as they waged their own modern political battles. While white southern commemorators knew little of Indian affairs, their enthusiasm for this particular historical episode influenced the defense and revitalization of Cherokee nationhood.

The Drama

Performing Cherokee Removal in the Termination Era

· ·

In July 1950, the outdoor drama *Unto These Hills* debuted in Cherokee, North Carolina, on the Qualla Boundary. The play, which recounted Cherokee history from European contact through removal, was an immediate success, drawing more than 100,000 spectators in its first summer season. It quickly became one of the most popular attractions in western North Carolina and an engine for the continued growth of the tourism industry on the Qualla Boundary. The Cherokee Historical Association (CHA), the group that produced the drama, went on to create a living history village, depicting Cherokee life in the eighteenth century, and it developed a tribal museum. Together, these attractions helped to convince a multitude of visitors each year to pause on the Boundary on their way to and from the Great Smoky Mountains National Park, allowing Cherokee to fulfill some of the economic potential created by the park's establishment in the prewar years.[1]

The CHA developed *Unto These Hills* during a significant moment in both Eastern Band history and the history of American Indian affairs. The early 1950s marked the high point of the termination policy, the federal government's campaign to remove tribal lands from federal trust and end the distinct status of Indian nations within the United States. After a brief period in the 1930s during which the BIA supported tribal autonomy and self-government, termination once again made the assimilation of Native people the primary goal of federal Indian policy.[2] The Eastern Band was not among the tribes targeted for immediate termination, so Cherokees did not face the most coercive version of the policy. During this period, however, federal officials raised the prospect of removing Cherokee property from trust, while making preparations to withdraw federal services like education and health care. These actions represented a potential crisis for the Eastern Band. While some Cherokees supported termination, many more worried that even a partial application of the policy would lead to the loss of tribal land and the erosion of the well-being of Cherokee communities. Tribal leaders like Principal Chief Osley Saunooke expressed strong opposition to the policy, insisting that Cherokees needed to foster economic development and address social problems within a continued trust relationship with the federal government. In the 1960s, this general outlook informed Native activism across the United States, which eventually compelled federal authorities to abandon the termination crusade and turn toward tribal self-determination as the goal of American Indian affairs.[3]

When placed in the context of the termination debate, *Unto These Hills* offered contradictory messages about the past and future of the Eastern Band. In its narrative, the drama celebrated Cherokee assimilation, employing language that strongly echoed that of termination advocates. Both the play and the policy belonged to a Cold War American culture that offered little room for the persistence of Indian communities as distinct peoples and self-governing nations. At the same time, *Unto These Hills* broadcast an immensely sympathetic image of North Carolina Cherokees, who appeared as a blameless people patiently suffering abuse at the hands of frontier whites and the federal government. That image, at the very least, suggested that federal officials should refrain from forcing new policies upon the Cherokees in the present. The commercial success of the drama, meanwhile, provided a practical argument against changing the Eastern Band's political status. Any policy that undermined the Cherokee community seemed also to threaten tourism, western North Carolina's most important industry. Non-Indians who might otherwise favor termination worried that changes in federal Indian policy would derail the region's economic development. The postwar tourism boom, driven by Cherokee heritage attractions, made termination inconvenient, which, in turn, helped the Eastern Band resist the policy.

Associated Communities

Unto These Hills grew from the work of the Western North Carolina Associated Communities (WNCAC), an organization of business and civic leaders formed to promote economic development in the counties west of Asheville. Established shortly after the end of World War II, the group sought to coordinate regionwide development efforts at a time when many residents were anxious about conversion to a peacetime economy. The war had drawn people away from the mountains, and local leaders worried that without rapid economic expansion, their communities would suffer either high unemployment or sustained population decline. "During the war this section was considered a labor supply area," a state employment officer observed. "War industries and the armed forces recruited heavily in this section. Now these persons are returning and there are not jobs for them."[4] Another state official called unemployment a "malignant growth" in the mountain counties, estimating that as much as 10 percent of the population was out of work in 1947.[5] The WNCAC looked mainly to tourism to mitigate this problem. Members anticipated a revival of the industry now that the war had ended, and they hoped that coordinated efforts to improve accommodations and advertise the region would help local businesses make the most of a new surge of visitors. Early projects of the WNCAC included a lobbying campaign aimed at convincing the federal government to finish the Blue Ridge Parkway and an effort to improve lodging and other amenities on the North Carolina side of the Great Smoky Mountains National Park. While the WNCAC eventually turned its attention to other industries, it pinned most of its early hopes on tourism.[6]

Like the boosters of the 1920s and 1930s, the WNCAC considered the Qualla Boundary a key asset to the regional economy. Cherokee was still North Carolina's doorway to the national park, and Americans' interest in Indians showed no signs of weakening. By the late 1940s, more than a million travelers passed through Cherokee each year. Tourism promoters worried, however, that accommodations in the town were inadequate to meet the needs of these visitors. Leasing tribal land proved difficult for outside developers, and tribal citizens generally lacked the capital to establish more than small tourist businesses. Cherokee's first motel, for instance, opened only in 1937, years after the rapid growth of automobile tourism began. A decade later, a federal agent could still describe "the present facilities" as "very meager, unattractive, and inadequate."[7] In late 1945, one promoter estimated that the Qualla Boundary turned away as many as three thousand potential guests per week for lack of sufficient lodging.[8] From the WNCAC's perspective, paltry amenities in Cherokee represented a problem for all of western North Carolina, not just a lost opportunity for the Eastern Band. They worried that communities on the Tennessee side of the national park offered travelers more rooms and better services. If North Carolina failed to keep pace, visitors would naturally spend most of their time and money in places like Gatlinburg, on the wrong side of the Smokies, a loss that would affect the entire region.[9]

Cherokee leaders shared at least some of these concerns, and, in the late 1940s, the tribal government became more directly involved in tourism development on the Qualla Boundary than in previous years. Principal Chief Jarrett Blythe led this effort, supported by Joe Jennings, the Eastern Band's federal agent and an early participant in the WNCAC. The leaders of the American Legion post at Cherokee were also involved, their contributions reflecting a desire to help returning Cherokee veterans secure employment.[10] In 1945, tribal leaders held meetings with BIA personnel and developers to discuss drafting a master plan for tourism on the Boundary. A short time later, Blythe, Assistant Principal Chief Henry Bradley, and the commander of the legion post traveled to Virginia to investigate accommodations in the Shenandoah Valley and Blue Ridge Mountains. They also cut across Virginia to visit the living history attractions at Williamsburg. The *State* magazine, always a booster, welcomed these developments as evidence that Cherokees were abandoning their "former aloofness" toward tourism and were now ready for "the great coming of the white man."[11]

During this same period, the Eastern Band moved to establish its first tribally owned tourist facility, an idea originally discussed in the late 1930s. Taking advantage of New Deal–era policies that promoted the expansion of tribal landholding, the Eastern Band purchased an 884-acre site known as the Boundary Tree Tract, with the goal of developing new accommodations for travelers. The site lay on the edge of the national park, just outside the main entrance, an ideal location for any business catering to visitors. In 1946, the tribe applied for a $150,000 loan from the BIA's revolving credit fund, proposing to build a tourist complex consisting of a lodge, a gas station, visitor cabins, a café, and a craft shop.[12] The WNCAC supported the project, explaining that it considered the development of better accommodations in Cherokee to be "most vital to the whole western section of the state."[13] The federal government approved the majority of the loan request, and the tribe completed the first stages of the project during the summer of 1948. Eastern Band citizens provided much of the construction labor, and Freeman Bradley, a Cherokee veteran of World War II, signed on as the Boundary Tree's first manager.[14] For decades, the complex was the first thing travelers encountered as they left the national park and entered the Qualla Boundary. In more recent years, the Eastern Band has refurbished the buildings and transformed the motor court into a Cherokee-language immersion school and offices for several of the tribe's education and cultural resources programs.[15]

The WNCAC, however, wanted more from Cherokee than just improved accommodations. They hoped to spur the creation of entirely new attractions, giving travelers more to consume and more reasons to linger in North Carolina. This was where the drama came in. When the founders of the WNCAC drew up their first list of potential projects, they included proposals for two new historical attractions: an Appalachian history museum and a historical pageant.[16] While the museum proposal never materialized, the pageant became the single biggest tourist draw in western North Carolina since the creation of the Great Smoky Mountains National Park.

Performing Cherokee History

Inspiration for the drama came from two sources. As I discuss in earlier chapters, historical pageantry already played a significant role in mountain tourism. In the 1930s, tourism promoters in Asheville, Knoxville, and Chattanooga mounted pageants as central features of local festivals, and these performances included significant Cherokee content. The Eastern Band put on a pageant of its own, "The Spirit of the Great Smokies," as part of the annual Cherokee Fall Fair in 1935 and as a summer tourist attraction in 1937. This practice continued after the war. In the late 1940s, for instance, a Waynesville resident created an operetta about removal based on Robert Frank Jarrett's "Occoneechee," an epic poem published in 1916 that told the story of young Cherokee lovers separated by the Trail of Tears.[17] While larger in scope and ambition than any of these pageants, *Unto These Hills* belonged to an established tradition in mountain communities of performing Cherokee history for visitors.

In addition to this local practice, the WNCAC drew inspiration from another North Carolina tourist region. In 1937, the town of Manteo, on the North Carolina coast, hosted the debut of *The Lost Colony*, a large-scale outdoor drama about early colonists in the Southeast. Written by Paul Green, a Pulitzer Prize–winning playwright who worked at the University of North Carolina, the play recounted the story of Walter Raleigh's doomed effort to establish an English colony on Roanoke Island in the 1580s. The idea for the play originally came from leaders of the Roanoke Colony Memorial Association, a local heritage group that purchased the presumed site of the colony in the 1890s, preserving it as a shrine and tourist attraction. In the 1920s, the association mounted pageants about the Roanoke colony as part of its annual commemorations of the birth of Virginia Dare, the first English child born in North America. The group asked Green to create a new and more polished rendition of the Roanoke story for the summer of 1937, which marked the 350th anniversary of Virginia Dare's birth.[18] Green used the commission to create what he called a "symphonic drama," a grand spectacle that combined traditions of historical pageantry with elements of contemporary professional theater. "By symphonic," he later wrote, "I mean the blending of all the arts and elements of stagecraft—music, dancing, folk song, choreographic movement, sound effects, pageantry, masks when needed, mental speech or what not—all working like the cooperative sections of a symphony orchestra."[19] Green's colleagues at the university's Carolina Playmakers helped to produce the pageant, aided by several federal programs under the Works Progress Administration. Workers employed by the Civilian Conservation Corps meanwhile built a large outdoor theater for the production. Well-received in its first run, the drama became a regular attraction, performed each summer during the height of the tourist season on the Atlantic Coast.[20] The play received a great deal of positive press, encouraging tourism promoters elsewhere to imagine replicating its success in their own communities. When members of the WNCAC began discussing new projects, they immediately identified the creation of an outdoor drama, "similar to 'The Lost Colony,'" as a key objective.[21]

In pursuing this goal, the WNCAC began by simply recruiting the people who created the play in Manteo. Paul Green was unavailable, but his colleagues in the Carolina Playmakers proved receptive. Kermit Hunter, a graduate student at the University of North Carolina, agreed to write a scenario for a Cherokee history play, and Samuel Selden, the director of the Carolina Playmakers, visited Cherokee to confer with WNCAC leaders.[22] According to an often-repeated story, Selden identified the perfect site for an outdoor theater during a tour of Cherokee conducted by Joe Jennings, the Eastern Band's federal agent. When led to a cove just above the tribal fairground, Selden supposedly declared, "This is the spot." The site was near downtown Cherokee, as well as the road leading to the national park, but the mountains enclosed it, creating a natural amphitheater. "The mountains themselves would be part of the scenery," Jennings recalled, "and would serve to shut out the sights and sounds of civilization, making the illusion of another time and people complete."[23] Thus encouraged, the WNCAC began raising funds to build the theater and produce the play's first season. Communities in the far western counties pledged donations for the project, and the state legislature approved a $35,000 loan. The Eastern Band promised to spend up to $5,000 to secure possessory rights to the land for the theater, while the BIA oversaw the construction of an access road and parking lot. The Carolina Playmakers, meanwhile, developed the entertainment itself. Kermit Hunter expanded his initial scenario into a full script, and another Playmaker, Harry Davis, signed on as director.[24] As this work proceeded, the WNCAC created a new organization—the Cherokee Historical Association (CHA)—to manage the drama and develop other Cherokee projects. Chartered in 1948, the CHA promised to "celebrate and depict by exhibitions, pageants, reproductions, and by broadcasting and publishing historic narratives and records, the history—both legendary and factual—of the Cherokee Indians and the early settlers other than the Indian."[25]

White businessmen dominated the CHA, as they did its parent organization. Its chairman, Harry Buchanan, was a Hendersonville merchant known for operating movie theaters. His political connections and skills as a fundraiser proved vital in staging the drama, but he seems to have had few dealings with the tribal community prior to his assuming leadership of the association. The vice chairman, Percy Ferebee, was a banker and local politician. The CHA's bylaws made the principal chief of the Eastern Band an ex officio member of the board of directors, but, in practice, Cherokee interest in the new enterprise received only indirect representation, through the presence of BIA personnel. Joe Jennings, the federal agent, served as the CHA's first treasurer, and his assistant at the agency, Molly Arneach, became the organization's secretary. Arneach was one of the few enrolled Cherokees to participate actively during the CHA's earliest years.[26] Dominated by non-Indians, the CHA leadership contrasted sharply with the organizers of the Cherokee Fall Fair, which remained a popular attraction for tourists and Cherokees alike. While the U.S. agent still served as the president of the fair association, the directors and most members of the executive committee were tribal citizens.[27] Cherokee political leaders like Jarrett Blythe backed the CHA and the creation of the outdoor drama, and, indeed, the project required their support. Without the approval of the tribal government and the BIA, the association could not produce the play on the Qualla Boundary. Once the enterprise began, however, tribal leaders exerted only limited influence over its operation.[28] The same could be said of the play's narrative and depiction of the Cherokees. Members of the Cherokee community, along with CHA leaders, reviewed drafts of Hunter's script, complaining when Hunter took liberties with tribal history. Hunter agreed to revise the drama, but he and Selden insisted that conveying the "spirit of the truth" in a popular entertainment required a certain amount of manipulation of historical fact.[29] Cherokees would have to trust in the Carolina Playmakers' ability to appeal to a mass audience, even if that meant distorting tribal history. The Eastern Band acted as a necessary partner in the creation of the CHA and *Unto These Hills*, but it was not the guiding hand. It made a crucial investment in the project, in the form of Cherokee land and a tacit endorsement of the association's use of tribal history and the Cherokee image. The drama, however, would be a non-Indian entertainment produced for a predominantly white audience, its authors more concerned with telling a story about the United States than about the Cherokees.

"We Are Americans!"

In developing the outdoor historical drama as a genre, the Carolina Play-makers attempted to create a patriotic theater of the people. They sought to fashion popular entertainment that would inspire faith in democracy and the nation, with a particular emphasis on early American history and the founding of communities and national institutions. In writing *The Lost Colony*, for instance, Paul Green celebrated the pioneer spirit of the Roanoke settlers, who braved terrible hardship in a strange land in the hope of "building a new nation in a new world."[30] The purpose of the drama was to renew that spirit of sacrifice and commitment in the contemporary audience. "Out of this play," Green wrote, "must come a sustaining faith, their faith, a purified statement of aim and intent, of human purpose, or then all was waste and sacrifice made vain."[31] Writing in the early 1950s, Samuel Selden acknowledged that this style of theater both appealed to Americans and served an important civic purpose. Americans "want to be reminded of those people whose thoughts and actions built the United States," Selden wrote. "In a period of cynicism and discouragement, especially, when our lives seem to be hemmed in on every side, we need to be reassured of the brave spirit which gave our early nation strength."[32] If successful, then, a historical drama would allow audience members to share in the "brave spirit" of their forebears, encouraging them to recommit themselves to American principles of freedom and democracy.

This style of popular culture, which the historian Richard M. Fried calls "patriotic pageantry," spread rapidly during the early stages of the Cold War. Fried uses the term to describe civic rituals, historical commemorations, and other forms of public theater that invited Americans to rededicate themselves to the nation's founding values. Examples of this phenomenon included events like Loyalty Day, the holiday invented by the American Legion to promote public expressions of patriotism, and enterprises like the Freedom Train, the popular exhibit of significant documents and other Americana that traveled the nation by rail in the late 1940s. Patriotic pageantry reflected a widespread anxiety that Americans might grow complacent during the Cold War, taking freedom and democracy for granted. Pageantry allowed Americans to renew their devotion to the United States, keeping them prepared ideologically for the struggle against communism.[33] The Carolina Playmakers' outdoor dramas offered audiences a similar experience of renewal, even if they lacked the paranoia and explicit politics of an event like Loyalty Day. They invited audiences to share in the spirit of early American founders, refreshing their faith in the nation and its democratic system. Writing in the early 1950s, Kermit Hunter suggested that a good historical drama could offer Americans moral clarity during the Cold War, making a fear of communism unnecessary. "One cannot imagine Jackson, or Jefferson, or Lincoln, or Daniel Webster being *afraid* of communism," he explained, "because they were too solidly convinced of the efficacy of democracy; for this reason it is good for us today to re-examine the beliefs and ideals of such men."[34]

This faith in American founders, however, posed an obvious problem when it came to the play the CHA proposed for the Qualla Boundary. If the drama were to focus on the Cherokees and the Trail of Tears, would not the founders and early American settlers provide the villains of the piece? Could the drama make sympathetic heroes of the Cherokees while still celebrating the nation that drove them west? Hunter resolved this dilemma by making *Unto These Hills* a story about America's struggle to overcome racial hatred, rather than a story of Cherokee resistance. In the play, the Cherokees suffer terribly at the hands of greedy, hateful whites, but they seldom retaliate, choosing instead to seek peace and friendship with the settlers. Along the way they find white allies who aid their efforts to remain in the mountains. While most Cherokees experience exile, some manage to stay, and gradually the newcomers accept them. In the end, the Cherokees become American citizens, their goodwill and forbearance rewarded with participation in the United States. Early frontier whites, then, do serve as the villains of Hunter's drama, but America remains innocent. The "basic thesis of the play," Selden observed, was that "different people of a growing country must learn to live together."[35] By the end of the drama, both Cherokees and their non-Indian neighbors understand that lesson, which allows *Unto These Hills* to remain a celebration of democracy and American nationhood. It is also a celebration of Indian assimilation. In the end, the peace and freedom Cherokees seek throughout the story can be secured only if they become Americans, rather than remain a distinct Indian people and an indigenous nation.

The opening of the drama portrays Cherokees as primitive, but content, a simple community living tranquilly in a bountiful environment. The play's first scene shows a busy Indian village, with frolicking children, women preparing food, and hunters mending their weapons. Dancers celebrate the harvest, giving thanks and showing the Cherokees' "deep kinship with the eternal God." A benevolent chief watches the scene from a raised chair. "In the beginning was the land," the Narrator intones. "In the beginning was freedom. . . . In the beginning was peace."[36] The arrival of Europeans disrupts this serenity, as "a seething tide of strange men with pale faces and restless hands" breaks across the Indian world. In the drama, Hernando de Soto represents the earliest arrivals. He and his men march into the village and immediately demand gold from the Cherokees. "Do as they say," Soto's Indian translator implores the chief, "or they will kill you!" The Cherokees manage to convince the Spanish to continue on their way, explaining that "the only gold we have is in the yellow cornfields." Still, the invasion has begun. "The white men kept coming."[37]

Hunter then moves the action forward several centuries to 1811. Tecumseh has arrived in the Cherokee country, seeking warriors to join his alliance against the United States. In the play, this scene represents a test of the Cherokees' inherent love of peace. "Like all who live close to the earth," the Narrator explains, "they had learned that no matter what a man's race or color might be, it is better to live with him in friendliness, because hatred bites into the souls of men."[38] Tecumseh, however, despises the whites, and, knowing that Cherokees, like all Indians, have suffered at the hands of the invaders, he tries to convince them to join him in an all-out war against the Americans. In the Cherokee council, Junaluska urges his people to refuse Tecumseh's offer, but White Path, whose own parents were killed by settlers, longs for war. "Here in the mountains you talk of peace," White Path exclaims, "but in Georgia the Cherokee are treated like animals! We must kill!"[39] For a time, it seems that White Path will carry the debate, but then Sequoyah arrives to save the day. In the drama, Sequoyah represents the "civilized" Cherokee. He is a Christian and understands "the wisdom of the white man," and he has started on his great invention of the syllabary. He reminds the council that Cherokees have already benefited from the presence of Europeans. "Years ago we lived in caves and grass huts—today we build warm houses," he observes. "Many times we used to starve through the long winter—now we plant big fields of corn and potatoes, and store food in barns for the winter. Our fathers prayed to the spirits of these mountains—now we go to church and worship the Christian God. *Where did the Red Man learn these things?*" Whites have brought the Cherokees many good things, Sequoyah explains, and, at any rate, Indians cannot hope to defeat the invaders. The only way forward is to avoid hostility and join the newcomers. "A good man never screams for revenge—he labors for peace!" he declares. "We are not Red Men! We are Americans!"[40]

Sequoyah plays the role of prophet in *Unto These Hills*. Understanding the whites, he knows that his people's destiny is to become part of the nation growing up around the Cherokees. At the end of the scene with Tecumseh, he swears an oath to live in peace with the Americans and convinces the rest of the Cherokee leaders (except White Path) to do the same. "You have taken the white man as your brother," he tells the council. "Let no man forget this day!"[41] The Cherokees keep their promise, the Narrator explains, and gradually some Americans begin to accept them. "With bitter self-denial and with strong determination, the Cherokee finally made their way into the confidence of the white men."[42] When the United States goes to war against the Creeks, the Cherokees join Andrew Jackson's army, taking up arms "against their own race." Junaluska even saves Andrew Jackson's life at the Battle of Horseshoe Bend. As time goes on, however, the Cherokees find themselves increasingly hemmed in by settlers. While they have gained friends among the newcomers, most Americans on the frontier remain hostile. As the Narrator explains, the Cherokees' "honest efforts to be friendly and peaceable seemed to be met more and more with greed and corruption—and hatred."[43] Finally, gold is discovered in northern Georgia. Disreputable prospectors pour into the Cherokee country, and the American government concludes that the Cherokees must give up their homes and go west.[44]

The drama covers the politics of removal in two scenes. The first shows the American agent John Schermerhorn working to negotiate a removal treaty with Cherokee leaders. Most refuse, but Elias Boudinot agrees to sign, hoping his people can find peace in the West, away from greedy frontier Americans. In the second, Junaluska and John Ross visit Washington to reason with Andrew Jackson, now the president. Boudinot and a small number of others have signed the Treaty of New Echota, but most Cherokees remain opposed to removal. Daniel Webster and Sam Houston appear in the scene, urging Jackson to repudiate the treaty. Junaluska, meanwhile, begs Jackson to protect the Cherokees, who are under assault by frontier whites. "My people are not safe in their homes!," Junaluska insists. "The very lowest classes of white men break in and beat our people with hickories, cowhides, and clubs!" Jackson, of course, refuses to listen. "Mr. Webster and his Whigs in the Senate can preach all day about justice, humanity, and civil rights—but the Cherokees have been offered a fair price—they voted to sell—and that's that!"[45]

As in earlier pageants, the story of Tsali's martyrdom provides the play's dramatic climax. It is the summer of 1838, and American soldiers have arrived to gather Cherokees for removal, imprisoning them in a stockade. Some go willingly, but others flee to hide in the mountains. Tsali has played a small role in earlier stages of the drama. He goes to war against the Creeks with Junaluska and fights at Horseshoe Bend, and several scenes introduce his wife, Wilani, and their children.[46] Now, as the family is conducted to the stockade, Wilani stumbles and drops her pack. A drunk soldier kills her with a blow to the head from the butt of his musket. Tsali leaps on the soldier and beats him to death with a rock, and he and his sons run from the stage. The soldiers want to hunt the family down, along with all of the other Cherokees still in hiding, but Junaluska makes a deal with their commander. If Tsali and his sons will give themselves up and face execution for the killing of the soldier, the army will depart, allowing any Cherokees still at large to remain in western North Carolina. Drowning Bear and Will Holland Thomas deliver the message, reminding Tsali that the Cherokees promised to live in peace with the whites. Back in the village, as a column of imprisoned Cherokees prepare to depart for the West, Tsali and his sons arrive and surrender. The Cherokees sing "Amazing Grace," and Elias Boudinot recites the 121st Psalm in Cherokee (translated into English by the Narrator). Tsali is led away and shot offstage.[47]

In drama's final scenes, the audience learns of the consequences of Tsali's sacrifice and of the realization of Sequoyah's vision of peace between Cherokees and whites. In Washington, Drowning Bear and Will Holland Thomas visit a new president, William Henry Harrison, asking him to grant the Cherokees American citizenship and to help them secure a reservation. "The Indian will never be safe until he is part of the government, like the white man himself," Drowning Bear pleads. "The day of the Red Man is passing. Sequoyah knew it thirty years ago. Junaluska told us that before he went into the West. Now Drowning Bear can see it too." The Cherokees' best hope lies in joining the United States.[48] Daniel Webster supports their request, insisting that the removal was a mistake and noting that "the ones who stayed behind have become part of the civilization of the whites."[49] Harrison is unsure if Americans will accept citizenship for Indians, but he is willing to work toward that goal. "Democratic government means nothing, as long as races continue to hate each other!" he declares. "I want Indians to become citizens, and Negroes too." He promises that the Cherokees will have the federal government's support.[50] Meanwhile, back in North Carolina, the Cherokees and local whites are holding a frontier dance, illustrating that they have indeed learned to live together. They are celebrating the birth of a child to Tsali's daughter and Drowning Bear's son. In the midst of the revelry, Junaluska, now an old man, returns home, having walked from Indian Territory back to the mountains. Drowning Bear tells him the good news, that the Cherokees are now safe in North Carolina, happy and at peace once more. "Now Tsali has a grandchild," Junaluska muses. "Tsali's grandchild will someday be an American citizen. Now Tsali lives again!"[51] As the music swells, and light floods the mountainside behind the stage, the Narrator offers a departing message.

> Once upon a time, out of the darkness of tragedy, a race of people looked beyond the years and devoted itself to the dream of its great leader, when he said, "It is not that a man's skin is black, or red, or white. Choose the way of peace. Take all men as your brothers."
> This, then, was the dream of the Cherokee.
> This, then, is America![52]

The drama thus ends on a triumphant note, in spite of Tsali's death and the removal of most of the Cherokee people. The victory, however, belongs less to the Cherokees than to the United States. Through their suffering and patient sacrifice, as well as their heartfelt desire to become citizens, the Cherokees have helped white Americans become more tolerant. They have shown the newcomers (and the audience) that people of different races can coexist in a democracy. Tolerance and understanding, the drama suggests, form the nation's true spirit. Daniel Webster and Sam Houston embody that democratic faith, as does a character named Major Davis, the officer in charge of carrying out removal in Junaluska's part of the mountains. Davis knows that removal is wrong. He performs his duty to expel the Cherokees, but, by the end of the play, he befriends those who remain in North Carolina. He even helps Will Holland Thomas buy land for Drowning Bear and his people.[53] The drama, then, manages to redeem the nation that dispossessed the Cherokees, even as it laments the Indians' loss.

Hunter achieves this maneuver by making removal a question of race and prejudice, rather than property and colonialism. Wicked frontier whites persecute the Cherokees because they cannot accept Indians as human beings equal to themselves. True, they covet Indian land, but the key problem, the drama suggests, is racial hatred. The Cherokees, meanwhile, want to assimilate into the United States. The wisest among them, like Hunter's version of Sequoyah, know that joining America is their destiny. In the drama, Cherokees struggle to maintain their commitment to peace, while convincing white Americans that they deserve to be equal participants in the new republic. They do not attempt to maintain a distinct tribal community or their own nationhood. Like most of the commemorations discussed in earlier chapters, the drama takes for granted American domination of the continent and the replacement of Indian nations with settler communities. The question is whether the United States will accept Indian people and permit them to assimilate once its domination is complete. Making removal a story about racial hatred allows Hunter to define the Trail of Tears as a tragic mistake, a violation of America's true spirit and principles. The play can then recognize that error, advocate tolerance, and, in doing so, celebrate the nation. The audience sympathizes with the much-abused Cherokees, while still experiencing the renewal of democratic faith authors like Hunter and Paul Green hoped to inspire through this new form of popular theater.

The drama's focus on racial prejudice reflected the emerging struggle over African American civil rights in the postwar era. Hunter's script did not acknowledge that context, except in the brief moment when President Harrison declares that "Negroes too" should one day be citizens. Nor did it note the presence of African American slaves in the removal-era Cherokee Nation. Like Georgia's commemoration at New Echota, however, *Unto These Hills* provided a public memory of Indian removal that resonated with the South's most important contemporary political issue. The play, meanwhile, reassured audiences that American race relations had improved over time and would continue to do so. Like the USIA broadcasts mentioned in chapter 4, *Unto These Hills* acknowledged America's history of racial oppression, while insisting that the United States had made steady progress toward the thorough realization of its founding ideals. This idea of the nation implied that African Americans would *someday* enjoy the full rights of citizenship, although it suggested that such equality would arrive only gradually. Like the Cherokees in the play, African Americans would have to suffer patiently, waiting for the slow perfection of American democracy. *Unto These Hills* turned the Trail of Tears into a celebration of Cherokee Americanness and an endorsement of Indian assimilation. In doing so, it anticipated moderate progress toward racial equality in the modern South.

The CHA underlined the drama's message of friendship and reconciliation in a remarkable publicity tour, mounted in preparation for the play's second season. In May 1951, a delegation of Cherokees, led by Assistant Principal Chief MacKinley Ross, retraced the Trail of Tears, following the main overland route used by Cherokees during the winter of 1838–1839. Organized by John Parris, a journalist working as the CHA's publicity director, the group included Arsene Thompson, who played Elias Boudinot in the drama, and Joseph Washington, a direct descendant of Tsali. They traveled through Tennessee, western Kentucky, southern Illinois, Missouri, and northwestern Arkansas, before arriving in eastern Oklahoma and the homeland of the Cherokee Nation. Pausing at dozens of towns along the way, they invited members of local communities to visit Cherokee that summer and attend a performance of *Unto These Hills*. Ross presented local dignitaries with white clay pipes, symbolizing friendship, and the delegates thanked the onlookers for kindness shown to Cherokees as they passed through during the removal. The gift of the pipes expressed the drama's main theme of peace and brotherhood among races. According to Parris, the trip was a resounding success. Large crowds greeted the visitors, and the local press gave them admiring coverage.[54]

In Oklahoma, the delegates visited the Will Rogers memorial in Claremore, where they sprinkled Rogers's grave with soil brought from the Qualla Boundary. The widow of Jesse Bartley Milam, the recently deceased chief of the Cherokee Nation, presented the visitors with a flag bearing the Cherokee Nation seal, which the delegates promised to fly at the Mountainside Theater when they returned home. From Claremore, they traveled to Oklahoma City, where they visited the state capitol and met with Governor Johnston Murray, who promised to visit Cherokee and take in a performance of the drama later that year.[55] During their time in Oklahoma, the delegates also arranged to receive coals from the sacred fire kept by one of the traditional Cherokee ceremonial grounds. According to Parris, the coals came from Stokes Smith, a significant leader among adherents to the Cherokees' traditional religion. The visitors brought the coals back to North Carolina, rekindling the fire and using it to light a gas flame at the Mountainside Theater on the night of the first performance of the 1951 season. Like the white clay pipes distributed by MacKinley Ross, the CHA turned the fire into an expression of the drama's message of universal brotherhood. On opening night, Chief Henry Bradley and Harry Buchanan, the CHA president, lit the flame together, creating what Parris called "a blazing symbol that men of two races can live side by side in friendship and peace."[56]

Tourism and Termination

By all accounts, *Unto These Hills* proved a spectacular success. More than 100,000 people saw the show in its first season from July through early September 1950, and attendance rose to around 150,000 the following summer. Those numbers surpassed attendance for *The Lost Colony* and for Paul Green's second outdoor drama, *The Common Glory*, a play about the American Revolution staged at Williamsburg. Over the next decade, attendance for *Unto These Hills* averaged about 130,000 each year.[57] The CHA paid off its debt after only one season, and its leaders quickly made plans to expand their operations. In 1951, the association began work on a living history museum, named the Oconaluftee Indian Village, depicting Cherokee life in the mid-eighteenth century. A year later, it purchased a privately owned museum with an extensive archeological collection, the Museum of the Cherokee Indian. Like the drama, the village and the museum proved popular and profitable.[58] Thanks to the CHA, the *State* magazine crowed, Cherokee was quickly becoming "the biggest single travel goal in North Carolina."[59] Indian agent Joe Jennings was even more enthusiastic, calling *Unto These Hills* the "greatest thing [that has] happened to the Cherokee Band since its start."[60]

The striking success of *Unto These Hills*, however, immediately raised questions about the extent to which Cherokee people benefited from the CHA's operations. White businessmen ran the association, after all, and the drama employed relatively few citizens of the Eastern Band. The association profited from its use of Cherokee history, but what did the tribe gain? In 1951, doubts like these inspired Cherokees to circulate a petition calling upon the CHA to transfer 10 percent of the earnings from *Unto These Hills* directly to the Eastern Band. The tribe could then use these funds to support better social services for the Cherokee community. The petition also demanded that the CHA employ more Cherokees.[61] The *State* criticized this development, insisting that Indians were already the greatest beneficiaries of the drama. Some Cherokees, the magazine remarked in a patronizing tone, had forgotten how diligently men of vision like Harry Buchanan had worked to create *Unto These Hills*. "From start to finish the idea, planning and execution of the pageant came from those who had a broader goal in view than the creation of a public grab-bag."[62] The CHA rejected the call for direct payments to the tribe, but it did make an effort to convince Cherokees that its presence contributed to the tribal community's well-being. It promised to hire as many Cherokees as possible, and it engaged in public good works, like the establishment of a scholarship program for Cherokee students. An official history of the WNCAC described the association in terms more appropriate to a charity than a tourism enterprise. "There is good reason to think that the Drama has renewed the Cherokees' pride in themselves," the authors observed. "Certainly it has tended to bring them out of the backwater in which they have lived for many scores of years."[63] The tribal government, meanwhile, managed to acquire a more direct benefit from the CHA. In the early 1950s, led by Chief Osley Saunooke, the Eastern Band secured an exemption from North Carolina's state sales tax for businesses on tribal land. It then established its own, identical levy, with the revenue going to fund tribal services. In the first years of the levy, the CHA was the single largest payer of this tax, providing close to a third of the revenue generated.[64]

During this same period, the CHA, and tourism generally, became part of an even more significant political issue, the question of whether the federal government would apply the termination policy to the Eastern Band. Termination was the post–World War II campaign to end the separate status of Indian tribes and, in the process, disentangle the federal government from Indian affairs. Terminating a tribe involved removing the trust status of reservation lands, dissolving the tribal government, and withdrawing special federal services from the Indian community.[65] As the federal government retreated, reservations would become subject to state regulation. States would extend civil and criminal jurisdiction over tribal lands within their borders, and state and county governments would assume responsibility for services like education. During this same period, under the policy known as relocation, the BIA encouraged Native Americans to migrate to cities, where presumably they would find greater economic opportunities than on rural reservations.[66] Together, these initiatives amounted to a comprehensive effort to end the special relationship between Indian nations and the United States.

For their supporters, these policies promised to bestow full equality upon Indian people by freeing them from a debilitating federal guardianship. Many Indian people, however, viewed the postwar policies as a renewed push for total assimilation and an attempt to destroy what remained of tribal landholdings. Relocation, they worried, would erode tribal communities, while termination would leave reservation lands subject to state and local taxation, which might compel the sale of tribal property. In seeking to eliminate tribal dependency, it appeared, the federal government had decided to eliminate the tribes. Those fears, along with the impoverishment suffered by communities that experienced termination, sparked a political response among Native Americans that proved to be as significant as the policies themselves. Individual tribes resisted government efforts to terminate them, while the National Congress of American Indians (NCAI) mounted a campaign to convince federal lawmakers to repudiate the policy. NCAI denounced termination as an abandonment of U.S. treaty obligations and an expression of colonialism, and it detailed the economic hardship that followed the policy's implementation. Some activists, meanwhile, began to insist that any alternative to termination should start with a stronger commitment to tribal self-government.[67]

In western North Carolina, the postwar expansion of the tourism industry provided arguments both for and against termination. Thanks to
tourism, North Carolina Cherokees appeared to enjoy greater economic
opportunities than did other tribes, suggesting they could prosper outside
of the federal trust relationship. At the same time, the fact that the Qualla
Boundary itself was a tourist attraction meant that business and civic leaders in the region found value in the Cherokees' tribal status and worried
that changes in Indian policy might disrupt this important element of the
mountain economy. Cherokee termination, they feared, might undermine
not only the tribal community, but the region as a whole. *Unto These Hills*
bore a similarly contradictory relationship to termination. While Kermit
Hunter's drama broadcast an assimilationist version of Cherokee history, the
success of *Unto These Hills* helped Cherokees thwart assimilationist policies
in the present.

In the late 1940s, federal officials identified the Eastern Band as a potential candidate for termination. In 1947, the BIA produced a report evaluat-
ing tribes' readiness for the removal of federal protection and services. The
bureau placed Indian communities in three categories: tribes it could terminate immediately; those that would be ready for termination within two
to ten years; and, finally, tribes whom the bureau would keep under federal supervision for the foreseeable future. The Eastern Band appeared in
the second group: federal investigators deemed the Cherokees substantially
acculturated to mainstream American society and almost prepared to stand
on their own.[68] Later that same year, North Carolina's state assembly considered a bill requesting an end to federal supervision over the Eastern Band,
a change amounting to a significant step toward termination. The bill failed
to make it out of committee, thanks in part to disapproval expressed by
tribal leaders, but the threat of a federal withdrawal remained. In the early
1950s, the BIA began negotiating the transfer of specific tribal services, such
as health care, away from federal responsibility. It also worked to persuade
state and local governments to take charge of Cherokee education. While
the Eastern Band did not face the kind of highly coercive termination effort suffered by tribes like the Klamath and Menominee, the bureau clearly
did intend to implement some form of the policy in the Cherokee country.[69]

The Eastern Band's elected leaders opposed termination, fearing that the
withdrawal of the federal government would lead to a loss of tribal land
and the erosion of the Cherokee community. "With the Cherokees," Joe Jennings reported, "the objection to Government withdrawal is not so much
because they do not want to pay taxes on their land, as the fear that with-

out Government help they may be cheated out of their land or otherwise become landless." In addition, "they do not want to lose the Government health, education, and agricultural services which they now enjoy."[70] Discussion of the termination policy in the press inspired great anxiety among tribal members, according to witnesses who spoke at a 1955 congressional hearing. Cherokees worried that the new policy was simply another effort to strip their people of their remaining property, or, as one witness put it, "get land divided up [so] white man can then buy up everything."[71] White Walkingstick, a former member of the tribal council, explained that most Cherokees preferred to keep the land in its current status. "It was put in there several years ago to protect Indians from white man coming in taking land," he recalled. "At that time, the Indians saw fit to put it in trust to United States Government and these fullblood Indians live peacefully under that today." Walkingstick urged federal authorities to continue the trust for at least another twenty-five years before they considered terminating the Eastern Band.[72] Cherokees needed greater economic opportunities, witnesses at the hearing recognized, but they hoped to pursue economic development while maintaining their current relationship with the federal government.[73]

A small segment of the tribe, however, supported the policy, finding in termination an opportunity to escape what they considered the oppressive paternalism of the BIA. The most prominent of these Cherokees was Fred Bauer, a former assistant principal chief of the Eastern Band, who advocated the abolition of the BIA and the immediate removal of trust status from tribal lands. The bureau, he believed, reduced Indian people to permanent wards of the government, keeping them poor and backward and preventing them from participating fully in American life. Cherokees and other Indians needed to become equal citizens of the United States, even if it meant the loss of some tribal property. In the 1930s, Bauer attacked John Collier's reform effort in Indian affairs as a socialist plot, and he helped to prevent the Eastern Band from adopting a new constitution under the Indian Reorganization Act. After World War II, he saw the emergence of the termination policy as an opportunity to revive his campaign against the BIA, liberating his people at last.[74] For Bauer and his allies, the tourism boom provided evidence that Cherokees could prosper, if only the federal government would let them run their own affairs. Trust status and BIA regulations limited the development of tribal land, they observed, preventing Cherokees from exploiting the economic opportunities afforded by the multitude of visitors passing through their community. Like members of the WNCAC, they regretted that towns like Gatlinburg, on the Tennessee side of the national park, offered better amenities than those available in western North Carolina. That situation would change, they argued, if the Cherokees freed themselves from their injurious relationship with the federal government. Termination would allow free enterprise to bloom on the Qualla Boundary.[75]

The positions taken by Bauer and his associates echoed the arguments of termination advocates nationally, who likewise defined the policy as a crusade for Indian liberty. One of the policy's great champions, for instance, famously likened termination to the abolition of slavery during the Civil War era. "Following in the footsteps of the Emancipation Proclamation," Senator Arthur V. Watkins wrote in 1957, "I see the following words emblazoned in letters of fire above the heads of the Indians—THESE PEOPLE SHALL BE FREE!"[76] Termination promised to grant Indian people equality within the United States by ending failed practices of federal guardianship. Living as wards of the United States, advocates like Watkins reasoned, kept Native Americans poor and powerless. Removing that status would allow them to join American society's prosperous mainstream. The Cold War frequently colored these arguments. Termination would bring Indians the full benefits of individual freedom and capitalist prosperity, values cold warriors associated with the United States in its international struggle. The policy, moreover, would end a form of collective landowning on reservations that, to some, looked like homegrown communism. While Cherokees like Bauer represented a minority within the Eastern Band, many federal officials and policy makers shared their basic outlook on American Indian affairs.[77]

In arguing for the emancipation of the Eastern Band, protermination Cherokees invoked their community's origins in the removal era, finding additional arguments for termination in their people's unique history. The Cherokees who founded Qualla, they noted, separated from the Cherokee Nation long before the Treaty of New Echota. They accepted North Carolina citizenship in order to remain on their preferred lands, following the treaties of 1817 and 1819. After removal, William Holland Thomas helped them purchase their land, but that property never constituted a reservation like those the federal government assigned to other tribes. By right, these Cherokee citizens should never have fallen under the BIA's authority in the first place. Following the Civil War, however, the federal government took control of the affairs of eastern Cherokees, under the flawed assumption that they were no different from the Indians of the West. Federal officials transformed these American citizens into wards. In the twentieth century, the BIA then perpetuated this error, in the interest of maintaining its power. For termination supporters, the policy provided an opportunity to correct this terrible mistake, returning the Cherokees of North Carolina to their rightful position as free American citizens.[78]

Toward the end of his life, Fred Bauer published a history of the Eastern Band that contrasted this account of Cherokee citizenship with the romantic story of Tsali's martyrdom, which Bauer called the "Mooney Myth." The writings of anthropologist James Mooney, he noted, first popularized the notion that the United States permitted Cherokees to remain in North Carolina as a consequence of Tsali's surrender and execution. This story hid the fact that the Cherokees at Qualla already held American citizenship at the time of Tsali's death. *Unto These Hills* perpetuated the Mooney Myth, broadcasting it to millions of visitors who knew little else of Cherokee history. It also misled many Cherokees about the origins of their community. The popularity of the drama, Bauer suggested, had the effect of strengthening those in the BIA who wanted to keep Cherokees as wards. "Our true early history should be our guide for the future, instead of a Myth portraying us as refugees being *given a reservation*," he wrote (emphasis in the original). "We were given nothing. We bought back a part of what Indians had given Caucasian settlers. We paid too much in gold and trouble for these lands, to find ourselves now demoted to mere *users* with *illusory possessory rights*."[79] North Carolina Cherokees were not a tribal people, Bauer insisted, but a community of American citizens held captive in a tribal status.

In some respects, *Unto These Hills* supported Bauer's view of Indian affairs, the Mooney Myth notwithstanding. As a work that celebrated Cherokee assimilation, the drama echoed the arguments used by termination advocates. In the play, Cherokees ask for citizenship and declare their destiny to be equal participation in the United States—precisely what Bauer and other termination supporters said they wanted for the Cherokee community. Tsali's sacrifice not only helps Cherokees remain in North Carolina but grants them an opportunity to become Americans. Drowning Bear asks the president to assign his people a reservation, but no one in the play says anything about trust status for Cherokee land or federal services for Indian communities. Cherokee characters do not discuss tribal self-government, other than with a brief mention of the Cherokees' preremoval constitution, and the drama does not depict the Eastern Band as a distinct Indian nation. In and of itself, *Unto These Hills* offers little to refute the logic of the termination campaign. Rooted in the same Cold War culture that informed the policy, the drama can only imagine a future in which Cherokees become more thoroughly integrated into the dominant society.

The popularity of *Unto These Hills*, however, helped the Eastern Band avoid termination. As the historian John Finger suggests, the postwar tourism boom made non-Indians wary of proposals to alter the Eastern Band's status. The success of the drama and the CHA's other projects reminded local whites of the tribe's commercial value as a tourist attraction, and they wanted that value preserved. In different circumstances, business leaders like the members of the WNCAC might reasonably have hoped to benefit from the removal of federal trust protection from tribal property. Termination would have eliminated barriers to developing the land and might have led to the sale of some or all of it. Instead, they worried that termination might undermine one of the region's great draws. As Joe Jennings reported, "many white leaders realize that the reservation is an asset to the State of North Carolina as well as to the Cherokees, and they are concerned lest in any withdrawal program the reservation will be broken up and the Cherokees lose their best chance for economic security along with their land."[80] The CHA's Harry Buchanan promised that the historical association would help the Eastern Band resist any federal policy that Cherokees deemed threatening. In the early 1950s, the CHA proposed a community development program for the Cherokees that sought to maintain collective ownership of tribal property, even if the BIA withdrew.[81] Fred Bauer, for his part, recognized the CHA as a key obstacle to termination. Men like Buchanan knew that their continued commercial success depended upon the maintenance of the status quo in Cherokee, so they encouraged both Indians and local whites to believe that termination represented a threat to the tourism industry. Bauer, of course, saw a sinister motive in the CHA's opposition to federal withdrawal. Buchanan and his colleagues, he suggested, simply wanted to maintain their own power on the Qualla Boundary and the CHA's dominant position in tourism development, not caring whether their enterprise benefited the Cherokees themselves.[82]

The sympathetic portrayal of the Cherokees by *Unto These Hills* also helped mitigate the threat of federal withdrawal. Hunter's play depicted the Cherokees as a peaceful, blameless people subjected to repeated wrongs by white Americans and the government of the United States. Applied to the politics of the postwar era, this version of Cherokee history suggested that, at a minimum, federal authorities should refrain from coercion in their dealings with the tribe. While the drama praised Cherokee assimilation, it also implied that it would be wrong to assimilate Cherokees by force. When federal authorities tried to impose new policies on the Eastern Band, they could appear to be repeating the mistakes of the past. In 1954, for instance, news that the BIA planned to close its agency in Cherokee drew angry de-nunciations, as the media in western North Carolina speculated that it her-alded an end to federal services for the Indian community. The *Asheville Citizen* warned of "another Trail of Tears" and insisted that an event like removal must never again take place.[83] The *State* concurred, worrying that, in termination, the Cherokees faced a "second Great Removal," this one coming "just as the tourists discover them."[84] The BIA quickly backtracked, insisting that it never intended to dismantle the Cherokee agency and that it merely sought to shift oversight of the Qualla Boundary office to a differ-ent regional division.[85] The controversy, however, illustrated the extent to which Cherokee history, popularized through tourism, could inform politi-cal debate in the termination era. Like many non-Indians, the editors of the *State* and the *Asheville Citizen* supported the general idea of termination and the goal of drawing Indian people more thoroughly into mainstream Amer-ican life. Yet they adamantly opposed any policy that looked as if it might bring about "another Trail of Tears." This phenomenon suggests that the memory of removal, reinforced each summer at the Mountainside Theater, represented a political resource for North Carolina Cherokees, as they ne-gotiated the dangerous politics of postwar Indian affairs. Cherokees and non-Indians agreed that removal was a tragedy and a crime, and they agreed that one could judge new policy initiatives in light of that historical aware-ness. As a consequence, Cherokees possessed, in this shared memory, a ready-made argument against any political action they considered threat-ening or ill advised.

The tourism boom by itself did not decide the termination issue in west-ern North Carolina. Several additional factors complicated the BIA's efforts to apply the policy to the Eastern Band. For one thing, the status of Chero-kee land proved confusing. The federal government held tribal property in trust, but the land also fell within the terms of the Eastern Band's corpo-rate charter from North Carolina. Changes in the status of tribal property would likely require both state and federal legislation, as well as tribal con-sent.[86] Western North Carolina, meanwhile, remained a relatively poor re-gion, raising doubts about the ability of surrounding communities to extend services to the Cherokees as the BIA withdrew. Education proved especially problematic. While some Cherokees already attended public schools in non-Indian communities, the local school systems lacked sufficient resources to educate all Eastern Band students.[87] Growing tension over school desegre-gation in the South further complicated the issue. In the era of massive re-sistance, the BIA's education officials worried that white schools would refuse to enroll Cherokees or that white racism would make attending those schools unbearable for Indian students. By the mid-1950s, the bureau halted its formal effort to withdraw from Cherokee education, although it still encouraged Cherokee families to enroll their children in off-reservation schools when possible.[88] For a variety of reasons, then, the Eastern Band proved a much greater challenge to the termination policy than BIA personnel initially estimated. John Finger, however, argues that concerns about tourism provided the single greatest obstacle to the policy. Both Cherokees and whites agreed that tourism provided the most likely foundation for prosperity in the region, and they recognized the significance of the Cherokee community as a tourist draw. White observers might have assumed that something like termination would eventually take place, but, for the immediate future, they preferred to avoid changes that could have negative consequences for the region's biggest business. That hesitation, coupled with the Eastern Band's opposition, kept the policy at bay in western North Carolina through the worst years of the termination campaign.[89]

Unto These Hills and southern Appalachian tourism offer a striking example of the ambivalence American culture has often displayed toward Indian peoples, an ambivalence rooted in the conception of Indians as a vanishing race. In Hunter's drama, the Trail of Tears remained a story about Indian disappearance. The play defined the Eastern Band as a relic and an anomaly, an Indian tribe whose persistence in the Southeast was unexpected. *Unto These Hills*, moreover, reassured audiences that Cherokees wanted to assimilate, in spite of their long history of abuse by white settlers and the American government. As Drowning Bear declares in the play, "the day of the Red Man is passing." Yet the Eastern Band's value to the tourism economy lay in their continued difference from other Americans and their possession of a unique status within the United States. Non-Indians prized the rare otherness of Native people, even as they favored policies that would erase Native American distinctiveness. The popularity of *Unto These Hills* testified to the first part of that contradiction, even as the drama's narrative often reflected the second. In the 1950s, the commercial value of Indianness proved high enough to help Cherokees mitigate the threat of termination. Cherokee heritage, made lucrative through tourism, became an argument against the federal government's postwar assimilation campaign.

6 The Remembered Community

Public Memory and the Reemergence of the Cherokee Nation in Oklahoma

. . . .

In western North Carolina, a popular play about the Trail of Tears, and the tourism industry that produced it, helped the Eastern Band of Cherokee Indians avoid the worst consequences of the postwar termination policy. In Oklahoma, a different story unfolded. Here, a version of tribal history informed the reconstruction of a Cherokee national government. The United States dismantled the Cherokee Nation's political system at the turn of the twentieth century, when it forced Cherokees to accept allotment and Oklahoma statehood. In essence, the federal government terminated Oklahoma Cherokees long before that expression entered the language of American Indian policy. By the mid-twentieth century, however, Cherokees began to reestablish a tribal administration, creating new institutions to provide services to Cherokees and to mediate between the Cherokee population and state and federal officials. By the mid-1970s, this new administration evolved into a full-fledged tribal government under a new Cherokee constitution.

Public memory contributed to these developments in several important ways. As Cherokee leaders established new tribal services, they sponsored public history projects devoted to the memory of the old Cherokee Nation. They created a yearly Cherokee holiday and developed a historical society modeled on the Cherokee Historical Association in North Carolina. They even produced an outdoor drama, engaging Kermit Hunter to write a sequel to *Unto These Hills*. These projects were tourism ventures, but they also bore political meaning. Tribal leaders invoked their people's nineteenth-century achievements as a means of promoting political cooperation among Cherokees. In particular, they pointed to the rebuilding of the Cherokee Nation after the Trail of Tears as a model for contemporary action. They also used the memory of the Indian republic to bolster their own legitimacy as tribal representatives, offering themselves as heirs to leaders like John Ross. They depicted their work as a campaign to restore the Cherokees' nineteenth-century greatness, applying tribal history to the task of building a modern Cherokee government.

The people who created this new government were affluent businessmen and professionals, civic leaders who enjoyed good political connections in the state and region. They were of Cherokee descent and took great pride in their Indian identities; however, few belonged to distinctly Native communities. Allotment and Oklahoma statehood opened a substantial gulf between Cherokees who embraced the new order and prospered within it and those who adhered to more traditional economic and cultural practices. While members of the economic elite of the old Cherokee Nation flourished in the new state, allotment drove many culturally traditional people into poverty and rural isolation. The leaders who built the new tribal government came from the former group, and, in most respects, they were indistinguishable from the politicians and businessmen who controlled the rest of Oklahoma. They belonged to the state's political and economic establishment, an establishment built upon the theft and exploitation of Indian property in the decades following allotment. Moreover, these leaders owed their positions as Cherokee representatives to the federal government, rather than to the Cherokee people. Tribal elections ended as part of the allotment process. Federal officials found it expedient to preserve the office of principal chief, but, for most of the twentieth century, the government filled that position by appointment. The American president selected the chief, and the chief received advice and counsel from whomever he chose to consult. This system meant that many Cherokees, especially those in small rural communities, simply did not recognize the individuals whom state and federal authorities considered their leaders, and they had little reason to trust them or affirm their legitimacy.

This arrangement helps to explain why public memory played so significant a role in the creation of a new tribal government. A proud heritage was one of the few things upon which a politically divided Cherokee populace could agree. Cherokee leaders appealed to a common historical identity as a way of encouraging their people to recognize their authority and participate in the creation of new tribal services. They invoked the memory of the reconstruction of the nation after removal as part of a broader effort to overcome the political divisions born of the allotment era. Some Cherokees, however, remained deeply skeptical of this effort, viewing the new tribal government as a vehicle for exploiting Cherokee communities. They saw the appointed leaders as agents of the Oklahoma establishment that defrauded Native people after allotment. These critics also invoked the Cherokee past, but in ways meant to challenge the growing power of the appointed leadership. Allotment and its devastating consequences, then, formed a crucial underlying subject of Cherokee public memory during this era. Historical commemoration became an arena in which Cherokees considered how best to heal the open wounds left by the destruction of the old Indian nation.

Age of the Grafter

The allotment policy sought to end the practice of communal landholding among Native Americans, a change that advocates hoped would prove a catalyst for the thorough assimilation of Indian people. Under the policy, federal officials broke the common lands of a given tribe into individual parcels, which they then distributed among its members. The federal government purchased any "surplus" land and made it available to American citizens. Tribal governments ceased to operate, and states expanded their jurisdictions to include the newly partitioned homelands. The United States held Indian allotments in trust, preventing their sale, but it promised to withdraw that protection eventually. By dividing the common lands, the federal government sought to initiate a process whereby the distinct status of Indian nations within the United States would come to an end.[1]

In the Indian Territory, leaders of the so-called Five Civilized Tribes (Cherokees, Choctaws, Creeks, Chickasaws, and Seminoles) steadfastly opposed allotment throughout the late nineteenth century. They argued that common ownership protected Indian homelands, and they urged the United States to recognize and support their right to self-government. Their people, they insisted, did not want to join a new American state, which non-Indians would surely dominate. The United States, moreover, had promised by treaty never to include the Five Civilized Tribes in a new state without their consent. When allotment bills began to appear in Congress in the late 1870s, the governments of the Five Tribes demanded that their people remain exempt from the policy. As a result of this lobbying, Congress excluded them from the provisions of the 1887 General Allotment Act, also known as the Dawes Act.[2]

This victory, however, proved only temporary, and, in the 1890s, the United States mounted an increasingly forceful effort to persuade the Five Civilized Tribes to accept allotment. In 1893, Congress created the Commission to the Five Civilized Tribes, charged with negotiating allotment agreements with the Cherokees and their neighbors. Commissioners warned tribal leaders that, if they did not cooperate, the United States would eventually impose the policy upon them. Congress then increased the pressure by passing the Curtis Act, which extended provisions of the Dawes Act to the Five Civilized Tribes and placed the Indian Territory under the federal government's legal jurisdiction. Faced with this threat, the tribes' resistance began to erode. By the end of the decade, leaders of the Choctaw, Chickasaw, Creek, and Seminole Nations all signed allotment deals. The Cherokee government held out the longest, but, with the passage of the Curtis Act, tribal leaders realized that allotment was coming, with or without their consent. In 1902, after several years of negotiation, Cherokees approved an allotment agreement.[3] Each tribal citizen would receive a forty-acre "homestead" and seventy acres of "surplus" land. Homesteads would remain untaxed and inalienable for twenty-one years, while surplus would be inalienable for five. The United States would sell the property of the tribal government, and the government itself would cease to exist in 1906.[4]

Despite this agreement, some Cherokees continued to fight the dissolution of the common lands. A portion of the Keetoowah Society, a group representing culturally traditional Cherokee communities, refused to register to receive allotments. Guided by the religious leader Redbird Smith, these "Nighthawk Keetoowahs" dodged federal enrollment officers and urged other Cherokees to reject their individual parcels of land. The United States government responded by dispatching federal marshals to enforce compliance with the 1902 allotment agreement. Smith and other Nighthawks were arrested and jailed in Muskogee, and rumors spread through eastern Oklahoma of an impending Indian "uprising." Smith eventually capitulated, accepting enrollment and encouraging his followers to do likewise. Today, however, some Cherokees remember that a portion of their people continued to resist, refusing allotments even after the Nighthawks began to register. These dissidents, they suggest, avoided enrollment entirely and, in the process, lost their right to claim a section of the fractured homeland.[5]

As resistance to the policy dwindled, a new and even worse struggle began. Many allottees spoke only their tribal language and lacked experience with American law. These factors left them vulnerable to fraud and manipulation as newcomers poured into Oklahoma in search of economic opportunity, and as the Indians' own representative institutions came to an end. Land speculators and other entrepreneurs, aided by officials in the new state and county governments, worked to gain control of as much Native property as possible, setting in motion what historian Angie Debo called an "orgy of plunder and exploitation probably unparalleled in American history."[6] Some "grafters," as they were known, offered to help Indian citizens select their "surplus" land. They then rented the land at very low rates and for very long terms. A careful businessman could assemble groups of contiguous rented allotments, which he could then lease to a third party at a profit. Grafters also worked to thwart restrictions on buying allotted land. When drawing up leases, for instance, they might include provisions allowing the renter to inherit the land upon the death of the allottee. The most egregious frauds involved minors with allotments. In 1908, Congress granted county courts in Oklahoma the authority to appoint guardians to manage Indian minors' property. Grafters promptly turned guardianship into a lucrative business. They found pliable county judges willing to grant them control of Indian children's land. They then leased the allotments for grazing or mineral development, keeping most or all of the proceeds for themselves.[7] Congress, meanwhile, aided the grafters by reducing restrictions on the sale of Indian land. Legislation in 1908 removed all restrictions from allottees considered less than one-half Indian "by blood," declaring their land alienable. For those listed on the rolls as one-half to three-quarters Indian by blood, the same law made surplus land alienable while leaving the homesteads restricted. This act opened a broad new field for the work of the grafters, and much of the newly alienable property passed quickly from the allottees' hands.[8] In the years following statehood, enterprising Oklahomans managed to strip the Five Tribes of much of their property. By 1930, around 1.5 million acres of restricted allotments remained, out of the approximately 20 million acres owned by the Five Tribes at the start of the century.[9]

The grafters often worked openly and enjoyed the approval of many of the new state's residents. Oklahoma's economic future, they reasoned, required the rapid development of the land and its resources. If Indians failed to make adequate use of their property, they should surrender their land for the good of the state. Stealing Native land became a public service, in this way of thinking. "The plunder of Indians," Debo observed, "was so closely joined with pride in the creation of a great new commonwealth that it received little condemnation."[10] Some members of the economic elite of the Five Civilized Tribes shared this outlook, and the grafter ranks included Native people. Oklahoma's first senator, Robert Owen, was a Cherokee citizen who served the tribal government in several capacities prior to allotment. As a federal legislator, Owen pushed for the removal of restrictions on the sale of allotted land, knowing full well that this change would result in the loss of much Cherokee property. Meanwhile, he used his ties to Native communities to assemble a large personal estate, offering to help Indians navigate the allotment process and then buying or leasing their surplus land at a minimal price.[11] Cherokees like Owen stepped directly from the old tribal elite into the highest ranks of political and economic power in Oklahoma, and for some that transition involved cheating their own people. As a Nighthawk Keetoowah leader recalled in the 1920s, the grafter era turned Cherokees against one another, as "a large number of their own blood, who had been fortunate enough to have received the advantages of literary training, now became the allies of the unscrupulous and exploiting hordes."[12]

Cherokee communities survived the grafters, and the allotment campaign failed in its goal of complete assimilation.[13] The policy, however, transformed Cherokee life in lasting ways. The loss of so much property intensified existing class and cultural divisions among Cherokees. Those who spoke English and were familiar with American law and economic ways could adapt readily, taking advantage of the opportunities afforded by statehood and the arrival of thousands of American citizens. Cherokees who adhered to more traditional practices and values, however, found themselves aliens in the new commonwealth. The old tribal government had managed to contain at least some of the divisions within the Cherokee Nation. In the nineteenth century, culturally traditional Cherokees participated in national affairs and enjoyed representation in the council and tribal administration. The tribal elite had to answer to Cherokee-speaking subsistence farmers who adhered to the old religion and communitarian value system. The new state government, in contrast, seldom included traditional people. Oklahoma belonged to the grafters. Allotment, then, was a political disaster, as well as an economic calamity. It drove many Cherokees to the margins of public life, and it fractured the Cherokee political community, making coordination extremely difficult in the years following statehood. As the Nighthawk Keetoowahs explained, allotment left Cherokees "factionalized and bitterly antagonistic toward one another, rendering impossible a united Cherokee effort for mutual benefit."[14] In confronting this reality, twentieth-century tribal leaders would look to the Cherokee past and the old Cherokee Nation for examples of both factionalism and cooperation. Public memory became a means of addressing allotment's terrible legacy.

Organizing after Statehood

When the United States destroyed the Cherokee government, it retained the office of principal chief. Federal officials preferred to have a tribal representative on hand for completing business left over from the allotment process, in particular the transfer of land from Cherokee to non-Indian ownership. For a decade following statehood, William C. Rogers, the last elected Cherokee chief, served in this capacity. After Rogers's death, federal authorities adopted the practice of periodically appointing a new chief when they needed someone to sign legal documents on behalf of the Cherokee Nation. The appointed leaders' terms in office were very brief, in most cases a single day. These "chiefs for a day," as they were known, included Andrew B. Cunningham, a Cherokee government official before allotment and mayor of Tahlequah after, and William Wirt Hastings, a nine-term Oklahoma congressman. While they came from the Cherokee population, federal officials selected them, and they served the needs of the BIA. Their position represented a logical extension of the allotment campaign more than it did a lingering expression of Cherokee self-government.[15]

The "chiefs for a day," however, were not the only Cherokee representatives operating during this period. Cherokee communities maintained a variety of institutions that continued to provide paths to leadership and forums for political discussion. Traditional religious organizations, like the Nighthawk Keetoowahs, remained a vital presence in eastern Oklahoma, while Cherokee Baptist churches served as focal points for many rural Indian communities. A portion of the Keetoowah Society, meanwhile, reorganized under a federal charter around the time of statehood. This "Keetoowah Society, Incorporated," selected its own chief and sought to represent Cherokee interests in Oklahoma, with a particular emphasis on securing funds owed Cherokees under the terms of the allotment agreement. In addition, Cherokees established voluntary associations after statehood that served to express a continued identification with the tribe. Former students of the Cherokee Male and Female Seminaries, for example, created an alumni group known as the Cherokee Seminary Students Association, which celebrated the memory of the old Cherokee Nation while preserving social connections among the descendants of the nineteenth-century tribal elite. While federal Indian agents preferred to work through the appointed "chiefs for a day," each of these groups produced leaders who could speak for at least a portion of the Cherokee population in Oklahoma.[16]

These organizations had varied agendas, but most agreed on at least one significant point: that the United States still owed their people large sums of money related to violations of the nineteenth-century treaties. In the early 1890s, for instance, federal commissioners compelled the Cherokee government to sell a large swath of land known as the "Cherokee Outlet," insisting on a price far below the territory's value. Cherokee leaders wanted to bring this grievance and others like it to the U.S. Court of Claims, in the hope of securing substantial monetary settlements. Distributed among the former citizens of the Cherokee Nation, these funds might help to ease the poverty afflicting rural Indian communities in the wake of allotment. Pursuing the claims became a political cause around which Cherokees from many different backgrounds could organize. A traditional religious leader and a member of the Seminary Students Association might have little experience in common, but both could agree that the United States should answer for its fraudulent dealings with the old Cherokee Nation.[17]

In the 1920s, members of several Cherokee groups began to hold periodic conventions, with the immediate goal of coordinating work on the claims cases. Historian Howard Meredith identifies these mass meetings as the start of the Cherokees' reemergence as a nation.[18] The Nighthawk Keetoowahs, for example, worked to build alliances with other Cherokee groups in the hope of securing better representation than that provided by a federally appointed chief. They hoped to select their own leaders, Cherokees who could explain the needs and interests of "fullbloods," by which they meant Cherokees who spoke the tribal language, adhered to traditional cultural and religious values, and lived in rural Indian communities.[19] In 1920, the Nighthawks chose Levi Gritts for the chief position. Gritts was a bilingual Cherokee, raised in a traditional community but educated in white-run schools. He lived in Muskogee, site of the federal government's agency for the Five Tribes. Following his selection, the Nighthawks invited the Keetoowah Society, Incorporated, and other Cherokee groups to join them in endorsing Gritts as chief, with the goal of "uniting all forces through the one proposed Representative."[20] Meredith interprets these actions as the start of an effort to reestablish a functioning tribal government. While some Cherokee groups declined to participate in this work, the Nighthawks and their allies clearly intended Gritts to speak for all Cherokee people in Oklahoma. They sought to rebuild the Cherokee Nation, replacing the appointed chiefs with a more legitimate and effective form of representation.[21]

The BIA, however, continued to work through the Cherokees' federally appointed leaders. Throughout the 1920s and 1930s, the federal government maintained the practice of periodically selecting a Cherokee to serve a short term, and federal authorities seem to have neither recognized Gritts nor endorsed the Keetoowahs' campaign.[22] It was only in the 1940s that the federal government finally began to alter its approach. In 1941, the principal chief's office became a permanent position, rather than a temporary assignment. That year, President Franklin Roosevelt named Cherokee businessman Jesse Bartley Milam as chief and granted him a one-year renewable commission, rather than a one- or two-day term. Milam was a bank president from Chelsea, Oklahoma, a member of a family that prospered during the transition from Indian Territory to American state.[23] He remained in office for much of the next decade, receiving annual reappointments from the Roosevelt and Truman administrations. This action suggests that the BIA now recognized the need for a permanent Cherokee representative, even if the chief remained an unelected position.[24] Later in the 1940s, Milam began advocating a further change, urging federal authorities to allow Cherokees to form a council to advise the chief. He hoped to establish an elected committee consisting of one or two members from each of the nine districts of the old Cherokee Nation. This committee would help the chief accurately convey the Cherokee population's views and interests, while providing a regular forum for political discussion. It would also, of course, be a substantial step toward the restoration of a Cherokee tribal government. Federal officials endorsed the idea of an advisory council, but they rejected the proposed elections. The new committee, like the chief, would be appointed. The federal government, in other words, acknowledged the need for better forms of Cherokee representation, but resisted practices that might make these institutions more thoroughly responsive to the Cherokee people.[25]

The persistence of appointed leaders proved crucial to subsequent tribal politics. Federal authorities found it more convenient to deal with an appointed chief than with organizations rooted in Cherokee communities. As a consequence, anyone selected as chief immediately gained influence with the BIA and other government agencies, something Cherokee people needed as they faced the aftermath of allotment and statehood. Continuing to create tribal leaders by federal appointment, however, undermined those leaders' authority, particularly at a time when Cherokees like the Keetoowahs cultivated their own forms of representation. An appointed leader might have been acceptable when the government merely needed an individual to sign documents, but such a leader could not attempt to speak for Cherokee communities without bringing his own legitimacy into doubt. In the years ahead, the chief's duties steadily expanded, and appointed leaders did, in fact, find themselves speaking for the Cherokee people. An appointed chief, then, faced the challenge of representing a divided Cherokee population while at the same time working to convince Cherokees that his interests lay with the tribe rather than with the federal officials who made him. Appealing to Cherokee history became one way of negotiating this contradictory political position.

Restoring an "Alert and Vigorous People"

Jesse Bartley Milam's career provides several examples of the interplay between public memory and Cherokee politics. For one thing, his participation in tribal affairs appears to have started with heritage work. In the 1920s and 1930s, he helped to underwrite research conducted by Cherokee historian Emmet Starr, and he assembled an impressive personal library of books on southeastern Indian history and Native American cultures.[26] In addition, he served as a leader of the Cherokee Seminary Students Association, the heritage group founded by alumni of the Cherokee Male and Female Seminaries. The seminaries were academies established by the Cherokee Nation in the mid-nineteenth century. They represented the crowning achievement of the Cherokee public school system, and, in memory, they symbolized the tribe's commitment to progress and civilization. In addition to being a social club, the Students Association acted as a Cherokee historical society. It lobbied the state government to preserve significant Cherokee sites, and members conducted research on nineteenth-century tribal history, paying particular attention to the Cherokee republic's political and economic elite—the Ross and Adair families, the Bushyheads and Boudinots.[27] By the 1930s, the Students Association also served as a forum in which Cherokees discussed tribal political affairs. At the group's annual reunions, held each May in Tahlequah, members heard reports on the claims cases and discussed legislation related to Indian policy. Milam's participation in the group helped to draw him into tribal politics, and members of the Students Association provided his main support after Roosevelt appointed him principal chief.[28]

The creation of Milam's Executive Committee, meanwhile, also involved historical memory in an important way. In July 1948, the chief and the BIA organized a convention in Tahlequah to select the members of the new Executive Committee. The meeting would also approve a new team of lawyers for the claims cases, which Cherokees revived after Congress created the Indian Claims Commission in 1946. In explaining the significance of these actions, the meeting's principal speakers repeatedly invoked the Cherokee past, citing the history of the nineteenth-century Indian nation as evidence that Cherokees should unite behind their appointed principal chief and his new advisors. The proceedings began, for instance, with a long recitation of tribal history by Oliver H. P. Brewer, a county judge from Muskogee who served as "chief for a day" in 1931.[29] Brewer provided an Oklahoman's version of the familiar Cherokee "civilization" narrative, emphasizing the tribe's rapid progress back in the Southeast and in the West after removal. The Cherokees, he explained, were an "alert and vigorous" people, always "striving to make their way to a plane of higher civilization."[30] He described the arrival of Christian missionaries in the early nineteenth century and the Cherokees' ready embrace of the education they provided. He recalled Sequoyah's great invention and the founding of the *Cherokee Phoenix* newspaper by the missionary Samuel Worcester and the young Elias Boudinot. Removal threatened this progress, Brewer noted, and it created terrible divisions among the Cherokee people. Yet, after the Trail of Tears, the tribe rebuilt its communities and labored on. Cherokees established a new constitutional government in the West and created a public education system, and, for a time, they flourished as an independent nation in Indian Territory. "Legislative and judicial departments were responding to every duty imposed upon them with probity, patriotism, and administrative ability," Brewer explained, and "economic development was so unusual as to bring entire satisfaction to the citizenship at large."[31] Unfortunately, the United States, driven by the same greed that inspired the removal policy, mounted a new assault upon the Cherokee Nation in the form of allotment and Oklahoma statehood. Some Cherokees, like Brewer himself, prospered under the new system, but allotment left many others impoverished and powerless. Cherokee claims, Brewer suggested, provided an opportunity to redress these injuries, but the Cherokees would only find success if they followed the example of their forebears. As they had after removal, they must overcome their differences and, working in common, return their people to a progressive course.[32]

Brewer's address contrasted an almost utopian memory of the old Cherokee republic with a present-day Oklahoma in which many Cherokees were powerless and poor. This particular use of the past became commonplace in Cherokee political discussions in the years to come, as tribal leaders summoned the memory of a prosperous, well-governed Indian nation to condemn U.S. abandonment of Native people since allotment. This history offered a clear political message to their fellow-Cherokees. In the old nation, it explained, Cherokees set aside their differences in pursuit of the common good, led by responsible tribal officials. Such unity, of course, was precisely what Milam and his allies wanted from their people in 1948. Cherokees attended the Tahlequah convention as members of multiple organizations and interest groups. Milam hoped they would leave the meeting agreed upon a single team of lawyers to prosecute the Cherokee claims and with a single Executive Committee to represent the tribe in its dealings with the federal government. Convention speakers like Brewer viewed themselves as the authorities around whom Cherokees should rally. Successful professionals and civic leaders, they were heirs to their people's tradition of statesmanship, the Rosses and Boudinots of the twentieth century. This memory of the old Indian republic, then, affirmed the legitimacy of Milam and his allies, while suggesting the benefits that would come to Cherokees should they support them.

Yet Cherokee unity proved elusive in 1948. The Nighthawk Keetoowahs refused to attend the Tahlequah convention, explaining that "we cannot accept the leaders that are sure to be elected." Milam and his allies, they implied, could not speak for the "fullblood" population.[33] Some of those who did participate in the meeting likewise rejected Milam's leadership. Midway through the proceedings, Levi Gritts, who remained active in Cherokee politics, complained that Milam's friends dominated the discussion. He suggested that Milam had orchestrated the convention to ensure that he and his preferred team of lawyers would win the right to prosecute the claims cases. Many Cherokees, he argued, did not understand the purpose of the Tahlequah meeting, implying that the convention could not legitimately act in the name of the Cherokee people. He wanted more discussion and time for those present to return to their communities to inform other Cherokees about the proceedings. Milam's allies responded by arguing that those complaints represented precisely the kind of factionalism that crippled their people in the past, and the convention defeated Gritts's motion to postpone the selection of lawyers. Later, Gritts charged that Milam, aided by the BIA, had tricked the Cherokees, using the convention to confirm decisions made ahead of time and in private. He characterized the meeting as a power grab by a chief who did not represent the Cherokee people. "He is after all appointed by the President," Gritts remarked, "and not by the authority of the Cherokees." Milam, he added, had no right to "dictate to the Cherokees." Unmoved by appeals to Cherokee history, Gritts dismissed Milam as the federal government's chief, rather than a legitimate representative of the Cherokee people. Far from the new John Ross, he was just another agent of the United States.[34]

The basic pattern on display in the summer of 1948 would recur in Cherokee politics for several decades to come. When appointed leaders took steps toward creating a new tribal administration, they invoked Cherokee history to frame their work, using the memory of the removal era and the old Indian nation to call for cooperation in the present. At each turn, however, they met resistance from Cherokees who rejected their authority and distrusted their intentions. These Cherokees worried that actions like the establishment of an Executive Committee belonged to an ongoing effort to concentrate power in the hands of unelected officials controlled by the federal government.

Cherokee "Self-Help" in the Termination Era

Milam died less than a year after the Tahlequah convention, and in 1949, at the Executive Committee's prompting, Harry Truman appointed William Wayne Keeler principal chief. Keeler was a forty-year-old corporate executive from Bartlesville, Oklahoma, who would occupy the principal chief's office for the next three decades. At the time of his appointment, he headed the refining division of the Phillips Petroleum company, and in later years he would rise through the Phillips hierarchy to become the company's president and chief executive officer. Keeler had little involvement in the Cherokee community politics of the prewar years, and his rise to the chief's office was something of an accident. He attended the 1948 convention as a representative of Texas Cherokees, who hoped to participate in the ongoing claims cases. That role led to his appointment to the Executive Committee, again as a representative of the Texas Cherokees. When Milam's declining health left him too weak to work after a few meetings of the committee, Keeler took over as its chair. That service then resulted in his selection as chief. While Milam created the new Executive Committee, Keeler quickly became its guiding hand, despite his status as a newcomer to Cherokee politics.[35]

During his long tenure, Keeler presided over the building of a new government for the Cherokee Nation, eventually becoming its first elected chief of the modern era. In this early period, however, nation building clearly did not enter his plans. Instead, he viewed his role as more philanthropic than political, stating that he wanted to use his office merely to improve Cherokees' physical and economic welfare. While Milam sought to revive a functioning tribal government, Keeler disavowed that project, informing Cherokee audiences on multiple occasions that the United States extinguished the Cherokee Nation at the time of Oklahoma statehood. The purpose of the appointed principal chief, he said, "was not to continue governmental powers and authority because that authority had already been destroyed."[36] Keeler's first years as chief, of course, coincided with the emergence of the termination policy. At a time when the United States worked to dissolve tribes, abolish the BIA, and abandon the trust relationship, it made little sense for the appointed chief to seek governmental powers. Keeler accepted the current direction of federal policy, stating that he simply wanted to use his position to see that needy Cherokees gained greater access to aid—an uncontroversial aim, even in the 1950s.[37]

The clearest expression of this philanthropic outlook came in the form of the Cherokee Foundation, a charity Keeler started shortly after his appointment as principal chief. The group was a nonprofit corporation designed to raise funds for direct aid and educational assistance to the poor. Keeler described its mission as Cherokee "self-help." Oklahoma Cherokees, led by successful businessmen like himself, would gather resources and distribute them among the needy in their own communities, making Cherokees less reliant on public welfare and the BIA. Much of the foundation's work focused on direct assistance, with special attention paid to young people. It distributed school clothing and shoes to Cherokee children, and it purchased eyeglasses for elementary school students. It also made small grants to older students attending boarding school or university. Like Keeler's insistence that the old Cherokee Nation was gone, this "self-help" approach suited the political climate of the termination era. It suggested that Cherokees might someday function without the BIA and the federal trust relationship.[38]

Yet the same version of Cherokee history recounted at the 1948 convention informed Keeler's work, and here a memory of Indian nationhood and self-government proved significant. Keeler and Executive Committee members frequently invoked the example of the nineteenth-century Cherokee Nation, reminding audiences that, in the past, Cherokees were independent and progressive. Like Oliver H. P. Brewer at the Tahlequah convention, they reviewed their people's nineteenth-century achievements: economic development, public schools, the national newspaper, and constitutional government. Keeler himself often added the point that, in the old nation, the Cherokees were self-sufficient. When Cherokees ran their own affairs, he noted, "there was little sickness and little poverty . . . they looked after one another; they were an independent people."[39] That memory stood in sharp contrast to the deplorable conditions many Cherokees continued to experience in the mid-twentieth century. The legacy of allotment and statehood had been the loss of land, declining health, and the narrowing of educational opportunities for many people living in rural sections of eastern

Oklahoma. Like other Cherokee representatives before him, Keeler blamed this state of affairs on the federal government, which had taken responsibility for Cherokee people and Cherokee problems away from the Indians themselves. Functions like education and poor relief became Washington's business, and the result in the present was that "many of the Cherokee people, who were once such a proud race and so independent, were going down the hill."[40] One of the Executive Committee's most frequently repeated messages during this time was that Cherokees needed to organize around their historical identity as a progressive community and work together for their people's welfare in Oklahoma.

Termination advocates found little to oppose in Keeler's public statements during this period. Cherokees should help themselves, the chief insisted, and work to escape the debilitating guardianship of the United States. That message echoed the federal government's goal of extricating itself from Indian affairs. At the same time, this analysis of the Cherokee past and present contained a strain of tribal nationalism. The problems of the twentieth century stemmed from U.S. refusal to let Cherokees manage their own affairs. The United States destroyed the institutions that Cherokees themselves had built to educate, protect, and care for their people, and the federal government established nothing as successful in their place. Transplanted to the 1960s or 1970s, this line of reasoning could sound like a call for self-determination and the revival of tribal government. After all, if the end of the Cherokee Nation represented the root cause of modern problems, one logical solution would be the nation's revival. Keeler's use of history, in other words, gestured toward national restoration even as the chief publicly accepted the termination policy.

Beginning in the early 1950s, Keeler and his associates pursued a number of public history projects that expressed this memory of the Cherokee Nation. They campaigned, for instance, to secure the return of Tahlequah's courthouse to Cherokee possession. Constructed in the late nineteenth century, it originally housed the Cherokee National Council. Keeler hoped to use part of the building as office space for the chief, while creating a Cherokee history museum in the area that remained.[41] Around the same time, they proposed staging an outdoor historical drama, an effort inspired by the success of *Unto These Hills* in North Carolina. Keeler and other Cherokee leaders visited the Qualla Boundary, corresponded with the Cherokee Historical Association, and recruited Kermit Hunter to write a script. The play would be a sequel to *Unto These Hills* and would dramatize Cherokee suffering and perseverance on the Trail of Tears, as well as the reconstruction of the Cherokee Nation in the West. Keeler and his allies lacked the funding necessary to mount the program, but for a time they hoped the drama would debut as part of the Oklahoma semicentennial in 1957.[42]

While the museum and the outdoor play failed to materialize in the 1950s, one very significant heritage project did come to fruition. In early September 1953, Tahlequah hosted the first Cherokee National Holiday, an annual event that continues to this day. Mounted by Keeler's Cherokee Foundation, and with the help of the Tahlequah Chamber of Commerce, the holiday commemorated the approval of the 1839 Cherokee Constitution, which declared the nation reestablished and reunited in Indian Territory after the Trail of Tears. It recalled, in other words, an act of Cherokee nation building in the wake of removal.[43] According to the local press, around four thousand people attended the first holiday, gathering in Tahlequah's courthouse square for speeches by Cherokee leaders and visiting dignitaries, performances of Indian music and dance, and a barbecue lunch. Attorney Earl Boyd Pierce provided an update on the Cherokees' ongoing claims cases, and Commissioner of Indian Affairs Glenn Emmons, who was visiting Oklahoma as part of a tour of western Indian communities, offered brief remarks describing the new Eisenhower administration's approach to Indian affairs.[44] In the evening, the celebration concluded with a pageant recounting the history of the Cherokee Nation and the town of Tahlequah. The performance was "amateurish," Keeler later remarked, "but so well received that we resolved to enlarge the production in the coming years."[45]

The first Cherokee National Holiday broadcast diverse and potentially conflicting political messages. While Emmons declined to discuss specific policies, his speech offered general support for the termination campaign. The goal of the Eisenhower administration, he remarked, would be to establish "a condition of parity or equality for the Indian people as compared with the rest of the population," and this status would require the eventual end of the federal government's trust relationship with Indian communities. "I sincerely hope," Emmons continued, "that the day will come when it is no longer necessary for the federal government to serve as a trustee for the property of any individual Indian or Indian tribal groups."[46] In the political environment of the early 1950s, this language represented a clear endorsement of termination. Other elements of the event, however, challenged this outlook, at least indirectly. Religious leaders Eli Pumpkin and Stokes Smith, speaking shortly after Emmons, encouraged their people to recommit themselves to their traditional culture, in particular the Cherokee religion. Young people spurned the old ways, Pumpkin complained, when they should unite with their fellow Cherokees, as dictated by their community's traditional spiritual values. The answer to Cherokee problems, Pumpkin and Smith implied, was not the individual equality and opportunity promised by postwar American Indian policy, but rather a renewed communal spirit within the practice of the old religion.[47]

The holiday itself, meanwhile, was replete with images of Cherokee nationhood and self-government. Members of the Executive Committee, for instance, introduced a new Cherokee Nation flag during the event, one that featured the national seal adopted by Cherokees in Indian Territory following the Trail of Tears. The speeches took place on Tahlequah's courthouse square, in the shadow of the old Cherokee capitol building. The historical pageant celebrated the reestablishment of the nation after the trauma of removal, while dramatizing Cherokee achievements in the West in the middle and late nineteenth century. And, as already mentioned, the day chosen for the event marked the anniversary of the approval of a Cherokee constitution, an act of political self-determination.[48] The organizers selected this date carefully. Early proposals for the holiday suggested holding the event in May, to coincide with the annual reunion of the Cherokee Seminary Students' Association. Keeler and his helpers rejected that idea in favor of staging the celebration on a date associated with tribal nationhood. A May event, they reasoned, might only appeal to Cherokees already associated with the alumni group, while they hoped to draw an audience whose members would represent all of the various Cherokee communities and political factions. The only memory that promised to inspire such broad participation was that of the nineteenth-century Cherokee Nation.[49] Keeler himself never challenged Emmons's vision of Indian affairs, with its broad support for termination. If anything, he endorsed it, encouraging those in attendance to listen closely to what the commissioner had to say.[50] The holiday he helped to create, however, hinted at alternatives to the postwar assimilation campaign. Termination advocates insisted that Indians could gain access to American prosperity and opportunity only as individual citizens, shorn of their special status as members of indigenous communities within the United States. In contrast, the holiday sometimes suggested that the Cherokees' strength lay in precisely that status. Cherokees, it implied, were at their best when they acted not as individual Americans, but as a distinct people and an Indian nation.

Public History and the New Cherokee State

In April 1961, after years of effort, the Cherokee Nation finally won a case before the Indian Claims Commission (ICC). In a ruling on the 1893 sale of the Cherokee Outlet, the ICC accepted the Cherokee position that federal officials had coerced the tribal government and paid too little for the land. The commission granted the Cherokee Nation a settlement of around $14.7 million. This decision represented a crucial moment in the development of a new Cherokee political administration, insofar as it enabled the appointed chief and his advisors to take on new responsibilities and an expanded authority in Cherokee affairs. Federal officials looked to Keeler and the Executive Committee for direction in determining how the funds would be distributed. Members of Keeler's circle, in fact, drafted some of the language of the congressional act that allocated the settlement money. That work required the appointed leaders to consult with various Cherokee communities and consider how to identify beneficiaries at a time when Cherokees lacked current tribal rolls. In other words, they had to define a Cherokee public and determine its will.[51] Moreover, a portion of the settlement funds went to the principal chief's office, giving Keeler and the Executive Committee their first significant tribal budget. Most of the settlement took the form of per capita payments (of around $280 each) to those listed on the final Cherokee allotment rolls, certified in 1906. Around $2 million of "residual funds," however, went to the chief's office.[52] With this money, Keeler and the Executive Committee initiated projects they identified as beneficial to Cherokees in Oklahoma. They developed a loan program for Cherokee students, began investing in tribal businesses, and made plans to develop an industrial site near Tahlequah.[53] Beyond its economic impact, this activity bore great political significance, since it led Keeler and the Executive Committee to behave like a permanent tribal government. The claims process encouraged the appointed leaders to become policy makers and providers of benefits, and it created new bureaucratic business that required Cherokee representation before federal authorities. Keeler and his associates remained unelected, and some Cherokees continued to doubt their legitimacy. Yet increasingly they acted like tribal officials. In the years following the ICC's decision, Keeler abandoned his tacit support for termination and became the key architect of what the anthropologist Circe Sturm calls a new "Cherokee state."[54]

In addition to the claims settlement, changes in federal Indian policy encouraged this new round of institution building. By the end of the 1950s, in response to Native American opposition, Congress and the BIA retreated from termination, promising not to force the policy on communities that did not want it. Many federal officials still assumed that some form of assimilation should be the ultimate goal of American Indian affairs, but the highly coercive termination crusade of the immediate postwar era came to a halt.[55] Indian activists and tribal leaders, meanwhile, increasingly advocated self-determination as their preferred policy alternative. The United States, they argued, should support tribal self-government and promote economic development within a continued federal trust relationship.[56] In the mid-1960s, tribal leaders then worked to align this position with the antipoverty crusade launched by Lyndon B. Johnson's administration. In particular, they hoped that the Community Action Program, with its goal of "maximum feasible participation," would allow tribal communities to create their own development and education programs and, in the process, help to make self-determination a reality. Tribal governments became significant conduits for new federal benefits, and the work of managing the programs gave new authority to tribal leaders. In eastern Oklahoma, the War on Poverty expanded the resources available to Keeler and the Executive Committee, allowing them to build an increasingly elaborate system of tribal services.[57]

This work, however, provoked considerable opposition from within Cherokee communities, and, at each stage, the expansion of the appointed leaders' influence inspired a corresponding wave of criticism. Some Cherokees objected to the idea of allowing settlement money to revert to the chief's office. They called for distribution of the residual funds on a per capita basis, even if individual payments amounted to only a few dollars each.[58] Others criticized the programs established with the residual funds, arguing that they helped few Cherokees and ignored the communities most in need of assistance. Later, when money from the War on Poverty began to flow into Oklahoma, critics accused Keeler and the Executive Committee of monopolizing the new federal aid to the detriment of grassroots community organizations. While this opposition addressed the practical question of how best to allocate available resources, it also involved a challenge to the basic authority of the chief and his advisors. As appointed officials, Keeler and his allies were not acting with the formal consent of the Cherokee people. Their status meant that any objection to their decisions could quickly become a rejection of the leaders' fundamental legitimacy. Keeler belonged to the BIA, rather than the Cherokee people, his opponents charged. He and his allies were "assimilated" Indians who knew little of the lives of

Cherokees belonging to more traditional, rural communities.[59] The Cherokee anthropologist Robert K. Thomas suggested that Cherokees from small, traditional communities would always distrust an appointed chief. Many traditional people admired Keeler personally, Thomas noted, but they viewed the appointed leadership as an arm of Oklahoma's "white society," the society that had destroyed the old nation and impoverished their people. Federal officials selected leaders whom they considered competent, and "a 'competent' man, in their sense, is one most removed from the full-blood and the most like a successful white man." The federal government could only resolve this issue by allowing Cherokees to develop their own government.[60] Keeler, of course, recognized this problem. In the 1950s, he and other Cherokee leaders discussed organizing an election for chief, and on two occasions he attempted to resign his position.[61] Federal officials ignored these requests, and Keeler recommitted himself to what he called his "Cherokee work." Yet the appointed leaders' basic vulnerability—the illogic of their position—would not go away. If anything, the protests grew louder as the principal chief and Executive Committee became more active, since each new initiative served to remind Cherokees that their leaders came from the federal government.

Public history provided a field for the politics of this emerging Cherokee state. One of the appointed leaders' first acts following the distribution of the claims settlement was to allocate $100,000 from the residual funds to the Cherokee National Historical Society (CNHS), a nonprofit corporation established in 1963. Modeled on the Cherokee Historical Association in North Carolina, the Society's goal was to develop a heritage center that would "preserve the history and traditions of the Cherokee tribe and stimulate general interest in its unique cultural development and accomplishments."[62] The center would eventually consist of a living history village depicting eighteenth-century Cherokee life back in the Southeast, an outdoor theater suitable for staging an epic historical drama about the Trail of Tears, a tribal history museum, and a Cherokee national archive.[63] The society's directors chose to build the center at the site of the old Cherokee Female Seminary in Park Hill, a few miles outside of Tahlequah. The state of Oklahoma purchased and preserved this land in the late 1940s, partly at Jesse Bartley Milam's urging. In the mid-1960s, Oklahoma leased the site to the CNHS, asking only $1 per year in rent. The Cherokee Nation's $100,000 helped the society begin work on the first two stages of its plan: the living history village and the outdoor theater.[64]

Cherokee principal chief William Wayne Keeler (left) with Martin Hargerstrand, director of the Cherokee National Historical Society, at the site of the Cherokee Female Seminary, where the historical society built the Cherokee Heritage Center, 1963. Courtesy Cherokee National Archives, Tahlequah, Oklahoma.

While legally distinct from the tribe, the CNHS expressed the appointed leaders' interests quite explicitly. The chief and several of his closest allies helped to organize the society, and Keeler served as the first president of its board of directors. During the 1960s, Keeler worked closely with the organization's executive director—a non-Indian from Tahlequah named Martin Hagerstrand—as the group developed a master plan for the cultural center and began construction. Keeler, in fact, subsidized Hagerstrand's salary during the society's early years, using the resources of the Cherokee Foundation.[65] The heritage center promised to create jobs for Cherokees, while improving the regional tourism economy. If successful, it would demonstrate the ability of the new tribal administration to foster economic development in eastern Oklahoma.[66] In addition, the center provided a means of broadcasting the kind of tribal history the appointed leaders had favored since Milam's day. Like the Cherokee National Holiday, it would recall the tribe's struggles and achievements, in particular the reconstruction of the Cherokee Nation after the Trail of Tears, with the goal of inspiring in contemporary Cherokees "a full sense of pride in the accomplishments of the nation."[67] This pride, Keeler and his allies hoped, would translate into cooperation among Cherokees and support for the new tribal administration.

Like the other projects started by the appointed leaders, the CNHS drew strong opposition. Some Cherokees objected to Keeler's choice of Hagerstrand as director, arguing that a white man should not be employed to head a Cherokee enterprise.[68] Others continued to oppose any allocation of claims funds for tribal programs, preferring that all available resources be distributed through per capita payments. When challenged in this way, Keeler and his allies responded by pointing out that Congress granted them the authority to handle the residual funds. This position, however, likely reinforced the impression that the Cherokee leadership answered to the federal government, rather than the Cherokee people. As long as the tribal budget remained under the control of an unelected chief and council, any use of Cherokee assets could be interpreted as corrupt.[69]

In 1967, a particularly strong condemnation of the heritage center came from a group of Cherokee activists who picketed the opening of the living history village. They distributed handbills denouncing the new attraction as a misuse of tribal funds and an insult to the Cherokee people. Addressed to tourists visiting the site, the leaflet featured a photo of Indian children standing in front of a dilapidated rural house. "While 10,000 of our people live like this," it read, "our own money has been squandered on this 'Cherokee Village.'" The CNHS, it noted, received $100,000 that "belongs to people who live in houses like this." The investment, it continued, was made by a "puppet government" appointed by the United States. "No Cherokee has a voice in choosing his tribal government nor in establishing the policy of the Cherokee National Historical Society." The appointed leaders spent the funds on behalf of Cherokee people, yet the CNHS provided little benefit to Cherokees beyond "a handful of degrading jobs at minimal wages from April to October." Making matters worse, the village presented Cherokee people as primitives. "We, who with our brother peoples *earned* the title of 'Five Civilized Tribes,' teach our children of the days when our prosperous nation had a constitutional government, fine schools, and financial solidity. Can you imagine how it pains us to be presented to you as unlettered savages?" In this protest, the activists invoked the same history of "civilization" so beloved of the appointed leaders. In this case, however, the memory of the "civilized tribe" served to condemn a "puppet government" more interested in building degrading tourist attractions than the restoration of the Cherokees' former glory.[70]

This demonstration reflected a significant broader development. By the mid-1960s, a new wave of Cherokee organizing began, as activists seeking to represent traditional Indian settlements worked to challenge the growing influence of Keeler's administration. The protest at the living history village emerged from the work of a group called the Original Cherokee Community Organization (OCCO), which had formed several years earlier during a controversy over hunting and fishing rights. Originally known as the Five County Northeastern Oklahoma Cherokee Organization (or Five County Cherokees), it attempted to express the grievances and political aspirations of traditional Cherokee communities. From 1965 until the early 1970s, the group pursued a variety of issues rooted in the experience of the settlements. It defended Cherokees who violated state hunting and fishing regulations in the name of treaty rights, and it broadcast Cherokee complaints against federal agencies like the Indian Health Service. It documented the continued erosion of the Cherokee land base and pressed for new treaty claims cases. Members of the National Indian Youth Council (NIYC) joined local residents in some of this work, demonstrating connections with broader networks of Native American activism. The NIYC, for instance, paid for the handbills protesting the living history village. The OCCO also worked with anthropologists sent by the University of Chicago to document rural Cherokee settlements as part of a project funded by the Carnegie Corporation. These scholars included Albert Wahrhaftig, who served as secretary to the Five County Cherokees, and Robert K. Thomas, the Cherokee anthropologist known for his writings on neocolonialism and for his work training Native American youth to become activists and community organizers.[71]

While the Five County Cherokees and OCCO aimed some of their complaints at state authorities and the BIA, they expressed particularly strong opposition to the appointed Cherokee leadership. Keeler and his allies, they suggested, ignored rural settlements and prevented more traditional Cherokees from benefiting from the federal government's antipoverty initiatives. The appointed leaders belonged to Oklahoma's political and economic establishment, and, in the activists' view, Keeler and the Executive Committee were incapable of representing the interests of traditional

Cherokee communities. Keeler's "tribal" projects, funded by claims money or the War on Poverty, served the needs of Oklahoma businessmen rather than those of poor rural settlements. The appointed leaders, in other words, took advantage of federal agencies' interest in Cherokee poverty to make themselves managers of lucrative new programs that did little to improve the lives of the poor. Cherokee communities and their problems became an exploitable resource for unelected officials. The heritage center stood as a particularly galling example of this phenomenon. Attractions like the village traded on the history and culture of the Cherokee people, but they did so in ways that helped few of the Cherokees who sustained that culture and who most needed assistance. Instead, the heritage center supported Tahlequah's business community, which activists suspected was the real purpose all along.[72]

Like Keeler and the Executive Committee, the Five County Cherokees and OCCO invoked their people's history in explaining their purpose. They remembered a time when Cherokees were free, well governed, and united, and they contrasted that memory with the present "time of darkness." "We know the place of the Cherokees in this world," an early statement declared. "For hundreds of years we ruled ourselves in peace and harmony. . . . We spoke with wisdom and dignity to our fellowmen. We learned of the world around us and made good use of its gifts. We taught people what we knew, while they taught us. For this we are called civilized." Like Keeler, the activists urged their people to unite, cooperating in the work of restoring Cherokees to their "rightful place." For the OCCO, however, the appointed leaders represented an obstacle to this work, rather than its logical authors. "Our government was never one man, or a few men," the activists explained. "Our government is all our people united." Today, "intruders, named without our consent, speak for the Cherokees." Cherokee revival, then, required not only the protection of remaining tribal lands and the assertion of treaty rights, but the creation of a new political system, one rooted in traditional Cherokee communities. "When the Cherokee government is the Cherokee people, we shall rest," the activists promised. "When we control our own destiny, we shall rest." For the OCCO, the growing power of men like Keeler prevented Cherokees from restoring true self-determination.[73]

The OCCO's heyday lasted only a few years, and by the early 1970s the group began to unravel. Significant differences arose among the activists over the group's objectives and organizational structure.[74] Keeler and his allies, meanwhile, worked to eliminate the OCCO as a political rival. They attacked the activists as radicals who threatened to disrupt the steady progress being made in Cherokee country under the new tribal administration. The chief's supporters likened OCCO leaders to the Black Panthers, suggesting they were subversives masquerading as members of traditional communities, and they urged Cherokees to avoid the group. They reserved particular disgust for the anthropologists, whom they condemned as outside agitators and likely communists.[75] As the activists struggled to respond to these attacks and to their own internal disputes, participation in the OCCO fell, which hindered the organization's efforts to secure outside funding for its initiatives. It finally disbanded in 1973.[76]

For a time, however, the group managed to mount a significant challenge to the expanding Cherokee state, and its particular use of history formed a central element of that challenge. Like Keeler, the activists looked to the tribal past for models of progress and sound government. Like Keeler, they spoke of restoring the Cherokees to their proper place as a great and renowned people. Yet, if the principal chief and Executive Committee equated themselves to the leaders of the old Cherokee Nation, the OCCO recognized a very different historical parallel. For the activists, Keeler and his allies were "intruders" who used their political influence to exploit Cherokee communities. They were like the grafters of the allotment era, rather than the chiefs who resisted removal. Far from the new John Ross, Keeler was the new Robert Owen, a member of the tribal elite who allied with non-Indians to rob the Cherokee people. The appointed leaders remembered the Trail of Tears and the rebuilding of the nation in the West, and they found in this history a model for their own work. The OCCO remembered allotment and the age of the grafter and rejected the appointed leaders' authority.

Cherokee Consensus History

In spite of the protests, the living history village at the heritage center opened as planned, drawing enough visitors in its first few seasons for Keeler and the CNHS to declare it a success. Two years later, the historical society completed its next phase when it debuted *The Trail of Tears*, an outdoor historical drama written by Kermit Hunter, who created *Unto These Hills* for the Cherokee Historical Association in North Carolina twenty years earlier.[77] A sequel to *Unto These Hills*, the new play dramatized the Cherokees' arrival in Indian Territory and their struggle to rebuild the nation after the trauma of removal. It broadcast, in other words, a version of tribal history the appointed Cherokee leadership had invoked for several decades. At the same time, the play ignored allotment and the struggles of the grafter era, erasing events that explained many of the challenges Cherokee communities faced in the present. In fact, the drama defined twentieth-century Oklahoma as a logical outgrowth of Cherokee and Native American history, rather than a polity born of theft and exploitation. The Cherokee story became an American triumph, an adaptation Hunter likely considered necessary to ensure the play would appeal to tourists. Like *Unto These Hills*, it became a narrative that celebrated Cherokee assimilation.

The drama's central theme was unity, or rather the terrible difficulty Cherokees experienced in reuniting their community in the era following their forced migration. The removal policy, it observed, gave rise to bitter factionalism among Cherokees, as the nation divided over whether to resist the United States or accept relocation. Those divisions persisted in the West, with pro- and antiremoval Cherokees fighting to control the new homeland and settle old political scores. Violence broke out soon after the arrival of the Cherokee majority in 1839, when allies of Chief John Ross killed Elias Boudinot, John Ridge, and Major Ridge, who had negotiated and signed the Cherokees' removal treaty. The United States brokered a peace between the factions a few years later; however, fighting resumed in the 1860s, when the American Civil War became, for Cherokees, "a sudden, diabolical opportunity for ancient semi-barbaric feuds and hatreds to burst once more into flame."[78] Because the Cherokees could not find peace and unity, the suffering of the removal era continued. "In a strange way," the play's narrator explained, "the whole world of the Cherokee seemed to become a trail of tears, leading nowhere."[79]

While Hunter's script identified the removal policy as the original cause of tribal factionalism, it blamed the Cherokees themselves for the persistence of their internal disputes and, by extension, the continued misery of their people. This theme provided a stark contrast with *Unto These Hills*, which portrayed Cherokees as thoroughly innocent. In *The Trail of Tears*, John Ross wanted to settle his quarrel with the Treaty Party, but his followers hungered for violent revenge. Proremoval Cherokees, for their part, hoped to dominate the Cherokee Nation in the West, deposing Ross and his allies. Sequoyah, making a brief appearance, counseled compromise and unity, while urging his people to build schools in order to continue their progress as a civilized people. Like *Unto These Hills*, the new drama portrayed Sequoyah as an advocate of Indian people emulating their Euro-American neighbors. Yet despite his great stature, he could not quell what he called the Cherokees' "old, strange passion to destroy ourselves."[80] Cherokees rebuilt their communities in the West, and the play affirmed the familiar image of the Cherokees as a "civilized tribe." Yet the Cherokees in Hunter's new drama continually undermined their own progress through their internecine conflicts. Among other consequences, this failure to work together left them powerless against their common enemies. "Do you know why the white man always wins?," a character named Sarah asked. "Because white children are taught a sense of duty! They learn the obligation to build a unified society!" The Cherokees, in contrast, placed their own desires ahead of the greater good. "All we have is wild independence," Sarah explained, "no obligation except our own personal desires. Unless we change this, we will be destroyed!"[81]

This call for unity echoed Keeler and the Executive Committee's most prominent message. In addition to promoting tourism, the play provided one more in a long line of arguments for Cherokees in the present to rally around the federally appointed leadership. The play's insistence that the Cherokees bore primary responsibility for their political problems, however, struck a new chord. At events like the 1948 convention, tribal leaders blamed allotment and the destruction of the Cherokee Nation for the poverty and marginalization of some of their people. Hunter's script, on the other hand, suggested that something in Cherokee culture or perhaps even the Cherokees' very nature undermined cooperation. A love of "wild independence" prevented Cherokees from working for the common good. These images, of course, drew upon some of the most pernicious Indian stereotypes, suggesting that Cherokee troubles stemmed from a lingering savagery, rather than American colonialism and hostile federal policies. The federal government, in fact, appeared in the play as an impartial judge, rather than the Cherokees' enemy. In a scene toward the end of the first act, President James K. Polk helped to mediate a settlement between the two main tribal factions, bringing temporary peace to the Cherokees in the 1840s. This scene acknowledged that removal was a tragedy instigated by the United States, but it implied that the U.S. government alone was capable of solving the lingering problems caused by removal. The same American empire that drove the Cherokees from their homeland would settle the conflicts sparked by that act of dispossession.[82]

The play's conclusion expressed this last message in particularly clear terms. Hunter's script ended with Oklahoma statehood, and it portrayed the Cherokees' inclusion in Oklahoma as the act that finally resolved the terrible divisions that plagued the tribe since the removal era. Like the promise of citizenship in *Unto These Hills*, inclusion in Oklahoma solved the

Cherokees' problems. At long last, the Cherokees found peace when they joined together in a new American state. "Back in the old days," a character named Dennis recalled, "they used to pray, Kaw at le os, tat gat eh: peace for the Cherokee. Now their dream has come true. Now we are Americans!"[83] Hunter's script, moreover, indicated that the ultimate significance of the Trail of Tears was that it contributed to the creation of Oklahoma. Dispossessed Cherokees brought "civilization" to a wild frontier, laying the foundation for the new state. Cherokee suffering, the play suggested, represented a sacrifice necessary for American progress, and Cherokee inclusion in Oklahoma symbolized that progress. "The march from North Carolina to Indian Territory was called the Trail of Tears," Dennis intoned in the play's final lines, "but I want to say that this trail has not ended in tears, but in triumph! . . . All of you: white, red, black . . . Choctaw, Seminole, or whatever you are, full-blood or half or anything, sing for Oklahoma—sing for America!"[84]

In this final scene, the play executed several astonishing narrative moves. It erased the history of Cherokee resistance to allotment and statehood, as well as the suffering of the grafter era. That suffering had provided a central element of the historical narratives Cherokee leaders recounted at events like the 1948 convention. In those public memories, allotment caused the problems Cherokees faced in the mid-twentieth century. The policy created the dire conditions that Cherokees hoped to improve by reviving a functioning Cherokee government. In Hunter's script, however, the allotment policy disappeared, and assimilation became the apparent answer to Cherokee problems. It is worth remembering, moreover, that the play's production was the work of Cherokee leaders who, at that very moment, were engaged in creating a new tribal administration, during a period when the United States had finally begun to abandon assimilation as the ultimate goal of American Indian policy. The creation of the play itself grew directly from the Cherokees' mid-twentieth-century political revival. In other words, a resurgent Cherokee Nation sponsored a version of tribal history that appeared to celebrate the destruction of Indian nationhood in an earlier era.

This contradictory narrative suited both the conventions of midcentury heritage tourism and the political needs of the appointed Cherokee leadership. As discussed in chapter 5, historical dramas like *Unto These Hills* or *The Trail of Tears* tended to follow the conventions of Cold War "patriotic pageantry." This form of public theater emphasized national unity during a period of perceived threats to American well-being, and it celebrated citizens who made willing sacrifices for the nation. If the United States were to defeat the enemies of democracy, Americans had to temper their love of individual liberty with a strong sense of patriotic duty.[85] The lines quoted above, in which the Cherokee character Sarah decried her people's "wild independence," fell squarely within this convention, while also echoing tribal leaders' more specific goal of convincing Cherokee people to cooperate (and accept their authority) in the present day. The celebration of Oklahoma statehood, meanwhile, reassured audiences that American history (even Native American history) was progressive. In the drama, Cherokees found peace with one another when they committed themselves to become citizens of the United States. The pain and violence of the removal era became a patriotic sacrifice, like the loss of soldiers in America's just wars. Erasing the dire consequences of allotment and statehood, *The Trail of Tears* offered a kind of Indian consensus history. It encouraged Cherokees to unite with one another, and it reminded non-Indian audiences that, in spite of terrible chapters like removal, their nation's history remained a story of progress and improvement.

The drama's idea of unity, moreover, implied that Cherokee dissidents were irrational and dangerous. If one applied the play's outlook to tribal politics in the late 1960s, a group like the OCCO became a modern expression of the Cherokees' "strange passion to destroy ourselves." Continued disputes among Cherokees, in this way of thinking, amounted to new versions of the old, sad factionalism, rather than legitimate arguments about the future of Cherokee communities. To be clear, *The Trail of Tears* never endorsed the principal chief or the new tribal administration explicitly. Its vision of history, however, proved fundamentally conservative, suggesting that established political structures were proper and legitimate. In Oklahoma at the end of the 1960s, that message encompassed the new Cherokee administration, as well as the state's broader power structure.

A Remembered Community

By the early 1970s, Keeler and the Executive Committee oversaw a complex network of new Cherokee agencies and services, which the Nation created with the support of the BIA and federal antipoverty programs. New tribal institutions included the Cherokee Nation Housing Authority, which drew on federal funds to subsidize construction of new homes, and job training programs like the Cherokee Skills Center and a Cherokee branch of the Neighborhood Youth Corps. Keeler and his allies also created Cherokee Nation Industries (CNI), a corporation that worked to draw manufacturing facilities to eastern Oklahoma. Critics questioned the impact of these initiatives, noting that many Cherokee communities remained poor and disadvantaged even as a river of new money flowed through the region. The tribal housing program, for instance, proved a windfall for Oklahoma's white-dominated construction industry, while making only modest improvements in living conditions in rural settlements. At CNI's new manufacturing plants, meanwhile, some Cherokees complained that non-Indians always secured the best jobs. In addition, charges of mismanagement and corruption dogged several early CNI projects, which only served to intensify criticism of the Cherokee leadership. One thing was certain, however. The programs launched during this period established the Cherokee Nation as a major economic force in eastern Oklahoma, and this growing influence helped Keeler and the Executive Committee solidify their control over tribal affairs.[86]

As this web of tribal programs expanded, the appointed leaders moved to create a full-fledged Cherokee government and to restore elections. In 1968, the chief invited Cherokee settlements to select local leaders to serve as advisors, creating what amounted to an informal tribal council. Two years later, these community representatives received voting privileges in the Executive Committee. Congress, meanwhile, authorized the Cherokee Nation to resume holding elections for principal chief, an action that reflected the continuing shift in federal Indian policy toward self-determination. In 1971, Keeler finally ran for the office he had occupied for over twenty years and won by a wide margin. Opponents observed that a majority of those Cherokees eligible to vote declined to participate, but Keeler understandably saw his victory as a mark of approval for his and the Executive Committee's work. Four years later, following his reelection as chief, he oversaw the drafting of a new Cherokee constitution, which replaced the Executive Committee with an elected council and provided for a new tribal judiciary. Ratified by Cherokee voters and approved by Congress in 1976, this constitution marked the full restoration of tribal government.[87]

At each stage, public memory and public history shaped the reemergence of the Cherokee Nation in Oklahoma. Heritage work drew leaders like Jesse Bartley Milam into tribal affairs. Before the nation was something he sought to reestablish, it was a proud memory and part of his personal history. For others, the memory of Cherokee achievements in the nineteenth century helped to motivate political action in the present. The knowledge that Cherokees had survived the Trail of Tears, rebuilt the nation, and thrived in the nineteenth-century West made the poverty and marginal status of some present-day Cherokee communities even more disgraceful. The memory of the old Indian republic gave added weight to the pursuit of claims cases and the demand for better social services. In the 1950s and 1960s, Keeler and the Executive Committee sponsored public history projects not only as a way of boosting tourism, but as a means of encouraging cooperation and validating their own authority. They positioned themselves as the heirs to the leaders of the old Cherokee Nation, suggesting that their people's history granted them a legitimacy their appointed status could not. Their opponents, meanwhile, attacked these public history projects as indicative of tribal leaders' failings. A principal chief who belonged to the BIA and Oklahoma's corporate establishment, they implied, endorsed a form of public history that could only serve non-Indian interests. If nations are "imagined communities," as Benedict Anderson famously wrote, then memories of the removal era and the old Cherokee republic proved crucial to the ways in which tribal leaders imagined, debated, and reconstructed the Cherokee Nation.[88]

Public history has remained a prominent element of Cherokee affairs since the rebuilding of the tribal government. In the mid-1970s, the CNHS completed the third stage of the Cherokee heritage center, when it finished construction of a tribal museum and archive. For a time, the facility only hosted temporary installations, like the "Trail of Tears Art Show," an annual exhibit and competition that continues today. In later years, the CNHS developed a permanent history exhibit for the museum, focusing on Cherokee life in the Southeast, the struggle against removal, and the rebuilding of the nation after the Trail of Tears.[89] The tribe and the city of Tahlequah, meanwhile, have continued to host the Cherokee National Holiday each September, and, if anything, the political significance of the event has grown in the years after the restoration of self-government. It has become, for instance, the setting for the annual State of the Cherokee Nation Address, in which the principal chief touts his or her achievements and outlines an agenda for the coming year. Today, the event is a fascinating mixture of political theater, historical commemoration, and celebration of cultural heritage. Finally, in the 1980s and 1990s, Cherokee Nation citizens and tribal leaders became significant participants in a federally sponsored commemoration of Cherokee removal, the Trail of Tears National Historic Trail. That development, which provided a catalyst for a new wave of removal commemoration, provides the subject of chapter 7.

The National Trail

· ·

In 1991, residents of Meigs County, Tennessee, launched a campaign to establish a memorial to Cherokee removal at a scenic spot on the Tennessee
River known as Blythe Ferry. The site was a well-documented section of
the Trail of Tears, where, in late 1838, Cherokee detachments camped before using the ferry to cross the river. As many as nine thousand Cherokees
paused at Blythe Ferry at the start of their long overland journey to Indian
Territory. That section of the Tennessee River remained fairly undeveloped
through the twentieth century, making it an ideal location for a park. The
land belonged to the Tennessee Valley Authority, and residents already used
the area for recreation. In 1998, heritage advocates secured twenty-nine
wooded acres on the eastern bank of the river near the old ferry landing.
With the help of the National Park Service, they transformed the spot into an
elaborate monument to the Trail of Tears. They established a visitor's center
and built an outdoor "history wall" with interpretive panels explaining the
story of Cherokee removal and the significance of Blythe Ferry. They created
an outdoor plaza with a map, embedded in the ground, showing the major
removal routes. Knowing that Blythe Ferry lies near the start of the removal
journey, one can stand in this space, looking down at the map, and gain a
sense of the great distance that lay before the Cherokees who stood there
in 1838. As a final feature, heritage workers added a stone monument
dedicated to the memory of the dispossessed Native people. Shaped as a
seven-pointed star, it lists each of the more than twenty-five hundred
names of Cherokee heads of household identified by federal officials in the
1835 removal census. If the map communicates the scale of the journey, the
monument attempts to convey the depth of Cherokee loss, the long register
of Indian families giving names to the absent.[1]

At Blythe Ferry, local historical memory intersected with a national heritage project. In 1987, Congress created the Trail of Tears National Historic
Trail (TOT-NHT), adding two Cherokee removal routes to the system of scenic paths and historic corridors overseen by the National Park Service in
cooperation with other federal agencies. The creation of the national trail
helped to inspire the Blythe Ferry campaign. Heritage advocates in Meigs

Cherokee Removal Memorial Park at Blythe Ferry, Meigs County, Tennessee.
Photo shows the visitors center and "history wall." Photo by author.

County already knew the history of the site and valued the memory of Cherokee removal. The national trail, however, encouraged them to concentrate
their attention on this particular aspect of the local past. It led them to
plan ambitiously for the site, since it suggested broad public interest in the
removal story. It offered them an opportunity to place Meigs County as
part of a national enterprise, an act the local leaders hoped would result in
increased heritage tourism in their community. They applied to the Park
Service to certify Blythe Ferry as an official trail site, and they persuaded
the NPS that the memorial park had the potential to become a significant
interpretive center. Park Service personnel helped the organizers plan the
memorial and historical exhibits, elaborating on a general design outlined
at the start of the park campaign. The memorial, then, was the product of
local heritage work translated through a national commemoration.[2]

This process, replicated in multiple communities across the South,
resulted in the rapid expansion of public history devoted to Cherokee
removal. The creation of the national trail sparked a new wave of memorialization, as heritage advocates like the group in Meigs County joined
in the effort to document the Trail of Tears and commemorate the Cherokee past. The national trail provided a framework in which local groups
of commemorators developed projects interpreting dozens of individual
sites. Communities that barely figured in the Cherokee removal story sought

to participate in the national trail, claiming the Trail of Tears as part of their local heritage. Elsewhere, places with established traditions of commemorating removal launched new campaigns or added new features to old memorials. A nonprofit advocacy group called the Trail of Tears Association (TOTA) formed to coordinate research on removal and promote public interpretation. While the NPS managed the national trail and provided oversight and some funding, commemoration relied heavily upon the work of volunteers. In each of the nine states containing segments of the trail, dedicated groups of heritage workers formed to study the migration routes and educate the public on the history of Indian removal. Driven by the kind of commitment displayed by the creators of the park at Blythe Ferry, the public memory of the Trail of Tears grew on the southern landscape.

The creation of the national trail contributed to a broader effort by the NPS to tell more complex and less celebratory narratives about the American past. In the 1990s, as the TOT-NHT developed, the Park Service worked to revise its approach to historical interpretation, seeking to include more diverse perspectives and the voices of underrepresented communities. According to Dwight Pitcaithley, chief historian of the NPS, the agency embraced the "new social history" during this period and made a concerted effort to place the struggles of traditionally marginalized groups in its interpretive plans.[3] This work involved recognizing American histories of racism and injustice, like African-American slavery and the violent dispossession of Native Americans. "The National Park Service must ensure that the American story is told faithfully, completely, and accurately," a 2001 NPS report stated. "The story is often noble, but sometimes shameful and sad."[4] Cherokee removal provided a ready example of the "shameful and sad" dimension of the American past. It was already a feature of the commemorative landscape in some parts of the South, and Americans had long used the removal story to epitomize the tragic elements of their history. The new historic trail offered the Park Service an opportunity to expand upon earlier state and local commemoration of Cherokee removal and, in the process, demonstrate the agency's commitment to its revised historical mission.

The heritage work inspired by the national trail, meanwhile, reflected another, related trend, the growing significance of grief and shame in American public memory. Americans have grown obsessively concerned with issues of memory in recent decades, a phenomenon the scholar Erika Doss calls "memorial mania." Commemoration of all kinds seems to be thriving in the contemporary United States, as diverse communities seek to claim and shape public interpretation of the past. One of the factors driving this trend is a growing desire on the part of Americans to acknowledge historical trauma, a development Doss credits to the twentieth-century civil rights movements.[5] The Cherokee Trail of Tears provides a ready vehicle for expressing this intensified concern with shameful episodes from the nation's past. Sites like the Blythe Ferry memorial invite one to contemplate Cherokee loss and suffering, and they allow visitors to act upon a contemporary obligation to acknowledge injustice. Cherokee removal was "one of the most regrettable episodes in our history," a brochure for the Blythe Ferry site states.[6] The memorial, and others like it along the national trail, grant visitors opportunities to experience that regret.

Yet, how different is this latest wave of commemoration from the earlier examples of memorial work I describe in this book? In the late 1930s, the organizers of Chattanooga's centennial commemoration expressed a similar regret for Cherokee loss. In the early 1960s, the Georgia state officials who dedicated the New Echota historic site spoke of their obligation to recognize their ancestors' crimes against the Cherokees. In both of those cases, the memory of Cherokee removal offered a politically innocuous way of acknowledging "shameful and sad" elements of American history. Both commemorations reinforced the assumption that Indian people no longer existed in these southern places in any meaningful way. How different is contemporary memorialization? Recently developed sites like Blythe Ferry provide more accurate and detailed accounts of Cherokee removal, and, in my own experience, visiting these places can be quite moving. The basic narrative, however, departs little from those told by earlier generations of commemorators. Newer sites frequently recount a version of the "civilized tribe" story, noting Cherokee achievements like Sequoyah's syllabary and the creation of the Cherokee national government. They detail the Cherokees' nonviolent resistance to removal and then describe their suffering on the journey west. They condemn the greed and hatred that drove the Cherokees from their homeland, but so too did earlier commemorations. Today, we have more commemoration of Indian removal, suggesting a general acceptance that this episode represents a significant part of American history. Yet the public narrative of the Trail of Tears seldom seems more complicated than before, and, in many places, it remains a story about vanishing Indians.

What does the recognition of Cherokee loss and suffering achieve in the present? Does it require anything of contemporary Americans other than the act of recognition itself? When NPS historians embraced revisionism in the 1990s, they did so with the familiar progressive goal of making history a foundation for civic dialogue and the cultivation of a more democratic society. "Understanding the past so that we can create a better, more equitable future, is what the study of history is all about," Pitcaithley wrote.[7] Acknowledging historical trauma, however, does not inevitably promote dialogue in the present, let alone action. Bearing witness to past trauma can have the effect of redeeming the present in an effortless manner.[8] Acknowledging a history of injustice suggests that we are better now. Indeed, the very act of recognition *proves* that we are better, since it demonstrates a moral sensibility superior to that of past generations. We reassure ourselves that contemporary Americans will not commit similar mistakes, and, with that reassurance, we render the very history we commemorate less relevant and less troubling. Much of the evidence I consider in this chapter suggests that the Trail of Tears remains a safe and settled topic among non-Indians, one that allows white Americans to acknowledge suffering and injustice in the national past without having to reconsider much of anything in the present.

In one very important way, however, the current wave of removal commemoration departs from earlier examples like the New Echota historic site or Chattanooga's centennial. Cherokees and other Native Americans have exerted considerably greater influence over the development of the TOT-NHT than they did over most of the commemorations discussed in earlier chapters. NPS conferred with the Cherokee Nation and the Eastern Band of Cherokee Indians throughout the study and planning process for the national trail, and Native Americans have played significant roles as advisors to the trail project and as leaders in the Trail of Tears Association. Citizens and representatives of other Indian nations have also participated. As the interpretation of the Trail of Tears evolved, this Native American presence resulted in a greater emphasis on tribal persistence and, in some cases, an effort to remind visitors of Native American sovereignty. If that trend continues, the public memory of removal may become less a story of Indian absence. It may also become a less settled (and more unsettling) topic for contemporary Americans.

Trails for America

The National Trails System began in the mid-1960s as part of a campaign by the federal government to promote outdoor recreation. In 1965, President Lyndon B. Johnson issued a statement on "natural beauty," in which he urged government action to protect ordinary citizens' access to the wonders of the American landscape. He lamented the plight of "the forgotten outdoorsmen," Americans who found their enjoyment of the natural environment compromised by urban development and the "tyranny" of automobiles. "For them," Johnson remarked, "we must have trails as well as highways."[9] Federal authorities, he suggested, should organize a coordinated system of hiking, bicycle, and bridle paths, starting with those already in place on federal lands.[10] In response, the Interior Department launched a national survey of trail resources and, in late 1966, issued a report titled *Trails for America*. The report proposed a network of long-distance scenic footpaths through landscapes of "national significance." The Appalachian Trail, running from northern Georgia to Maine, would be the first unit of this new system, with others to follow as directed by Congress.[11] The Interior Department drafted legislation implementing this idea, and, in 1968, Congress passed the National Trails System Act. As approved, the law designated two national hiking trails (the Appalachian Trail and the Pacific Crest Trail) and identified fourteen additional routes for study and later consideration.[12]

While the system's original purpose was to help Americans enjoy the natural environment, its creation inspired a host of proposals that focused more on history than the landscape. When listing potential additions to the network, the Interior Department included routes like Lewis and Clark's journey from St. Louis to the Northwest Coast, the Mormon migration route from Illinois to Utah, and the early American trading path known as the Santa Fe Trail. Heritage advocates in the South lobbied for a trail devoted to Hernando De Soto's travels, while westerners hoped to commemorate frontier cattle drives by including the Chisholm Trail in the system. These were not hiking paths, but commemorative projects tracing old migration and commercial ways. Each route included places of natural beauty, but their significance derived from the history of exploration and the American frontier.[13] In 1978, Congress made this concern for history explicit, amending the original act to create a formal classification of National Historic Trails. The new category would recognize routes significant to the history of American expansion, commerce, military campaigns, and migration.[14]

The idea of commemorating Cherokee removal with a national trail appeared quite early in the system's development. In 1965, shortly after Johnson's "natural beauty" message, Senator Mike Monroney of Oklahoma contacted the Interior Department to "nominate" the Trail of Tears for the new network. Monroney counted a great many Cherokees among his constituents, and he was likely aware of the Cherokee Nation's efforts during this period to develop new heritage attractions. "Although none of us can be very proud of this incident in our history," he remarked, "it is of such significance that the Trail should be developed as part of the national system."[15] Federal planners responded by incorporating the proposal into the *Trails for America* report, identifying the Trail of Tears as a potential future project.[16] Congressman Roy Taylor, one of the architects of the trails system, endorsed the idea. Taylor chaired the House Subcommittee on National Parks and Recreation, and his district, in the far western corner of North Carolina, included the lands of the Eastern Band of Cherokee Indians. Taylor became a key sponsor of the 1968 act, and his committee oversaw the trails system's development. He seconded Monroney's proposal, noting that the Trail of Tears began near his own North Carolina home.[17] In 1979, shortly after Congress created the category of National Historic Trails, Taylor's successor in the House of Representatives submitted a bill authorizing a study of the Cherokee removal route, the first step toward adding it to the trails network. The bill stalled, but the provision for a Trail of Tears report became part of a bundle of legislation submitted during subsequent sessions. In 1983, Congress voted to authorize the study as one of several investigations of potential new trails. The National Park Service would identify a route, assess historic and natural resources along the trail, and gauge public reactions to the idea of a national commemoration of Cherokee removal.[18]

Though it originally focused on the natural landscape, the trails system became a catalyst for heritage campaigns, as particular communities sought to knit their homes and histories into a new national project. The Trail of Tears study set a similar process in motion. When federal officials announced their interest in commemorating Cherokee removal, local heritage advocates across the South responded by seeking room for their communities on the proposed trail. They remembered a Cherokee history of southern places, in many cases drawing upon earlier rounds of removal commemoration. They claimed the removal story as part of their local past, and as new projects and proposals emerged, the public memory of removal began to expand on the southern landscape.

"Overwhelming Public Interest"

To investigate the Trail of Tears, the NPS created a working group headquartered at the agency's regional office in Atlanta. Park service historians conducted research on Cherokee removal and traced the overland and river routes traveled by Cherokees in their journey west, while a group of "outdoor recreation planners" studied environmental impacts and assessed the potential for tourism development along the trail corridors. In addition to this study group, the agency formed an advisory committee to provide data and help coordinate public dialogue about the project. This committee included tribal representatives, such as Robert Youngdeer, the principal chief of the Eastern Band, and Duane King, an anthropologist and public historian then working as director of the Cherokee National Historical Society in Oklahoma. King would later become one of the principal researchers responsible for providing the NPS with information on the various removal routes. State governments also provided advisors, one from each of the states through which the trail might pass. Among other duties, these officials helped investigators identify local heritage advocates, whom the NPS then consulted by mail and through a series of public workshops. With this design, the Park Service sought to synthesize its own research with ideas drawn from state governments, the Cherokee tribal communities, and a variety of local organizations from places along the trail's potential route.[19]

This work met with immediate and widespread public approval. Investigators found "overwhelming public interest" in the proposed trail among the communities they consulted, noting that they received "no negative comments throughout the scoping process." While differences arose over the ideal route for a national trail, all parties agreed that Cherokee removal merited a federally sponsored commemoration, a unanimity NPS workers considered unprecedented.[20] This popular approval, investigators reasoned, stemmed from the Cherokees' reputation as a "civilized tribe," along with an awareness of the hardship and sorrow Cherokees experienced on their journey west. "Fascination with the Cherokee removal," they wrote, "can be explained by the success of the Cherokees in adapting to the 'Old South' lifestyle of the whites who surrounded them, embracing Christianity, becoming literate through the use of Sequoyah's syllabary, resistance to removal through legal means, and the suffering and mortality of the detention and forced exile on the Trail of Tears."[21] Americans already knew a version of the removal story, the study group discovered, and they valued that memory.

For the local heritage advocates who responded to the study, a national trail promised to help them place their particular communities in the familiar narrative of the Trail of Tears. In their letters to the NPS, they argued for the importance of their home places to Cherokee history and, in some cases, identified specific projects they hoped to see integrated into the national trail. As the Park Service shaped its case for the Trail of Tears' significance, local heritage groups sought to convince the NPS that their particular communities deserved starring roles in any commemoration. In far western North Carolina, for instance, residents of the town of Murphy hoped the national trail might help them realize a longstanding ambition to develop a historic site. Murphy was the location of Fort Butler, one of the network of small military installations established by the United States to facilitate removal. Cherokees forced to depart North Carolina passed through Fort Butler before traveling to deportation camps in Tennessee. For some years, residents had discussed creating a "historical park" at the site, ideally with a reconstruction of the fort. Local heritage workers now urged the NPS to help in this effort, suggesting that Murphy represented the starting point of the Trail of Tears. Murphy was "the main stage of this sad drama in state and national history," one wrote, and deserved to feature prominently in any commemorative effort by the park service. A restored Fort Butler, local residents suggested, could serve as an interpretive center for the new national trail.[22]

Heritage advocates in southeastern Tennessee, meanwhile, advertised their own region as the beginning of the Cherokee removal route. James Corn of Cleveland, Tennessee, was a retired lawyer and local historian who led a campaign in the 1960s and 1970s to create a state park at Red Clay, where the Cherokee National Council met in the period just before removal. He considered the starting point of the Trail of Tears to be Rattlesnake Springs, a few miles north of Cleveland, where detachments traveling overland to Indian Territory departed in autumn 1838. This spot, he insisted, deserved recognition as the *true* beginning of the trail. "Please don't let anyone tell you the Trail of Tears started anywhere but Rattlesnake Springs," he wrote the NPS in 1985. "That's where the military commanders signaled 'forward,' that's where the teamsters shouted and cracked their whips, and that's where the Cherokee members of each melancholy column took a last look at their beloved homeland and started their trek to an unknown land in the far west."[23] In statements like these, heritage workers argued for the primacy of their local places to the history NPS now proposed to commemorate. The study provided a forum for these local memories, drawing them into debate, as different groups of heritage activists worked to persuade federal authorities to accept their particular understandings of the past.

As Corn's letter suggests, a sense of competition developed among communities seeking inclusion in the national trail. Heritage advocates in Dent County, Missouri, for instance, felt aggrieved when it seemed the study group might propose a route for the Trail of Tears that bypassed their part of the state. Cherokees followed several different roads through Missouri, they noted, and, in fairness, all of these should be recognized. "While we applaud the Park Service's intent to commemorate the Indians who were treated so unjustly, we believe it is a disservice to them and to the public to create the impression that the Indians had only to follow the route of interstate 44 to their new homeland."[24] A heritage advocate in Arkansas, meanwhile, challenged the entire state of Missouri's claim to preeminence when it came to the removal route. "It has been the popular thing to tag the one trek of Indians, through Missouri, as the 'Trail of Tears,'" Marguerite Turner observed, yet Cherokees also migrated by river across Arkansas. Ignoring this water route would have excluded places like her own home in Pope County, which combined scenic beauty with sites of great historical significance. "Every trail woven by the misplaced Cherokee Indians was, indeed, a 'trail of tears,'" she declared, "and the whole of the Removal should be so designated."[25] These letters expressed the kind of possessiveness I explored in my discussion of Chattanooga's centennial. Removal belonged to Cherokee history, but these predominantly non-Indian communities claimed it as their local heritage. The national trail study invigorated these claims, promising to validate local knowledge while also threatening rejection.

In June 1986, the NPS study group issued its final report and recommendations. It found that Cherokee removal represented an event of national significance, and it proposed that Congress should designate a "water route" and one overland corridor as a new historic trail. The water route would start at Ross's Landing in Chattanooga, follow the Tennessee River and the Ohio to the Mississippi, and then cut across Arkansas on the Arkansas River. Among other things, this path would grant Marguerite Turner her wish to see Pope County included in the national trail. The overland corridor, meanwhile, would follow the Cherokees' "northern route," which began near Charleston, Tennessee. Following James Corn's advice, the report identified Rattlesnake Springs as one of the starting points for the overland journey. The northern route ran northwest through Nashville and into western Kentucky. It then cut across the tip of southern Illinois before passing through Missouri and the northwest corner of Arkansas to arrive in Oklahoma. In addition to these main corridors, the NPS recommended identifying three "side trails" to represent the paths taken by Cherokees as the military gathered them for the forced migration. One of these side trails would start in Murphy, North Carolina, and the site of Fort Butler, while a second would reach into Georgia as far as the New Echota state historic site. The side trails would converge in southeastern Tennessee and the starting points of the two main routes. Together, these trails reflected an effort by the study group to include as many interested communities and existing heritage sites as possible, while still maintaining a coherent trail corridor that travelers could readily trace.[26] In December 1987, a little more than a year after the NPS issued its report, Congress designated the Trail of Tears National Historic Trail along the lines recommended by the Park Service study.[27]

Two Graves in Kentucky

In places like Murphy, North Carolina, the trail study enlivened existing heritage ideas, as local advocates sought to persuade the Park Service of the significance of their communities to Cherokee history. Elsewhere, the national trail project led heritage workers to *find* a Cherokee history in places only briefly influenced by the nineteenth-century Cherokee Nation. Hopkinsville, Kentucky, provides a vivid example of this second phenomenon, one that merits more detailed analysis. Hopkinsville played only a small role in the Trail of Tears story. Cherokee detachments rested there and resupplied while traveling the northern route in late 1838. During this era, the town was a regionally significant crossroads and commercial center, but it was not a Cherokee community. Cherokees merely passed through on their way to Indian Territory. In the 1980s, however, residents of Hopkinsville organized one of more substantial removal commemorations in the South, motivated by the prospect of inclusion in the national trail. That commemoration shifted the public historical identity of the town, while also influencing the development of the national trail itself.

The Hopkinsville commemoration began with two removal-era Cherokee graves. In 1838, two Cherokee political leaders, Whitepath and Fly Smith, died while camped near Hopkinsville, and their people buried them near the Little River a short distance from town. In the decades following removal, Hopkinsville residents retained a memory of those particular deaths, which helped to remind them, in turn, that thousands of Cherokees had once passed through their area. Local histories generally highlighted the fact that this section of Kentucky was the final resting place of prominent Cherokee "chiefs," and, as one writer noted in the 1880s, "many can point out the spot where these noble red men sleep their last, long sleep."[28] In the twentieth century, the town expanded to encompass the land residents identified as the site of the burials, but the graves themselves remained undisturbed. White landowners cared for the site informally and, in the process, helped to perpetuate the memory of Cherokee visitors and the Trail of Tears.[29]

In the 1980s, that memory became a focus of public commemoration through the efforts of a white Kentuckian named Beverly Baker. Baker ran a bookkeeping business in Hopkinsville with her husband, Walter, while also working in local advertising and public relations. In the latter pursuit, she participated in efforts during the mid-1980s to promote tourism in Hopkinsville and its immediate region, and this interest in tourism apparently drew her attention to the Trail of Tears. In December 1985, Baker read a newspaper story explaining that the National Park Service was considering adding one or more of the Cherokee removal routes to the National Trails System. This chance discovery gave her the idea of developing a removal-themed historic site at Hopkinsville. Like many residents, she recalled that exiled Cherokees had traveled through this part of Kentucky, and she knew about the "chiefs'" graves. Moreover, members of her husband's family believed themselves to be of Cherokee descent, and this may have provided Baker with a particular stake in the Native American past. A Trail of Tears historic site, she concluded, would illustrate a distinct feature of local history while encouraging tourists to stop in the area. And perhaps the NPS would provide some of the money to create it. "If there are plans for a 'Trail of Tears' Museum," Baker wrote, "why not [build it] in Hopkinsville?"[30]

Baker brought her idea to the attention of the local tourism commission, while securing the endorsement of the city and county governments. Other residents joined in the effort, and together they wrote letters to the state government, Congress, and the NPS making the case that Hopkinsville should be the site of a memorial and interpretive center for the Trail of Tears. While the NPS proved unable to provide money for the construction of museums, Baker and her allies formed a nonprofit "Trail of Tears Commission" and began raising funds on their own. They secured a donation of the land that contained the grave sites, along with several acres of adjacent property, and they bought a log cabin to serve as the interpretive center. With the help of Michael Abram, a physician and art collector who ran a gallery in Cherokee, North Carolina, they created the museum exhibit, which included historical objects, craft items, and contemporary Native American art. The commission also began to stage annual powwows at the site, which served both as a fund-raising method and as a way of publicizing the project. The result of all this work was the Trail of Tears Commemorative Park, which today features markers recounting the removal story, the log cabin museum, and two life-sized bronze statues depicting the Cherokee leaders whose graves form the focal point of the commemoration.[31]

Statues of Whitepath and Fly Smith, Trail of Tears Commemorative Park, Hopkinsville, Kentucky. Photo by author.

Baker and her allies, however, did more than develop the local attraction. During this same period, they played a significant role in securing the establishment of the Trail of Tears National Historic Trail. Recognizing that the national project could only help their local commemoration, they organized a public relations campaign aimed at convincing Congress and the NPS to complete the work of designating a national trail memorializing Cherokee removal. To help with this effort, they enlisted Hopkinsville school children and their teachers. More than five hundred middle-school students wrote letters to Congress in support of the national trail proposal as part of special history lessons on the Cherokees and the Trail of Tears. Baker and the other adults, meanwhile, cultivated the local media and convinced one of Kentucky's senators, Wendell Ford, to introduce the bill adding the Trail of Tears to the National Historic Trails System. When that bill became law in late 1987, Hopkinsville was one of four specific locations identified as sites related to Cherokee removal.[32] Congress would have likely approved the national trail eventually, with or without the Kentuckians' efforts. As already noted, the NPS recommended designation of the Trail of Tears in its study, and there were other constituencies supporting the idea.[33] Yet Baker and her allies provided the immediate stimulus for the inclusion of the removal route in the trail system. In doing so, they ensured that Hopkinsville would figure prominently in the national effort to remember Cherokee removal.

This commemorative work had the effect of greatly magnifying the Cherokee history of the town and its surrounding region. As residents promoted the local memorial and then the national trail, their sense of the Cherokees' significance to the area grew, a process Baker's correspondence illustrates quite vividly. Her initial letters exploring the memorial idea simply noted that the Cherokee migration route passed through Hopkinsville and that Whitepath and Fly Smith were buried there. As the work continued, however, she began to argue that the Cherokees "played an important part in the history of this area" and that "many lives here were touched by that forced march."[34] Later, in discussing the schoolchildren's letter-writing campaign, she suggested that students should emphasize that the Trail of Tears "bears strong historical significance to western Kentucky." She also encouraged them to note that "many area citizens," like her husband, could claim Cherokee descent.[35] The idea of the memorial, in other words, led Baker to reimagine the historical character of her home place, finding a more pronounced Indian identity for the predominantly white southern town.

Through this work, moreover, Baker herself changed. From her start as a local tourism booster, she grew into a significant heritage activist, and commemorating removal became a cause that helped to define the last three decades of her life. In the early 1990s, she joined an advisory council established by the Park Service to support the Trail of Tears Historic Trail, and, over the next decade, she drew other Kentucky residents into Cherokee commemoration. She oversaw efforts to certify additional locations in Kentucky as significant trail sites, helping to define those places as part of Cherokee history, much as she had for Hopkinsville. When she died in 2010, she was remembered as a founder of the national trail and as an evangelist for removal commemoration. Baker exemplified the double transformation at work in much heritage advocacy. In commemorating removal, she remade the historical identity of her home community, and in conducting this work, she remade herself.[36]

A Flood of Proposals

In the late 1980s and early 1990s, the NPS began developing the national trail, following the recommendations made in its earlier study. It mapped an "auto tour," consisting of modern highways that followed the general corridor of the overland northern route. Marked with the agency's brown road signs, the tour would allow travelers to retrace the Cherokee migration, all the way from southeastern Tennessee to eastern Oklahoma.[37] The NPS also began working with established museums and historic sites to create exhibits recounting the Trail of Tears story, while devising a system for designating official Trail of Tears sites. The earliest of these "certified sites" were existing heritage attractions like New Echota and Red Clay, but over time additional places joined the list of official trail components. For many of these sites, the Park Service and community groups created wayside exhibits, small clusters of outdoor signage detailing both local events and the broader story of removal.[38] Historian Duane King continued his research to pinpoint the routes followed by Cherokee detachments, and the NPS established an advisory council to coordinate public participation in the trail. This council included state and tribal representatives and members of heritage organizations interested in Cherokee commemoration.[39] They, in turn, oversaw the creation of a larger volunteer group, the Trail of Tears Association (TOTA). Chartered as a nonprofit in 1993, TOTA sought to promote trail research, contribute to the development of new historic sites, and educate the public about the history of Indian removal. Over time, these activities formed the foundation for a diverse partnership involving the NPS, tribal representatives, professional historians like King, and a variety of volunteers and local heritage advocates.[40]

Initial work on the Trail of Tears took place during several significant changes in NPS practice. As noted earlier, the agency revised its approach to historical interpretation during this period, paying greater attention to American histories of racism, violence, and injustice. At the behest of Congress, it launched a series of new projects devoted to exploring what one NPS advisor called the "negative lessons" of American history, including several initiatives addressing the violence of American westward expansion.[41] In 1989, for instance, Congress changed the name of the Custer Battlefield National Monument to the Little Bighorn Battlefield National Monument, while directing NPS to transform the site from a shrine to George Armstrong Custer to an institution where visitors might learn about all of the peoples who fought there. This act set off a vigorous debate over the meaning of the site and the legacies of American conquest.[42] A few years later, the Park Service created the Washita Battlefield National Historic Site, where American cavalry (again led by Custer) launched a devastating attack on a group of Southern Cheyenne.[43] African American slavery, meanwhile, also began to play a greater role in Park Service histories. In the 1990s, the NPS altered its interpretation at Civil War battlefields to include discussion of slavery as the central cause of the conflict. Prior to this time, battlefield museums tended to restrict their narratives to the movement of armies and the experience of common soldiers, setting aside the causes and politics of the war.[44] Other projects during this time included a national historic site at Manzanar, one of the internment camps used to imprison Japanese Americans during World War II, a memorial at the site of the Oklahoma City bombing, and the Selma to Montgomery National Historic Trail, which commemorates the struggle for African American voting rights.[45] Taken together, these sites of memory constitute a wide-ranging effort to recognize histories of suffering and injustice, particularly those tied to race. The Park Service and its advisors began developing the Trail of Tears as this transformation took hold, and the language of the planning documents reflected the new emphasis on confronting violence and trauma in American history. They defined removal as a "tragic experience" and a "culturally devastating episode" for Cherokees. The goal of the national trail, they stated, would be "to instill understanding and sensitivity" in the public with regard to the struggle and loss suffered by those subjected to removal.[46] A national commemoration of the Trail of Tears, then, fit easily within the agency's revised mission.

Planning for the Trail of Tears, meanwhile, reflected another change at the NPS, a greater commitment to collaborating with Indian nations. In the late 1980s, the NPS approved new policies requiring consultation with Native American authorities when agency projects involved the lands, history, and cultural patrimony of indigenous peoples. The NPS adopted this mandate in response to the turn toward self-determination in federal Indian policy, as well as Native American activism related to issues like repatriation of human remains and the protection of sacred sites.[47] Throughout the drafting of the TOT-NHT management plan, the NPS conferred with representatives of the Eastern Band and Cherokee Nation, and the principal chiefs of the two tribes were invited to join the advisory council. Wilma Mankiller, the principal chief of the Cherokee Nation, played a particularly significant role in the early stages of the planning. As NPS workers David Gaines and Jere Krakow recalled, Mankiller impressed upon the planners the need to remain respectful toward the Cherokee people who suffered and died during removal. That principle meant limiting tourism development along the trail and emphasizing education over leisure. While trail sites would be places of public recreation, Mankiller suggested, the NPS needed to take care to avoid trivializing the deeply traumatic experience the trail was meant to commemorate.[48] This degree of tribal consultation marked a contrast with many of the earlier commemorations discussed in this book. The organizers of the New Echota State Historic Site, for instance, communicated with Cherokee leaders, but felt little need to include them as authors of the restoration. Cherokees participated at several stages of the site's development, but only on terms defined by the non-Indian planners. In creating the national trail, the NPS provided at least some space for meaningful consultation, and, through the advisory council, Cherokee authorities had a chance to shape the project. In Gaines and Krakow's estimation, Cherokee contributors did, in fact, influence the trail from the start.[49]

This organizational work provoked a flood of new ideas for historic sites, commemorations, and exhibits. Like the earlier trail study, the NPS planning process became an open invitation to members of the public to place their local communities in the Cherokee removal story. Actual work on the national trail proceeded very slowly in the 1990s, owing mainly to the lack of resources available to the Park Service's Long Distance Trails Office.[50] The public interpretation of removal, however, expanded as heritage advocates continued to bring their community histories to bear upon the national trail project. Residents of several states, for instance, sought to establish new trail corridors, complaining when the Park Service paid what they considered insufficient attention to their home places. Heritage advocates in North Carolina felt that the national trail neglected their state's western region, and they argued that the TOT-NHT should include the network of forts used in rounding up Cherokees in the mountains. "This story must start in Western North Carolina," one insisted.[51] Residents of Tennessee and Arkansas encouraged NPS to recognize two additional overland routes passing through substantial parts of those states. The Park Service supported research on these routes; however, progress proved slow, and some heritage advocates took what they considered the neglect of the corridors as a personal slight. *"There are more miles of the Trail of Tears in Arkansas than any other state,"* wrote one (emphasis in the original), *"yet Arkansas has less certified miles than any other state."* For some history enthusiasts, the failure of the NPS to acknowledge all removal routes was not only an error, but an injustice.[52]

In northern Alabama, meanwhile, a campaign to gain recognition for another neglected trail route led to an entirely new form of removal commemoration, an annual event known as the "Trail of Tears Commemorative Motorcycle Ride." In the summer of 1838, low water levels on the Tennessee River forced a detachment of Cherokees originally scheduled to travel west by boat to follow an overland route instead. They journeyed from the Chattanooga area across northern Alabama to Waterloo, near the Mississippi border. There, they boarded boats and continued on by river.[53] In the early 1990s, a Scottsboro, Alabama, resident named Jerry Davis launched a campaign to recognize this route as part of the Trail of Tears. Working through the Alabama Waterfowl Association, a nonprofit hunters' group, he lobbied officials in the state government, the Alabama Historical Association, and the Alabama Indian Affairs Commission. He hoped to designate State Highway 72, which ran close to the path taken by Cherokees during removal, as a Trail of Tears route.[54] To publicize this idea, Davis and a friend, Bill Cason, who lived near Chattanooga, organized a motorcycle ride in October 1994. Gathering around two hundred riders from motorcycle clubs in the immediate region, they drove their bikes from Chattanooga to Waterloo, a journey of about two hundred miles. The ride, some participants reported, helped them to empathize with the Cherokees. "When we would start going up some of those hills," one rider said, "you think of those people who had to do it on foot."[55]

The commemorative ride proved popular, and Davis and Cason repeated it the following year and each autumn thereafter. Davis formed a new nonprofit to support the enterprise, the Alabama-Tennessee Trail of Tears Corridor Association. By the early 2000s, the group reported more than 100,000 riders taking part for at least portions of the route, and ride leaders started billing the event as the "Largest Organized Motorcycle Ride in History."[56] Organizers sold T-shirts and other merchandise and accepted donations, which they then used to fund scholarships for Native American students and to erect historical markers commemorating the Trail of Tears. They placed these markers in communities throughout the trail corridors in Alabama and in other locations related to the history of Indian removal. While the group that manages the motorcycle ride is not affiliated with the Park Service or TOTA, its work has made this relatively minor route through northern Alabama one of the more heavily commemorated features of the Cherokee removal story.[57]

As some heritage workers pushed for additional routes, others developed new exhibits and interpretive sites, seeking help from the Park Service and its advisors. Personnel from the Long Distance Trails Office helped to plan exhibits on removal for the Cherokee National Historical Society in Tahlequah and the Red Clay State Historical Park in Tennessee, and they collaborated with fellow NPS workers to create removal exhibits for the Fort Smith National Historic Site, in western Arkansas.[58] In western Tennessee, the city of Savannah developed wayside exhibits interpreting the Trail of

Tears for its main municipal park on the banks of the Tennessee River. Savannah was located on the national trail's designated water route, while the overland Bell route passed through the city. A new museum in Savannah also became involved in removal commemoration. In the mid-1990s, the city's Tennessee River Museum began developing an exhibit on Cherokee removal and Savannah's role in the Trail of Tears. The Long Distance Trails Office helped with planning and review. The material on removal became part of the museum's permanent exhibit, alongside displays devoted to the town's first non-Indian settlers, the Tennessee River's role in the Civil War, and industry in Savannah. The museum, in other words, highlighted the Trail of Tears as one of the more significant episodes from the local past, even though the Cherokees' main role in Savannah's history was simply to pass through on their journey west.[59] Residents of Golconda, Illinois, on the banks of the Ohio River, pursued a similar project, working to create interpretive exhibits on Berry's Ferry (also known as Lusk Ferry). Cherokees used this river crossing while traveling the northern route as they left Kentucky.[60] In Faulkner County, Arkansas, the local historical society proposed adding exhibits on the Trail of Tears to the Cadron Settlement, a small park on the site of one of the state's earliest European settlements. Cadron lay on the banks of the Arkansas River and, thus, was part of the TOT-NHT's water route.[61] In these places, and others like them, the evolution of the national trail encouraged heritage workers to magnify the significance of Cherokee removal to their local history. While the NPS could devote only limited resources to these projects, the very fact of the national trail's existence spurred the growth of removal commemoration.

Not all projects, however, met with the approval of the NPS and the trail advisory group. Residents of Ozark, Arkansas, for instance, proposed an ambitious memorial for a site on a bluff overlooking the Arkansas River. The "Trail of Tears Memorial Park" would feature a fifteen-foot-high bronze statue of a Cherokee mother holding a baby, facing the river and "looking into the heavens." The statue would be seen to weep, water dripping from her eyes to collect in a pool at her feet. "Our goal," one of the planners explained, "is to tell the story to the viewers with just one look at the statue." In case that proved insufficient, the history of Cherokee removal would be etched into bronze tablets mounted on a stone wall forming a semicircle around the statue. In time, the planners hoped to add a museum to the site and surround it with extensive park facilities.[62] NPS officials responded politely, explaining the process of certifying national trail sites; however, members of the advisory council found the weeping statue distasteful and declined to offer assistance. The Park Service's Jere Krakow and David Gaines recalled that the Cherokee members of the council, in particular, disliked the plan.[63]

The groundswell of new initiatives confirmed the Park Service's expectation that the national trail would meet with broad public approval. While trail planners balked at some proposals, even the rejected ideas (like the weeping statue) testified to a public willingness to recognize Cherokee loss and suffering. A desire to promote tourism, of course, informed most of these proposals. The national trail promised to bring new visitors to communities that could demonstrate a connection to the removal story and make that connection manifest in the form of signs, historic sites, and wayside exhibits. The people proposing new trail features clearly also hoped the Park Service would provide financial support for new heritage attractions. Commemorating the Trail of Tears, however, made sense to these communities for reasons other than economics. Heritage advocates embraced the idea that contemporary Americans bore an obligation to recognize histories of injustice and suffering. They accepted the reasoning behind the Park Service's turn toward historical revisionism, at least when it came to the removal episode. "We want to show that this injustice to the Cherokees is not going unnoticed," a local official in Tennessee remarked of the Blythe Ferry site.[64] Bearing witness to removal, they assumed, would encourage Americans to become more tolerant in the future. "Let us learn from this mistake," urged a brochure for the commemorative motorcycle ride, "accept each other as we are, and walk together in peace."[65] Erika Doss argues that sentiments like these form an increasingly prominent element of American cultures of memory. Contemporary Americans display a heightened rights consciousness, and this awareness has made the recognition of past violence and injustice an obligation of American citizenship.[66] While the development of the national trail contributed to the Park Service's new mandate to include "negative lessons" of American history, it also provided the public opportunities to participate in acknowledging those lessons. If Doss is correct that such acts have become a public obligation, then the national trail offered both the promise of tourism and the satisfaction of fulfilling a civic responsibility.

Consensus and Participation

This widespread enthusiasm for the national trail raises an obvious, but important, point: Cherokee removal was simply not a topic that inspired public controversy. Both Cherokees and non-Indians proved eager to commemorate removal, and they agreed on the general meaning of the event. Removal was a tragic injustice caused by greed and a disregard for Cherokee rights. It was a shameful episode that contemporary Americans needed to remember, in order to guard against such abuses in the future. Local communities competed for the privilege of depicting the disgraceful treatment of the Cherokees by the United States, and heritage advocates only grew angry when it seemed the Park Service might overlook the role played by their particular town or county in this shameful episode. Few people, it seems, objected to the idea of memorializing the Trail of Tears in the first place.

This lack of opposition appears noteworthy when considered in light of several well-known historical controversies fought during this same period. The development of the national trail coincided with the so-called history wars, a series of bitter public arguments over the representation and teaching of the American past. Several of the most conspicuous of these debates involved Native Americans and the history of colonization and American expansion. In 1991, for instance, the Smithsonian's National Museum of American Art provoked outrage with its exhibit *The West as America*, which offered a critical examination of iconic images of the American frontier. The exhibit paired works by artists like Frederick Remington and Charles Bird King with interpretive panels that called attention to the ways in which traditional frontier images served to justify violent conquest and exploitation. Political conservatives condemned the exhibit as anti-American, characterizing it as a radical assault on the nation's founding principles. This criticism became part of a broader backlash against "political correctness" and multicultural education.[67] Around the same time, planning for the Columbus Quincentenary provoked even greater public debate, as Native Americans protested observations that appeared to celebrate colonialism and the destruction of indigenous peoples. Indigenous activists declared 1992 a "year of mourning" and condemned Columbus as a facilitator of genocide, slavery, and environmental destruction. Conservative commentators responded with predictable anger, attacking the protests as the work of radicals. The controversy effectively derailed the quincentenary before it even began, as public history institutions and funding agencies began to avoid projects related to an event that now seemed dangerously contentious.[68] The NPS drafted its plans for the Trail of Tears in the midst of these arguments, yet the debates seem not to have colored public reactions to the agency's campaign to commemorate removal. Non-Indians did not condemn the Park Service for bowing to "political correctness" in this case. Instead, they petitioned to have their communities included in the project. Even during the history wars, the Trail of Tears remained a politically safe topic.

A comparison with another NPS initiative from this era may prove helpful in explaining the broad acceptance of the Trail of Tears. In the 1990s, as I mentioned earlier, the Park Service revised its interpretive strategies at Civil War battlefields to include discussion of slavery as the war's primary cause. Prior to that time, national battlefields focused almost entirely on military actions. They avoided discussion of the causes of the war to focus on the heroism and sacrifice of combatants on both sides. The new emphasis on slavery and the politics of the war struck some history enthusiasts as a distraction and others as distasteful or even threatening. The Park Service had succumbed to "political correctness," critics charged. Cherished historic sites were now "bashing the South," taking sides and casting dishonor on those who fought for the Confederacy. The harshest criticism came from adherents to the old Lost Cause ideology, which denied the connection between slavery and the Civil War. While most academic historians had dismissed the Lost Cause interpretation by this time, it still shaped the thinking of heritage groups like the Sons of Confederate Veterans. For those who viewed the Confederacy as a noble defense of states' rights, the new emphasis on slavery seemed to erase the true history of the conflict and to do so in a way that cast disgrace upon southern ancestors. The introduction of slavery to battlefield interpretation, then, sparked outrage because it challenged some Americans' personal heritage and fundamental conceptions of the past.[69] The Cherokee Trail of Tears was a very different matter. There were no "Sons of Cherokee Removers" in the South in the 1990s, no community that considered removal a heroic cause or whose members made the rectitude of the removal policy a core element of their personal sense of history. Many Americans, of course, descended from families or belonged to communities that benefited directly from Cherokee dispossession, but they did not celebrate removal (or their own privilege) in the way that some southerners still honored the Confederacy. Even guardians of Andrew Jackson's memory, like the organization that preserved his home, the Hermitage, in Nashville, could recognize the "tragedy" of removal while still venerating the "People's President."[70] When it came to the public memory of the Trail of Tears, the only partisans were those who wanted to honor Cherokee loss and acknowledge the injustice of American policy. It is difficult to start a history war when the only people invested in the events in question concur upon their basic meaning.

The absence of controversy, however, should not be taken as evidence of public indifference. On the contrary, those who embraced the national trail often found deep personal meaning in the Cherokee removal story. While few Americans appear to have been offended by the idea of a national removal commemoration, a great many people forged personal connections to the trail. For Cherokees, the project represented an official acknowledgment of the unjust treatment of their people by the United States. As John Ketcher, deputy principal chief of the Cherokee Nation, remarked at a meeting of the advisory council, the creation of the national trail meant that "the Federal Government realized their mistakes of the past and were willing to recognize this tragic and historic event."[71] Sites along the trail, meanwhile, offered Cherokees opportunities to honor their ancestors and remember their suffering. "It still hurts to know that my great-great-grandfather was pulled from North Carolina," a citizen of the Cherokee Nation said in reference to the creation of an interpretive site in Arkansas. To honor that memory, "we need to go where the history was."[72] Remembering removal and the persistence of Indian communities might also help to inspire and comfort Cherokees in the present. Planning documents for the national trail spoke of the "triumph of the five tribes," calling their efforts to rebuild their communities after a removal "a tribute to their spiritual strength."[73] Wilma Mankiller concurred, noting that remembering the Trail of Tears helped her to face challenges in her own life. "Going back in time and space can sometimes help remedy a person's troubles," she observed. "Remembering those Cherokees and others who were forced to move to Indian Territory and how they persisted brings me at least some relief whenever I feel distressed or afraid."[74]

For other participants, family history and genealogy provided a personal link to the removal story. Some of the most active members of TOTA were not tribal citizens, but rather individuals who identified Cherokees or other Native Americans among their ancestors. Working on projects related to the national trail provided a way to express and cultivate this family connection to the Cherokee past. Shirley Lawrence, one of the creators of the Blythe Ferry site, provides an example. Interviewed in 2011, Lawrence credited her grandmothers with first inspiring her interest in history. While one grandmother recounted the family's participation in the Civil War, the other "told me about my Indian side."[75] This family history led Lawrence to research her Cherokee ancestry and later to delve into Cherokee history more broadly. When the NPS began developing the Trail of Tears National Historic Trail, she started researching routes and sites in eastern Tennessee.

Trail of Tears Commemorative Walk, Pea Ridge National Military Park, Arkansas.
Photo: National Park Service.

She and another Cherokee descendent, the Oklahoma-born Shirley Hoskins, began attending the Trail of Tears advisory meetings and later helped establish TOTA's Tennessee state chapter. Throughout this time, Lawrence and Hoskins also worked on the Blythe Ferry site. For Lawrence, then, family history led to a deeper engagement with Cherokee history and, eventually, an avocation as a researcher and public history activist.[76] Dola Davis, a longtime supporter of the national trail in Georgia, offers a similar example, although in her case an awareness of her husband's family history, rather than her own, led to her involvement in removal commemoration. Her husband Dan Davis descended from a Cherokee family that received a land reserve in northern Georgia in the early nineteenth century. The family lost this land during the years prior to removal, but they stayed in the area, maintaining an identification with their Cherokee origins. Acting on this personal connection, Dola Davis began working with TOTA shortly after its establishment, serving on the association's national board and then helping to organize a state chapter in Georgia.[77] Today, TOTA members frequently cite genealogy work or research on family history as the experience that drew them to the association. "We hear that all of the time," a TOTA officer remarked, " 'my great-great-grandma was a Cherokee' . . . people feel a connection because they have a family connection, or think they have a family connection."[78]

For some heritage advocates, this sense of Cherokee ancestry extended to their local communities. TOTA members in Georgia and Tennessee, for instance, reported that their particular towns included families with roots in the preremoval Cherokee population. The oldest families, they recalled, traced their origins to both early non-Indian settlers and Cherokees who managed to avoid expulsion.[79] In northern Alabama, organizers of the commemorative motorcycle ride spoke of Cherokees "escaping" the trail when low river levels forced detachments traveling by boat to pause in places like Waterloo. "Many area residents," they noted, "can trace their Native American ancestry to those who fled."[80] Residents of southeast Missouri told similar stories, recalling that some Cherokees left the trail at this middle point of the northern route and joined non-Indian settlements. The most dramatic of these stories concerned Cherokee children lost or orphaned on the trail and then adopted by local white families. These oral traditions managed to illustrate the cruelty and injustice of removal, while offering a local memory of white residents taking pity on abused Indians.[81] In my own work with TOTA, I have heard members of other communities located along the removal routes recount similar narratives of Cherokees "escaping the trail" to settle with whites. These memories express a sense of community genealogy, finding submerged Indian origins in contemporary towns and counties. Of course, they also establish a kinship with Cherokees, rather than with the non-Indian beneficiaries of the removal policy.

In her recent work on Cherokee "racial shifting," the anthropologist Circe Sturm notes that "self-identified Cherokees" often reference the Trail of Tears when asserting an indigenous identity. For these individuals, remembering removal provides a way to fashion themselves as Cherokee.[82] This phenomenon has worried some contributors to the national trail. Tribal citizens express concern that "wannabes" might dominate commemoration as new interpretive sites and exhibits evolve. In 2004, for example, an official from the Cherokee Nation complained that "local non-Indians posing as Cherokees" were trying to influence a new art installation related to Cherokee history and culture on the waterfront in Chattanooga. The city should work with the federally recognized Cherokee tribes, he insisted, and refuse proposals from "wannabes."[83] For tribal officials, one of the attractions of the national trail is the promise that the Park Service will consult with the federally recognized Cherokee tribes on new projects. NPS policy regarding collaboration with Indian peoples provides some reassurance that Cherokee interests will take precedence over those of other sectors of the public.[84]

One does not need to possess or claim Cherokee ancestry, however, to forge personal ties to the Trail of Tears. For many participants, local history has provided a strong enough association to justify working on a trail site or joining TOTA. As I noted earlier, local heritage workers have expressed a sense of ownership and competitiveness when it comes to removal routes and historic sites in their communities. North Carolina residents insisted that the trail began on *their* side of the Smoky Mountains, rather than in eastern Tennessee. Arkansans felt slighted when the NPS appeared to neglect their state. For these advocates, commemorating removal was a personal matter, regardless of whether they identified as Cherokee, because it involved their own homes. For others, removal commemoration has provided a means of pursuing a deeper engagement with the histories and identities of their local places. Jeff Bishop, a leader in TOTA's Georgia state chapter, noted that the association's events frequently attract residents who want to know more about their local past. Individuals encounter some reminder of the Native American history of their community or even their own land and come to the chapter meetings to learn more. "I think definitely there is the local aspect of it," Bishop remarked, "the fact that these artifacts are washing up in my yard, the fact that these events occurred on my street."[85] Bishop himself traces his interest in removal to a particularly powerful encounter with local history. In the 1990s, he and his family lived in Rome, Georgia, where he worked as a journalist. In 1996, his wife gave birth to their daughter in a hospital in Rome located on land that once belonged to John Ross, near the meeting of the Coosa and Oostanaula Rivers. When Bishop accompanied his wife to the hospital, he happened to bring a copy of *The Trail of Tears*, John Ehle's popular history of removal. As he waited in the labor and delivery ward, reading Ehle's work, he quickly realized that some of the scenes the book recounted took place just a short distance from where he sat. "The events being described happened right there where I was sitting in that hospital," he recalled, "right there on the river." Bishop knew the general story of removal, but this local connection deepened his awareness of that history and its significance. "It had an immediacy for me," he explained. Several years later, in his work as a journalist, he reported on research conducted by members of TOTA to pinpoint the location of removal forts in northern Georgia. He volunteered to help with the work, and, from there, became one of the most active historians in the Georgia chapter and, later, the chapter president.[86] The feeling of "immediacy" he described reflects a common experience for TOTA members. They engage in this heritage work, in part, because it affords a richer involvement with specific local places.

Shirley Lawrence provided an especially vivid illustration of this last point when I interviewed her in 2011. I asked her why she thought it was important to preserve sites like Blythe Ferry. What made this place worthy of the years of labor she and her friends invested in it? In answering, she spoke of the "emotional connection" one could experience at the site to the Cherokee people who paused there almost two hundred years before. "You can feel a closeness . . . it's like there's an echo or a footprint," she said. "I can just sit down there when it's peaceful and quiet . . . and I can almost see the people crossing." While one can read about removal and understand the relevant history, places like Blythe Ferry provide a feeling for past human lives. "Those emotions are stored there," she explained.[87]

In their study of popular history making, David Thelen and Roy Rosenzweig observe that contemporary Americans tend to embrace history that can be made intimate and participatory. Through genealogical research, collecting, travel, and other practices, Americans cultivate personal relationships with elements of the past.[88] The Trail of Tears National Historic Trail provides opportunities for this kind of personal work. It allows Cherokees to form stronger bonds of empathy with their forebears, while seeking public acknowledgment of their people's suffering and survival. It invites Cherokee descendants to explore an element of their family history, and, for some, commemoration has become a way to lay claim to a Cherokee identity. For a variety of other participants, working on the trail has offered new ways of relating to homes and local places. The uncontroversial nature of the Trail of Tears within American public memory has helped foster the development of those personal bonds. As Thelen observes, political battles over history can hinder the development of what he calls a "participatory historical culture," as individuals and communities avoid disputed subjects.[89] The Trail of Tears has seldom been contested history. The heritage workers involved in developing the trail have disagreed about many things, but they share a sense of the basic meaning of Cherokee removal and an obligation to bear witness to this particular injustice. Commemoration has been less a debate about historical events than a practice of deepening one's experience of a past already known.

The Power and Limits of Recognition

Commemoration of Cherokee removal has continued to grow, structured by the national trail and driven by the work of the Trail of Tears Association. Today, there are more than seventy certified trail sites and interpretive centers, ranging from roadside features with a few signs to museums with significant exhibits on Cherokee history. Recent additions include the site of the Cedar Town Camp, in Polk County, Georgia, one of the small posts established by military forces charged with evicting Cherokees from their homes in the summer of 1838. Interpretive signs explain that militia used the camp to gather every Cherokee they could find within a ten-mile area. They then transferred those assembled to the larger post at New Echota and, from there, to the internment camps in Tennessee.[90] In Charleston, Tennessee, near the sites of those camps, the newly established Hiwassee River Heritage Center includes substantial material on Cherokee history and the Trail of Tears. Interpretive panels explain that Charleston was the location of the Cherokees' U.S. agency in the early nineteenth century, as well as General Winfield Scott's headquarters during removal. The exhibit describes the camps that stretched along the river in the vicinity of Charleston and the departure of Cherokee detachments from the area in the summer and fall of 1838.[91] Further west, along the trail routes, a variety of recent exhibits convey specific stories from the journey. At the Camp Ground Cemetery, near Jonesboro, Illinois, wayside signage notes that as many as ten thousand Cherokees traveled the road adjacent to the site during the winter of 1838–1839. It also speculates that the cemetery, established just prior to removal, contains Cherokee graves.[92] In Waynesville, Missouri, exhibits in the town's main park, along Roubidoux Creek, identify the area as a camping spot for Cherokee detachments, "a resting place for the weary."[93] Similar signs in New Madrid, Missouri, erected on the levy overlooking the Mississippi River, describe the experience of Cherokees who traveled the water routes to Indian Territory.[94] At the far western end of the national trail, the NPS, TOTA, and local communities have even marked the locations of "dispersal camps," the depots in Indian Territory where Cherokee detachments disbanded.[95] As the Park Service certifies new sites each year, the public memory of removal continues to grow upon the landscape.

Meanwhile, the national trail itself has grown. In 2006, Congress ordered the Park Service to study the feasibility of adding new components to the trail, including the paths followed by the Bell and Benge detachments and the "round-up routes" used by the military to transport Cherokees to the internment camps in eastern Tennessee. For years, heritage advocates had expressed disappointment that the original trail designation included only two major corridors, and researchers working with the Park Service and TOTA spent countless hours tracing the neglected components. Drawing this research together, the NPS recommended expanding the national trail to include all documented paths used in the removal.[96] In 2009, Congress accepted these findings, adding around twenty-eight hundred miles to the national trail. Designation of the Bell and Benge routes greatly increased TOT-NHT mileage in Tennessee and Arkansas, while the addition of the "round-up routes" integrated North Carolina and Georgia more thoroughly into the trail. The new paths included so-called "water land components," overland sections used by Cherokee detachments that otherwise traveled by boat. The largest of these sections covered the corridor through northern Alabama commemorated by the yearly motorcycle ride. The 2009 act also embraced additional river mileage and several "dispersal" routes, paths taken by Cherokees as they left their detachments at the end of the journey and traveled to new settlements. In all, these new routes and sections amounted to a massive expansion. The 2009 act more than doubled the size of the Trail of Tears, opening a wealth of new opportunities for site development and interpretation.[97]

Taken as a whole, the national trail represents a remarkable achievement. In an era of shrinking preservation budgets, a partnership consisting of the Park Service, Cherokee tribes, and a variety of local heritage advocates created what surely constitutes the largest commemoration of Native American history in the South, and possibly the largest in the nation. Today, one can follow the overland northern route by automobile and stop every few hours at a new interpretive site. These exhibits allow one to cultivate a fine-grained sense of the Cherokee journey, as one physically retraces the slow progress of the overland detachments. The other routes offer less interpretation, with the exception of the corridor adopted by the motorcycle riders; however, the rapid accretion of new certified sites promises to integrate these routes into the national trail more thoroughly in coming years. This work has made Indian removal a part of the public historical identity of dozens of communities that might otherwise offer little recognition of an indigenous past.

When I consider the national trail, however, I find myself troubled by the earlier commemorations discussed in this book. For much of the twentieth century, these monuments, rituals, and historic sites told stories of a vanishing people, offering sympathy and regret for absent Cherokees. In mounting these commemorations, white heritage workers deepened their possession of Cherokee places. By recognizing Indian founders and forebears, and then narrating their absence, white residents made themselves the native people of these stolen lands. They relegated Native Americans to the past, reinforcing the assumption of a biracial South. Many sites along the contemporary national trail still act as monuments to absence. Indeed, they cannot help but do so, since so many of them commemorate stories of Cherokee people either leaving southern places or merely passing through on their journey into the West. Signs and exhibits along the trail employ a visual language that would be familiar to earlier commemorators. Visitors see long columns of Cherokees, huddled against the cold, walking slowly by. Wagons recede into the distance. Recent exhibits sponsored by TOTA and the NPS usually include a reminder that Cherokee communities survived the Trail of Tears. Newer wayside exhibits, for example, note that the Five Tribes, today, "stand as successful sovereign nations, proudly preserving cultural traditions, while adapting to the challenges of the twenty-first century."[98] The weight of interpretation, however, emphasizes Indian decline and retreat. After all, for most of the communities involved in the national trail, removal is still a story about Native Americans going away. It is worth asking, then, whether even the most accurate and thorough removal commemoration can avoid reinforcing old ideas of Indian disappearance.

Much of the current heritage work, meanwhile, ignores the place of African Americans in Cherokee history, continuing a long-standing practice of erasing black slavery from public memories of the removal-era Cherokee Nation. This practice helps to distance Cherokee history from the history of the biracial South, by divorcing the removal-era Cherokee Nation from an institution that defined the South as a region. It also helps to keep the removal memory uncontroversial by separating the Trail of Tears from the contemporary debate over the rights of "freedmen," descendants of Cherokee slaves who have long pursued citizenship in the Cherokee Nation. The Vann plantation house in Chatsworth, Georgia, offers a notable exception to this tendency to erase slavery. There, a state historic site has begun interpreting the lives of black workers enslaved by the Cherokee Vann family, prompted by research conducted by the historian Tiya Miles. At many other sites, however, slavery still goes unnoticed, in spite of the steady growth of Cherokee public history.[99]

Moreover, contemporary commemoration tends to define Indian removal in a way that diminishes its significance to American history, even as it acknowledges the injustice of the removal policy. Removal, these commemorations suggest, was a tragic mistake committed by an otherwise just nation. A 2004 NPS interpretive plan, for instance, states that "the history of the Trail of Tears warns how a nation founded on the principles of equality and guaranteed protection under law fell prey to greed, racism, and disregard for human rights to serve special interests." Contemporary Americans, it concludes, must remain "eternally vigilant to prevent this happening again."[100] That lesson is laudable, of course, and the public memory of removal may indeed remind Americans to live up to their better ideals. Defining the Trail of Tears as an aberration, however, overlooks the fundamental role played by episodes like Cherokee removal in the creation of the United States. As a settler nation, the United States required the vacating of Indian land for its existence. Settlers fashioned the United States by replacing indigenous peoples with their own communities.[101] From this perspective, acts like the coerced removal of the southeastern tribes were not violations of American principles of freedom and equality, but the very foundation upon which freedom and equality rested for white American citizens. Defining removal as a tragic error acknowledges injustice, but, in doing so, it redeems the United States and erases the colonial origins of American nationhood. The habit of viewing removal as an aberration, meanwhile, is part of what keeps the memory of the Trail of Tears uncontroversial. If removal merely represents a terrible mistake, one need only acknowledge the injustice and promise not to repeat it. The episode remains safely distant from contemporary political concerns.

It is probably asking too much to expect the Park Service to interpret the past in a manner that questions the legitimacy of American nationhood. But perhaps the partnership that has overseen the impressive development of the national trail can at least work to make the public memory of removal more challenging, asking more of contemporary Americans than simply the recognition of old crimes. The current practice of including references to the sovereignty of Indian nations suggests one way of pursuing that goal. Perhaps removal commemoration can serve as a forum for not only celebrating the fact of Cherokee persistence, but discussing the ongoing work of Indian nations to restore their political, economic, and cultural autonomy in the present. For non-Indians, such commemoration would require more than the recognition of American injustice. It would demand support for the efforts of contemporary indigenous communities to gain greater control over their own futures. Americans have acknowledged the injustice of removal for a long time. We must either do more with the public memory of the Trail of Tears or find new stories to tell about the Native American past and present.

Epilogue

••

In 2012, small white signs began appearing next to monuments and roadside markers related to Cherokee history in western North Carolina and southeastern Tennessee. In red letters, printed in both the Cherokee syllabary and English, they stated simply, "we are still here." I first noticed one of the signs on my commute to work. It showed up one day next to a North Carolina roadside marker indicating the boundary of Cherokee territory established by a land cession in 1802. The state marker was a typical colonial monument. It commemorated the transfer of territory from an indigenous people to the new settler nation, invoking Cherokees in order to account for their erasure. The new sign, however, deftly reworked the old, reminding passersby that this place is still Cherokee ground and that the Cherokee people remain present.

As I learned a short time later, the signs belonged to a project created by the artist Jeff Marley, a member of the Eastern Band, who used the small temporary notices to challenge what he termed the "finality" expressed by memorials to Native history created by the dominant society. Historic sites, he observed, suggest that the history of Native peoples has ended. By adding "new information" to old monuments, he sought to question that assumption, reminding viewers that "history and culture are not static, but growing and developing daily."[1] He kept his signs small, so that the original markers would dwarf the new. This disparity served as a reminder that Indian people—and their histories and ways of knowing—remain marginal in the contemporary United States. Over several months, Marley placed the signs next to a variety of markers and memorials, while documenting the growing project through photography. The signs appeared next to roadside markers devoted to the "Rutherford Trace," the route taken by North Carolina's Revolutionary militia when they invaded Cherokee territory in 1776, and at Ross's Landing in Chattanooga, a departure point on the Trail of Tears. He placed one at the site of a Revolutionary Era military post in the town of Old Fort, North Carolina, and another beside the state marker indicating the spot where Tsali was executed.[2] The small white signs provided ironic

Jeff Marley, "We Are Still Here," Old Fort, North Carolina. Courtesy Jeff Marley.

footnotes to the older monuments, politely correcting long-established narratives of Indian disappearance. "By the way," they seemed to remark, "Cherokees did not vanish—this history is not finished."

Like Marley's project, some of the most fascinating recent work in Native public history involves Indian people and tribal communities repossessing historical memories and, in the process, transforming them. I conclude this study by briefly describing three Cherokee examples of this phenomenon—a monument, a tribal history course, and a reclaimed place. Each of these examples involves or alludes to the history of Cherokee removal, but their purpose is less to recognize the injustice of that episode than to strengthen Cherokee people and communities in the present.

A Repatriated Memorial

In Robbinsville, North Carolina, a group of Cherokees from the Snowbird community have created a memorial that operates like a permanent and more detailed version of Jeff Marley's signs, a new monument that talks back to and revises something old. In 1910, the Daughters of the American Revolution (DAR) placed a monument at the gravesite of the Cherokee leader Junaluska. An iron tablet bolted to a rough boulder, it honored Junaluska's service to the United States in the Creek War of 1813–1814. During those years, several hundred Cherokees joined militia troops led by Andrew Jackson in a campaign to destroy the nativist Creek movement known as the Red Sticks. At the war's climactic battle, tradition held, Junaluska rescued Jackson from certain death by killing a Creek warrior who had assaulted the general. This legend became an important part of local memory, in part because Junaluska's service to Jackson provided a poignant contrast to Jackson's espousal of the removal policy in later years. The DAR memorial invoked the legend and noted that, "for his bravery and faithfulness," the state of North Carolina made Junaluska a citizen and granted him land in the mountains in the years following removal.[3]

In the 1990s, Cherokees from the Snowbird community remade the site, organizing a campaign to create a new memorial and to persuade the government of the Eastern Band of Cherokee Indians to purchase the land where Junaluska lies. Around the grave they placed seven additional markers describing Junaluska's life in greater detail and emphasizing his determination to remain in what became western North Carolina. In particular, they brought Junaluska into the history of Cherokee removal, highlighting his role as a resistance leader. Captured in 1838 and started on the journey west, he and his brother Wachacha led about fifty Cherokees in an escape attempt, leaving their detachment and heading back toward the mountains. While Wachacha and others made it home, Junaluska was retaken and forced on the long journey to Indian Territory. Within a few years, however, he returned, walking back to the southern highlands, reversing the Trail of Tears. Only then did North Carolina decide that his "faithfulness" to the United States merited citizenship and the gift of a small portion of the Cherokees' stolen homeland.[4]

Like Marley's signs, the new memorial at Junaluska's grave responds to the old marker, creating a dialogue between two very different historical memories. The DAR monument represented both a gesture of respect and an act of possession. It drew Junaluska into the history of the United States, but only on terms that emphasized American nationalism and white munificence. It defined Junaluska as an agent of the empire he and other Cherokees resisted, making the replacement of Cherokees with settler communities appear natural and preordained. The newer memorial revises the old, repatriating Junaluska. It works to restore his reputation as a Cherokee who served his own people, regardless of what he might have done for Andrew Jackson. The fact that the gravesite now belongs to the Eastern Band, moreover, reminds visitors that Cherokees remain in their homeland, thanks to the labors of people like Junaluska. Annual commemorative events at the site reinforce that message of service and persistence. Each November, Cherokees lay a wreath at the grave in a ceremony that emphasizes the sacrifices made by Junaluska's generation to maintain a Cherokee presence in the Southeast. In recent years, the site has also served as the destination for a commemorative walk that follows the route of a road cut by the United States to facilitate removal. In 1838, Cherokees from the Robbinsville area walked the road as North Carolina militia transported them to the deportation camps in Tennessee. The commemorative walk reverses that course, with participants hiking from a mountain gap through which Cherokees left the area back to the Junaluska memorial.[5] Both events emphasize Cherokee youth and leadership. The commemorative walk raises money for a scholarship fund, while the wreath-laying ceremony, in recent years, has been led by the Junaluska Leadership Council, a Cherokee youth organization. At the 2013 wreath ceremony, the chair of the Eastern Band Tribal Council explained what she considered the message of the site. "Just like this man here [Junaluska] and our forefathers who fought in and around this area and spilled their blood here we are connected genetically, spiritually and otherwise to this place," Terri Henry said. "We will never leave because it is our home."[6] The Junaluska memorial, then, refers to removal, but with its new features in place, it is no longer a monument to absence.

History as Nation Building

In 2000, the government of the Cherokee Nation began sponsoring a short, intensive class on federal Indian law and Cherokee political history. The "Cherokee Nation History Course" surveyed colonial and American legal doctrines, the history of U.S. Indian policy, and the Cherokee Nation's long struggle to defend its land and autonomy. The nation offered the class free of charge while making it a mandatory training exercise for tribal employees. First taught in Oklahoma, the course later began to travel to communities across the United States, providing university-level instruction in Native American history to both Cherokee Nation citizens and any other member of the public interested enough to commit forty hours to the endeavor. Since its launch, several thousand tribal employees, Cherokee citizens, and non-Cherokees have taken the class.[7]

Led by Cherokee Principal Chief Chad Smith, the organizers of the course designed it explicitly as an exercise in nation building. They sought to encourage Cherokees, in particular those employed by the tribe, to think of themselves as citizens of a sovereign Indian nation by instructing them in the history of Cherokee self-government. The course emphasized the Cherokees' long record of innovation and the extent to which Cherokee persistence required careful adaptation to a world transformed by colonialism and American power. Course lessons discussed many of the developments that non-Indians traditionally cited as evidence of the Cherokees' nineteenth-century "civilization," such as Sequoyah's syllabary, the development of the Cherokee government, and the postremoval Cherokee national school system. They interpreted those developments, however, as examples of successful Cherokee experimentation rather than efforts to emulate and assimilate into the dominant society. As personnel with Harvard University's Project on American Indian Economic Development commented, the class encouraged tribal employees to see the Cherokees as a "people of excellence" and to bring that spirit into their work with the nation.[8]

The "Cherokee Nation History Course" paid significant attention to the removal era and the Trail of Tears, but it did not reduce removal to a story merely of loss and decline. Instead, it presented the removal era as the context for the development of the Cherokees' constitutional government, while emphasizing the persistence of both Cherokee people and Cherokee sovereignty. Like the mid-twentieth-century tribal leaders I discussed in chapter 6, the course narrated the reconstruction of the Cherokee Nation in the West as a model of perseverance and political action.[9] Indeed, the course represented a logical continuation of those earlier tribal leaders' use of public history, since it, too, focused on building consensus in support of the Cherokee national government revived in the postwar era. While William Wayne Keeler and his allies hoped to inspire Cherokees to cooperate in their efforts to build a new tribal administration, the class encouraged Cherokees to become active tribal citizens, participating in the ongoing project of building a Cherokee Nation.

The Mother Town

Finally, there is Kituwah. In 1996, the Eastern Band purchased three hundred acres along the Tuckaseegee River, a short distance from the Qualla Boundary. Known locally as Ferguson Fields, this land was the site of Kituwah, the town Cherokees identify as their origin place as a people. Here, Cherokee ancestors received the sacred fire that provides a central element of traditional religious life and, with it, knowledge of how to live properly in the world. A mound rose from the center of Kituwah, supporting a polygonal council house. At the center of that building lay the hearth and the fire. According to Cherokee tradition, the people used fire from Kituwah to rekindle the sacred fires of the other Cherokee towns once each year. Kituwah, then, stands at the center of things, a place of paramount sacred and historical importance. In the early nineteenth century, when the Cherokee Nation ceded the surrounding territory to the United States, Cherokees tried to preserve Kituwah, along with other significant places, by taking individual land reserves. North Carolina, however, dispossessed Cherokees of most of that property, including Kituwah, and the land passed into the hands of white settlers. Over the next century and a half, agriculture and erosion reduced the mound to a gentle rise of five or six feet, and the mother town became Ferguson Fields. Cherokees, however, did not forget. Keepers of traditional knowledge in both the mountains and the West remembered Kituwah and its significance. Tom Belt, who grew up in Oklahoma and who helped lead the effort to acquire the site, recalls learning of Kituwah from his father and grandmother, who never saw the place. In the mid-1990s, the white family that farmed the land for generations offered to sell the property to the Eastern Band, and, with that act, the mother town returned. After some initial discussion of possible commercial uses for the land, the tribal government decided simply to preserve the site. A few years ago, the Tribal Council passed a resolution affirming Kituwah's standing as a sacred place, in effect promising that no new development would occur there.[10]

Today, Cherokees cultivate gardens along the river and use the site for a variety of events and gatherings. Meanwhile, Kituwah has become a destination for Cherokees visiting their people's original homeland from other places. Each June, the Eastern Band hosts the Annual Kituwah Celebration, an event that draws together Cherokees from around the country. The celebration features performances of traditional dance and music, while providing an opportunity to educate the public about ongoing efforts to preserve and revitalize tribal culture. Kituwah is a heritage site, but more importantly, it is now, once again, a living Cherokee place. In recent years, Eastern Band officials have worked to reacquire other important locations, starting with Cowee, a town site on the Little Tennessee River. With these purchases, Cherokees are protecting culturally significant places, but they are also reclaiming the Cherokee homeland.[11]

Removal, and the broader history of Cherokee dispossession, form unavoidable elements of public memory at sites like Kituwah. At the dedication of the site, following its reacquisition, Tom Belt noted that "over a century and a half ago, my great-grandmother and great-grand-father left these mountains, never to return."[12] It is difficult to stand at Kituwah or Cowee and not think of how little of the surrounding country belongs to the Cherokees, the people who have the best claim upon it. One cannot help but remember the Revolutionary militia who burned these sacred places in the name of liberty, or the soldiers who gathered Cherokees for the long march into the West. Yet Kituwah is not a site of memory that speaks of Indian absence. On the contrary, it is a place of renewal and possibility. After Cherokees dedicated the site, Principal Chief Joyce Dugan wrote of the Eastern Band's responsibility to protect important places like Kituwah on behalf of those Cherokees whose ancestors had to leave their homeland. The Cherokees who went west on the Trail of Tears, she wrote, "entrusted the preservation of these resources to us." North Carolina Cherokees had the honor and the duty "to protect our homeland until the time they might return. That time is now."[13] Removal was not the end, and Kituwah's people do return. As Belt remarked, "We are only separated by a short distance and a little time."[14]

Notes

Abbreviations

BBP	Beverly Baker Papers, Sequoyah National Research Center, University of Arkansas, Little Rock, Arkansas
BHP	Barbara Heffington Papers, Sequoyah National Research Center, University of Arkansas, Little Rock, Arkansas
CAR	RG 75, Bureau of Indian Affairs, Cherokee Agency, General Records, National Archives, Southeast Region, Morrow, Georgia
CFR	Cherokee Foundation Records, Cherokee Heritage Center, Tahlequah, Oklahoma
CNHS	Cherokee National Historical Society Records, Cherokee Heritage Center, Tahlequah, Oklahoma
CNR	Cherokee Nation Records, Cherokee Heritage Center, Tahlequah, Oklahoma
CSR	RG 75, Bureau of Indian Affairs, Cherokee School, 1907–1939, National Archives, Washington, D.C.
GHCR	Georgia Historical Commission Records, RG 61, series 1, Georgia State Archives, Morrow, Georgia
GSMNPL	Great Smoky Mountains National Park Library, Gatlinburg, Tennessee
KRC	King Research Collection, Museum of the Cherokee Indian, Cherokee, North Carolina
MPR	Missouri State Parks Records, Missouri Department of Natural Resources, Jackson, Missouri
MWP	Marie Wadley Papers, Cherokee Heritage Center, Tahlequah, Oklahoma
NESHS	New Echota State Historic Site, Calhoun, Georgia
OIHC	Oklahoma Indian Pioneer History Collection, Oklahoma Historical Society, Oklahoma City, Oklahoma
TOTA	Trail of Tears Association Papers, Sequoyah National Research Center, University of Arkansas, Little Rock, Arkansas
WNCAC	Western North Carolina Associated Communities Papers, Hunter Library, Western Carolina University, Cullowhee, North Carolina
WWKP	William Wayne Keeler Papers, Cherokee Heritage Center, Tahlequah, Oklahoma

Introduction

1. Significant works on early nineteenth-century Cherokee history and removal include McLoughlin, *Cherokees and Missionaries* and *Cherokee Renascence in the New Republic*; Wilkins, *Cherokee Tragedy*; Anderson, *Cherokee Removal*; Norgren, *Cherokee Cases*; Perdue, *Cherokee Women*; Garrison, *Legal Ideology of Removal*; Perdue and Green, *Cherokee Nation and the Trail of Tears*.

2. See, for example, Blight, *Race and Reunion*; Brundage, *Where These Memories Grow* and *The Southern Past*; Shackel, *Memory in Black and White*; and Yuhl, *Golden Haze of Memory*.

3. Tiya Miles's work on the Vann plantation in Georgia represents an exception. See Miles, *House on Diamond Hill* and "Showplace of the Cherokee Nation."

4. See, for example, Wilson, *In the Footsteps of Our Ancestors*; Elliot, *Custerology*; Jacoby, *Shadows at Dawn*; Kelman, *Misplaced Massacre*; and Cothran, *Remembering the Modoc War*.

5. For discussion of the "Native South" and recent historiography of southern Indians, see Saunt, "The Native South." For recent literature on slavery among southern Indians, see Saunt, *Red, White, and Indian*; Miles, *House on Diamond Hill* and *Ties That Bind*; Naylor, *African Cherokees in Indian Territory*; Snyder, *Slavery in Indian Country*; and Krauthamer, *Black Slaves, Indian Masters*.

6. See, for example, Brundage, *Southern Past*, 7–10, and "No Deed But Memory," 10–11; Bishir, "Landmarks of Power," 139–42; Clark, "Celebrating Freedom" and *Defining Moments*; Horton and Crew, "Afro-Americans and Museums."

7. O'Brien, *Firsting and Lasting*, 55–57.

8. Wolfe, *Traces of History*, 10.

9. Martin, "'My Grandmother was a Cherokee Princess,'" 134–42.

10. Hale, *Making Whiteness*, 284–85.

11. Osburn, "The 'Identified Full-Bloods' in Mississippi," 423–25; Lowery, *Lumbee Indians in the Jim Crow South*, 20–24, 28–31.

12. Doss, *Memorial Mania*, 1–2, 13–15, 254–58.

13. See, for example, Wolfe, "Land, Labor, and Difference" and "Settler Colonialism and the Elimination of the Native"; Hixson, *American Settler Colonialism*.

14. Glassberg, *Sense of History*, 6–7, 18–21. See also Hayden, *The Power of Place*.

15. Foreman, *Indian Removal*, 308; Mooney, *History, Myths, and Sacred Formulas*, 132–33; King, *Cherokee Trail of Tears*, 111–12, 130–31.

16. *Jackson Cash-Book*, August 22, 1935; *Southeast Missourian*, October 10, 1962; *Kennett Democrat*, January 5, 1962; Laura Hinkebein (Otahki Girl Scouts, Inc.), personal communication, June 29, 2004; Exler, *Tears of the Trail*, 9; John S. Kochtitzky, "Removal of the Cherokee Indians in 1838–1839: An Account of Their Passing through Cape Girardeau County, Mo.," typescript, 1935, Trail of Tears, Special Collections, Kent Library, Southeast Missouri State University, Cape Girardeau, Missouri, 17–20; Gilbert, *Trail of Tears across Missouri*, 57–59.

17. Minutes, State Parks Board, February 5, August 6, 1954, May 4, 1956, July 1, 1957, Report on the Master Plan for the Trail of Tears State Park, July 1957, MPR; "Trail of Tears State Park," brochure, 1958, Trail of Tears Booklets, Special Collections, Kent Library, Southeast Missouri State University, Cape Girardeau, Missouri; *Southeast Missourian*, January 13, 14, March 14, 24, 1956.

18. Program, Dedication Ceremony, Princess Otahki Memorial, May 27, 1962, MPR; *Southeast Missourian*, October 11, 1961, May 28, 29, 1962.

19. "Heritage Interpretation Conceptual Plan," February 27, 1980, MPR; Larry Grantham to H. G. Riggs, May 29, 1991, Booker Rucker to Brick Autry and Thomas Holloway, July 27, 1992, MPR; Jesse Bushyhead to Duane H. King, December 12, 1993, KRC; "Bushyhead Memorial," interpretive signs, Trail of Tears State Park, Cape Girardeau County, Missouri; Foreman, "Aunt Eliza of Tahlequah."

20. "Certified Sites on the Trail of Tears NHT," National Park Service website, https://www.nps.gov/trte/learn/management/certified-sites-on-the-trail-of-tears-nht.htm, accessed July 12, 2015.

21. *Trail News*, June 2009, 1; National Park Service, *Trail of Tears National Historic Trail Additional Routes*.

22. *TOT-NHT Newsletter*, March 2014, 1, 3.

Chapter One

1. Raymond Fogelson, "Cherokee in the East," in Fogelson, *Southeast*, 337–38.

2. For Kituwah, see Duncan and Riggs, *Cherokee Heritage Trails Guidebook*, 73–75; Riggs, "In the Service of Native Interests," 26–29.

3. For Cherokee-British relations in the colonial era, see Hatley, *Dividing Paths*; Oatis, *A Colonial Complex*; Tortora, *Carolina in Crisis*.

4. Calloway, *American Revolution in Indian Country*, 26–64, 182–211; Hatley, *Dividing Paths*, 179–203, 217–19, 222–28.

5. Prucha, *Great Father*, 35–60, 89–158; Berkhofer, *White Man's Indian*, 38–49.

6. During the 1820s and 1830s, Cherokees invoked the memory of Washington and those early policies to argue against the removal campaign. Denson, *Demanding the Cherokee Nation*, 28–33.

7. Wolfe, "Settler Colonialism and the Elimination of the Native," 387–90.

8. McLoughlin, *Cherokee Renascence*, 21–40, 58–76; McLoughlin, *Cherokees and Missionaries*, 34–36, 101–6, 124–49, 150–53; Perdue, *Cherokee Women*, 115–34.

9. McLoughlin, *Cherokee Renascence*, 139–42, 224–27, 284–95, 394–401; Strickland, *Fire and the Spirits*, 40–66; Champagne, *Social Order and Political Change*, 92–107, 127–43.

10. Foreman, *Sequoyah*, 3–7; Cushman, *Cherokee Syllabary*, 26–36; Bender, *Signs of Cherokee Culture*, 25–41; Parins, *Literacy and Intellectual Life in the Cherokee Nation*, 34–44.

11. Prucha, *Great Father*, 195–97; Perdue and Green, *Cherokee Nation and the Trail of Tears*, 42–46; Sheehan, *Seeds of Extinction*, 148–81; Dippie, *Vanishing American*, 165–90.

12. Prucha, *Great Father*, 186, 197–98; McLoughlin, *Cherokee Renascence*, 217–20; Garrison, *Legal Ideology of Removal*, 59–102.

13. Prucha, *Great Father*, 191–94; Norgren, *Cherokee Cases*, 46–48.

14. Prucha, *Great Father*, 200–201.

15. Perdue and Green, *Cherokee Nation and the Trail of Tears*, 60–67.

16. Ibid., 74–78; McLoughlin, *Cherokees and Missionaries*, 248–57; McLoughlin, *Cherokee Renascence*, 428–38.

17. Denson, *Demanding the Cherokee Nation*, 27–38.

18. Norgren, *Cherokee Cases*, 49–62, 98–122.

19. Ibid., 123–33.

20. National Park Service, *Trail of Tears (The Cherokee Removal Route/1838–1839): Draft National Trail Study*, chap. 2, 2–3.

21. Perdue and Green, *Cherokee Nation and the Trail of Tears*, 99–100; Wilkins, *Cherokee Tragedy*, 249–52.

22. Perdue and Green, *Cherokee Nation and the Trail of Tears*, 74.

23. Federal officials made the annuities payable to individual Cherokees, rather than the Nation. Most Cherokees never claimed the payments. McLoughlin, *Cherokee Renascence*, 438; Perdue and Green, *Cherokee Nation and the Trail of Tears*, 100–101.

24. McLoughlin, *Cherokees and Missionaries*, 298–302.

25. Elias Boudinot, "Letters and Other Papers Relating to Cherokee Affairs: Being a Reply to Sundry Publications by John Ross," 1837, in Perdue and Green, *Cherokee Removal*, 153; Wilkins, *Cherokee Tragedy*, 233–41.

26. Wilkins, *Cherokee Tragedy*, 243–49, 62–63; Perdue and Green, *Cherokee Nation and the Trail of Tears*, 96–98.

27. Wilkins, *Cherokee Tragedy*, 266–76; Perdue and Green, *Cherokee Nation and the Trail of Tears*, 102–10.

28. Wilkins, *Cherokee Tragedy*, 285–90; Perdue and Green, *Cherokee Nation and the Trail of Tears*, 112–13.

29. Wilkins, *Cherokee Tragedy*, 292.

30. Perdue and Green, *Cherokee Nation and the Trail of Tears*, 117–22.

31. Letter of Evan Jones, 1838, quoted in McLoughlin, *Champions of the Cherokees*, 174.

32. Prucha, *Great Father*, 237–40; Denson, *Demanding the Cherokee Nation*, 39–41.

33. Perdue and Green, *Cherokee Nation and the Trail of Tears*, 123–24; National Park Service, *Trail of Tears National Historic Trail Additional Routes*, 7–8.

34. Letter of Evan Jones, 1838, quoted in McLoughlin, *Champions of the Cherokees*, 174.

35. Butrick, *Journal of Rev. Daniel S. Butrick*, 6.

36. Perdue and Green, *Cherokee Nation and the Trail of Tears*, 127–28; King, *Cherokee Trail of Tears*, 47–50; National Park Service, *Trail of Tears National Historic Trail Additional Routes*, 16–17.

37. Butrick, *Journal of Rev. Daniel S. Butrick*, 6.

38. King, *Cherokee Trail of Tears*, 170–71; Perdue and Green, *Cherokee Nation and the Trail of Tears*, 128.

39. L. H. Jordan to Lyde, July 22, 1838, Correspondence Pertaining to Cherokee Removal, M1475, microfilm, RG 75 Bureau of Indian Affairs, National Archives; Perdue and Green, *Cherokee Nation and the Trail of Tears*, 129.

40. Perdue and Green, *Cherokee Nation and the Trail of Tears*, 129–30; King, *Cherokee Trail of Tears*, 170–71.

41. King, *Cherokee Trail of Tears*, 89–136.

42. Ibid., 53–87.

43. Ibid., 139–57.

44. Ibid., 170–72.

45. *New York Observer*, January 26, 1839, quoted in King, *Cherokee Trail of Tears*, 102–3.

46. Butrick, *The Journal of Rev. Daniel S. Butrick*, 52.

47. King, *Cherokee Trail of Tears*, 165–68; Thornton, *Cherokees*, 73–76.

48. Perdue and Green, *Cherokee Nation and the Trail of Tears*, 143–48.

49. McLoughlin, *After the Trail of Tears*, 2–4.

50. Ibid., 11–22.

51. Ibid., 22–58; Denson, *Demanding the Cherokee Nation*, 42–49.

52. McLoughlin, *After the Trail of Tears*, 52, 60–69, 86–96.

53. Ibid., 168–75, 192–95, 205–17; Thornton, *Cherokees*, 90–95. See also Confer, *Cherokee Nation in the Civil War*.

54. McLoughlin, *After the Trail of Tears*, 245–50.

55. Prucha, *Great Father*, 737–57; Denson, *Demanding the Cherokee Nation*, 201–42.

56. Finger, *Eastern Band*, 10–11.

57. Ibid., 11–14.

58. Ibid., 16–19.

59. Abraham Eustis to Winfield Scott, July 3, 1838, Correspondence Pertaining to Cherokee Removal.

60. Ibid.; Robert Anderson to C. H. Larned, September 17, 1838, Correspondence Pertaining to Cherokee Removal.

61. C. H. Larned to Winfield Scott, October 3, 1838, Correspondence Pertaining to Cherokee Removal.

62. George Porter to Major Kirby, June 18, 1838, Larned to Scott, September 16, 1838, Correspondence Pertaining to Cherokee Removal; Duncan and Riggs, *Cherokee Heritage Trails Guidebook*, 208.

63. Finger, *Eastern Band*, 21–28; Jurgelski, "New Light on the Tsali Affair."

64. Finger, *Eastern Band*, 29.

65. Howe, " 'The Ancient Customs of Their Fathers.' "

66. Finger, *Eastern Band*, 44–45, 62–63, 69–70.

67. Ibid., 35–37, 41–42.

68. Ibid., 102–6.

69. Ibid., 111–12, 118–25.

70. For the sake of clarity, I will use the term Bureau of Indian Affairs (BIA) to designate the administrative unit charged with managing federal Indian relations. In the nineteenth century, federal authorities generally used the term Office of Indian Affairs, or simply Indian Office. Other names, however, were also used, including Indian Bureau, Indian Service, and Indian Department. By the 1920s and 1930s, the terms Indian Bureau and Bureau of Indian Affairs began to appear more frequently in administrative records and legislation. In 1947, the Interior Department formally adopted the name Bureau of Indian Affairs for the unit, ordering its personnel to dispense with the earlier designations. Prucha, *Great Father*, 1227–29.

71. Finger, *Eastern Band*, 107–8, 114–15.

72. Ibid., 155–56.

73. Jackson, *Century of Dishonor*, 270.

74. Ibid., 270–71.

75. Herbert Welsh, "The Indian Question Past and Present," 1890, Indian Rights Association Papers, printed matter, IRA pamphlets, 1883–1892, microfilm roll 102, 7.

76. Barrows, *Indian's Side of the Indian Question*, 71.

77. Dawes, "The Indian Territory," 96.

78. Letter of Dennis W. Bushyhead, *New York Independent*, February 24, 1881, reprinted in *Cherokee Advocate*, April 13, 1881.

79. Ibid.

80. Batteau, *Invention of Appalachia*, 38–85; Harkins, *Hillbilly*.

81. Davis, "Qualla," 582.

82. Ibid., 583.

83. Ibid., 586.

84. Zeigler and Grosscup, *Heart of the Alleghenies or Western North Carolina*, 17.

85. Ibid., 36.

86. Doak, *Wagonauts Abroad*, 231–32.

87. Mooney, *History, Myths, and Sacred Formulas*, 8–13. See also Moses, *Indian Man*.

88. Mooney, *History, Myths, and Sacred Formulas*, 11–12.

89. Ibid., 131, 157–58.

90. Ibid., 158; Finger, *Eastern Band*, 28; Jurgelski, "New Light on the Tsali Affair," 134–40.

91. Finger, *Eastern Band of Cherokees*, 10–13, 16–19, 26–28; King, "Origin of the Eastern Cherokees as a Social and Political Entity."

Chapter Two

1. "Great Smoky Mountains National Park: The Rooftop of Eastern America," *Tennessee Wildlife* (1939), clipping, Publicity Files, GSMNPL, 7–27, quotations 7, 12, 15, 26.

2. Ibid., 8–9.

3. Urry, *Tourist Gaze*, 1–3.

4. See Becker, *Selling Tradition*, 7–10.

5. Katherine Osburn suggests that segregation helped to create a "market" for Indianness in the South. Osburn, "The 'Identified Full-Bloods' in Mississippi," 423–25.

6. Discussions of Cherokee tourism often focus on the question of whether tourist performances are authentic representations of tribal culture and history. See, for instance, Finger, *Cherokee Americans*, 98–104; Martin, *Tourism in the Mountain South*, 62–65; French and Hornbuckle, *Cherokee Perspective*, 35–40. For a more nuanced approach, see Beard-Moose, *Public Indians, Private Cherokees*. Anthropologist Edward M. Bruner suggests authenticity is a "red herring," distracting attention from the complexity of tourist cultures. Bruner, *Culture on Tour*, 5–7.

7. Starnes, *Creating the Land of the Sky*, 9–34; Martin, *Tourism in the Mountain South*, 1–41.

8. Finger, *Cherokee Americans*, 20–21, 32.

9. French and Hornbuckle, *Cherokee Perspective*, 35.

10. Martin, *Tourism in the Mountain South*, 106–8; Starnes, *Creating the Land of the Sky*, 53–56. See also Preston, *Dirt Roads to Dixie*.

11. Finger, *Cherokee Americans*, 55–56.

12. Song sheet, undated, Great Smoky Mountains Conservation Association scrapbooks, GSMNPL.

13. Pierce, *Great Smokies*, 37, 40–42, 56–88, 109–11.

14. Ibid., 45–55.

15. Ibid., 89–153; Starnes, *Creating the Land of the Sky*, 118–21.

16. Finger, *Cherokee Americans*, 78–79; *Knoxville News-Sentinel*, April 24, 1927; *Appalachian Journal*, March, April 1932.

17. *Raleigh News and Observer*, August 15, 1930.

18. Ibid.

19. *Asheville Citizen*, October 15, 1915; Finger, *Cherokee Americans*, 32; Chiltoskey, *Cherokee Fair and Festival*, 5–8; Cherokee Superintendent to *Asheville Citizen*, October 12, 1914, Cherokee Superintendent to Cato Sells, October 25, 1915, October 30, 1916, Cherokee Superintendent to Commissioner of Indian Affairs, August 4, 1917, CAR.

20. *Asheville Citizen*, October 4, 9, 1920, October 3, 1921, October 3, 7, 1922, October 10, 11, 1924, October 6, 8, 9, 1926, October 5, 1927, October 4, 1927, October 3, 4, 5, 6, 1928, October 8, 9, 10, 1929; *Charlotte Observer*, October 6, 1929; *State*, October 1, 1938.

21. James Henderson to Commissioner of Indian Affairs, August 4, December 17, 1917, CAR; Chiltoskey, *Cherokee Fair and Festival*, 5–10.

22. "Indian Fair at Cherokee Most Colorful Event," *Charlotte Observer*, October 6, 1929.

23. Ibid. Owl noted a similar adaptation when he mentioned that the dance ground featured a large tipi as stage dressing.

24. Finger, *Cherokee Americans*, 161–63; Beard-Moose, *Public Indians, Private Cherokees*, 80–86.

25. *Charlotte Observer*, October 6, 1929.

26. Finger, *Cherokee Americans*, 44–51.

27. "The Great Smoky Mountains National Park," 1928, Publicity Files, GSMNPL, 13, 31, 38.

28. "A National Park in the Great Smoky Mountains," undated [circa 1926], Publicity Files, GSMNPL, 7.

29. Ibid.

30. "Guide to the Great Smoky Mountains National Park," 1933, Publicity Files, GSMNPL, 116–20.

31. "The Great Smokies: A Vast National Park in the Land of the Sky," undated [circa 1930], Publicity Files, GSMNPL, 3–14; "The Qualla Reservation," *Touring the Land of the Sky* 5 (1938), Publicity Files, GSMNPL, 6–7, 28.

32. "The Cherokee Indians of the Qualla Reservation," 1937, Special Collections, Hunter Library, Western Carolina University, Cullowhee, N.C.

33. "Guide to the Great Smoky Mountains National Park," 1933, 71; "A National Park in the Great Smoky Mountains," undated [circa 1926], 2, 10, 12–13; "The Great Smokies," undated [circa 1930], 3–14, Publicity Files, GSMNPL.

34. Martin, "To Keep the Spirit of Mountain Culture Alive," 256.

35. "Taming 'Old Smoky' for a National Park," *New York Times Magazine*, March 25, 1928.

36. "Guide to the Great Smoky Mountains National Park," 1933, 112, 114.

37. Mason, *Lure of the Great Smokies*, 267.

38. "The Great Smokies," undated [circa 1930].

39. *Baltimore Sun*, February 2, 1930, clippings, Great Smoky Mountains Conservation Association scrapbook, GSMNPL. This essay was published by several newspapers. "Preserving a Land of Tragedy" was the title used by the *Baltimore Sun*.

40. Ibid.

41. Mooney, *History, Myths, and Sacred Formulas*, 131, 157–58.

42. "Cherokee Indians of the Qualla Reservation," 24.

43. James P. Welsh, "These Smokies," *Mountaineer* 1 (February 1941) 3–4, in Publicity Files, GSMNPL; Thornborough, *Great Smoky Mountains*, 67, 70–71.

44. *Asheville Citizen*, October 2, 4, 1935, July 4, 1937; "The Spirit of the Great Smokies: A Pageant Commemorating the One-Hundredth Anniversary of the Great Removal, 1835–1935," Kansas State Historical Society, Topeka, Kansas; Program, "The Spirit of the Great Smokies: A Cherokee Indian Pageant," July–August 1937, CSR.

45. Glassberg, *American Historical Pageantry*, 1–5, 43–101.

46. *Asheville Citizen*, June 2, 4, October 6, 1931.

47. "Spell of the Smokies," October 1933, notes on Spell of the Smokies, Edith Harrington Papers, Southern Historical Collection, University of North Carolina, Chapel Hill, N.C.

48. Prucha, *Great Father*, 954–68; Finger, *Cherokee Americans*, 79–82.

49. Finger, *Cherokee Americans*, 51–52, 79–80.

50. Harold Foght, "Preliminary Organization of Activities: Cherokee Indian Reservation," October 1934, CSR, 3–4, 5, 11; Finger, *Cherokee Americans*, 82–84. John Collier was himself an enthusiastic supporter of Native American cultural performance. See Schwartz, "Red Atlantis Revisited."

51. Program, "Cherokee Indian Fair and Folk Festival," 1935, CAR; Williams, *Staging Tradition*, 11–15. For Lunsford and the Mountain Dance and Folk Festival, see Starnes, *Creating the Land of the Sky*, 158–61; Jones, *Minstrel of the Appalachians*; Whisnant, "Finding the Way between Old and New."

52. *State*, February 22, 1936.

53. Harold Foght to John Collier, June 18, July 17, 1935, CAR; *Chilocco Indian School Journal*, May 1924; *Haskell Indian Leader*, September 18, 1931; *Kansas City Times*, October 23, 1948, June 30, 1949.

54. "The Pageant of Great Gifts," October 9–10, 1930, "Wa-gthe' Ce Shpi-zho: A Pageant of Indian Education," November 3, 1933, Kansas State Historical Society, Topeka, quote on page 2; Speelman, "Pageantry in Indian Schools."

55. "Spirit of the Great Smokies," 6–12; Glassberg, *American Historical Pageantry*, 105–50.

56. "Spirit of the Great Smokies," 7.

57. Ibid., 8.

58. Ibid., 9–11.

59. Ibid., 12.

60. Witthoft, "Will West Long, Cherokee Informant," 355–59, quote on 358; Speck and Broom, *Cherokee Dance and Drama*, xvii–xx.

61. *Asheville Citizen*, June 2, 4, 1931; Programs, National Folk Festival, May 1935, June 1926, Sarah Gertrude Knott Papers, Folklife Archives, Kentucky Library and Museum, Western Kentucky University, Bowling Green. For the National Folk Festivals, see Williams, *Staging Tradition*.

62. Speck and Broom discussed the Green Corn Dance and Eagle Dance, for instance, which Long and other Cherokees also performed for tourists. Speck and Broom, *Cherokee Dance and Drama*, 39–44, 45–54.

63. "Spirit of the Great Smokies," 2, 14; Speelman to Clyde Blair, April 17, 1939, CAR.

64. Harold Foght to John Collier, August 17, 1937, CAR; Program, "The Spirit of the Great Smokies: A Cherokee Indian Pageant"; *Asheville Citizen*, July 4, 6, 1937.

65. Finger, *Cherokee Americans*, 100.

66. For a more detailed description of the memorial campaign, see Denson, "Gatlinburg's Cherokee Monument."

67. *Knoxville News-Sentinel*, February 21, 1937; Herbert Ravenel Sass, "Land of the Cherokee," *Collier's*, February 20, 1937, 57–62. The *Collier's* piece was itself based on an earlier example of Sass's writing. In 1936 Sass included a chapter on Tsali in a book titled *Hear Me, My Chiefs!*, which consisted of a series of vignettes describing famous individuals and events from Indian history.

68. *Knoxville News-Sentinel*, February 21, 1937.

69. Ibid.

70. Ibid.

71. Ibid.

72. Ibid., February 26, 1937.

73. Ibid., February 26, 27, 28, March 2, 1937; Pierce, *Great Smokies*, 104–5.

74. *Knoxville News-Sentinel*, March 3, 8, 9, 15, 1937.

75. Ibid., May 5, 1937.

76. Ibid.

77. *Knoxville News-Sentinel*, June 20, 22, 23, 26, 1937; *Knoxville Journal*, June 26, 27, 1937.

78. *Knoxville News-Sentinel*, June 20, 1937; Brad Lawrence to Clyde Blair, April 17, 1939, Harold Foght to J. L. Waters, August 17, 1937, CAR; Harold Foght to John Collier, July 31, 1937, CSR.

79. Brad Lawrence to Clyde Blair, December 7, 1838, April 17, 1939, Clyde Blair to John Collier, April 19, May 9, 1939, CAR; Brad Lawrence to John Collier, April 21, 1939, CSR.

80. Clyde Blair to John Collier, May 9, 1939, Brad Lawrence to Clyde Blair, June 9, 1939, CAR; Brad Lawrence to John Collier, April 21, 1939, CSR.

81. Brad Lawrence to John Collier, April 21, 1939, CSR; Brad Lawrence to John Collier, May 8, 1939, John Collier to Brad Lawrence, May 31, 1939, CAR.

82. *Knoxville News-Sentinel*, April 19, 1940.

83. Bruner, *Culture on Tour*, 22–23.

Chapter Three

1. For the Chickamauga and Chattanooga battles, see McDonough, *Chattanooga*; Cozzens, *This Terrible Sound* and *Shipwreck of Their Hopes*; and John Bowers, *Chickamauga and Chattanooga*.

2. Govan and Livingwood, *Chattanooga Country*, 108–9.

3. Susman, *Culture as History*, 153–57.

4. Govan and Livingwood, *Chattanooga Country*, 12–14, 18–21; Calloway, *American Revolution in Indian Country*, 26–64. For life in the region prior to European contact, see Lewis and Lewis, *Prehistory of the Chickamauga Basin*.

5. Duncan and Riggs, *Cherokee Heritage Trails Guidebook*, 273, 284–85; "Return Jonathan Meigs," *Tennessee Encyclopedia of History and Culture*, tennesseeencyclopedia.net, accessed March 27, 2012; McLoughlin, *Cherokees and Missionaries*, 109–10.

6. Duncan and Riggs, *Cherokee Heritage Trails Guidebook*, 251–60, 275, 278–82; Wilkins, *Cherokee Tragedy*, 242, 247, 252, 254.

7. Govan and Livingwood, *Chattanooga Country*, 115–58.

8. Cozzens, *This Terrible Sound*, 21–60, 357–477, 520–21; Cozzens, *Shipwreck of Their Hopes*, 8–22, 39–43, 51–100, 159–78, 244–81.

9. Ezzell, "Yankees in Dixie," 13–74, 197–229.

10. Ibid., 74–114; Potts, "Unfulfilled Expectations," 112–28.

11. Govan and Livingwood, *Chattanooga Country*, 385–91, 449–64; Livingwood, *History of Hamilton County*, 385–405.

12. *Chattanooga Times*, September 18, 1938; Kaser, *At the Bivouac of Memory*, 81–130; Smith, *Golden Age of Battlefield Preservation*, 51–85. See also Smith, *Chickamauga Memorial*.

13. *Tennessee State History of the Daughters of the American Revolution*, 124, 154–55; Cummings and Smothers, *Historical Markers Placed by the Tennessee Society, Daughters of the American Revolution*, 490.

14. *Tennessee State History of the Daughters of the American Revolution*, 51; Cummings and Smothers, *Historical Markers Placed by the Tennessee Society, Daughters of the American Revolution*, 4–5, 413–18, 439; *Chattanooga Times*, November 26, 1924, November 2, 1933; *Lookout* (Chattanooga Centennial Edition), June 10, 1938; Armstrong, *History of Hamilton County and Chattanooga, Tennessee*, 63.

15. For the founding of the Daughters of the American Revolution, see Gibbs, *DAR*, 30–56; Strayer, *DAR: An Informal History*, 1–31.

16. Calloway, *American Revolution in Indian Country*, 26–64, 182–97; Hatley, *Dividing Paths*, 179–203.

17. *Tennessee State History of the Daughters of the American Revolution*, 40–43, 47–48, 76–77, 80, 81, 82, 95, 153, 154; Cummings and Smothers, *Historical Markers Placed by the Tennessee Society, Daughters of the American Revolution*, 33, 34, 52, 53–54, 139–40, 141, 369, 392–93, 474–75.

18. Hatley, *Dividing Paths*, 217–19; Calloway, *American Revolution in Indian Country*, 188–97.

19. Calloway, *American Revolution in Indian Country*, 197–211; Hatley, *Dividing Paths*, 222–28.

20. Perdue, *Cherokee Women*, 38–39, 55–56.

21. Ibid., 54, 61; Conley, *Cherokee Nation*, 59–60, 68–70.

22. A. A. Taylor, "Early Days in Tennessee," in Justi, *Official History of the Tennessee Centennial Exposition*, 66–67.

23. "Work of the Chapters," *Daughters of the American Revolution Magazine*, October 1925, 638, 646.

24. *Cleveland Herald*, October 26, 1923; *Cleveland Banner*, October 27, 1923.

25. *Chattanooga Times*, November 26, 1924.

26. Ibid.

27. State Historian's Report, *Proceedings of the Thirty-Eighth State Conference, National Society Daughters of the American Revolution, Georgia* (n.p., 1936), 54–55.

28. *Dalton Citizen*, May 30, 1935.

29. Ibid., June 13, 1935.

30. *Dalton Citizen*, June 27, November 14, 1935; *Chattanooga Times*, July 28, November 17, 1935; *Cleveland Daily Banner*, November 5, 1935; Charles Lusk to Mrs. William Becker, October 23, 1935, William Snell Papers, History Branch, Cleveland Public Library, Cleveland, Tennessee.

31. Lusk to Becker, October 23, 1935.

32. *Chattanooga Times*, February 6, March 27, 29, 1938, April 13, 1965; Official Program, Chickamauga National Celebration, 1938, Local History Collections, Chattanooga Public Library, Chattanooga, Tennessee, 7; Armstrong, *History of Hamilton County and Chattanooga.*

33. *Chattanooga Times*, March 29, 30, August 4, 1938.

34. Ibid., August 25, September 16, 19, 20; Official Program, Chickamauga National Commemoration, 19–20, 61; Mary Cecelia Freeland, "The Drums of Dixie," pageant script, Local History Collections, Chattanooga Public Library, Chattanooga, Tennessee, 18–22, 30–33.

35. *Chattanooga Times*, August 3, 8, September 11, 17; Official Program, Chickamauga National Celebration, 19–20, 59, 61, 63, 65.

36. *Chattanooga Times*, April 6, June 19, 1938.

37. Armstrong, *History of Hamilton County and Chattanooga*, 31–34. See also Allen, *Historic Chattanooga*, 25; *Lookout* (Chattanooga Centennial Edition), June 10, 1938.

38. *Chattanooga Times*, March 21, 23, 1930; Cummings and Smothers, *Historical Markers Placed by the Tennessee Society Daughters of the American Revolution*, 422–23.

39. Armstrong, *History of Hamilton County and Chattanooga*, 54–62; *Tennessee State History of the Daughters of the American Revolution*, 142.

40. *Chattanooga Times*, September 18, 1938.

41. Ibid., September 18, 1938; Walker, *Torchlights to the Cherokees.*

42. Glassberg, *American Historical Pageantry*, 236–37, 260–63, 275–76; Freeland, "Drums of Dixie," 34.

43. Glassberg, *American Historical Pageantry*, 139–40, 185–86.

44. Freeland, "Drums of Dixie," 5–7, 9–10, 11–13; Official Program, Chickamauga National Celebration, 34–35, 37–38, 39–40; *Chattanooga Times*, September 15, 16, 1938.

45. Freeland, "Drums of Dixie," 13–18.

46. Ibid., 7–9; Official Program, Chickamauga National Celebration, 41.

47. Freeland, "Drums of Dixie," 19–20.

48. Ibid., 18.

49. *Chattanooga Times*, September 20, 1938. At this time, the principal chief of the Cherokee Nation was appointed by the U.S. president, but groups of Cherokees in Oklahoma often identified their own leaders as well. In August 1938, a convention of Cherokees named Milam its chairman. Later, in 1941, Franklin Roosevelt appointed Milam to the principal chief's office. Meredith, *Bartley Milam*, 39–40, 53–54.

50. *Chattanooga Times*, September 20, 22, 25, 1938; Official Program, Chickamauga National Celebration, 20.

51. *Chattanooga Times*, September 21, 22, 1938.

52. Ibid., September 22, 25, 1938.

53. Ibid., September 21, 1938; Official Program, Chickamauga National Celebration, 20.

54. Peers, *Playing Ourselves*, xv–xxi.

55. *Chattanooga Times*, September 23, 1938; Official Program, Chickamauga National Celebration, 20.

56. *Chattanooga Times*, September 23, 1938.

57. Ibid., September 22, 23, 25, 1938.

58. Ibid., September 18, 1938.

59. Ibid.; *Chattanooga Free Press*, September 21, 1938; Jones, "Class Consciousness and Worker Solidarity in Urban Tennessee"; Jones, "Strikes and Labor Organization in Tennessee"; Potts, "Unfulfilled Expectations"; Lamon, *Black Tennesseans*, 20–30.

60. *Chattanooga Times*, September 19, 1938.

61. Ibid., September 19, 20, 1938.

62. Blight, *Race and Reunion*, 386. Historian Caroline E. Janney has recently challenged this emphasis on reconciliation, noting the emergence in the 1930s of a southern nationalist critique of reconciliation in Civil War memorialization. Janney, "War over a Shrine of Peace."

63. Blight, *Race and Reunion*, 381–91.

64. *Chattanooga Times*, September 20, 1938.

65. *Chattanooga Free Press*, September 25, 1938.

66. *Chattanooga Times*, September 18, 1938. African Americans made up 32.6 percent of Chattanooga's population in 1920 and 27.8 percent ten years later. This drop reflected the city's policy in the 1920s of annexing outlying neighborhoods, most of which were dominated by whites. Livingwood, *History of Hamilton County*, 383–84.

67. *Chattanooga Times*, September 16, 1938.

68. Brundage, *Southern Past*, 5–11.

69. Levine, *Unpredictable Past*, 209.

70. Dickstein, *Dancing in the Dark*, 215–310.

71. Levine, *Unpredictable Past*, 207–21.

72. Ibid., 218–19; Susman, *Culture as History*, 155.

Chapter Four

1. "Acts Relating to Cherokee Indians Repealed" (No. 712), February 27, 1962, *Acts and Resolutions of the General Assembly of the State of Georgia, 1962*, 154–55. This act repealed specific sections of the removal-era state laws. Much of the legislation from the 1820s and 1830s dealt with the extension of state jurisdiction over Cherokee land and the distribution of that land to Georgia citizens. Those sections could not be repealed, since Georgia obviously did not intend to return the northern part of the state to the Cherokee Nation. The General Assembly struck provisions that restricted Indians' right of assembly, freedom of movement, and ability to testify in state courts. In drafting Resolution 712, however, legislators overlooked some of the anti-Indian provisions still subject to repeal. A second act, passed in 1980, repealed

additional sections of the removal-era laws. "Georgia State Commission of Indian Affairs Abolished" (No. 738), March 18, 1980, *Acts and Resolutions of the General Assembly of the State of Georgia, 1980*, 346–48.

2. *Atlanta Constitution*, May 13, 1962; Memo, Georgia Historical Commission, n. d. [1962], press release, April 24, 1962, NESHS.

3. "Acts Relating to Cherokee Indians Repealed," 154–55; Resolution, Commending the Renovation of New Echota by the Georgia Historical Commission, and for Other Purposes, HR 600, 1962, GHCR.

4. *Savannah Morning News*, February 13, 1962.

5. Resolution, Commending the Renovation of New Echota by the Georgia Historical Commission.

6. Tuck, *Beyond Atlanta*, 101–4, 119–26, 140–42, 147–53.

7. *Atlanta Constitution*, February 14, 1962; *Atlanta Inquirer*, February 3, 10, 1962; *Pittsburgh Courier*, February 10, 1962.

8. Miles, " 'Showplace of the Cherokee Nation' "; Ruskin, *John Ross*; Bishop, *Myth and History*, 162–76.

9. Finger, *Cherokee Americans*, 114–17, 138–19.

10. James Corn to Penelope Allen, January 30, 1950, William Snell Papers, Cleveland Public Library, Cleveland, Tennessee; *Chattanooga Times*, January 19, 1961; *Cleveland Daily Banner*, September 26, 1979; *Tennessee Historical Markers*, 24, 152–53, 155, 162–64.

11. "Trail of Tears State Park," brochure, 1958, Trail of Tears Booklets. Special Collections, Kent Library, Southeast Missouri State University, Cape Girardeau, Missouri; Program, Dedication Ceremony, Princess Otahki Memorial, May 27, 1962, "Heritage Interpretation Conceptual Plan: Cultural Complex, Trail of Tears State Park," February 27, 1980, MPR.

12. Jakle, *Tourist*, 185–90.

13. Clark, *Emerging South*, 138–48; Starnes, "Introduction," in Starnes, *Southern Journeys*, 6–7.

14. Kammen, *Mystic Chords of Memory*, 533–34, 538–44, 558–60, 587–88.

15. Ibid., 549–52, 590–610.

16. *Atlanta Constitution*, April 20, 1954; R. D. Self to Charles Gregory, April 13, 1953, GHCR.

17. Malone, "New Echota"; McLoughlin, *Cherokee Renascence in the New Republic*, 277–301, 388–410, 450–51.

18. R. D. Self, pamphlet, "New Echota: Cherokee National Capitol," 1953, NESHS; Malone, "New Echota," 11 (photo of Worcester house in 1930s); Press release, April 24, 1962, NESHS.

19. "Marker on Site of New Echota, Former Capital of Cherokee Indians," April 7, 1930, H. Rep 1085, 71 Cong., 2 sess., U.S. Serial 9192; *Atlanta Constitution*, April 20, 1954; R. D. Self to Charles Gregory, April 13, 1953, Minutes, May 15, 1953, GHCR; "People Who Led the Effort to Preserve the Site of New Echota," n.d., NESHS; Pitts, *History of Gordon County, Georgia*, 19–25.

20. R. D. Self to C. E. Gregory, April 13, 1953, GHCR; Minutes, May 15, October 18, 1953, GHCR; *Calhoun Times*, May 28, October 22, November 12, 1953.

21. *Calhoun Times*, January 1, 7, 1954; Recommendations for the Development of New Echota, March 11, 1955, NESHS; Charles Gregory to R. D. Self, January 6, 1953, Joseph Caldwell, "Preliminary Report on New Echota Excavations," May 29, 1954, GHCR.

22. *Calhoun Times*, January 6, 1955; Clemens de Baillou to Charles Gregory, August 12, 1954, Joseph Cumming to GHC, May 12, 1955, Joseph Cumming to Clemens de Baillou, October 10, 1955, Report, New Echota Restoration, 1969, GHCR. The 1969 report included a review of the history of the historic site's development.

23. Charles Gregory to Joseph Cumming, July 7, 1953, September 3, 1958, Joseph Cumming, Memorandum to GHC, December 3, 1957, Mary Jewett to Joseph Cumming, January 5, 1960, March 7, 1961, GHCR.

24. *Cartersville Daily Tribune News*, February 17, 1959; *Calhoun Times*, October 8, 1959; Charles Gregory to Joseph Cumming, June 18, 1957, Tom Little, "Ground Rules for the Reconstruction of the Cherokee Indian Capitol City of New Echota," 1958, in Report, New Echota Restoration, 1969, GHCR.

25. Clemens de Baillou to Joseph Cumming, October 30, 1957, Charles Gregory to Joseph Cumming, April 15, 1958, GHCR.

26. Arthur Kelly to Joseph Cumming, April 29, 1958, GHCR.

27. Tom Little to Charles Gregory, December 27, 1957, H. C. Foreman to Charles Gregory, November 5, 1957, January 25, 1958, Charles Gregory to Clemens de Baillou, March 3, 1958, GHCR.

28. The GHC based the reconstruction on a Cherokee law that dictated the dimensions of the building, along with several general contemporary descriptions of New Echota. *Calhoun Times*, October 22, 1953; "Recommendations for the Development of New Echota," November 1955, New Echota Museum Plans, December 1963, NESHS.

29. Mary Jewett to Sylvan Meyer, March 29, 1961, GHCR.

30. Press release, April 24, 1962, NESHS; *Calhoun Times*, February 2, 1958; *Atlanta Constitution*, May 13, 1962.

31. Clemens de Baillou, Notes on the Council House, September 1955, Mary Jewett to Joseph Cumming, February 12, March 24, 1959, Report on Council House, April 7, 1971, GHCR; Steven Baker, Report on New Echota Archeology, January 31, 1970, NESHS.

32. Tuck, *Beyond Atlanta*, 101–2, 110–53; Roche, *Restructured Resistance*, 71, 76–77; Brown-Nagin, *Courage to Dissent*, 136–49, 158–64, 175–208.

33. Tuck, *Beyond Atlanta*, 99–100.

34. *Calhoun Times*, September 4, 1958.

35. Tuck, *Beyond Atlanta*, 101–2; Brown-Nagin, *Courage to Dissent*, 309–26; Roche, *Restructured Resistance*, 158–72, quote on 165.

36. Roche, *Restructured Resistance*, 178–86.

37. Ibid., 190.

38. Gerstle, *American Crucible*, 4–5.

39. Ibid., 249–50, 270–77. The internment of Japanese Americans during World War II might also have contributed to this uneasiness with racial nationalism. For internment in the South, see Howard, *Concentration Camps on the Home Front*.

40. Gerstle, *American Crucible*, 246–48, 280–81.

41. For public criticism and the politics of "southern inferiority" during this era, see Maxwell, *Indicted South*, 167–210.

42. Press Release, April 24, 1962, Program, New Echota Dedication, May 12, 1962, Press Release and Text of Vandiver's Address, May 12, 1962, NESHS; *Calhoun Times*, May 10, 12, 1962.

43. Foote, *Shadowed Ground*, 6–18, 111–44.

44. Press Release and Text of Vandiver's Address, May 12, 1962, Text of Address, May 12, 1962, NESHS. The document does not identify the speaker of this second text. It may be the speech delivered by Secretary of State Ben Fortson.

45. *Rome News-Tribune*, May 9, 1962.

46. Press Release and Text of Vandiver's Address, May 12, 1962, NESHS.

47. *Atlanta Constitution*, May 13, 1962.

48. Earl Boyd Pierce to William Wayne Keeler, April 2, 1958, N. B. Johnson to William Wayne Keeler, August 8, 1958, WWKP.

49. Ruskin, *John Ross, Chief of an Eagle Race*, 76.

50. See, for example, Horton and Crew, "Afro-Americans and Museums: Towards a Policy of Inclusion"; Brundage, *Southern Past*, 7–10; Shackel, *Memory in Black and White*, 11–16.

51. Joseph Cumming to Henry Alexander, October 2, 1952, GHC Minutes, November 12, 1952, Joseph Cumming to Mary Jewett, September 2, 1958, July 31, 1961, Joseph Cumming to GHC, August 3, 1961, GHCR. These complaints reflected the enduring contentiousness of the memory of the Civil War, a phenomenon the Civil War Centennial demonstrated on a much larger scale during this period. See Fried, *The Russians Are Coming!*, 119–32; Cook, *Troubled Commemoration*, 15–37, 51–119.

52. Mary Jewett to Sylvan Meyer, March 20, 1961, Mary Jewett to Joseph Cumming, July 31, 1961, Joseph Cumming to GHC members, August 3, 1961, GHCR; *Calhoun Times*, April 25, 1957, September 4, 1958, July 7, 1960; *Gainesville Daily Times*, March 13, 1961; *Atlanta Journal*, July 21, 1961.

53. Georgia created a State Commission of Indian Affairs in 1977. At that time, an executive order identified the Georgia Tribe of Eastern Cherokee Indians, Inc., and the Lower Muscogee Tribe—East of the Mississippi, Inc., as "legal tribal organizations" for the state's Cherokee and Creek people, respectively. Memorandum, Office of the Governor, April 27, 1977, Department of Human Resources, Governor's Subject Files, RG 80, series 30, Georgia State Archives, Morrow, Georgia. For Georgia state recognition of Indian tribes, see Koenig and Stein, "Federalism and State Recognition of Native American Tribes," 118–20.

54. Dudziak, *Cold War Civil Rights*, 12–13, 18–78. See also Borstelmann, *Cold War and the Color Line*; Plummer, *Black Americans and United States Foreign Affairs*; Von Eschen, *Race against Empire*.

55. Recent works on Native American politics and the Cold War include Cobb, *Native Activism in Cold War America*; Cobb, "Talking the Language of the Larger World"; Rosier, "'They are ancestral homelands'"; Rosier, *Serving Their Country.*

56. For the development of the USIA, see Elder, *Information Machine*; Dizard, *Strategy of Truth.*

57. *Questions and Answers*, September 12, 1963, Voice of America Scripts, USIA, Library of Congress, Washington, D.C.

58. *The American Indian: Past and Present*, "The Indian of the Future," August 14, 1965, Voice of America Scripts, USIA, Library of Congress, Washington, D.C.

59. For an extended discussion, see Denson, "Native Americans and Cold War Public Diplomacy."

60. *Atlanta Constitution*, July 12, 1956; *Atlanta Journal-Constitution Magazine*, September 4, 1960; *Rome News-Tribune*, October 1, 8, 15, 1961, February 11, 1962; *Gainesville Tribune*, February 21, 1962.

61. *Rome News-Tribune*, May 1, 1956, February 11, 1962; *Atlanta Journal and Constitution*, February 11, 1962; *Atlanta Constitution*, February 14, 1962.

62. *Atlanta Constitution*, May 11, 1962.

63. Doss, *Memorial Mania*, 253–60, 302–12, quote on 307.

Chapter Five

1. For *Unto These Hills* and postwar tourism in Cherokee, see Finger, *Cherokee Americans*, 98–117; Beard-Moose, *Public Indians, Private Cherokees*, 18–49; Thompson, "Staging 'the Drama'"; Smithers, "Cherokee Epic."

2. Prucha, *Great Father*, 1013–84.

3. Finger, "Termination and the Eastern Band of Cherokees," 154–58, 162–64.

4. Henry Parker to Office of Civilian Production, February 28, 1947, correspondence, Boundary Tree tribal enterprise, CAR.

5. Simon Davis, Labor Market Digest, 1947, excerpt in Henry Parker to Office of Civilian Production, February 28, 1947, correspondence, Boundary Tree tribal enterprise, CAR.

6. Simpson and Herring, *Western North Carolina Associated Communities*, 16–23; Minutes, July 17, 1946, WNCAC.

7. Joe Jennings to Carl Compton, March 3, 1947, Boundary Tree tribal enterprise, CAR; Finger, *Cherokee Americans*, 100–102.

8. *State*, December 15, 1945.

9. Francis Heazel to Carl Compton, February 27, 1947, Boundary Tree tribal enterprise, CAR; Simpson and Herring, *Western North Carolina Associated Communities*, 35–36.

10. *State*, December 15, 1945.

11. Ibid.

12. Finger, *Cherokee Americans*, 112–14; Plan of Operation, correspondence, Boundary Tree tribal enterprise, CAR.

13. Justification for the Project, 1947, Boundary Tree tribal enterprise, CAR.

14. Finger, *Cherokee Americans*, 113; Minutes, April 15, 1947, WNCAC; Joe Jennings to C. O. Ensign, March 13, 1947, Joe Jennings to E. C. Hemingway, December 23, 1947, Boundary Tree tribal enterprise, CAR.

15. Finger, *Cherokee Americans*, 113; Kituwah Preservation and Education Program, www.newkituwahacademy.com/our-history.html, accessed June 12, 2015.

16. Minutes, July 17, August 8, 1946, WNCAC; Simpson and Herring, *Western North Carolina Associated Communities*, 16–17.

17. Stringfield, *Occoneechee*, 1–11; Jarrett, *Occoneechee*.

18. Powell, *Paradise Preserved*, 113–30, 146–48.

19. Paul Green, "Playmaker's Progress," excerpted in Free and Lower, *History into Drama*, 125.

20. Powell, *Paradise Preserved*, 146–60.

21. Simpson and Herring, *Western North Carolina Associated Communities*, 16–17; Umberger, "History of *Unto These Hills*," 5–8.

22. Minutes, November 22, 1946, January 14, 1947, WNCAC; Simpson and Herring, *Western North Carolina Associated Communities*, 25–26; Umberger, "History of *Unto These Hills*," 10–17.

23. Simpson and Herring, *Western North Carolina Associated Communities*, 26.

24. Ibid., 24–30; Minutes, February 24, July 30, November 30, 1948, April 14, 1949, WNCAC.

25. Simpson and Herring, *Western North Carolina Associated Communities*, 27; Minutes, December 2, 1947, WNCAC.

26. Finger, *Cherokee Americans*, 114–15; "Buchanan, Harry Eugene," "Ferebee, Percy Bell," Encyclopedia of North Carolina, *NCpedia.org*, accessed June 8, 2015; Joe Jennings, Eastern Cherokee Indians, Recent Progress, 1954, Joe Jennings Collection, Archives of Appalachia, East Tennessee State University, Johnson City, Tennessee.

27. Program, Thirty-Second Annual Cherokee Indian Fair, 1949, Program, Thirty-Third Annual Cherokee Indian Fair, 1950, *Cherokee Traditions*, Western Carolina University, http://www.wcu.edu/library/DigitalCollections/CherokeeTraditions, accessed January 7, 2015.

28. Finger, *Cherokee Americans*, 114.

29. Umberger, "History of *Unto These Hills*," 45.

30. Green, *Lost Colony*, 5.

31. Ibid., vii.

32. Selden, "American Drama in the Open Air," in Free and Lower, *History into Drama*, 126.

33. Fried, *The Russians Are Coming!*, 3–9, 23–28, 30–45, 55–62.

34. Hunter, "Some Aspects of Outdoor Historical Drama, with Special Reference to 'Unto These Hills,'" in Free and Lower, *History into Drama*, 136.

35. Umberger, "History of *Unto These Hills*," 45.

36. Hunter, *Unto These Hills*, 5.

37. Ibid., 9–10, 12.

38. Ibid., 12.

39. Ibid., 16.

40. Ibid., 17–20.

41. Ibid., 21.

42. Ibid.

43. Ibid., 30.

44. Ibid., 30–31.

45. Ibid., 40–48, 53, 55.

46. Ibid., 20, 28–29, 58–60.

47. Ibid., 71–72, 74–75, 78–87.

48. Ibid., 91.

49. Ibid., 88.

50. Ibid., 92.

51. Ibid., 99.

52. Ibid.

53. Ibid., 95.

54. Umberger, "History of *Unto These Hills*," 83–85; Thompson, "Staging 'the Drama,'" 49–51.

55. *Asheville Citizen*, May 20, 1951.

56. *Sylva Herald*, June 28, 1951.

57. Umberger, "History of *Unto These Hills*," 75; Thompson, "Staging 'The Drama,'" 49.

58. Finger, *Cherokee Americans*, 137–38. See also Beard-Moose, *Public Indians, Private Cherokees*, 133–49, 104–15.

59. *State*, November 22, 1952.

60. Minutes, October 24, 1950, WNCAC.

61. Thompson, "Staging 'The Drama,'" 53–54.

62. *State*, September 8, 1951.

63. Simpson and Herring, *Western North Carolina Associated Communities*, 32–33; Joe Jennings, Eastern Cherokee Indians, Recent Progress, 1954.

64. Finger, *Cherokee Americans*, 130; Umberger, "History of *Unto These Hills*," 101–2.

65. Works examining the termination era in American Indian policy history include Burt, *Tribalism in Crisis*; Prucha, *Great Father*, 1013–84; Fixico, *Termination and Relocation*; and Philp, *Termination Revisited*.

66. Fixico, *Termination and Relocation*, 111–57; Prucha, *Great Father* 1044–46, 1079–84. See also Philp, *Termination Revisited*, 140–52.

67. Cobb, *Native Activism in Cold War America*, 11–17; Wilkinson, *Blood Struggle*, 64–86, 104–6; Cowger, "'The Crossroads of Destiny,'" 128–38; Cornell, *Return of the*

Native, 123–27, 192. For the termination debate in individual tribes, see Burt, *Tribalism in Crisis*, 29–47; Hood, "Termination of the Klamath Tribe in Oregon," 379–92; Peroff, *Menominee Drums*; Dahl, "The Battle over Termination on the Colville Indian Reservation," 29–53; Metcalf, *Termination's Legacy*; Beck, *Struggle for Self-Determination*, 129–78.

68. Finger, "Termination and the Eastern Band of Cherokees," 155–56.

69. Ibid., 162–63.

70. Report, Investigation of the Bureau of Indian Affairs, September 20, 1954, H. Rpt. 2680 (83 Cong., 2 sess.), U.S. Serial 11747, 281.

71. Hearing, House Subcommittee on Indian Affairs, September 17, 1955, 40–41.

72. Ibid., 40.

73. Ibid., 59–62.

74. Finger, "Termination and the Eastern Band of Cherokees," 154; Finger, *Cherokee Americans*, 88–97.

75. Finger, "Termination and the Eastern Band of Cherokees," 154–55; *State*, September 28, 1946.

76. "Senator Watkins on the Termination Policy, May 1957," in Prucha, *Documents of United States Indian Policy*, 240.

77. For Cold War language in the termination debate, see Cobb, *Native Activism in Cold War America*, 13, 17–22; Wilkinson, *Blood Struggle*, 67–69.

78. Hearing, House Subcommittee on Indian Affairs, September 17, 1955, 5; Bauer, *Land of the North Carolina Cherokees*, 10–24, 29–34, 55.

79. Bauer, *Land of the North Carolina Cherokees*, 24–25, 54–55.

80. Report, Investigation of the Bureau of Indian Affairs, September 20, 1954, 283.

81. Finger, "Termination and the Eastern Band of Cherokees," 164–65.

82. Bauer, *Land of the North Carolina Cherokees*, 57.

83. *Asheville Citizen*, November 12, 1954.

84. *State*, July 31, 1954.

85. Finger, "Termination and the Eastern Band of Cherokees," 164.

86. Report, Investigation of the Bureau of Indian Affairs, September 20, 1954, 282.

87. Ibid., 281; Hearing, House Subcommittee on Indian Affairs, September 17, 1955, 22.

88. Finger, "Termination and the Eastern Band of Cherokees," 162–63.

89. Ibid., 162.

Chapter Six

1. Prucha, *Great Father*, 659–71.

2. Denson, *Demanding the Cherokee Nation*, 214–30; Prucha, *American Indian Policy in Crisis*, 387.

3. Prucha, *American Indian Policy in Crisis*, 232–341.

4. Cherokee Agreement, 1902, in *Annual Report of the Commission to the Five Civilized Tribes*, 101–9.

5. Hendrix, "Redbird Smith and the Nighthawk Keetoowahs," 73–81; Thomas, "The Redbird Smith Movement."

6. Debo, *And Still the Waters Run*, 91.

7. Ibid., 95–96, 103–7, 113–14, 182–83; Carter, *Dawes Commission*, 139–40.

8. Debo, *And Still the Waters Run*, 179–80.

9. Ibid., 6, 281–87, 379; Carter, *Dawes Commission*, 173–77.

10. Debo, *And Still the Waters Run*, 92.

11. Ibid., 98–99, 137; Carter, *Dawes Commission*, 174.

12. Sam Smith to Levi Gritts, December 9, 1920, reprinted in Emmet Starr, *History of the Cherokee Indians*, 485.

13. See, for example, Stremlau, *Sustaining the Cherokee Family*.

14. Resolution, Illinois Fire, November 10, 1920, OIHC, vol. 6, 240.

15. Conley, *Cherokee Encyclopedia*, 63–64, 78, 115–16; Meredith, *Bartley Milam*, 24–25.

16. Meredith, *Bartley Milam*, 25–26, 35; Leeds, *United Keetoowah Band*, 10.

17. Meredith, *Bartley Milam*, 41–43.

18. Ibid., 35–36.

19. Resolution, Illinois Fire, November 10, 1920, OIHC, vol. 6, 242.

20. Ibid.; Sam Smith to Levi Gritts, December 9, 1920, in Starr, *History of the Cherokee Indians*, 486; Cherokee Meeting, Tahlequah, Oklahoma, January 31, 1921, Resolution of the Keetoowah Society, Incorporated, January 31, 1921, Resolution, Cherokee Executive Committee, January 31, 1921, OIHC, vol. 6, 243–44, 246, 249; *Ada Weekly News*, March 17, 1921.

21. Meredith, *Bartley Milam*, 35–37; Duncan, "Keetoowah Society," 253–54; Zissu, *Blood Matters*, 91–92.

22. Meredith, *Bartley Milam*, 26–27; Conley, *Cherokee Nation*, 204. This approach remained in place even after reformers began to remake federal Indian policy in the 1930s. In 1934, Congress passed the Indian Reorganization Act (IRA), which repudiated allotment and allowed tribes to draft new constitutions. While the law did not apply to Oklahoma, Congress extended some IRA provisions to the state two years later in the Oklahoma Indian Welfare Act (OIWA). Almost immediately following passage of the OIWA, the Keetoowah Society, Incorporated, began efforts to gain recognition as a tribal organization under the new law. Yet, in spite of these developments, Cherokee relations with the federal government remained the province of an appointed leader. Prucha, *Great Father*, 971–73; Leeds, *United Keetoowah Band*, 14–15; Blackman, *Oklahoma's Indian New Deal*, 78–103.

23. Meredith, *Bartley Milam*, 3–6, 9–14; Conley, *Cherokee Nation*, 204–5. In 1938, Milam had been selected as "permanent chairman" of a group of Cherokee representatives working on the claims cases. Meredith likens this position to that of principal chief. Meredith, *Bartley Milam*, 40.

24. Meredith, *Bartley Milam*, 52–55; Conley, *Cherokee Nation*, 205.

25. Meredith, *Bartley Milam*, 86–87, 95–96, 100, 102.

26. Ibid., 27–28, 46–48.

27. Ibid., 29–30; *Tulsa World*, April 26, 1936; Programs, Cherokee Seminaries Homecoming, May 7, 1937, 1938, Jesse Bartley Milam Papers, University of Tulsa, Tulsa, Oklahoma.

28. Meredith, *Bartley Milam*, 30–31, 95; Milam, "President's Report," J. B. Milam Papers, University of Tulsa, Tulsa, Oklahoma.

29. Conley, *Cherokee Encyclopedia*, 39.

30. Transcript, Convention of Duly Enrolled Cherokees by Blood in Oklahoma, July 30, 1948, CNR, 3, 9.

31. Ibid., 9–13.

32. Ibid., 14–16.

33. Interview with Stokes Smith, July 19, 1948, quoted in Tyner, "Keetoowah Society in Cherokee History," 95.

34. Transcript, Convention of Duly Enrolled Cherokees by Blood in Oklahoma, CNR, 41, 43–44, 47–51, 55–56; *Muskogee Times-Democrat*, August 2, 1948; *Tahlequah Democrat-Star*, August 5, 1948.

35. Conley, *Cherokee Nation*, 210–11; Conley, *Cherokee Encyclopedia*, 133–34; Minutes, Cherokee Executive Committee, December 4, 1948, CNR.

36. Minutes, Cherokee Executive Committee, February 15, 1953, CNR, 2.

37. Keeler to W. O. Roberts, January 14, 1949, Minutes, Cherokee Executive Committee, April 16, 1950, February 15, 1953, CNR.

38. Minutes, Cherokee Foundation, December 3, 1951, April 27, October 6, 1952, *TSA-LA-GHI GAH-NAH-SE-DAH* (*The Cherokee Ambassador*), January 1955, September 1959, Cobb to Cherokee Foundation, December 10, 1959, Cherokee Foundation Expenditures (review of foundation projects, 1952–1962), undated, CFR.

39. Minutes, Cherokee Executive Committee, March 1, 1953, CNR, 14.

40. Ibid., 15.

41. *TSA-LA-GHI GAH-NAH-SE-DAH* (*The Cherokee Ambassador*), July 1956, CFR; Keeler to John Gillespie, October 21, 1959, WWKP.

42. Minutes, Cherokee Foundation, February 6, June 15, August 1, 1954, *TSA-LA-GHI GAH-NAH-SE-DAH* (*The Cherokee Ambassador*), July 1956, CFR; Keeler to George Cochran, December 21, 1953, W. W. Keeler to Kermit Hunter, February 1, 1954, WWKP.

43. Minutes, Cherokee Foundation, December 3, 1951, July 18, October 6, 1952, CFR; Keeler to Elmer Davis, October 9, 1952, press release [August 1953], Keeler to Earl Boyd Pierce, September 17, 1953, WWKP.

44. *Muskogee Phoenix*, September 6, 1953; program, First Annual Cherokee National Holiday, September 6, 1953, Cherokee National Holiday Collection, Cherokee Heritage Center, Tahlequah, Oklahoma.

45. Keeler to George Cochran, December 21, 1953, WWKP.

46. *Muskogee Phoenix*, September 7, 1953.

47. Ibid.

48. *Muskogee Phoenix*, September 6, 1953; program, First Annual Cherokee National Holiday, Cherokee National Holiday, Cherokee Heritage Center, Tahlequah, Oklahoma.

49. Minutes, Cherokee Executive Committee, June 11, 1950, CNR; minutes, Cherokee Foundation, December 3, 1951, July 18, 1952, CFR.

50. *Muskogee Phoenix*, September 7, 1953.

51. Minutes, Cherokee Executive Committee, July 22, September 2, October 11, 1961, March 24, 1962, CNR; Report of a Cherokee Meeting Held at Sallisaw, Oklahoma, December 7, 1964, MWP.

52. Fact Sheet Concerning Authorized Cherokee Programs, February 4, 1966, WWKP; Disposition of Judgment Funds to Cherokee Nation, Pub. L. No. 87-775, October 9, 1962. If a person on the allotment rolls had died since 1906 (as was the case with many), the payment was divided among that person's heirs. Unclaimed payments, payments to deceased heirs of $10 or less, and inherited shares of $5 or less reverted to the Cherokee Nation. The $2 million of "residual" funds represented that money, plus the interest on those funds accrued between the settlement and the completion of distribution.

53. Minutes, Cherokee Executive Committee, May 8, 1965, CNR; Fact Sheet Concerning Authorized Cherokee Programs, February 4, 1966, WWKP.

54. Sturm, *Blood Politics*, 91.

55. Cobb, *Native Activism in Cold War America*, 21–29; Castile, *To Show Heart*, 3–18.

56. Cobb, *Native Activism in Cold War America*, 11–17; Wilkinson, *Blood Struggle*, 64–86, 104–6; Cowger, " 'Crossroads of Destiny,' " 128–38; Cornell, *Return of the Native*, 123–27, 192.

57. Cobb, *Native Activism in Cold War America*, 90–94, 120–24, 130–33, 142–46; Wahrhaftig, "Making Do with the Dark Meat," 470, 474–75; Minutes, Cherokee Executive Committee, February 24, June 23, 1966, May 10, 1967, MWP; Minutes, Cherokee Executive Committee, June 21, 1967, CNR.

58. Report of a Cherokee Meeting Held at Sallisaw, Oklahoma, December 7, 1964, MWP; Jim Pickup to Keeler, December 26, 1964, WWKP.

59. Wahrhaftig, "Making Do with the Dark Meat," 476–84; Leeds, *United Keetoowah Band*, 48–49.

60. Robert Thomas to Helen Peterson, October 2, 1957, copy in WWKP.

61. Keeler to Stokes Smith, September 7, 1954, WWKP; C. C. Victory to Keeler, May 27, 1956, CNR; *Tulsa World*, September 8, 1957; minutes, Cherokee Executive Committee, January 25, 1966, MWP.

62. Cherokee Cultural Center Project, December 31, 1965, WWKP.

63. Prospectus, Cherokee National Historical Society, n.d. [ca. 1965], CNHS.

64. The Cherokee National Historical Society, Inc.: A History through 1978, n.d. [1978], CNHS, 2.

65. Ibid., 1; Fact Sheet Concerning Authorized Cherokee Programs, February 4, 1966, WWKP; Minutes, Cherokee Executive Committee, January 15, 1966, June 23, 1966, MWP.

66. Prospectus, Cherokee National Historical Society, n.d. [ca. 1965], CNHS; Cherokee Cultural Center Project, December 31, 1965, WWKP.

67. Program, Dedication of Cherokee Village, June 24, 1967, MWP.

68. Mildred Ballenger to Keeler, December 22, 1965, WWKP.

69. Minutes, Cherokee Executive Committee, January 15, 1966, CNR; Earl Boyd Pierce to Eva Walker, December 23, 1965, Marie Wadley, Memo, December 29, 1965, Fact Sheet Concerning Authorized Cherokee Programs, February 4, 1966, WWKP.

70. Handbill, [1967], WWKP.

71. Wahrhaftig and Lukens-Wahrhaftig, "New Militants or Resurrected State?" 231–39; Wahrhaftig, "Making Do with the Dark Meat," 481–82; Cobb, *Native Activism in Cold War America*, 157.

72. Wahrhaftig and Lukens-Wahrhaftig, "New Militants or Resurrected State?," 228–29, 238–39; Wahrhaftig, "Making Do with the Dark Meat," 482–83.

73. "Declaration of the Five County Northeastern Oklahoma Cherokee Organization," in Wahrhaftig, "In the Aftermath of Civilization," 162–63.

74. Wahrhaftig and Lukens-Wahrhaftig, "New Militants or Resurrected State?," 239–40.

75. Ibid., 235; *Cherokee Nation News*, June 24, August 19, 26, 1969; Cobb, "Devils in Disguise."

76. Wahrhaftig and Lukens-Wahrhaftig, "New Militants or Resurrected State?," 240.

77. The Cherokee National Historical Society, Inc.: A History through 1978, n.d. [1978], CNHS, 4–5.

78. Kermit Hunter, "The Trail of Tears," typescript, 1966, CNHS, 39. This was labeled the second draft of the script, copyrighted 1966 (the date of the first draft), but likely written later.

79. Ibid., 2. When Hunter wrote a new version of the play in 1973, he eliminated this statement. Kermit Hunter, "The Trail of Tears," typescript, 1973, CNHS.

80. Kermit Hunter, "The Trail of Tears," typescript, 1966, CNHS 21.

81. Ibid., 19.

82. Ibid., 22–28.

83. Ibid., 56.

84. Ibid. The 1973 script eliminated this language, but still depicted Oklahoma statehood as inevitable and suggested statehood offered Cherokees a "rebirth." Kermit Hunter, "The Trail of Tears," typescript, 1973, CNHS, 58–61.

85. Fried, *The Russians Are Coming!*, 17–28, 101–17.

86. Wahrhaftig, "Making Do with the Dark Meat," 480–81, 485, 491–93, 499–500.

87. Sturm, *Blood Struggle*, 90–94; Wahrhaftig, "Making Do with the Dark Meat," 486–88; Strickland and Strickland, "Beyond the Trail of Tears," 130–32.

88. Anderson, *Imagined Communities*. Anthropologist Circe Sturm makes a similar point, applying Anderson's analysis to the activities of Keeler and his allies. Sturm, *Blood Politics*, 93.

89. The Cherokee National Historical Society, Inc.: A History through 1978, n.d. [1978], CNHS, 6, 7, 10; Cherokee Heritage Center, www.cherokeeheritage.org /attractions/totas/, accessed July 10, 2015.

Chapter Seven

1. Blythe Ferry Pamphlet, "Cherokee History & the Trail of Tears: Cherokee Removal Memorial," n.d., author's collection; National Park Service, Cherokee Removal Memorial Park, Conceptual Design Charette, March 2002, BHP, 1–27; www .cherokeeremoval.org/news.htm, accessed May 7, 2015.

2. Interview, Shirley Lawrence, November 3, 2011; Cherokee Removal Memorial Park, Conceptual Design Charette, March 2002, BHP, 1–5; Brochure, Cherokee Memorial Park, [1991], BHP.

3. Pitcaithley, "National Parks and the Interpretive Message," 444–45.

4. National Park Service, *Rethinking the National Parks for the Twenty-First Century*, www.nps.gov/policy/report.htm, accessed May 10, 2015.

5. Doss, *Memorial Mania*, 2, 32–37, 57–60.

6. Blythe Ferry Pamphlet, "Cherokee History & the Trail of Tears," n.d., author's collection, 1.

7. Pitcaithley, "National Parks and the Interpretive Message," 447.

8. Doss, *Memorial Mania*, 307–8.

9. *Trails for America*, 3; Elkinton, *National Trail System*, 8–9.

10. *Trails for America*, 3, 6; Elkinton, *National Trail System*, 8–9.

11. *Trails for America*, 13–14.

12. National Trails System Act, Pub. L. No. 90-543, October 2, 1968; Elkinton, *National Trail System*, 10–12.

13. *Trails for America*, 14–15; National Trails System Act, Pub. L. No. 90-543, October 2, 1968.

14. Elkinton, *National Trails System*, 14–18; National Parks and Recreation Act, Pub. L. No. 95-625, November 10, 1978; National Trails System, www.nps.gov/nts /nts_trails.html, accessed June 10, 2015.

15. A. S. Mike Monroney to Edward Crafts, July 9, 1965, RG 368, Bureau of Outdoor Recreation, Special Area Studies: Roads and Trails, National Archives, College Park, Maryland.

16. *Trails for America*, 15.

17. Roy A. Taylor to Edwards Crafts, March 4, 1966, RG 368, Bureau of Outdoor Recreation, Special Area Studies: Roads and Trails, National Archives, College Park, Maryland.

18. Public Bills and Resolutions, October 24, 1979, *Congressional Record* 125, 29466; National Trails System Act Amendments, Pub. L. No. 98-11, March 28, 1983. Taylor's successor was Asheville lawyer V. Lamar Gudger.

19. National Park Service, *Trail of Tears (The Cherokee Removal Route/1838–1839): Draft National Trail Study*, chap. 1, 2–3, chap. 11, 3–5.

20. Ibid., chap. 11, 2.

21. Ibid., appendix, 10.

22. Alice White to Wallace Brittain, February 14, 1986, Nell White to NPS, February 24, 1986, National Park Service, *Trail of Tears (The Cherokee Removal Route/1838–1839): Final National Trail Study*, appendix D, 78, 100–101.

23. James Corn to Sharon Keane, December 30, 1985, National Park Service, *Trail of Tears (The Cherokee Removal Route/1838–1839): Final National Trail Study*, appendix D, 107.

24. E. A. Gill to NPS, February 10, 1986, National Park Service, *Trail of Tears (The Cherokee Removal Route/1838–1839): Final National Trail Study*, appendix D, 80.

25. Marguerite Turner to National Park Service, February 22, 1986, National Park Service, *Trail of Tears (The Cherokee Removal Route/1838–1839): Final National Trail Study*, appendix D, 96.

26. National Park Service, *Trail of Tears (The Cherokee Removal Route/1838–1839): Final National Trail Study*, chap. 3, 1–2.

27. National Trails System Act Amendment, Pub. L. No. 100-192, December 16, 1987.

28. Perrin, *Counties of Christian and Trigg, Kentucky*, 38; Meacham, *History of Christian County, Kentucky*, 63–65; Foreman, *Indian Removal*, 303.

29. *New York Times*, December 21, 1987.

30. Beverly Baker to Carroll Hubbard, February 27, 1986, BBP; *Trail News*, February 2005; "Historical Data—Trail of Tears Commission, Inc.," Scrapbook, Kentucky Chapter, TOTA, Hopkinsville, Kentucky.

31. "Historical Data-Trail of Tears Commission, Inc.," Program, Park Dedication, May 14, 1988, Scrapbook, Kentucky Chapter, TOTA, Hopkinsville, Kentucky; Beverly Baker to Wendell Ford, August 12, 1987, Beverly Baker to Robert E. Thompson, July 5, 1988, Baker Collection; Press Release, [1992], BBP; *Kentucky New Era*, September 16, 26, October 8, 1987, May 3, 1988, September 20, 1989; "Video Tour—Trail of Tears Park and Museum" (Trail of Tears Commemorative Park, n.d.), author's personal collection. When completed, the museum included both the Cherokee-themed exhibit and a "western room" featuring art and craft items from a variety of other tribal communities. This room was meant to represent the variety of Native Americans who participated in the annual powwow.

32. *Trail News*, February 2005; Beverly Baker to Leon Roberts, July 28, 1986, Beverly Baker to Senator Mitch McConnell, October 2, 1986, BBP; National Trails System Act Amendment, Pub. L. No. 100-192, December 16, 1987.

33. National Park Service, *Trail of Tears (The Cherokee Removal Route/1838–1839): Final National Trail Study*, vi, section 2, 5–6, section 3, 1–2, section 11, 1–2, appendix D, 4.

34. Beverly Baker to Carroll Hubbard, February 27, 1986, Beverly Baker to Ray Emmanuel, May 23, 1986, BBP.

35. Beverly Baker to Leon Roberts, July 28, 1986, Beverly Baker to Jane Adams and Clyde Wallace, August 28, 1986, BBP.

36. *Trail News,* February 2005.

37. National Park Service, *Trail of Tears National Historic Trail: Comprehensive Management and Use Plan,* 41.

38. Ibid., 36–39; Minutes, Trail of Tears Advisory Council, March 30–31, 1995, October 23, 2001, BHP.

39. National Park Service, *Trail of Tears National Historic Trail: Comprehensive Management and Use Plan,* 3–6, 106; *Trail of Tears National Historic Trail Newsletter,* November 1989; NPS Press Release, Draft Trail of Tears Management Plan Available for Public Review, August 29, 1991, Minutes, Trail of Tears Advisory Council, September 17–18, 1991, March 30–31, 1995, October 23, 2001, BHP; Duane H. King, Report to the National Park Service on the Mapping and Site Inventory of the Cherokee Trail of Tears National Historic Trail, January 6, 1990, KRC; Gaines and Krakow, "Trail of Tears National Historic Trail," 162–64.

40. National Park Service, *Trail of Tears National Historic Trail: Comprehensive Management and Use Plan,* 49; Minutes, Trail of Tears Advisory Council, May 27–28, 1993, BHP; *Trail News,* May 2003, 3, 10–11.

41. Winks, "Sites of Shame," 23.

42. Pitcaithley, "National Parks and the Interpretive Message," 444; Elliot, *Custerology,* 42–45.

43. Pitcaithley, "National Parks and the Interpretive Message," 444; Doss, *Memorial Mania,* 349–50.

44. Pitcaithley, "'A Cosmic Threat.'"

45. Pitcaithley, "National Parks and the Interpretive Message," 444; Doss, *Memorial Mania,* 169–71, 298–301; Linenthal, *Unfinished Bombing.*

46. National Park Service, *Trail of Tears National Historic Trails: Comprehensive Management and Use Plan,* iii, 7, 33.

47. Crespi, "Native American Relationships Policy," 38–39; Keller and Turek, *American Indians and the National Parks,* 233–35; Wray et al., "Creating Policy for the National Park Service," 43–46.

48. Gaines and Krakow, "Trail of Tears National Historic Trail," 163; Minutes, Trail of Tears Advisory Council Meeting, September 17–18, 1991, BHP.

49. Gaines and Krakow, "Trail of Tears National Historic Trail," 168.

50. Barbara Heffington to Bob Stanton, January 26, 1998, BHP; Santa Fe Superintendent's Response to January 14, 2002, Memorandum from Bobbie Heffington, n.d. [2002], BHP.

51. David C. Little to Jonathan Taylor, August 11, 1993, KRC; *Asheville Citizen-Times,* September 1, 1996; Mary Ann Thompson to David Gaines, September 20, 1996, North Carolina Chapter Archives, TOTA.

52. National Park Service, *Trail of Tears National Historic Trail: Comprehensive Management and Use Plan*, 20; Bill Woodiel to Marynell Kalkbrenner, n.d. [August 1999], BHP.

53. National Park Service, *Trail of Tears National Historic Trail Additional Routes*, 8, 15, 16–17.

54. *Scottsboro Daily Sentinel*, August 24, October 28, 1994.

55. *Scottsboro Daily Sentinel*, October 11, 1994; interview, Bill Cason, December 5, 2011; Trail of Tears Commemorative Motorcycle Ride, http://al-tn-trailoftears.net, accessed July 17, 2014.

56. Trail of Tears Commemorative Motorcycle Ride; Brochure, Trail of Tears 2000, BHP.

57. Trail of Tears Commemorative Motorcycle Ride; interview, Bill Cason, December 11, 2011; Richard Sheridan to Dawnena Darnell, April 17, 1995, Jerry Davis to Riley Bock, May 25, 1995, Alabama Chapter Archives, TOTA.

58. National Park Service, Trail of Tears National Historic Trail—Current Projects, 1998, Andrea Sharon to Barbara Heffington, December 15, 1998, BHP.

59. City of Savannah, Recreation Trails Grant Application, 1993, KRC; National Park Service, Trail of Tears National Historic Trail—Current Projects, 1998, BHP; Tennessee River Museum, www.tennesseerivermuseum.org, accessed May 10, 2015.

60. National Park Service, Trail of Tears National Historic Trail—Current Projects, 1998, BHP; King, *Cherokee Trail of Tears*, 107–9.

61. National Park Service, Trail of Tears National Historic Trail—Current Projects, 1998, BHP.

62. Preliminary Site Plan, Trail of Tears Memorial Park, n.d. [1993], BHP.

63. David Gaines to Dusty Helbling, December 28, 1993, BHP; Gaines and Krakow, "Trail of Tears National Historic Trail," 168.

64. *Chattanooga Times Free Press*, March 13, 2005.

65. Brochure, Trail of Tears 2000, BHP.

66. Doss, *Memorial Mania*, 36–37.

67. Tyler-McGraw, "Some Thoughts Provoked by *The West as America*," 51–52; Truettner, "Ideology and Image."

68. Summerhill and Williams, *Sinking Columbus*, 116–26.

69. Pitcaithley, "'A Cosmic Threat,'" 169–86.

70. See thehermitage.com/learn/andrew-jackson/president/presidency, accessed May 3, 2015. The home is still managed by the Ladies' Hermitage Association, the heritage activists who preserved and restored the house starting in the late nineteenth century.

71. Minutes, Trail of Tears Advisory Council, September 17–18, 1991, BHP.

72. Press clipping, n.d. [2003], TOTA.

73. National Park Service, *Trail of Tears National Historic Trail Interpretive Plan*, 5.

74. Mankiller, *Mankiller: A Chief and Her People*, 77.

75. Interview, Shirley Lawrence, November 3, 2011.

76. Ibid.

77. Minutes, Georgia TOTA meeting, November 22, 1997, Memo to Georgia TOTA members, January 10, 1998, Georgia Chapter Archives, TOTA. The TOTA papers in Little Rock, Arkansas, include files and records from the various state chapters.

78. Interview, Jeff Bishop, November 22, 2011.

79. Indian Removal Questionnaires, 2001, BHP.

80. Brochure, Trail of Tears 2000, BHP.

81. Exler, *Tears of the Trail*, 3-9.

82. Sturm, *Becoming Cherokee*, 102-3.

83. Richard Allen to Vicky Karhu, October 11, 2004, Tennessee TOTA to Chadwick Smith, October 17, 2004, Tennessee Chapter Archives, TOTA.

84. National Park Service, *National Historic Trail Feasibility Study Amendment*, 28, 35-38.

85. Interview, Jeff Bishop, November 22, 2011.

86. Ibid.

87. Interview, Shirley Lawrence, November 3, 2011.

88. Rosenzweig and Thelen, *Presence of the Past*, 15-36.

89. Ibid., 190. The term comes from Thelen's section of the book's "afterthoughts."

90. *Trail News*, March 2015; interpretive signage, Cedar Town Camp, Cedartown, Georgia, www.nps.gov/trte/learn/historyculture/unveiling_cedartown_cavespring .htm, accessed April 2, 2015.

91. *Chattanooga Times Free Press*, May 16, 2013; NPS Brochure, Trail of Tears in Tennessee, author's collection; Amy Kostine, amykostine.wordpress.com (blog), accessed June 23, 2015.

92. Interpretive signage, Camp Ground Cemetery and the Trail of Tears, Union County, Illinois, www.nps.gov/trte/learn/historyculture/trte_campground_church .htm, accessed April 2, 2015.

93. Interpretive signage, Laughlin Park, Waynesville, Missouri, www.nps.gov /trte/learn/historyculture/laughlin-park.htm, accessed April 2, 2015.

94. Interpretive signage, New Madrid and the Trail of Tears, New Madrid, Missouri, www.nps.gov/trte/learn/historyculture/new_madrid.htm, accessed April 2, 2015.

95. Interpretive signage, Stilwell and the Trail of Tears, Stilwell, Oklahoma, Westville and the Trail of Tears, Westville, Oklahoma, www.nps.gov/trte/learn/history culture/exhibits_dispersal.htm, accessed April 2, 2015.

96. National Park Service, *Trail of Tears National Historic Trail Additional Routes*, 1-3.

97. Ibid., 10-19, 27-30; *Trail News*, June 2009, 1.

98. See, for instance, interpretive signage, Cedar Town Removal Camp, Cedar Town Georgia, www.nps.gov/trte/learn/historyculture/trte_exhibits_removal.htm, accessed April 2, 2015.

99. For the Cherokee freedman issue, see Sturm, *Blood Politics*, 168-200. For the Vann house, see Miles, " 'Showplace of the Cherokee Nation' "; Miles, *House on Diamond Hill*.

100. National Park Service, *Trail of Tears National Historic Trail Interpretive Plan*, 5.

101. Anthropologist Patrick Wolfe argues that the elimination of indigenous peoples serves as the central organizing principle of settler societies like that of the United States, referring to this principle as "the logic of elimination." Wolfe, "Settler Colonialism and the Elimination of the Native," 387–89.

Epilogue

1. Jeff Marley, "We Are Still Here," jeffmarley.com/gallery/we-are-still-here, accessed July 17, 2015; *Cherokee One Feather*, June 1, 2012.

2. Jeff Marley, "We Are Still Here."

3. "Junaluska," *Daughters of the American Revolution Magazine* 39 (July 1911): 64–66.

4. Duncan and Riggs, *Cherokee Heritage Trails Guidebook*, 118–23; interpretive markers, Junaluska Memorial and Museum, Robbinsville, N.C.

5. Duncan and Riggs, *Cherokee Heritage Trails Guide*, 118–23; *Cherokee One Feather*, June 8, 2011, November 8, 2013.

6. *Cherokee One Feather*, November 8, 2013.

7. "Cherokee Nation History Course," Native Nation's Institute, University of Arizona, nnidatabase.org/text/cherokee-nation-history-course, accessed June 20, 2015; "Cherokee Nation History Course," course reader, 2000, author's personal collection; author's course notes, July 2005. I attended versions of the course, and taught sessions as a guest instructor, in 2005 and 2006.

8. Citation, Honoring Nations Award, Harvard Project on American Indian Economic Development, 2002, copy at "Cherokee Nation History Course," Native Nations Institute nnidatabase.org/db/attachments/text/honoring_nations/2002_HN _Cherokee_Nation_history_course.pdf, accessed June 20, 2015.

9. Author's course notes, July 2005.

10. Duncan and Riggs, *Cherokee Heritage Trails Guidebook*, 73–75; Riggs, "In the Service of Native Interests," 26–29; *Cherokee One Feather*, December 16, 2013.

11. Duncan and Riggs, *Cherokee Heritage Trails Guidebook*, 73–75; *Cherokee One Feather*, June 6, 2013, June 6, 2015, June 15, 2015; Middleton, *Trust in the Land*, 175–85.

12. Quoted in Duncan and Riggs, *Cherokee Heritage Trails Guidebook*, 73.

13. *Cherokee One Feather*, October 15, 1997.

14. Quoted in Duncan and Riggs, *Cherokee Heritage Trails Guidebook*, 73.

Bibliography

Archival Collections

Bowling Green, Kentucky
    Folklife Archives, Kentucky Library and Museum, Western Kentucky University
        Sarah Gertrude Knott Papers
Calhoun, Georgia
    New Echota State Historic Site
        New Echota State Historic Site Papers
Cape Girardeau, Missouri
    Kent Library, Southeast Missouri State University
        Trail of Tears Booklets
Chapel Hill, North Carolina
    Wilson Library, University of North Carolina
        Southern Historical Collection
            Edith Harrington Papers
Chattanooga, Tennessee
    Chattanooga Public Library
        Local History Collections
Cherokee, North Carolina
    Museum of the Cherokee Indian
        Duane King Research Collection
Cleveland, Tennessee
    Local History Branch, Cleveland Public Library
        James F. Corn Papers
        William Snell Papers
College Park, Maryland
    National Archives II
        RG 368, Bureau of Outdoor Recreation, Special Area Studies: Roads and Trails
Cullowhee, North Carolina
    Hunter Library, Western Carolina University
        Western North Carolina Associated Communities Papers
Gatlinburg, Tennessee
    Great Smoky Mountains National Park Library
        Great Smoky Mountain National Park Scrapbooks
        Publicity Files

Hopkinsville, Kentucky
    Kentucky Chapter, Trail of Tears Association
        Kentucky Chapter Scrapbook
Jackson, Missouri
    Missouri Department of Natural Resources
        Missouri State Parks Records
Johnson City, Tennessee
    Archives of Appalachia, East Tennessee State University
        Joe Jennings Collection
Little Rock, Arkansas
    Sequoyah National Research Center, University of Arkansas, Little Rock
        Beverly Baker Papers
        Barbara Heffington Papers
        Trail of Tears Association Papers
Morrow, Georgia
    Georgia State Archives
        Georgia Historical Commission Records
    National Archives, Southeast Region
        RG 75, Bureau of Indian Affairs, Cherokee Agency Records
Oklahoma City, Oklahoma
    Oklahoma Historical Society
        Indian Pioneer History Collection
Philadelphia, Pennsylvania
    Historical Society of Pennsylvania
        Indian Rights Association Records. Microfilm
Tahlequah, Oklahoma
    Cherokee Heritage Center
        Cherokee Foundation Records
        Cherokee National Historical Society Records
        Cherokee National Holiday Collection
        Cherokee Nation Records
        Marie Wadley Papers
        William Wayne Keeler Papers
        William Wayne Keeler Scrapbooks
Topeka, Kansas
    Kansas State Historical Society General Library
Tulsa, Oklahoma
    McFarlin Library, University of Tulsa
        Jesse Bartley Milam Papers
Washington, D.C.
    National Archives
        RG 75, Bureau of Indian Affairs Cherokee School, 1907–1939
        RG 75, Bureau of Indian Affairs. Correspondence Pertaining to Cherokee
            Removal. M1475. Microfilm

Library of Congress
U.S. Information Service, Voice of America Scripts, Microfilm

Newspapers and Periodicals

Asheville Citizen (N.C.)
Asheville Citizen-Times (N.C.)
Atlanta Constitution
Atlanta Inquirer
Atlanta Journal
Charlotte Observer
Chattanooga Free Press
Chattanooga Times
Chattanooga Times-Free Press
Cherokee Nation News (Tahlequah, Okla.)
Cherokee One Feather (Cherokee, N.C.)
Cherokee Phoenix (Tahlequah, Okla.)
Chilocco Indian School Journal (Chilocco, Okla.)
Cleveland Daily Banner (Tenn.)
Cleveland Herald (Tenn.)
Dalton Citizen (Ga.)
Daughters of the American Revolution Magazine (Washington, D.C.)
Decatur-Dekalb News (Ga.)
Dekalb New Era (Ga.)
Gainesville Daily Times (Ga.)
Haskell Indian Leader (Lawrence, Kans.)
Jackson Cash-Book (Mo.)
Jackson County Journal (Sylva, N.C.)
Kansas City Times
Kennett Democrat (Mo.)
Kentucky New Era (Hopkinsville, Ky.)
Knoxville News-Sentinel
Lookout (Chattanooga, Tenn.)
Muskogee Phoenix (Okla.)
New York Times
Pittsburgh Courier
Rome News-Tribune (Ga.)
Savannah Morning News
Scottsboro Daily Sentinel (Ala.)
Southeast Missourian (Cape Girardeau, Mo.)
State (Raleigh, N.C.)
Sylva Herald (N.C.)
Waynesville Mountaineer (N.C.)

National Park Service Reports and Planning Documents

Bishop, William J. *Myth and History: The John Ross House through Time*, 2007.

Elkinton, Steven. *The National Trail System: A Grand Experiment*, 2008.

Rethinking the National Parks for the Twenty-First Century, 2011.

Trail News (Trail of Tears National Historic Trail / Trail of Tears Association newsletter), 2002–2016.

Trail of Tears (The Cherokee Removal Route/1838–1839): Draft National Trail Study and Environmental Assessment, 1985.

Trail of Tears (The Cherokee Removal Route/1838–1839): Final National Trail Study, 1986.

Trail of Tears National Historic Trail Additional Routes, 2007.

Trail of Tears National Historic Trail: Comprehensive Management and Use Plan, 1992.

Trail of Tears National Historic Trail Interpretive Plan, 2004.

Trail of Tears National Historic Trail Newsletter, 1989–2002.

Interviews

Bishop, Jeff. November 22, 2011.

Cason, Bill. December 11, 2011.

Heffington, Barbara. June 26, 2012.

Lawrence, Shirley. November 3, 2011.

Murphree, Alice. September 19, 2011.

Websites

Cherokee Heritage Center (Tahlequah, Okla.): www.cherokeeheritage.org.

Cherokee Nation History Course. Native Nations Institute, University of Arizona: nnidatabase.org/text/cherokee-nation-history-course.

Cherokee Removal Memorial Park (Blythe Ferry, Meigs County, Tenn.): www .cherokeeremoval.org.

Jeff Marley: Jeffmarley.com.

Tennessee River Museum (Savannah, Tenn.): www.tennesseerivermuseum.org.

Trail of Tears Commemorative Motorcycle Ride: al-tn-trailoftears.net.

Trail of Tears National Historic Trail: www.nps.gov/trte.

Books, Articles, and Dissertations

Allen, Penelope Johnson. *Historic Chattanooga: A Brief Description of the Places of Historical Interest in and around Chattanooga*. Chattanooga: Daughters of 1812, 1935.

Anderson, Benedict. *Imagined Communities: Reflections on the Origin and Spread of Nationalism*. New York: Verso, 1991.

Anderson, Peggy. *The Daughters: An Unconventional Look at America's Fan Club, the DAR*. New York: St. Martin's Press, 1974.

Anderson, William L. *Cherokee Removal: Before and After*. Athens: University of Georgia Press, 1991.

Annual Report of the Commission to the Five Civilized Tribes. Washington, D.C.: Government Printing Office, 1902.

Armstrong, Zella. *The History of Hamilton County and Chattanooga, Tennessee*. Chattanooga: Lookout Publishing Company, 1931.

Barrows, William. *The Indian's Side of the Indian Question*. 1887. Reprint, New York: Books for Libraries, 1972.

Batteau, Allen W. *The Invention of Appalachia*. Tucson: University of Arizona Press, 1990.

Bauer, Fred B. *Land of the North Carolina Cherokees*. Brevard, N.C.: George Buchanan, 1970.

Beard-Moose, Christina Taylor. *Public Indians, Private Cherokees: Tourism and Tradition on Tribal Ground*. Tuscaloosa: University of Alabama Press, 2009.

Beck, David R. M. *The Struggle for Self-Determination: History of the Menominee Indians since 1854*. Lincoln: University of Nebraska Press, 2005.

Becker, Jane S. *Selling Tradition: Appalachia and the Construction of an American Folk, 1930–1940*. Chapel Hill: University of North Carolina Press, 1998.

Bender, Margaret. *Signs of Cherokee Culture: Sequoyah's Syllabary in Eastern Cherokee Life*. Chapel Hill: University of North Carolina Press, 2002.

Berkhofer, Robert. *The White Man's Indian: Images of American Indians from Columbus to the Present*. New York: Knopf, 1978.

Bird, S. Elizabeth, ed. *Dressing in Feathers: The Construction of the Indian in American Popular Culture*. New York: Westview Press, 1996.

Bishir, Catherine W. "Landmarks of Power: Building a Southern Past in Raleigh and Wilmington, North Carolina, 1885–1915." In *Where These Memories Grow: History, Memory, and Southern Identity*, edited by W. Fitzhugh Brundage, 139–68. Chapel Hill: University of North Carolina Press, 2000.

Blackman, Jon S. *Oklahoma's Indian New Deal*. Norman: University of Oklahoma Press, 2013.

Blight, David W. *Race and Reunion: The Civil War in American Memory*. Cambridge, Mass.: Harvard University Press, 2001.

Borstelmann, Thomas. *The Cold War and the Color Line: American Race Relations in the Global Arena*. Cambridge, Mass.: Harvard University Press, 2001.

Bowers, John. *Chickamauga and Chattanooga: The Battles That Doomed the Confederacy*. New York: Harper Collins, 1994.

Brown-Nagin, Tomiko. *Courage to Dissent: Atlanta and the Long History of the Civil Rights Movement*. New York: Oxford University Press, 2011.

Brundage, W. Fitzhugh. "Introduction: No Deed but Memory." In *Where These Memories Grow: History, Memory, and Southern Identity*, edited by W. Fitzhugh Brundage, 1–28. Chapel Hill: University of North Carolina Press, 2000.

——. *The Southern Past: A Clash of Race and Memory.* Cambridge, Mass.: Harvard University Press, 2005.

——, ed. *Where These Memories Grow: History, Memory, and Southern Identity.* Chapel Hill: University of North Carolina Press, 2000.

Bruner, Edward M. *Culture on Tour: Ethnographies of Travel.* Chicago: University of Chicago Press, 2005.

Burt, Larry W. *Tribalism in Crisis: Federal Indian Policy, 1953–1961.* Albuquerque: University of New Mexico Press, 1982.

Butrick, Daniel S. *The Journal of Rev. Daniel S. Butrick, May 19, 1838–April 1, 1839.* Park Hill, Okla.: Trail of Tears Association, Oklahoma Chapter, 1998.

Calloway, Colin G. *The American Revolution in Indian Country: Crisis and Diversity in Native American Communities.* New York: Cambridge University Press, 1995.

Carter, Kent. *The Dawes Commission and the Allotment of the Five Civilized Tribes, 1893–1914.* Orem, Utah: Ancestry.com, 1999.

Castile, George Pierre. *To Show Heart: Native American Self-Determination and Federal Indian Policy.* Tucson: University of Arizona Press, 1998.

Champagne, Duane. *Social Order and Political Change: Constitutional Governments among the Cherokee, the Choctaw, the Chickasaw, and the Creek.* Stanford, Calif.: Stanford University Press, 1992.

Chiltoskey, Mary Ulmer. *Cherokee Fair and Festival: A History thru 1978.* Asheville, N.C.: Gilbert Printing Company, 1979.

Clark, Kathleen. "Celebrating Freedom: Emancipation Day Celebrations and African American Memory in the Early Reconstruction South." In *Where These Memories Grow: History, Memory, and Southern Identity*, edited by W. Fitzhugh Brundage, 107–32. Chapel Hill: University of North Carolina Press, 2000.

——. *Defining Moments: African American Commemoration and Political Culture in the South, 1863–1913.* Chapel Hill: University of North Carolina Press, 2005.

Clark, Thomas D. *The Emerging South.* New York: Oxford University Press, 1961.

Cobb, Daniel M. "Devils in Disguise: The Carnegie Project, the Cherokee Nation, and the 1960s." *American Indian Quarterly* 31 (Summer 2007): 465–90.

——. *Native Activism in Cold War America: The Struggle for Sovereignty.* Lawrence: University of Kansas Press, 2008.

——. "Talking the Language of the Larger World: Politics in Cold War (Native) America." In *Beyond Red Power: American Indian Politics and Activism since 1900*, edited by Daniel M. Cobb and Loretta Fowler, 161–77. Santa Fe, N.M.: SAR Press, 2007.

Cobb, Daniel M., and Loretta Fowler, eds. *Beyond Red Power: American Indian Politics and Activism since 1900.* Santa Fe, N.M.: SAR Press, 2007.

Confer, Clarissa. *The Cherokee Nation in the Civil War.* Norman: University of Oklahoma Press, 2007.

Conley, Robert J. *A Cherokee Encyclopedia.* Albuquerque: University of New Mexico Press, 2007.

——. *The Cherokee Nation: A History.* Albuquerque: University of New Mexico Press, 2005.

Cook, Robert. *Troubled Commemoration: The American Civil War Centennial,*
    1961–1965. Baton Rouge: Louisiana State University, 2007.

Cornell, Stephen. *The Return of the Native: American Indian Political Resurgence.*
    New York: Oxford University Press, 1988.

Cothran, Boyd. *Remembering the Modoc War: Redemptive Violence and the Making*
    of American Innocence. Chapel Hill: University of North Carolina Press, 2014.

Cowger, Thomas W. " 'The Crossroads of Destiny': The NCAI's Landmark Struggle
    to Thwart Coercive Termination." *American Indian Culture and Research*
    Journal 20 (1996): 128–38.

Cox, Karen L., ed. *Destination Dixie: Tourism and Southern Memory.* Gainesville:
    University Press of Gainesville, 2012.

———. *Dixie's Daughters: The United Daughters of the Confederacy and the*
    Preservation of Confederate Culture. Gainesville: University Press of Florida, 2003.

Cozzens, Peter. *The Shipwreck of their Hopes: The Battles for Chattanooga.* Urbana:
    University of Illinois Press, 1994.

———. *This Terrible Sound: The Battle of Chickamauga.* Urbana: University of
    Illinois Press, 1992.

Crespi, Muriel. "Native American Relationships Policy, an Evolving Script."
    Courier: Newsmagazine of the National Park Service 32 (December 1987): 38–39.

Cummings, Martha Lynn Fuquay, and Ida Garrett Herod Smother. *Historical*
    Markers Placed by the Tennessee Society, Daughters of the American Revolution.
    Knoxville: Tennessee Valley Publishing, 2007.

Cushman, Ellen. *The Cherokee Syllabary: Writing the People's Perseverance.*
    Norman: University of Oklahoma Press, 2011.

Dahl, Kathleen. "The Battle over Termination on the Colville Indian Reservation."
    American Indian Culture and Research Journal 18 (1994): 29–53.

Davis, Rebecca Harding. "Qualla." *Lippincott's Magazine of Popular Literature and*
    Science 16 (November 1875): 576–86.

Dawes, Henry L. "The Indian Territory." In *Proceedings of the Thirteenth Annual*
    Meeting of the Lake Mohonk Conference of Friends of the Indian, 95–99. New York:
    Lake Mohonk Conference, 1895.

Debo, Angie. *And Still the Waters Run: The Betrayal of the Five Civilized Tribes.*
    Princeton, N.J.: Princeton University Press, 1940.

Deloria, Philip. *Playing Indian.* New Haven, Conn.: Yale University Press, 1998.

Denson, Andrew. *Demanding the Cherokee Nation: Indian Autonomy and American*
    Culture, 1839–1900. Lincoln: University of Nebraska Press, 2004.

———. "Gatlinburg's Cherokee Monument: Public Memory in the Shadow of a
    National Park." *Appalachian Journal* 37 (Winter 2010): 28–43.

———. "Native Americans and Cold War Public Diplomacy: Indian Politics,
    American History, and the U.S. Information Agency." *American Indian Culture*
    and Research Journal 36 (2012): 3–21.

———. "Reframing the Indian Dead: Removal-Era Cherokee Graves and the
    Changing Landscape of Southern Memory." In *Death and the American South,*

edited by Craig Thompson Friend and Lorri Glover, 250–74. New York: Cambridge University Press, 2015.

———. "Remembering Cherokee Removal in Civil Rights–Era Georgia." *Southern Cultures* 14 (Winter 2008): 85–101.

Dickstein, Morris. *Dancing in the Dark: A Cultural History of the Great Depression.* New York: W. W. Norton, 2009.

Dippie, Brian. *The Vanishing American: White Attitudes and American Indian Policy.* Middletown, Conn.: Wesleyan University Press, 1982.

Dizard, William P. *The Strategy of Truth: The Story of the U.S. Information Service.* Washington, D.C.: Public Affairs, 1961.

Doak, Henry Melvil. *The Wagonauts Abroad.* Nashville, Tenn.: Southwestern Publishing House, 1892.

Doss, Erika. *Memorial Mania: Public Feeling in America.* Chicago: University of Chicago Press, 2010.

Dudziak, Mary L. *Cold War Civil Rights: Race and the Image of American Democracy.* Princeton, N.J.: Princeton University Press, 2000.

Duncan, Barbara, and Brett Riggs. *Cherokee Heritage Trails Guidebook.* Chapel Hill: University of North Carolina Press, 2003.

Duncan, James W. "The Keetoowah Society." *Chronicles of Oklahoma* 4 (September 1926): 251–54.

Elder, Robert. *The Information Machine: The United States Information Agency and American Foreign Policy.* Syracuse, N.Y.: Syracuse University Press, 1968.

Elliot, Michael A. *Custerology: The Enduring Legacy of the Indian Wars and George Armstrong Custer.* Chicago: University of Chicago Press, 2007.

Ellis, Clyde. "'More Real than the Indians Themselves': The Early Years of the Indian Lore Movement in the United States." *Montana* 58 (Autumn 2008): 3–22.

Exler, Marie. *Tears of the Trail.* Cape Girardeau: Center for Regional History, Southeast Missouri State University, 2000.

Ezzell, Timothy Paul. "Yankees in Dixie: The Story of Chattanooga, 1870–1898." Ph.D. diss., University of Tennessee, 1996.

Finger, John R. *Cherokee Americans: The Eastern Band of Cherokees in the Twentieth Century.* Lincoln: University of Nebraska Press, 1991.

———. *The Eastern Band of Cherokees, 1819–1900.* Knoxville: University of Tennessee Press, 1984.

———. "Termination and the Eastern Band of Cherokees." *American Indian Quarterly* 15 (Spring 1991): 153–70.

Fixico, Donald. *Termination and Relocation: Federal Indian Policy, 1945–1960.* Albuquerque: University of New Mexico Press, 1986.

Fogelson, Raymond E., ed. *Southeast.* Vol. 14 of *Handbook of North American Indians.* Washington, D.C.: Smithsonian Institution Press, 2004.

Foote, Kenneth. *Shadowed Ground: America's Landscapes of Violence and Tragedy.* 1997. Rev. ed., Austin: University of Texas Press, 2003.

Foreman, Carolyn Thomas. "Aunt Eliza of Tahlequah." *Chronicles of Oklahoma* 9 (March 1931): 43–55.

Foreman, Grant. *Indian Removal: The Emigration of the Five Civilized Tribes of Indians*. Norman: University of Oklahoma Press, 1935.

———. *Sequoyah*. Norman: University of Oklahoma Press, 1938.

Foster, Gaines F. *Ghosts of the Confederacy: Defeat, the Lost Cause, and the Emergence of the New South*. New York: Oxford, 1987.

Free, William, and Charles Lower, eds. *History into Drama: A Source Book on Symphonic Drama, Including the Complete Text of Paul Green's* The Lost Colony. New York: Odyssey Press, 1963.

Freeman, David B. *Carved in Stone: The History of Stone Mountain*. Macon, Ga.: Mercer University Press, 1997.

French, Laurence, and Jim Hornbuckle. *The Cherokee Perspective*. Boone, N.C.: Appalachian Consortium Press, 1981.

Fried, Richard M. *The Russians Are Coming! The Russians Are Coming! Pageantry and Patriotism in Cold War America*. New York: Oxford University Press, 1998.

Gaines, David M., and Jere L. Krakow. "The Trail of Tears National Historic Trail." *Landscape and Urban Planning* 36 (1996): 159–69.

Garrison, Tim Allen. *The Legal Ideology of Removal: The Southern Judiciary and the Sovereignty of Native American Nations*. Athens: University of Georgia Press, 2002.

Gerstle, Gary. *American Crucible: Race and Nation in the Twentieth Century*. Princeton, N.J.: Princeton University Press, 2001.

Gibbs, Margaret. *The DAR*. New York: Holt, Rinehart, and Winston, 1969.

Gilbert, James. *Writers and Partisans: A History of Literary Radicalism in America*. 1968. Reprint, New York: Columbia University Press, 1972.

Gilbert, Joan. *The Trail of Tears across Missouri*. Columbia: University of Missouri Press, 1996.

Glassberg, David. *American Historical Pageantry: The Uses of Tradition in the Early Twentieth Century*. Chapel Hill: University of North Carolina Press, 1990.

———. *Sense of History: The Place of the Past in American Life*. Amherst: University of Massachusetts Press, 2001.

Govan, Gilbert E., and James W. Livingwood. *The Chattanooga Country, 1540–1962*. Rev. ed., Chapel Hill: University of North Carolina Press, 1962.

Green, Paul. *The Lost Colony, a Symphonic Drama of American History*. Chapel Hill: University of North Carolina Press, 1954.

Hale, Grace Elizabeth. "Granite Stopped Time: The Stone Mountain Memorial and the Representation of White Southern Identity." *Georgia Historical Quarterly* 82 (Spring 1998): 22–44.

———. *Making Whiteness: The Culture of Segregation in the South, 1890–1940*. New York: Vintage, 1998.

Harkins, Anthony. *Hillbilly: The Cultural History of an American Icon*. New York: Oxford University Press, 2004.

Harmon, David, ed. *People, Places, and Parks: Proceedings of the 2005 George Wright Society on Parks, Protected Areas, and Cultural Sites.* Hancock, Mich.: The George Wright Society, 2006.

Hatley, Tom. *The Dividing Paths: Cherokees and South Carolinians through the Revolutionary Era.* New York: Oxford University Press, 1995.

Hayden, Dolores. *The Power of Place: Urban Landscapes as Public History.* Cambridge, Mass: MIT Press, 1995.

Haywood, John. *The Civil and Political History of the State of Tennessee from Its Earliest Settlement Up to the Year 1796, Including the Boundaries of the State.* 1823. Reprint, Knoxville: Tenase Company, 1969.

Hendrix, Janey B. "Redbird Smith and the Nighthawk Keetoowahs." *Journal of Cherokee Studies* 8 (Spring 1983): 22–29; (Fall 1983): 73–85.

Hixson, Walter. *American Settler Colonialism: A History.* New York: Palgrave Macmillan, 2013.

Hood, Susan. "Termination of the Klamath Tribe in Oregon." *Ethnohistory* 19 (Fall 1972): 379–92.

Horton, James Oliver, and Spencer R. Crew. "Afro-Americans and Museums: Towards a Policy of Inclusion." In *History Museums in the United States: A Critical Assessment,* edited by Warren Leon and Roy Rosenzweig, 215–36. Urbana: University of Illinois Press, 1989.

Horton, James Oliver, and Lois E. Horton, eds. *Slavery and Public History: The Tough Stuff of American Memory.* Chapel Hill: University of North Carolina Press, 2006.

Howard, John. *Concentration Camps on the Home Front: Japanese Americans in the House of Jim Crow.* Chicago: University of Chicago Press, 2008.

Howe, Tyler B. " 'The Ancient Customs of Their Fathers': Cherokee Generational Townhouse Politics of Mid-19th Century Western North Carolina." *Journal of Cherokee Studies* 29 (2011): 3–13.

Hunter, Kermit. *Unto These Hills: A Drama of the Cherokee.* Chapel Hill: University of North Carolina Press, 1950.

Jackson, Helen Hunt. *A Century of Dishonor: A Sketch of the United States Government's Dealings with Some of the Indian Tribes.* 1881. Reprint, St. Clair, Mich.: Scholarly Press, 1977.

Jacoby, Karl. *Shadows at Dawn: An Apache Massacre and the Violence of History.* New York: Penguin, 2008.

Jakle, John A. *The Tourist: Travel in Twentieth Century America.* Lincoln: University of Nebraska Press, 1985.

Janney, Caroline E. *Burying the Dead, But Not the Past: Ladies' Memorial Associations and the Lost Cause.* Chapel Hill: University of North Carolina Press, 2008.

——. "War over a Shrine of Peace: The Appomattox Peace Monument and Retreat from Reconciliation." *Journal of Southern History* 77 (February 2011): 91–120.

Jarrett, Robert Frank. *Occoneechee: The Maid of the Mystic Lake.* 1916. Reprint, Atlanta: Lithograph Company, 1946.

Jones, James B., Jr. "Class Consciousness and Worker Solidarity in Urban Tennessee: The Chattanooga Carmen's Strikes of 1899–1917." *Tennessee Historical Quarterly* 52 (Summer 1993): 98–112.

———. "Strikes and Labor Organization in Tennessee during the Depression of 1893–1897." *Tennessee Historical Quarterly* 52 (Winter 1993): 256–64.

Jones, Loyal. *Minstrel of the Appalachians: The Story of Bascom Lamar Lunsford.* Boone, N.C.: Appalachian Consortium Press, 1984.

"Junaluska." *Daughters of the American Revolution Magazine,* July 1911, 64–66.

Jurgelski, William Martin. "New Light on the Tsali Affair." In *Light on the Path: The Anthropology and History of the Southeastern Indians,* edited by Thomas J. Pluckhahn and Robbie Ethridge, 133–64. Tuscaloosa: University of Alabama Press, 2006.

Justi, Herman, ed. *Official History of the Tennessee Centennial Exposition.* Nashville: Tennessee Centennial Committee on Publication, 1898.

Kammen, Michael. *Mystic Chords of Memory: The Transformation of Tradition in American Culture.* New York: Alfred Knopf, 1991.

Kaser, James A. *At the Bivouac of Memory: History, Politics, and the Battle of Chickamauga.* New York: Peter Lang, 1996.

Keller, Robert H., and Michael F. Turek. *American Indians and the National Parks.* Tucson: University of Arizona Press, 1998.

Kelman, Ari. *A Misplaced Massacre: Struggling over the Memory of Sand Creek.* Cambridge, Mass.: Harvard University Press, 2013.

King, Duane H., ed. *The Cherokee Indian Nation: A Troubled History.* Knoxville: University of Tennessee Press, 1979.

———. *The Cherokee Trail of Tears.* Portland, Ore.: Graphic Arts, 2008.

———. "The Origin of the Eastern Cherokees as a Social and Political Entity." In *The Cherokee Indian Nation: A Troubled History,* edited by Duane H. King, 164–80. Knoxville: University of Tennessee Press, 1979.

Koenig, Alex, and Jonathan Stein. "Federalism and State Recognition of Native American Tribes: A Survey of State-Recognized Tribes and State Recognition Processes across the United States." *Santa Clara Law Review* 48 (January 2008): 79–153.

Krauthamer, Barbara. *Black Slaves, Indian Masters: Slavery, Emancipation, and Citizenship in the Native American South.* Chapel Hill: University of North Carolina Press, 2013.

Lamon, Lester. *Black Tennesseans, 1900–1930.* Knoxville: University of Tennessee Press, 1977.

Leeds, Georgia Rae. *The United Keetoowah Band of Cherokee Indians in Oklahoma.* New York: Peter Lang, 1996.

Lefler, Lisa J., and Frederic W. Gleach, eds. *Southern Indians and Anthropologists: Culture, Politics, and Identity.* Athens: University of Georgia Press, 2002.

Leon, Warren, and Roy Rosenzweig, eds. *History Museums in the United States: A Critical Assessment.* Urbana: University of Illinois Press, 1989.

Levine, Lawrence. *The Unpredictable Past: Explorations in American Cultural History.* New York: Oxford University Press, 1993.

Lewis, Thomas M. N., and Madeline D. Kneberg Lewis. *The Prehistory of the Chickamauga Basin in Tennessee.* 2 vols. Knoxville: University of Tennessee Press, 1995.

Lindgren, James M. *Preserving the Old Dominion: Historic Preservation and Virginia Traditionalism.* Charlottesville: University Press of Virginia, 1993.

Linenthal, Edward. *The Unfinished Bombing: Oklahoma City in American Memory.* New York: Oxford University Press, 2001.

Livingwood, James W. *A History of Hamilton County, Tennessee.* Memphis, Tenn.: Memphis State University Press, 1981.

Lowenthal, David. *The Heritage Crusade and the Spoils of History.* New York: Cambridge University Press, 1998.

Lowery, Malinda Maynor. *Lumbee Indians in the Jim Crow South: Race, Identity, and the Making of a Nation.* Chapel Hill: University of North Carolina Press, 2010.

Malone, Henry T. "New Echota: Capitol of the Cherokee Nation." *Early Georgia* 1 (Spring 1955), 6–13.

Mankiller, Wilma. *Mankiller: A Chief and Her People.* New York: St. Martin's Press, 1993.

Martin, C. Brenden. "To Keep the Spirit of Mountain Culture Alive: Tourism and Historical Memory in the Southern Highlands." In *Where These Memories Grow: History, Memory, and Southern Identity,* edited by W. Fitzhugh Brundage, 249–70. Chapel Hill: University of North Carolina Press, 2000.

———. *Tourism in the Mountain South: A Double-Edged Sword.* Knoxville: University of Tennessee Press, 2007.

Martin, Joel W. " 'My Grandmother Was a Cherokee Princess': Representations of Indians in Southern History." In *Dressing in Feathers: The Construction of the Indian in American Culture,* edited by S. Elizabeth Bird, 129–48. New York: Westview Press, 1996.

Mason, Robert Lindsay. *The Lure of the Great Smokies.* Boston: Houghton Mifflin, 1927.

Maxwell, Angie. *The Indicted South: Public Criticism, Southern Inferiority, and the Politics of Whiteness.* Chapel Hill: University of North Carolina Press, 2014.

McDonough, James Lee. *Chattanooga: A Death Grip on the Confederacy.* Knoxville: University of Tennessee Press, 1984.

McLoughlin, William G. *After the Trail of Tears: The Cherokees' Struggle for Sovereignty.* Chapel Hill: University of North Carolina, 1993.

———. *Champions of the Cherokees: Evan and John B. Jones.* Princeton, N.J.: Princeton University Press, 1990.

———. *Cherokee Renascence in the New Republic.* Princeton, N.J.: Princeton University Press, 1986.

———. *Cherokees and Missionaries, 1789–1839.* New Haven, Conn.: Yale University Press, 1984.

Meacham, Charles Mayfield. *A History of Christian County, Kentucky: From Oxcart to Airplane*. Nashville, Tenn.: Marshall and Bruce, 1930.

Meredith, Howard L. *Bartley Milam: Principal Chief of the Cherokee Nation*. Muskogee, Okla.: Indian University Press, 1985.

Meringolo, Denise D. *Museums, Monuments, and National Parks: Toward a New Genealogy of Public History*. Amherst: University of Massachusetts Press, 2012.

Metcalf, Warren. *Termination's Legacy: The Discarded Indians of Utah*. Lincoln: University of Nebraska Press, 2002.

Middleton, Beth Rose. *Trust in the Land: New Directions in Tribal Conservation*. Tucson: University of Arizona Press, 2011.

Miles, Tiya. *The House on Diamond Hill: A Cherokee Plantation Story*. Chapel Hill: University of North Carolina Press, 2010.

———. "'Showplace of the Cherokee Nation': Race and the Making of a Southern House Museum." *The Public Historian* 33 (November 2011): 11–34.

———. *Ties That Bind: The Story of an Afro-Cherokee Family in Slavery and Freedom*. Berkeley: University of California Press, 2005.

Mills, Cynthia, and Pamela H. Simpson, eds. *Monuments to the Lost Cause: Women, Art, and the Landscape of Southern Memory*. Knoxville: University of Tennessee Press, 2003.

Mooney, James. *History, Myths, and Sacred Formulas of the Cherokees*. 1891, 1900. Reprint, Asheville, N.C.: Bright Mountain Books, 1992.

Moore, Lynda, ed. *Chewani (The Faithful): Cherokee Indian Materials Collected by Gertrude McDaris Ruskin*. Darien, Ga.: Darien News, 1975.

Moses, L. G. *The Indian Man: A Biography of James Mooney*. Urbana: University of Illinois Press, 1984.

Naylor, Celia. *African Cherokees in Indian Territory: From Chattel to Citizens*. Chapel Hill: University of North Carolina Press, 2008.

Norgren, Jill. *The Cherokee Cases: The Confrontation of Law and Politics*. New York: McGraw-Hill, 1996.

Oatis, Steven J. *A Colonial Complex: South Carolina's Frontiers in the Era of the Yamasee War, 1680–1730*. Lincoln: University of Nebraska Press, 2004.

O'Brien, Jean M. *Firsting and Lasting: Writing Indians Out of Existence in New England*. Minneapolis: University of Minnesota Press, 2010.

Osburn, Katherine M. B. *Choctaw Resurgence in Mississippi: Race, Class, and Nation Building in the Jim Crow South, 1830–1977*. Lincoln: University of Nebraska Press, 2014.

———. "The 'Identified Full-Bloods' in Mississippi: Race and Choctaw Identity, 1898–1918." *Ethnohistory* 56 (Summer 2009): 423–47.

Parins, James W. *Literacy and Intellectual Life in the Cherokee Nation, 1820–1906*. Norman: University of Oklahoma Press, 2013.

Peers, Laura. *Playing Ourselves: Interpreting Native Histories at Historic Reconstructions*. New York: Altamira, 2007.

Pells, Richard H. *Radical Visions and American Dreams: Culture and Social Thought in the Depression Years*. New York: Harper and Row, 1973.

Perdue, Theda. *Cherokee Women: Gender and Culture Change, 1700–1835*. Lincoln: University of Nebraska Press, 1998.

Perdue, Theda, and Michael D. Green. *The Cherokee Nation and the Trail of Tears*. New York: Viking, 2007.

Perdue, Theda, and Michael D. Green, eds. *The Cherokee Removal: A Brief History with Documents*. New York: Bedford–St. Martin's, 1995.

Peroff, Nicholas. *Menominee Drums: Tribal Termination and Restoration*. Norman: University of Oklahoma Press, 1982.

Perrin, William Henry. *The Counties of Christian and Trigg, Kentucky: Historical and Biographical*. Chicago: F. A. Battey, 1884.

Philp, Kenneth R. *Termination Revisited: American Indians on the Trail to Self-Determination, 1933–1953*. Lincoln: University of Nebraska Press, 1999.

Pierce, Daniel S. *The Great Smokies: From Natural Habitat to National Park*. Knoxville: University of Tennessee Press, 2000.

Pitcaithley, Dwight T. " 'A Cosmic Threat': The National Park Service Addresses the Causes of the American Civil War." In *Slavery and Public History: The Tough Stuff of American Memory*, edited by James Oliver Horton and Lois E. Horton, 169–86. Chapel Hill: University of North Carolina Press, 2006.

———. "National Parks and the Interpretive Message since 1990." In *People, Places, and Parks: Proceedings of the 2005 George Wright Society on Parks, Protected Areas, and Cultural Sites*, edited by David Harmon, 444–48. Hancock, Mich.: George Wright Society, 2006.

Pitts, Lulie. *History of Gordon County, Georgia*. Calhoun, Ga.: Press of the Calhoun Times, 1933.

Pluckhahn, Thomas J., and Robbie Ethridge. *Light on the Path: The Anthropology and History of the Southeastern Indians*. Tuscaloosa: University of Alabama Press, 2006.

Plummer, Brenda Gayle. *Black Americans and United States Foreign Affairs, 1935–1960*. Chapel Hill: University of North Carolina Press, 1996.

Potts, Nancy J. "Unfulfilled Expectations: The Erosion of Black Political Power in Chattanooga, 1865–1911." *Tennessee Historical Quarterly* 49 (Summer 1990): 112–28.

Powell, William. *Paradise Preserved*. Chapel Hill: University of North Carolina Press, 1965.

Preston, Howard Lawrence. *Dirt Roads to Dixie: Accessibility and Modernization in the South*. Knoxville: University of Tennessee Press, 1991.

Proceedings of the Thirty-Eighth State Conference, National Society Daughters of the American Revolution, Georgia. N.p.: Daughters of the American Revolution, Georgia State Society, 1936.

Prucha, Francis Paul. *American Indian Policy in Crisis: Christian Reformers and the Indian, 1865-1900.* Norman: University of Oklahoma Press, 1976.

———. *Documents of United States Indian Policy.* Lincoln: University of Nebraska Press, 1975.

———. *The Great Father.* Lincoln: University of Nebraska Press, 1984.

Riggs, Brett. "In the Service of Native Interests: Archaeology for, of, and by Cherokee People." In *Southern Indians and Anthropologists: Culture, Politics, and Identity,* edited by Lisa J. Lefler and Frederic W. Gleach, 19-30. Athens: University of Georgia Press, 2002.

Roche, Jeff. *Restructured Resistance: The Sibley Commission and the Politics of Desegregation in Georgia.* Athens: University of Georgia Press, 1998.

Rosenzweig, Roy, and David Thelen. *The Presence of the Past: Popular Uses of History in American Life.* New York: Columbia University Press, 1998.

Rosier, Paul C. *Serving Their Country: American Indian Politics and Patriotism in the Twentieth Century.* Cambridge, Mass.: Harvard University Press, 2009.

———. " 'They Are Ancestral Homelands': Race, Place, and Politics in Cold War Native America." *Journal of American History* 92 (March 2006): 1300-26.

Ruskin, Gertrude McDaris. *John Ross, Chief of an Eagle Race.* Atlanta, Ga.: Gertrude Ruskin, 1963.

———. *Sequoyah: Cherokee Indian Cadmus.* Weaverville, N.C.: Crowder's Press, 1970.

Sass, Herbert Ravenel. *Hear Me, My Chiefs!* New York: William Morrow and Company, 1936.

Saunt, Claudio. "The Native South: An Account of Recent Historiography." *Native South* 1 (2008): 45-60.

———. *Red, White, and Indian: Race and the Unmaking of an American Family.* New York: Oxford University Press, 2005.

Schwartz, E. A. "Red Atlantis Revisited: Community and Culture in the Writings of John Collier." *American Indian Quarterly* 18 (Fall 1994): 507-31.

Shackel, Paul A. *Memory in Black and White: Race, Commemoration, and the Post-Bellum Landscape.* Walnut Creek, Calif.: Altamira, 2003.

Sheehan, Bernard. *Seeds of Extinction: Jeffersonian Philanthropy and the American Indian.* Chapel Hill: University of North Carolina Press, 1973.

Simpson, George L., and Harriet L. Herring. *Western North Carolina Associated Communities.* Cherokee, N.C.: Cherokee Historical Association, 1956.

Sims, Anastasia. *The Power of Femininity in the New South: Women's Organizations and Politics in North Carolina, 1880-1930.* Columbia: University of South Carolina Press, 1997.

Smith, Timothy B. *A Chickamauga Memorial: The Establishment of America's First Civil War Military Park.* Knoxville: University of Tennessee Press, 2009.

———. *The Golden Age of Battlefield Preservation: The Decade of the 1890s and the Establishment of America's First Five Military Parks.* Knoxville: University of Tennessee Press, 2008.

Smithers, Gregory D. "A Cherokee Epic: Kermit Hunter's *Unto These Hills* and the Mythologizing of Cherokee History." *Native South* 8 (2015): 1–30.

Snyder, Christina. *Slavery in Indian Country: The Changing Face of Captivity in Early America.* Cambridge, Mass.: Harvard University Press, 2010.

Speck, Frank G., and Leonard Broom. *Cherokee Dance and Drama.* 1951. Reprint, Norman: University of Oklahoma Press, 1983.

Speelman, Margaret Pearson. "Pageantry in Indian Schools." *Indians at Work* 3 (August 1935): 23–25.

Stanley, Sam, ed. *American Indian Economic Development.* The Hague: Moulton Publishers, 1978.

Starnes, Richard D. *Creating the Land of the Sky: Tourism and Society in Western North Carolina.* Tuscaloosa: University of Alabama Press, 2005.

———, ed. *Southern Journeys: Tourism, History and Culture in the Modern South.* Tuscaloosa: University of Alabama Press, 2003.

Starr, Emmet. *History of the Cherokee Indians and Their Legends and Folklore.* 1921. Reprint, Millwood, N.Y.: Kraus Reprint Company, 1977.

State of Georgia. *Acts and Resolutions of the General Assembly of the State of Georgia, 1962.* Atlanta: State Printer, 1962.

———. *Acts and Resolutions of the General Assembly of the State of Georgia, 1980.* Atlanta: State Printer, 1980.

Strayer, Martha. *The DAR: An Informal History.* 1958. Reprint, Westport, Conn.: Greenwood Press, 1973.

Stremlau, Rose. *Sustaining the Cherokee Family: Kinship and the Allotment of an Indigenous Nation.* Chapel Hill: University of North Carolina Press, 2011.

Strickland, Rennard. *The Fire and the Spirits: Cherokee Law from Clan to Court.* Norman: University of Oklahoma Press, 1975.

Strickland, Rennard, and William M. Strickland. "Beyond the Trail of Tears: One Hundred Fifty Years of Cherokee Survival." In *Cherokee Removal: Before and After,* edited by William L. Anderson, 112–38. Athens: University of Georgia Press, 1991.

Stringfield, Margaret. *Occoneechee: Fair Maid of the Forest.* Waynesville, N.C.: Margaret Stringfield, 1948.

Sturm, Circe. *Becoming Cherokee: The Struggle over Cherokee Identity in the Twenty-First Century.* Santa Fe, N.M.: SAR Press, 2010.

———. *Blood Politics: Race, Culture, and Identity in the Cherokee Nation of Oklahoma.* Berkeley: University of California Press, 2002.

Summerhill, Stephen J., and John Alexander Williams. *Sinking Columbus: Contested History, Cultural Politics, and Mythmaking during the Quincentenary.* Gainesville: University Press of Florida, 2000.

Susman, Warren I. *Culture as History: The Transformation of American Society in the Twentieth Century.* New York: Pantheon, 1984.

Tennessee State History of the Daughters of the American Revolution. Knoxville: S. B. Newman and Co., 1930.

Thomas, Robert K. "The Redbird Smith Movement." In *Symposium on Cherokee and Iroquois Culture*, edited by William N. Fenton and John Gulick, 161–66. *Smithsonian Institution Bureau of Ethnology Bulletin* 180. Washington, D.C.: Government Printing Office, 1961.

Thompson, Matthew D. "Staging 'the Drama': The Continuing Importance of Cultural Tourism in the Gaming Era." Ph.D. diss., University of North Carolina, Chapel Hill, 2009.

Thornborough, Laura. *The Great Smoky Mountains.* 1937. Rev. ed., New York: Thomas Y. Crowell Company, 1942.

Thornton, Russell. *The Cherokees: A Population History.* Lincoln: University of Nebraska Press, 1990.

Tortora, Daniel J. *Carolina in Crisis: Cherokees, Colonists, and Slaves in the American Southeast, 1756–1763.* Chapel Hill: University of North Carolina Press, 2015.

Trails for America. Washington, D.C.: Bureau of Outdoor Recreation, 1966.

Truettner, William H. "Ideology and Image: Justifying Westward Expansion." In *The West as America: Reinterpreting Images of the Frontier, 1820–1920*, edited by William H. Truettner, 27–53. Washington, D.C.: Smithsonian Institution Press, 1991.

Tuck, Stephen G. N. *Beyond Atlanta: The Struggle for Racial Equality in Georgia, 1940–1980.* Athens: University of Georgia Press, 2001.

Tyler-McGraw, Marie. "Introduction: Curating History in Museums: Some Thoughts Provoked by *The West as America.*" *The Public Historian* 14 (Summer 1992): 51–53.

Tyner, Howard Q. "The Keetoowah Society in Cherokee History." Master's thesis, University of Tulsa, 1949.

Umberger, Wallace Randolph. "A History of *Unto These Hills*, 1941–1968." Ph.D. diss., Tulane University, 1970.

Urry, John. *The Tourist Gaze.* London: Sage, 1990.

Von Eschen, Penny. *Race against Empire: Black America and Anti-Colonialism, 1937–1957.* Ithaca, N.Y.: Cornell University Press, 1997.

Wahrhaftig, Albert L. "In the Aftermath of Civilization: The Persistence of the Cherokee Indians in Oklahoma." Ph.D. diss., University of Chicago, 1975.

——. "Making Do with the Dark Meat: A Report on the Cherokee Indians in Oklahoma." In *American Indian Economic Development*, edited by Sam Stanley, 409–510. The Hague: Mouton Publishers, 1978.

Wahrhaftig, Albert L., and Jane Lukens-Wahrhaftig. "New Militants or Resurrected State? The Five County Northeastern Oklahoma Cherokee Organizations." In *The Cherokee Nation: A Troubled History*, edited by Duane H. King, 223–46. Knoxville: University of Tennessee Press, 1979.

Walker, Robert Sparks. *Torchlights to the Cherokees: The Brainerd Mission.* New York: Macmillan, 1931.

West, Patricia. *Domesticating History: The Political Origins of America's House Museums*. Washington, D.C.: Smithsonian Institution Press, 1998.

Whisnant, David E. "Finding the Way between Old and New: The Mountain Dance and Folk Festival and Bascom Lamar Lunsford's Work as a Citizen." *Appalachian Journal* 7 (1979–1980): 135–54.

Wilkins, Thurman. *Cherokee Tragedy: The Ridge Family and the Decimation of a People*. 1970. Rev. ed., Norman: University of Oklahoma Press, 1986.

Wilkinson, Charles. *Blood Struggle: The Rise of Modern Indian Nations*. New York: Norton, 2005.

Williams, Michael Ann. *Staging Tradition: John Lair and Sarah Gertrude Knott*. Urbana: University of Illinois Press, 2006.

Wilson, Waziyatawin Angela. *In the Footsteps of Our Ancestors: The Dakota Commemorative Marches of the 21st Century*. St. Paul, Minn.: Living Justice Press, 2006.

Winks, Robin. "Sites of Shame: Disgraceful Episodes from Our Past Should be Included in the Park System to Present a Complete Picture of Our History." *National Parks* 68 (March–April 1994): 22–24.

Witthoft, John. "Will West Long, Cherokee Informant." *American Anthropologist* 50 (April–June 1948): 355–59.

Wolfe, Patrick. "Land, Labor, and Difference: Elementary Structures of Race." *American Historical Review* 106 (June 2001): 866–905.

———. "Settler Colonialism and the Elimination of the Native." *Journal of Genocide Research* 8 (2006): 387–409.

———. *Traces of History: Elementary Structures of Race*. New York: Verso, 2016.

Wray, Jacilee, Alexa Roberts, Allison Pena, and Shirley Fiske. "Creating Policy for the National Park Service: Addressing Native Americans and Other Traditionally Associated Peoples." *The George Wright Forum* 26 (2009): 43–50.

Yuhl, Stephanie. *A Golden Haze of Memory: The Making of Historic Charleston*. Chapel Hill: University of North Carolina Press, 2005.

Zeigler, Wilbur G., and Ben S. Grosscup. *The Heart of the Alleghenies or Western North Carolina*. Raleigh, N.C.: Alfred Williams & Co., 1883.

Zissu, Erik M. *Blood Matters: The Five Civilized Tribes and the Search for Unity in the Twentieth Century*. New York: Routledge, 2001.

Index

CPSIA information can be obtained
at www.ICGtesting.com
Printed in the USA
LVHW09s1243150918
590075LV00007BA/388/P